JAMES KNOWLES
VICTORIAN EDITOR
AND ARCHITECT

FRONTISPIECE: Sir James Knowles, KCVO, *c.* 1903, photograph by his son

JAMES KNOWLES
VICTORIAN EDITOR AND ARCHITECT

BY

PRISCILLA METCALF

CLARENDON PRESS · OXFORD
1980

Oxford University Press, Walton Street, Oxford OX2 6DP

OXFORD LONDON GLASGOW
NEW YORK TORONTO MELBOURNE WELLINGTON
KUALA LUMPUR SINGAPORE JAKARTA HONG KONG TOKYO
DELHI BOMBAY CALCUTTA MADRAS KARACHI
NAIROBI DAR ES SALAAM CAPE TOWN

Published in the United States by
Oxford University Press, New York

British Library Cataloguing in Publication Data
Metcalf, Priscilla
    James Knowles, Victorian editor and architect.
    1. Knowles, *Sir* James
    2. Journalists – England – Biography
    3. Architects – England – Biography
    I. Title
    805   PN5123.K/   79-40266

ISBN 0-19-812626-3

Printed and bound in Great Britain by
Morrison & Gibb Ltd, London and Edinburgh

To

the memory of Eirene Skilbeck, James Knowles's granddaughter,
who so gladly furnished materials for this book
and to Kathleen Tillotson, Nikolaus Pevsner, and John Summerson
who saw the point of it

Preface

'MEDALS OF CREATION' was a phrase young James Knowles used in 1855 for new Victorian buildings, adapting the title of a book of 1844 by Gideon Mantell that had introduced him to the wonders of geology. And *Building News* in 1858 called the new Victorian architecture 'a national compound . . . as capable of giving out clear fresh harmonies as bronze'. And 'strokes of the great Victorian clock' was a phrase of Henry James's for Victorian periodicals, in remembrance of the *Cornhill* sounding into the London world of 1860 and after. Such ringing metallic metaphor tells the tone of Victorian apprehensions, almost hallucinatingly intense sometimes and heavy with overtones. Biography is one way of tuning in to that world, especially in the rare case of a subject who produced both buildings and periodicals. Sir James Knowles, as he became, was James Thomas Knowles junior, 1831–1908, ARIBA 1853, FRIBA 1876, KCVO 1903, son of James Thomas Knowles senior, 1806–84, FRIBA 1847. Eclectics and reconcilers both. Victorian opportunism in its more energetic, deserving, and sometimes amusing aspects has seldom been more variously or more purposefully put to good use than in these two lives. James Knowles's most successful creation—for which Tennyson suggested the title, and for which the KCVO was eventually bestowed—was his monthly review the *Nineteenth Century*, a power in its time, Victoria's last quarter-century when Knowles was most in tune with his time.

The random nature of the survival of papers often plays such havoc with biographical balance, it was great luck to find letters written over a long period. For the use of a packet of letters and travel journals with their strong sense of what it was like to be young and curious in the 1850s, as well as for other material, I am deeply indebted to James Knowles's granddaughter, the late Eirene Skilbeck, who for a while before I knew her edited the *Twentieth Century*. During the first five years of my research when it seemed a mountainous enterprise, she spurred things on with jolly lunches and helpful reminiscence at her flat in Orsett Terrace—familiar to the many writers she knew, with its view over a then-picturesque Victorian churchyard in Paddington— much as her grandfather had spurred his authors on at Queen Anne's Lodge. She very nicely put up with early stages of the book that were bound to interest her less than the great editorial period she could just barely remember and through her parents knew a good deal about. Through her I met or corresponded with other helpful relations, Arthur Knowles's daughters Mrs. Roger Tilley and the late Lady Harvey, and Isabella Knowles's granddaughters Lady Elkins and the late Miss Flint. I am much indebted to Eirene Skilbeck's cousin and executor Cuthbert Skilbeck for allowing me continued use of such material as remained in family hands and for falling in with my suggestion that it should be deposited in Westminster (at the Public Reference Library in Buckingham Palace Road where the Westminster historical collections are kept) except for certain papers relating to Tennyson deposited in the Tennyson Research Centre at Lincoln, where were already most of Knowles's letters to Tenny- son. For much helpful information about Tennyson's letters to Knowles I am most grateful to Professor Cecil Lang at the University of Virginia, while he was in course of preparing all of Tennyson's letters for publication. I was fortunate in being a London-dweller and so able with least pain to draw upon almost thirty years of letters from Knowles to Gladstone in the Glad- stone Papers at the British Library and from Knowles to Huxley in the Huxley Papers at Imperial College; the use of material from them to him is cited in the acknowledgements and in the footnotes. Much of my chapter on the *Nineteenth Century* is based on his previously unpublished correspondence with these three men. (Most unfortunately, but perhaps just as well for me, not being young when I started, much miscellaneous *Nineteenth Century* correspondence was destroyed in various quarters during and since the last war; other papers were dispersed at Sotheby's in April 1928.) My main work on that chapter was done before the relevant volume of the *Wellesley Index to Victorian Periodicals* came out, but that great index has been useful in my book's final stages. In view of the Wellesley editors' embargo on poetry, I have provided at the end of this book a list of poems published by Knowles. There is also a list of buildings by him and his father, for in their day and ever since, these architects were and are sometimes confused with one another.

The chapter called 'Turning-point' on the designing of Aldworth and the founding of the Metaphysical Society—not considered together before, though they ought to be—was a sort of turning-point in this book too, and appears pretty much as written in 1970. I talked a bit with Sir Charles Tennyson in 1965 and 1970, finding him sympathetic and humorous as everyone did, and I regret not having shown the chapter to him before he died in 1977, although we were in touch shortly before about his own account of Aldworth. After I came to know Professor Kathleen Tillotson in 1973, her interest made me feel I was on the right track. Luckily, when the late Mr. and Mrs. Suren were living at Aldworth, they were glad to show it to me, for now under another owner the house is not shown. And there were other pleasant perambulations. At Reigate, prepared by maps and deeds in the Surrey Record Office, one could still nose along Church Walk and find the 'running stream' sliding along. When I called on Sir Francis Cook (4th baronet, d. 1978) on the island of Jersey in 1965 he kindly brought out great Edwardian albums that were compensation for my being unable to go to Portugal, sumptuous photographs of Monserrate showing every room as once furnished and full of works of art, and he not only showed me much else that fed my narrative but gave me specially taken photographs of drawings in his possession, while his nephew Alexander Hamilton-Fletcher gave me photographs he had recently taken of Monserrate. As for London, I can only repeat Henry James's florid phrasing that my book 'was unmistakably the ripe round fruit of perambulation . . . pedestrian gaping having been from childhood prevailingly my line'. And I am glad to acknowledge the helpful and informative interest of Eric E. Smith of the Clapham Antiquarian Society ever since my first walks around Clapham Common in the 1950s.

When one finishes a book that has been in and out of the typewriter for more than ten years, and the fascinating millstone rolls away at last, it is a relief to look back on its much-cumbered progress. The architectural aspect had to be tackled first (while looking beyond it too), mainly because it came first organically, as it were; also because buildings are more vulnerable to destruction than papers already in careful hands, and because it became possible to proceed under the loyal supervision of Sir Nikolaus Pevsner, while eking out the bread-and-cheese with free-lance editing (how writers do have to live off one another). For the three years 1967–9 I was able to work on the book full time with a research fellowship in Victorian studies from the University of Leicester: to the Board of Studies there I am grateful for their tolerance of research only partly performed at Leicester, where however the library's fine array of Victorian periodicals served me well. It is a pleasure to record that the research funds of that university and of the Courtauld Institute of Art in the University of London were of much assistance to me. After the laborious typing of a bulky thesis in 1970, a commission to write the Victorian book in Cassell's London series had to be dealt with in 1971; the friends who helped my material existence during 1970–1 know how grateful I was to them. In 1972 I went back to making a book out of Knowles, until a totally unexpected full-time commission descended on me to write the history of a unique site in the City for the Fishmongers' Company, and Knowles was again suspended. During 1977, however, the embattled typescript was completely overhauled and became a book which Oxford University Press accepted. The chief character, except in spots where the reader can see through him a little too well, might have been pleased.

I gratefully acknowledge the gracious permission of Her Majesty the Queen to quote from certain royal correspondence; the kindness of Sir William Gladstone, Bart., in permitting me to quote from Gladstone's drafts for three letters; that of Professor Sir Andrew Huxley, F.R.S., in allowing use of a lost sketch by Thomas Huxley, and of Mrs. Rosalind Huxley for my quotations from Leonard Huxley's *Life* of his father; that of the late Sir Francis Cook, Bart., and of Mr. Wilfrid Hodgson to show drawings Knowles Sr. made for their great-grandfathers, as well as permission from Lord Tennyson, the Tennyson Research Centre, and the R.I.B.A. Drawings Collection to reproduce drawings, and from the National Monuments Record to use Crown Copyright photographs.

Contents

LIST OF ILLUSTRATIONS   xiii

ABBREVIATIONS   xv

I. KNOWLES AND SON UNTIL 1860

Family tree, 2.

1. Master Craftsmen of Reigate   3

2. Knowles the Elder: the Making of an Early Victorian   11
   Architect to the peerage and gentry, 19. Clapham Park
   and the way to professional status, 30. Architect to the
   middle station, 43.

3. Knowles the Younger: Learning About the World   61
   Early influences, 63. The *Clapham Magazine*, 1850, 65.
   Faith, fossils, art and comets, 71. Grand Tour, 1854, 87.
   Searching for a motive, 112.

4. The Grosvenor Style: a Mid-Victorian Synthesis   129
   The Grosvenor Hotel at Victoria Station, 130. Cook's
   villa at Cintra, 143. The end of a style, 150.

II. JAMES KNOWLES AFTER 1860

Nursery sketch by Tennyson, 158.

5. King Arthur and Bread & Cheese   159
   Literary interlude: Malory modernized, 160. The Jones,
   Woodgate, and Flower developments, 166. Life and art
   1862–8, 187.

6. Turning-point: Aldworth and the Metaphysical Society   197
   A Victorian Camelot, 198. Knowles as impresario, 208.

7. The *Contemporary Review* and Bread & Cheese   228
   First years of editing, 232. Public interlude: the Paris Food
   Fund, 240. Estate development at West Brighton, 245.

Baron Grant: was he Melmotte? 247. Friendship with Tennyson, 254. An outlet for Gladstone, 261. Parting company with Strahan, 268.

8. The *Nineteenth Century*: a Late Victorian Success   274
Questionable title, unquestionable success, 276. Two practices ended, 286. At home in Westminster: Queen Anne's Lodge, 298. Midwife to Gladstone and Huxley, and to the Royal Family, 308. Misunderstandings with the Tennysons and others, 336. Turn of the century: *and After*, 348.

9. A Wonderful Medium of Communication   352

BUILDINGS DESIGNED BY THE KNOWLESES   364
INDEX TO POETRY PUBLISHED BY KNOWLES   368
INDEX   371

List of Illustrations

Frontispiece, Sir James Knowles, *c.* 1903

(AT END)

1. Bell Street, Reigate, Surrey, *c.* 1900
   Knowles the Elder, 1860
   Knowles the Younger, *c.* 1877

2. Silverton Park, Devon, 1839–1845
   Long section for hall, *c.* 1840–1843

3. Friday Grove, Clapham Park, 1845
   View of hall during demolition (one)
   View of hall during demolition (two)

4. Broadstairs, August 1853
   Messrs. Cook's warehouse, 1854

5. Drawing for Chancery Lane front, 1854
   Design for an International Hotel, 1858
   Design for the Grosvenor Hotel, 1860

6. Grosvenor Hotel at Victoria Station, 1858–1862
   Original window-tracery, 1863

7. Grosvenor Hotel, frieze and cornice in 1964
   Window-tracery, Cedars estate, Clapham Common, 1860

8. Monserrate, Sintra, Portugal, rebuilding 1863–1865
   Exterior, 1965

9. Thatched House Club, St. James's Street, Westminster, 1861–1864
   Street view and detail of foliage carving, 1864

10. Sketch by Tennyson, inscribed 'for Aldworth', 1867?
    Aldworth, Sussex, 1867–1869

11. Aldworth, three details of carved frieze, 1868–1877

12. St. John Evangelist, Redhill, Surrey, 1842–1843
    St. Saviour's, Cedars Road, Clapham, 1862–1864

13. Hedsor, Buckinghamshire, 1865–1868
    West Brighton (Stanford) estate, Hove, Sussex, sea-front terraces, 1871–1872
    Kensington House, 1873

14. Fountain in Leicester Square, 1874
    Knowles at the Reform Club, 1885

15. Demon and Gadarene pig sketched by Huxley, 1890
    Original drawing for title-page of *Nineteenth Century and After*, c. 1896

16. The Hollies, Clapham Common North Side
    Queen Anne's Lodge, No. 1 Queen Square Place, Westminster, c. 1900

    Pencil Sketch by Tennyson, for Beatrice Knowles, 1872, p. 158

Abbreviations

APSD	*Architectural Publication Society Dictionary*, 1853–92
AR	*Architectural Review*, 1896–
Benét	W. R. Benét, *The Reader's Encyclopaedia*, 1948
BL	British Library
Bldr	*Builder*, 1842–
BM	British Museum
BN	*Building News*, 1854–
Boase	F. Boase, *Modern English Biography*, 1892–1901, 1908–21
Brown	A. W. Brown, *The Metaphysical Society*, 1947
CBA	*Companion to the British Almanac*, 1827–
CEAJ	*Civil Engineer and Architect's Journal*, 1837–
CEO	Crown Estate Office
CG	*Clapham Gazette*, 1853–71
ChCom	Church Commissioners (former Ecclesiastical Commissioners)
CL	*Country Life*, 1897
Colvin	H. Colvin, *Biographical Dictionary of English Architects 1660–1840*, 1954; and rev. edn. as . . . *British Architects 1600–1840*, 1978
CR	*Contemporary Review*, 1866–
DNB	*Dictionary of National Biography*
GL	Guildhall Library
GLRO	Greater London Record Office
Graves	A. Graves, *Royal Academy of Arts . . . Contributors 1769–1904*, 1905–6
GS	Geological Survey maps
HLRO	House of Lords Record Office
ILN	*Illustrated London News*, 1842–
LRS	London Record Society
MBW	Metropolitan Board of Works
Minet	Minet Library, Surrey Collection
NC	*Nineteenth Century*, 1877–1900, . *Nineteenth Century and After*, 1901–50, *Twentieth Century*, 1951–74
NMR	National Monuments Record (former National Buildings Record)
OS	Ordnance Survey maps
RIBA	Royal Institute of British Architects
Ricks	C. Ricks, ed., *The Poems of Tennyson*, 1969
S of L	Survey of London volumes
SAC	*Surrey Archaeological Collections*
SRO	Surrey Record Office, Kingston
SRS	Surrey Record Society
TRC	Tennyson Research Centre, Lincoln

VPN   *Victorian Periodicals Newsletter*
VS   *Victorian Studies*
WIVP   *Wellesley Index to Victorian Periodicals*, vols. I and II
WPL   Westminster Public Library, Buckingham Palace Road, London S.W.1

I

KNOWLES AND SON UNTIL 1860

Knowles descent in Kingston, Reigate, and London

poss. William Knowles, d. Kingston 1579
?
Jacob, d. Reigate 1602
tinker, pewterer, and brazier

William, b. Reigate 1586 tinker of Reigate	Jacob, b. Reigate 1588 haberdasher of Kingston	John, b. Reigate 1597 (bequest Kingston 1667 to bro. James of Reigate)	James, b. Reigate 1600 shoemaker, d. Reigate 1668 m. Mary Eaton

Israel, b. Kingston 1621
master carpenter St. Paul's *et al.*
d. City of London 1705

Jacob, 1645–1704
glazier of Reigate
(poss. apprent. to a Thomas Fisher)

James, d. 1736
in Fleet Prison

Thomas, 1667–1735
glazier of Reigate
m. Ann Pullen

bros. incl. 2 Jameses, d.
young; John, apprent. to
Israel in London 1686;
Daniel, admin. cousin
James's property and named
a son Israel

James, 1702–66
glazier of Reigate
(w. a bro. Thomas)
m. Sarah Coleman

Jacob, 1728–87
glazier of Reigate
(w. a bro. Thomas)
m. Ann ----

James, 1757–95
glazier of Reigate
(w. a bro. Thomas)
m. Elizabeth ----

James, 1778–1813
glazier of Reigate
(w. a bro. Thomas)
m. Maria Gale

James Thomas Knowles, b. Reigate 1806
d. Russell Square, London, 1884
plumber and glazier *c.* 1830–6
architect *c.* 1836–84, FRIBA 1847
m. Susannah Brown 1831

James Thomas Knowles, b. Reigate 1831
d. Brighton 1908
ARIBA 1853, FRIBA 1876, KCVO 1903
editor *Contemporary Review* 1870–6
editor *Nineteenth Century* 1877–1908
m. (1) Jane Emma Borradaile 1860 (d. 1863)
(2) Isabel Mary Hewlett 1865 (d. 1918)

I

Master Craftsmen of Reigate

'The snug little borough . . . has the Surrey chalk hills
close to it on the north, and sand hills along on its
south. . . . [And from] the tip-top of Reigate Hill . . .
there is one of the finest views in the whole world.'
William Cobbett, *Rural Rides*, 25 September 1826,
30 July 1823, 26 October 1826

THE OLD SURREY MARKET TOWN OF REIGATE sits in a
valley between the North Downs height where Cobbett
liked to pause and a chain of lower hills commanding
views toward the South Downs. From a cluster of headstones
carved with the family name of Knowles, before the west door of
the parish church high above Chart Lane, there are tree-framed
views toward the northern escarpment, grander in scale than the
term Home County implies. Whatever the new building styles
now refacing parts of the High Street, the situation of Reigate
with its castle ruins and enfolding hills is still, here and there,
such (to quote a local historian at the time of Napoleon's wars)
'as to render the prospect very romantic'.[1]

In 1854 the future editor of the *Nineteenth Century*, in Rome
aged 22, recorded in the customary tourist journal his solemn
sensations on the customary moonlit visit to the Colosseum: 'I got
into a solitary place, and sitting down, thought Byron and history
intently . . . and thinking—unutterable things—mournful yet
deeply full of pleasure . . . a delight which ranks with my recollections of the primroses and foxgloves, hayfields, and Park-hills
of which my earliest impressions and happiest are composed.'
That is (trailing intimations perhaps of Wordsworth too),
recollections of Reigate which he had left at the age of eight. For
'Park-hills' was the old name of the high places south of Reigate

[1] David Hughson, *London and its Neighbourhood* (1805–9), v. 335.

Priory where a natural terrace commanded 'extensive and delightful views' (another local historian in 1830) well within small-boy scrambling distance of Bell Street where the family lived.[2]

Whether a traveller's surge of feeling for the hills of home included some archetypal sense of origin—Knowles, knolls, high places—is the sort of question James Knowles probably never asked himself in later life when, for him, Reigate receded into limbo. Home, nevertheless, for seven or more generations of his family until the 1830s was a certain plot in Bell Street, beside a 'running stream'. Still today the only street going south from the old Town Hall, Bell Street (Pl. 1) in the early nineteenth century was part of the Brighton coach road, where 'the mails' dashed through with news of Wellington's victories, where the Regent *en route* to his Pavilion stopped at the White Hart, and Cobbett snorted at 'great parcels of stock-jobbers [who] skip backward and forward on the coaches' between Brighton and the City of London. For the first two hundred yards south of the market-place, buildings lined both sides, houses and shops and inns; then came the Priory garden wall along the west side, opposite a crowded row of houses on the east side, small houses flush with the pavement in front but with long back gardens. Today the occupiers on both sides have changed, yet the scale of Bell Street has remained much the same (at least in 1977) from Castle Hill at the north end to Cockshut Hill at the south end. Much of the east side is still bordered by the gables or cornices of two-storey houses, with even the faceless new buildings still in scale, and there is open air above the Priory wall opposite, once lined with trees. The present No. 41 Bell Street, a two-gabled front of about 1851 with a shop inserted, nearly opposite the northern verge of the Priory grounds, has the width of frontage of two medieval houses.

Behind the back premises of No. 41 were, for centuries, large open greens known as Ship Field and Fridays Mead, until recently kept entirely green and open, and still partly so. Along their far side runs a footpath, Church Walk (approached at the north end from Church Street to the left of a Gothick gateway marked Barons Park). Along Church Walk generations of newly

[2] Travel journal, chap. 3, n. 37 below. Map in Wilfrid Hooper, *Reigate* (1945), p. 54, also pp. 47, 72. Thomas Allen, *History of Surrey and Sussex* (1830), ii. 269.

joined couples walked down and newly laden coffins were carried up. About halfway, a brook slides from a culvert under the path, and among tree-roots and half-wild grasses flows toward Bell Street, to be culverted again between the rear premises of Nos. 41 and 43. On an important local survey map of 1786 the boundary between those houses is marked 'Stream of water', and on a conveyance plan of 1851 this is 'the Running Stream'. Here less than a yard wide, having risen as a spring on Wray Common below Reigate Hill, to end in a pond in the Priory grounds, the stream crossed Bell Street in the open till 1815, when it was taken under the road, though the modern drainage it now joins under Bell Street came only in the 1870s. From Church Walk one can still see it (in 1977 anyway) rushing along after a rainstorm or sluggish in a dry season. At No. 41, the glazier's house that drained into it and drank from it, in 1795 and again in 1813 two successive James Knowleses died in their thirties, the former quickly followed by his wife—in the summer.[3]

By the late sixteenth century there were Knowleses in various parts of Surrey as there were in other counties (too many for all the Knowleses in England to have been one clan). In 1579 a William Knowles died in Kingston, and in the 1580s Surrey muster rolls listed another William in the Kingston area, while in the Reigate parish register there appeared Jacob Knowles, tinker. Between 1586 and 1602, as Jacob's children are born or die, he is 'tynker' or 'pewter & brasier' (maker as well as mender); with the birth of his son James in 1600, he is 'the tinker', and so at his own death in 1602. In a market town, with increasing domestic use of pewter instead of wooden vessels, the tinker need not have been a travelling man. Was christening a country-town tinker's child James in 1600 a distant tribute to the heir to the throne? Jacob as Christian name in six generations of the family—in the seventeenth century often as brother to a James—was of course Biblical in origin, given unaware of any Jacobean Latinizing of James.[4]

[3] On this stream as a possible source of Reigate's name, Hooper, p. 23. Map with William Bryant MS. 'List and State of Reigate Burgages 1786', SRO. Map with lease 1851, Earl Somers to James Fisher, SRO 792/5/65. In early summer 1795 there were not unusually many deaths in the parish (registers now at SRO; fortunately I was in time to see them at the church).

[4] Surrey muster rolls (printed SRS 1914–17) III.17. Reigate and Kingston (transcript) parish registers SRO.

Jacob the tinker's first son William carried on as a tinker in Reigate. Two other sons, Jacob and John, seem to have moved fifteen miles away to Kingston, whence their father may originally have come, along the road through Ewell. Of John we only know that he bequeathed 'my wearing Apparrell to my brother James Knolles of Reygate'. This James, the youngest and longest-surviving son (d. 1668), was a shoemaker. He had a son Jacob (b. 1645), apparently a Reigate glazier of that name who in 1686 apprenticed a son John to a cousin in London: to Wren's master carpenter, Israel Knowles—son of Jacob Knowles, haberdasher, of Kingston. Israel (1621–1705), sometime Master of the Carpenters' Company, was one of the rebuilders of St. Paul's, seven City churches, and indeed much of the City of London after the Great Fire. His Christian name out of Genesis (32:28) he probably owed to a Puritan element in Kingston parish where he was christened in the parish church. His splendid signature as church-warden of St. Mary Magdalene, Old Fish Street, near St. Paul's, attests his superiority to his Surrey relations. Yet Israel's only son James was to die, probably a debtor, in the Fleet Prison. Now, their cousin Jacob the glazier of Reigate (father of Israel's apprentice) must have been 15 at the Restoration in 1660: whether he apprenticed in London himself, until the Plague and Fire years, is not recorded (though the great master carpenter's shop did glazing and painting too); but Reigate at this time did have a glazier to whom Jacob could have been apprenticed, a Thomas Fisher. Jacob's wife was producing children in Reigate from 1667 on—the eldest christened, for a change, Thomas, a name that then continued in the family. Besides Thomas's brother John who was apprenticed in London, there was their brother Daniel, who named one of his own children Israel and who administered the doubtless depleted property of his 'cousin-german twice removed', the James Knowles who died in the Fleet.[5]

[5] John Knolles of Kingston, will dated 1664, proved June 1667 Surrey Arch-deaconry 44. James appears on Reigate protestation roll Mar. 1642 (HLRO, printed SAC vol. 59, 1962) though not in hearth-tax assessments of 1664 when a James Knowles appears for Richmond (SRS vol. 17), but he died and was buried in Reigate in 1668 (parish register). Carpenters' Company apprentices entry books 1654–94 printed in Bower Marsh, *Records* of that company, vol. I (1913) index *sub* Israel Knowles. For him, Kingston parish registers transcript at SRO; Wren Society vol. XIV, verso dedication page (but apprenticed 1639 not 1649, company records) and index vol. XX; parish registers St. Gregory by St. Paul's (pre-Fire) and St. Mary Magdalene, Old Fish Street (post-Fire), GL MSS. 10,233

That is, Jacob the Elizabethan tinker of Reigate seems to have been grandfather to that pillar of the City of London, Israel Knowles. While Israel was scaffolding the crypt and choir vaults of the slowly rising cathedral, he lived and owned property near by in Carter Lane, at the corner of Do Little Alley, subsequently called Knowles Court (now obliterated by the new processional way south of St. Paul's). In 1852 a Reigate-born descendant of Jacob the tinker, James the shoemaker, Jacob the glazier, and Thomas his son—James Thomas Knowles, architect—was to rebuild the rear premises of Messrs. Cook's warehouse on Knowles Court, Carter Lane, quite possibly knowing himself kin to the great craftsman—not that he would have said so. Over the centuries, while masons travelled with Reigate stone to build Westminster Abbey and while other large works went on in London or its surrounding countryside, Surrey was continually criss-crossed by migrant craftsmen.

Whether those Elizabethan and Jacobean Knowleses lived in Bell Street we cannot be sure. Perhaps a workshop beside the stream became necessary only when Jacob the first glazier set up his trade and his furnace about 1667. We know that his son Thomas, glazier, was occupying the house by the stream in Bell Street by 1710, if not sooner. Jacob died poor during a time of fevers and poverty in 1704. Thomas had his troubles in the years following, but his sons James and John benefited from a charitable bequest of 1700 to the parish school (later Reigate Grammar School) for 'the free teaching of four poor boys'. All five generations between 1700 and 1820 probably attended this school until they were fourteen or fifteen.[6]

In Thomas's time the inhabitants of Reigate Borough were tenants of houses held on burgage-tenure by owners resident elsewhere, such tenure enabling such absentees to vote here in parliamentary elections, for Reigate sent two Members to Westminster. During the period of intense political rivalry, between the elections of 1698 and 1722 especially, such vote-bearing tenements were briskly changing hands at inflated prices

---

and 10,221; churchwardens' accounts for latter church, GL MS. 1341/1; LRS, *London Inhabitants Within the Walls 1695*, p. 176; will proved 1708, 1 Poley 492; for son James, admin. Spurway Mar. 1736. Fisher family of Reigate glaziers: parish registers from 1615; a James Fisher, glazier, acquired Knowles's Bell Street lease after 1840.

[6] Account book of John Bird, vicar and schoolmaster, pupils 1711–15, SRO.

among a mixed crowd of Londoners, over the tenants' heads. The state of ownership and tenure became in some cases an almost trackless tangle. This, so to say, over-ripe property market (until two more stable proprietors later in the eighteenth century divided the borough between them) is nicely illustrated by a series of transactions involving Albyns, a house in Bell Street temporarily subdivided into two tenements. At one point, the owner of Albyns, a biscuit-maker of Wapping, sold half his holding to a City of London joiner after his own bankruptcy trustees had already disposed of the whole of Albyns to someone else; the joiner's son, a City grocer, collected rents on his half for twenty years before the legal owner caught on—while the voteless tenants went on living their lives. But by 1741 we find James Knowles, glazier, Thomas's son, taking a ninety-nine-year lease on Albyns (no longer divided) from the then landlord the Earl of Wilmington: the house stood next door northward to the one the Knowleses had been occupying beside the stream. Thereafter the two houses, eventually altered as one, remained the family home until 1837, and the premises of the family glazing and plumbing business until that lease ran out in 1840.[7]

In the churchyard the earliest surviving gravestone in the Knowles family group, between two old chestnut trees overlooking the road, is that of James the leaseholder (d. 1767)—carved stone having been beyond his forebears' means. Better education, the increasing prosperity of the eighteenth century in general and more building activity in particular, as well as the shift of Reigate property into fewer and more responsible landlords' hands, all helped to mellow the struggle for existence. The Bell Street leases were to last the family out, until this James's great-great-grandson took his measured steps into professional life and on to London. In surviving vestry records we have glimpses of Georgian Knowleses attending Reigate Borough vestry meetings in one almost continuous family performance, with four or more generations serving intermittently as churchwardens or overseers of the poor. Yet James of the long lease and the carved headstone died intestate, so apparently did his son Jacob, and his grandson James left only an unwitnessed note. The next James, however, made a proper will just before he died at 35 in 1813, having

---

[7] Bell Street deeds, and Bryant list and map, SRO. Hardwicke papers at BL. Add. MS. 36232.

between 1806 and 1810 acquired four freeholds in 'the Foreign' outside the borough. Property, the real possession of property, concentrates the mind. Not only his real estate, but his large table-tomb (now gone) and a 'gentleman' brother-in-law (the town auctioneer) as executor, suggest a rise in shrewdness, opportunities, and status.[8]

From the 1660s on, all were glaziers (or plumbers, painters, and glaziers), Jacob, Thomas, James, Jacob, James, James—and James Thomas for a few years before he began to call himself architect and never looked back. Reigate sandpits had long been a source of white sand for glassmakers and builders, as Reigate quarries were a famous source of stone. When Early Victorian James Thomas specified cements and mortars for his buildings, he knew their ingredients in his bones. His ownership of a freehold field, with a sandpit in it, in Chart Lane gave him a vote after the first Reform Act. Glazing in the days of lead-casement windows had involved leadwork; then, when sash windows arrived (in this provincial area perhaps only from the first Georgian James's time), glazing involved paintwork. With a new age after 1800 of glass-and-iron conservatories and increasingly skylighted buildings, the combined trade of plumbers, painters, and glaziers became one of those from which contracting for a whole building was the next step. In 1803 James Knowles aged 24 knew no better than to approve, with fellow-craftsmen and vestry members, the removal of the main beams of the parish church; James Thomas his son at the same age would hardly have been so innocent of the rules of construction. In defence of young James in 1803, it should be noted that the master craftsman in charge was an old friend of his father's, as no doubt were churchwardens and vicar—the beam in their eyes was the snag.[9]

[8] Vestry minutes: at SRO (Foreign), Town Hall (Borough), and one sheet 1744 in Hardwicke papers (as in n. 7 above). Wills and administrations: James, admin. PCC Torriano Dec. 1767; Jacob (d. 1787), none found; James, unwitnessed will 30 Mar. 1795, burial 27 June, probate Surrey Archdeaconry 5 July 1795, widow buried 30 July; James, will dated 3 July 1813, burial 2 Aug., probate 21 Feb. 1814 PCC Bridport 76. No tomb for that James survives, but William Ridgeway's MS. history of Reigate (1816 with notes up to 1827, BL Add. MS. 34237) mentions one, and visible in old photographs. On his freeholds, Land Tax assessments Reigate Foreign 1805–10, and Returns of Freeholders for Juries 1802–13, SRO. On executors, chap. 2.

[9] Vestry minutes, Reigate Foreign, Mar.–Sept. 1803, 19 Apr. 1808, SRO. Hooper, p. 53 on 'this meddlesome folly', pp. 47, 106, on Reigate sand. On field in Chart Lane, chap. 2, n. 5 below.

Down the generations, the master craftsman in a small town controlled his jobs and his workshop, owned his own tools, bought his own materials, and worked alone or with an apprentice and mate, selling his services through no middle man. The latest building techniques could be picked up on country-house work alongside men from London. And pattern-books will have accumulated in the glazier's workshop from generation to generation. A sale catalogue of 1886 includes forty titles that apparently represent the remainder of the family working library.[10] For example, 'Price's British Carpenter 1735' and 'Langley's Builder's Treasury 1740' could have belonged to James of the long lease and the carved headstone, while his great-grandson could have acquired 'Atkinson s Picturesque Cottages 1805' and 'Gyfford's Designs for Cottages 1806'—unless young James Thomas picked them up at his uncle's country-house auction sales in the 1820s, along with such souvenirs of clients' long-past grand tours as 'Borbone Roma Antica e Moderna 1754' and 'Bastien, Maison Rustique, Paris 1798', and such inspiration for the future as 'Miller's Country Gentleman's Architect 1793' and 'Salmon's Palladio Londinensis 1734'. That James Thomas produced architectural drawings himself in the 1830s need not surprise us, for working draughtsmanship had been part of the artisan's skill since the middle ages.

The legacy of such forebears was not small. All down the line, except for the usual apprenticeship and sometimes journeyman years, they worked for themselves and as they saw fit. However tossed by circumstances, survival depended on their own energies and practical judgement, their own vein of Surrey iron. They became sound local figures, pillars of the church—even if they saw no harm in removing the beams. And dormant in their temperaments lay a feeling for grandeur, for large-scale projects, for the view from Reigate Hill.

---

[10] Hodgson sale catalogue, 2 Mar. 1886, seen at Chancery Lane and now in BL, includes a library of an unnamed 'eminent architect', with so many titles pertinent to interests of both J. T. Knowles Sr. (d. 1884) and his son (then closing down his practice) as to seem fairly safely identifiable as theirs, even though this sale also included another library as well.

2

Knowles the Elder: the Making of an Early Victorian

> 'Great inducements are offered to the ambitious
> student of our art, we live in a great country & a
> palmy period of our history—great buildings are
> daily rising round us, and those who are most con-
> spicuous for ability & learning & diligence cannot
> fail to reap every desired advantage from our profes-
> sion in due time.' Professor C. R. Cockerell at the
> Royal Academy, 3rd lecture, 1842 (RIBA MS.
> collection)

THE SENIOR JAMES THOMAS KNOWLES was born in
Bell Street a year after Trafalgar, and grew up to the sound
of the London coaches. He was not quite seven when his
father died, poisoned perhaps by the common stream beside the
house, and the mother was left with six children, her youngest a
few months old. The executors were three citizens of Reigate
Borough, the auctioneer, a brewer, and a tallow-chandler. The
first, Mrs. Knowles's brother Samuel Emly Gale, was named in
the will only as 'Gentleman': his occupation, in town directories
of the 1820s, will have brought him in close touch with country-
house families round about, on the same confidential footing as a
solicitor. The executors were to invest the proceeds of 'all my
Real Estate' for the children's benefit 'in placing them out as
Apprentices or in other Situations to enable [them] to gain their
own Livelihood'. Uncle Gale may have been able to arrange
country-house work for his eldest nephew when the time came.
Meanwhile, Maria Knowles, as many a master craftsman's
widow had done before, turned to and ran the plumbing and
glazing business, apparently until her eldest son was able to do so:

an old neighbour knew her in 1816 as 'Mrs Knowles, Widow, Glaizer and Plumber'; ten years later, trade directories were still listing her under 'Painters, Plumbers and Glaziers'.[1]

By the end of 1830, James Thomas was attending vestry meetings after a gap of seventeen years since his father's presence there. And of the young man during those seventeen years we know nothing at all about schooling or apprenticeship—the latter probably from 1821 to 1827, perhaps to his mother, or in London—nor about that of his two younger brothers. All three may have worked for their mother. Attendance at the parish school until the age of 15 must have been the limit of their formal education.[2] James Thomas very likely spent the first years after his apprenticeship working for a master craftsman in or near London—the magnet, as in Israel Knowles's time. Great building works were going forward there between 1827 and 1830: Buckingham Palace, Carlton Terrace, Regent's Park, the Bank of England, University College, St. George's Hospital, the General Post Office, the British Museum, the Athenaeum Club, and other splendours for an observant craftsman to study, whether actually employed on any of them or on some suburban development near by, or only on rare visits from Reigate fortified by study in new books such as Britton and Pugin's *Public Buildings of London* and Elmes's *Metropolitan Improvements*, along with the new pattern-books of architectural detail for studious artisans. In London, the tag end of the Georgian era was a time of building excitement, whatever political crises impended.

In the countryside, within working distance of Reigate, large houses were rising or altering, for example at Deepdene near Dorking; and a Surrey artisan's field of action could by then include jobs on houses in Sussex and Hampshire and Kent, wherever horse and cart could take materials and tools over the improved roads. Building accounts for some Georgian brick houses in Reigate itself probably showed work by successive Knowleses, and a full building history of Reigate Priory might mention the whole series of master glaziers and plumbers from over the road. And there were a few local stimuli in the mid-

[1] Will 1813 cited chap. i, n. 8. (Gale himself died 1827.) Directories SRO. Ridgeway MS. cited chap. i, n. 8.

[2] Borough vestry minutes, Town Hall, Dec. 1830–Oct. 1836. Reigate Grammar School: no attendance records survive for period just before 1821 (Headmaster, 29 Jan. 1968).

1820s, besides the noisy passage of the Brighton–London coaches. It must have been exciting to watch the boring of the road-tunnel at the top of Bell Street, just when serious plans for the much grander Thames Tunnel were being talked about. And we may suppose that the carved late twelfth-century foliage inside Reigate church, seen Sunday after Sunday—while the sermon shaped modes of expression in other ways—had its effect when the Grosvenor Hotel design was assembled, once the foliage-vogue of the 1850s reminded the architect of it. Sermons and, subsequently, meetings of the vestry and local societies will have supplied not only a mode of oral flow, but a taste for turning it on with a straight face, enormously helpful to a young man naturally disposed to a craftsman's emphasis on deeds-not-words in a town where he and his talents were known with little social effort on his part, yet who was intelligent enough and determined enough to seek a larger sphere. His marriage on the edge of London, attended by a friend who was already calling himself an architect in the very centre of London, suggests that the larger sphere was already in view.

It was in January 1831 that Knowles married Susannah, daughter of a surgeon and apothecary, George Brown of Paradise Street, Rotherhithe. Perhaps, in this mariners' neighbourhood, a former ship's surgeon? In any case, there seems to have been a father-to-son craftsman-rising-to-professional tradition in that family too, in a locality of as marked character as Reigate though soon due for more ruthless change. At the end of the eighteenth century Rotherhithe had been 'remarked for the salubrity of its air, and the infrequency of infectious disorders there; a circumstance which has been accounted for from the flux and reflux of the tides passing through the common sewers'. Fifty years on, the Thames was the great common sewer, and meanwhile there came the railway line to Greenwich and the building-over of market gardens. But Paradise Street, near the river and the parish church, must still have been a pleasant and bracing place to live in Mrs. Knowles's girlhood before 1831. And inescapably there emerges, from later descriptions of her and in certain delightful traits she seems to have transmitted to her children, a sense of some potent strain of charm, imagination, and humour, perhaps Celtic or Gallic, somewhere in the Brown family. But no more is heard of the Browns, whether they emigrated, hyphenated, died of cholera, or were quietly dropped. At any rate, they soon moved away from Rotherhithe, as the stenches rose and social tone declined. Knowles's groomsman John Stanford was an architect, of no known works, listed in directories from 1831 at 21 Downing Street, Westminster, later as an artist at 49 Pall Mall. The family of the bridesmaid Ann Lainson we shall meet again.[3]

James Thomas and Susannah, as a modern couple of the 1830s, were to name their daughters Isabella Susannah, Julia Maria, and Emmeline Mary (born 1834–8), in contrast to the homespun names of his sisters Maria, Harriet, and Eliza (born 1802–8); recurring names of Knowles wives down the two preceding centuries had been Mary, Elizabeth, Sarah, and Ann, though in 1591 Jacob the tinker and his wife Alice had named a daughter Susanna. The new Knowles sons were to be James Thomas Jr. and George Henry; the senior James Thomas had been the first man in the family to have two Christian names, though neither of his brothers did. From the start he was equipped for more pretentious life.[4] At first, however, the couple settled down in Bell Street where he took up the family trade. The leasehold double house had increased in value, being no doubt improved by him; by the late 1830s its estimated rental value as 'House Shop Garden' was two and a half times that of a generation before. He owned the freehold of a three-acre meadow in Chart Lane on which Albion Road was laid out after his time: it gave him a supply of sand (the Ordnance Survey of 1870 showing an 'Old Sand Pit' there) and its ownership made him one of the thirty-one electors of Reigate Foreign.[5]

In the autumn of 1831 when the first child, the future editor,

---

[3] Rotherhithe parish register, transcript GLRO. George Brown: Returns of Freeholders for Juries 1806, electoral register 1834, directories, SRO. Cf., e.g. Erasmus Wilson's father, a Scottish naval surgeon who settled as parish surgeon at Dartford (on Wilson, chap. 8, n. 26); and Charlotte Eaton, *Rome in the Nineteenth Century*, preface to 1820 edn., on superior manners of an English apothecary's wife. Lainson, n. 18 below. Rotherhithe: Lysons, *Environs of London* (1796), i. 475; *ILN*, 15 Sept. 1849, p. 195.

[4] Reigate parish registers SRO. 'Thomas' may have been conferred in 1806 to honour an uncle who took in the orphans of 1795, the name having been borne (as the only Christian name) by one of each generation since the Thomas born 1667, then possibly named after Thomas Fisher, a glazier to whom his father may have been apprenticed (chap. 1, n. 5).

[5] Borough rate book 1838, Town Hall; house rebuilt *c.* 1850 by Knowles's successor. Meadow on Chart Lane: tithe map 1843, SRO; OS maps surveyed 1870, 1933, sheet 26.15; GS sheet 286, 1967. Electoral registers SRO.

was born, life in Reigate was not easy. A market town could hardly be unaware of farm-workers' discontents seething in the countryside roundabout since the 'Swing' riots of 1830. After the House of Lords threw out the Reform Bill in early October 1831, riots broke out in many towns: in Reigate, between the child's birth on 13 October and his christening on 18 November, there were threats of trouble in the streets near the church. St. Crispin's Day, 25 October, was in Reigate a traditional day of wild disorder—in lingering celebration of Agincourt?—Crispin being the ancient patron of local leather-tanners, as in the time of the Jacobean James Knowles, shoemaker. And there was illness in the glazier's cottage in Bell Street: on 22 October, the young father's brother Charles aged 18 was buried, and a few weeks later died the other brother Henry, aged 21; perhaps the drain-fed water supply still claimed its victims. In February the borough vestry met to consider how to 'avert if possible the introduction into this parish of the Disease called Cholera Morbus', it having appeared 'in the Metropolis'—the beginning of the epidemic of 1832. During 1833–4 young Mr. Knowles served as the borough's last overseer of the poor under the old Poor Law.[6]

By this time there were signs of a future for him beyond the familiar ancestral round. About 1833 he seems to have designed and supervised the construction of a complete house, coated with metallic-sand cement and dressed with Ionic columns, 'on the borders of Hampshire, not far distant from the sea', perhaps on his landlord's property at Hamble. 1833 was the year Loudon's *Encyclopaedia of Cottage, Farm and Villa Architecture* came out: a good deal of Knowles's work was drawn from that bible during the next few years. In January 1834 he became one of the original group of members of a new Reigate lodge of Freemasons with young Lord Monson, of nearby Gatton Park, as Master, Knowles thereupon signing as 'Gentleman'; four years later he became Master himself (1838–40), as well as treasurer of a new Provincial Grand Lodge for the county. Twice he chaired vestry meetings, before he was 30, in the Vicar's absence. The open vestries where any responsible inhabitant had a vote were nurseries of the conviction that one man's vote was as good as another's, as well as

---

[6] Burial register, vestry minutes, SRO. Hooper, p. 173, on St. Crispin's Day (in the previous century Dr. Johnson complained, 'the feast of Crispin passes by without any mention of Agincourt', but he was editing *Henry V* in London).

of the principle that some could chair the meeting better than others. He must have had presence, with a quick ear for the forms of formal occasions and the uses of a superior accent, time spent in London having perhaps quickened his Surrey vowels. And from 1834, we shall find, he kept one foot in London. In 1836, the year he was 30, his mother died; later that year, he attended his last vestry meeting. The Bell Street lease was not due to fall in until Michaelmas 1840, but other avenues were opening.[7]

Trade directories at first listed him as his mother had been, and the baptismal register for the first four children from 1831 until late 1835 gave his occupation as plumber. But by late 1836 or early 1837, directories gave this dual entry: 'Knowles J. T. Cockshut Hill Architect & Surveyor', 'Knowles James Thomas Bell st. Plumber'. By 1838, the Coronation year, we find him only as architect, or architect and surveyor: on drawings for two lordly clients in March and June, and at the baptism of the fifth child in April, as well as in Reigate directories. Although the earliest entry in a London directory appeared late in 1839, for chambers at No. 1 Raymond Buildings, Gray's Inn, the records of the Inn show him as a subtenant there by 1834: perhaps at first a part-time arrangement as a convenience for clients and as a stepping-stone for himself.[8] Journeying to building sites in other counties was often easier from London (the London hub-effect, for the metropolis had a double, centrifugal–centripetal pull for a practical ambitious man, it was the place to be seen coming from). Just then, an institute of architects was being formed there, though he could not join it yet. In the years 1834–45 he must have been often away from home: young James's deep feeling for his mother was founded then. In these years James senior was responsible for houses in Devon and Somerset and west Sussex, enlarging upon those first Ionic colonnades in Hampshire near the sea. His son

---

[7] House *c.* 1833: 'erected about seventeen years ago . . . it is the oldest work of my own to which I can refer' (Knowles to RIBA in 1850, as n. 33 below; 'executed in a most masterly manner . . . which left nothing to be desired', said he). Freemasonry: John Lees, *History of the Surrey Lodge . . . Established at Reigate 1834* (1884), pp. 74, 62, 22; Hooper, p. 159. Vestry meetings: on the open vestry see W. E. Tate, *The Parish Chest* (3rd edn. 1969); an expanding London suburb like Streatham in the 1840s–50s had a select vestry, with elected members. Maria Knowles died in April 1836 aged 61, leaving £300 (admin. PCC Capes August 1836).

[8] Drawings 1838 for Lord Egremont and Lord Monson, n. 14 below. Gray's Inn, n. 37 below.

did not set eyes on the sea—a morning's journey from Reigate on the Brighton coach—until his twentieth year, on the family's first seaside holiday from suburban London, in 1851. There was to be no travel for pleasure in this family until its head had established himself.

Two 'buildings of the future', for architects like this, had been completed in London early in the 1830s, two Italian *palazzi*, Soane's State Paper Office and Barry's Travellers' Club, both actually designed—just—in the reign of George IV. But the particular magnet in 1834 was that fire-sent chance for architects, the burning of the Houses of Parliament in October. Knowles may well have stood in the excited crowd with his friend from Pall Mall, watching the flames and thinking his practical ambitious thoughts. At any rate, he entered the ensuing competition and in the spring of 1836 his designs were hung between Bunning's and Lamb's in Room Two of the still unfinished National Gallery in Trafalgar Square. In drawing his perspective view, a finished river-scene now in the Victoria and Albert Museum, it is possible that he had the help of his artist friend Stanford. According to the catalogue his outsize plan was to include a 'great staircase', a feature of which he became fond. And three entrance-towers on the river front were to be 'so arranged that carriages may conveniently pass through them': the principle of the towered *porte cochère* (or sidelong gatehouse) was 'in the air' then and could be had from the Wilkinses' neo-Tudor houses; Barry was to Italianize it for a house at Walton-on-Thames. Knowles's practical arrangements for M.P.s were to include 'ample provision . . . for the escape of the impure air from the House of Lords', through ornamental bosses in the ribbed ceiling, as well as strict attention to 'the laws of acoustics' in the Commons. These drawings must have occupied much of his time during the second half of 1835. Some of his external Gothic ornament, seemingly emulating the church of St. Peter at Brighton, suggests that he was already aware of earlier work by the winner of the Parliamentary competition, Charles Barry, whose works and society he was to admire and cultivate.[9]

Meanwhile, Knowles moved his expanding family out of Bell

---

[9] Houses of Parliament competition: *Catalogue of the Designs . . . now exhibiting in the National Gallery* (1836), p. 43; Knowles's perspective drawing is illustrated in *The Houses of Parliament*, ed. M. H. Port (1976), p. 37.

Street (probably right after his mother's death in 1836, with £300 she left), up to Cockshut Hill, the southward continuation of Bell Street and loftier both topographically and socially, nearer to the 'Park-hills'. He probably took a short lease, on which house is not clear, perhaps a still existing, stuccoed two-storey detached house, with trellised tent-canopied veranda but the deep window-reveals of an older cottage, quite likely altered by himself. Except for James the eldest, the children on growing up probably remembered nothing of the Bell Street house or the workshop by the stream, or indeed of any life that was not comfortable. Cockshut Hill to their father was one more stepping-stone. For by 1840, the family was installed in a leasehold house facing Clapham Common—only sixteen miles from Reigate as crows fly across Surrey but, in a sense, a world away—and Knowles was entirely free of the old Bell Street connection, with his office fully established at No. 1 Raymond Buildings as for some thirty years to come. By 1847 he could be proposed as a Fellow of the Institute of British Architects: in spite of earlier self-assigned professional status, he carefully waited until his great-great-grandfather's lease on the plumber's-and-glazier's premises ran out at Michaelmas 1840, before measuring the seven years of professional practice required of a Fellow.[10] Not all the burgeoning new architects of the 1840s aspired or bothered to join the Institute, but this one was a 'joiner'. To adapt Professor Cockerell's prescription for success at the head of this chapter, Knowles was ambitious and diligent, sure of his abilities, and learning was to be got along the way.

The stepping-stones of a minor architect's early existence may seem hardly worth lingering over, yet how often are chapter and verse for professional and social emergence just then so fully available? He was ready for metamorphosis just at the moment when the times were ready for him. Both bold and cautious, he was in a sense an Early Victorian from birth, and the timeliness of everything that happened to him from the 1830s to the 1860s, compared with his obscurity when he died in the 1880s, reveals that watershed about 1870 between the Early and Late Victorians.

[10] No architect to be eligible 'who had any interest in any Trade or Contract connected with Building', Institute prospectus 1834–5; years of practice soon extended from five to seven. Cockshut Hill, Reigate directory for 1837. Clapham address: electoral register 1841 for Reigate Foreign; Batten's Clapham Directory 1841.

In contributing to the landscape his generation left behind, he laid the stepping-stone for his son's now better-known career.

In appearance the elder Knowles was below middle height, fair hair always parted on the left and, as time went on, side-whiskers framing his shrewd, plain face—keen, small brown eyes, long upper lip, wide mouth shut tight like a trap—a long-headed, determined, self-reliant and self-satisfied, rather silent man, very much on his dignity, quite humourless. Professionally, his chief concern was to combine functional efficiency with ceremonious effect in a building, whatever its style. His own tastes were classical-empirical; his politics, in those days of open voting, perhaps conservative-empirical, while remaining a close-mouthed radical at heart.[11] His first clients of whom we are aware were retired naval officers, country gentry, Tory peers. If any of them at first told their friends, as people do, that they had-a-little-man-who etc., the majesty of Mr. Knowles's demeanour, the efficiency of his arrangements, and/or his breath-taking scenic effects, soon inspired esteem.

ARCHITECT TO THE PEERAGE AND GENTRY

'Indeed, the time for such [large] villas is rapidly passing away . . . and [they will] only be referred to by architects to afford hints for smaller villas, and for inns of recreation.' J. C. Loudon prophesying the end of great houses, *Encyclopaedia of Cottage, Farm, and Villa Architecture* (1833), p. 790

By early 1837, Knowles had formed a gratifying connection. Captain the Honourable George Francis Wyndham R.N. (1785–1845) of Bramley House in Surrey was heir to his uncle the

[11] Electoral registers never gave political affiliations and John Vincent's *Poll-books* (1967), p. 1, says no poll-books are known for any London seat after 1841. Political affiliations at Reigate probably related only to Hardwicke–Somers control of borough property in Knowles's time. Vincent includes architects as epiphenomena of a mainly Tory landed ruling class, with no disrespect for their sincerity but as part of the pattern of life until open voting ended in 1872. Building craftsmen he found mainly radical, probably without differentiating between the recently risen and the rest. Knowles may have been a reader of the radical *Westminster Review*: a set, 1827–81, was in the 1886 book sale (chap. 1, n. 10); his St. John, Redhill, was discussed and illustrated in the *Westminster* in 1844; his son's youthful opinions seem to have been influenced by it (see chap. 3 on *Clapham Magazine*). Family lore from the late Miss Flint. Appearance from portraits, n. 36 below.

third Earl of Egremont, solely because the Earl had not bothered
to marry until after his sons were born: the natural sons, or 'right
heirs', could inherit the great Sussex house of Petworth, but only
the 'heir-at-law', his nephew, could have the title. Some sketches
in the Wyndham papers, among others by Knowles and dated in
May 1837, probably refer to Captain Wyndham's Surrey house.
In November 1837 the third Earl died. The fourth Earl inherited
Wyndham estates in Devon and Somerset, including the medieval
–Tudor–Queen Anne house, Orchard Wyndham, near Williton,
between Taunton and the Bristol Channel, near Watchet and the
church of St. Decuman's with its Wyndham Chapel, where he
was to be buried some seven years later. He succeeded just in time
to take part in the Coronation of 1838, but kept no permanent
London house. His portrait on the inn sign at Williton, in peer's
robes over naval uniform, after a painting at Orchard Wyndham,
shows a commanding personage as such portraits do. He had
married in 1820 a daughter of the Vice-Provost of Eton. (Her
brother Captain Roberts R.N. was married to one of the
Sargents of Lavington Park whose three nieces were to marry,
respectively, two Wilberforces and the local curate Mr. Manning.)
Wyndham had reached post-rank in 1812, when the future
William IV was Admiral of the Fleet. Via the network of naval
acquaintance Wyndham will have known the Earl of Hardwicke,
admiral and landlord of half Reigate in the 1830s, for whose
family successive Knowleses had done building jobs in Reigate
and possibly in Hampshire, where that first Ionic-colonnaded
house may well have been commissioned for some well–connected
naval officer. At any rate, Knowles at 30 knew the uses of the
grapevine.[12]

Bramley House, or Bramley Park, near the village south-east
of Guildford, was an eighteenth-century or older building when
Captain Wyndham acquired it in 1825, but in 1837 he rebuilt it as
'a noble erection of Brick and Slate, covered with Metallic
Cement, in imitation of Stone . . . of commanding elevation, and
on either side . . . a long Colonnade'. The house combined the

---

[12] 4th Earl of Egremont: *Complete Peerage*, vol. 5 (1926); O'Byrne, *Naval
Biographical Dictionary* (1849). Hardwicke accounts to 1807 (as chap. 1, n. 7) show
unspecified work by Knowles's father and grandfather on Yorke–Hardwicke
property; the Yorke house at Hamble, Sydney Lodge, was by Soane but might
incorporate lesser subsequent work by Knowles (e.g. conservatory with inept
apse); for information on this house I am grateful to Miss Stroud.

ceremonious with the functional, in a rather elementary symmetry of main rooms either side of the sixty-foot length of the entrance hall, and in the provision of no fewer than five water-closets on the ground floor. With its one-storey Ionic colonnades and Doric-pilastered upper storey (an inexperienced sequence of orders) this was probably a test-piece in more ways than one, for the architect was trying out a new patent cement facing material at the time. Bramley Park was demolished in 1951. It is better known as the childhood home of Gertrude Jekyll the great garden-designer: here from 1848 to 1868 she formed her lifelong attachment to Surrey.[13]

In 1837 Bramley Park prepared its architect's way to giant projects in the west country. For the new Lord Egremont, exalted at last in status and property, went slightly building-mad. Knowles had arrived just in time. His clients were often to be older men with new titles, new money, or new wives. For this patron he designed buildings large and small: a vast Greek-colonnaded 'Egremont Castle' intended to be 600 feet long (twice as long as Petworth, that prize denied), for a waterless plateau near Orchard Wyndham, designed in March 1838 but never built; the somewhat less vast, Grecian-colonnaded Silverton Park near Exeter, built between 1839 and 1845, but left unfinished; a giant semi-detached (back-to-back) pair of towered Italianate mansions, one for the Earl and one for the local Rector, built on an exposed height at Blackborough in Devon during 1838–44; a Gothic box of a church at Blackborough, started in 1838; an unexecuted rebuilding design for Williton church; rectories at Rewe, Kentisbeare, and Silverton, and the vicarage (Eastfield) at Williton. In the same years Knowles made ambitious designs for other clients. There remains a signed drawing of June 1838 for one elevation of a monster villa, influenced perhaps by Wilkins's Downing College at Cambridge and Barry's Royal Institution at Manchester, for Knowles's brother-Freemason, Lord Monson. This was probably intended for Gatton Park near Reigate,

---

[13] Bramley (demolished): much kind information from Lord Hamilton of Dalziel; sale particulars 1868, BL Maps, Surrey vol. II, 137.b.4(13); electoral registers and tithe map, SRO; fragment among Wyndham drawings deposited in RIBA Drawings Collection; old photographs now at NMR, and in F. Jekyll, *Gertrude Jekyll, A Memoir* (1934); wrongly captioned in Strong, Binney, and Harris, *The Destruction of the Country House* (1974), fig. 137, as 'for Ricardo family', much later owners.

where elaborate constructions of the 1830s are said to have included a marble hall modelled on the interior of the Corsini Chapel in St. John Lateran at Rome, doubtless by Knowles from engravings. There was also Dangstein, a large Greek temple of a country house with an enormous staircase, built about 1839 (demolished 1933) not far from Lavington Park in Sussex for a Captain James Lyon. And there was the church of St. John, Redhill, near Reigate, endowed by Lord Somers. Although Knowles had his *pied-à-terre* at Gray's Inn, the drawings of 1838 are inscribed from Reigate where he then still had the home drawing-office, more convenient for driving over to Bramley and Gatton when their lordships were in Surrey. But for journeys to building-sites in Devon and Somerset the point of departure was London, the coach from Piccadilly to Exeter taking almost twenty-four hours until the railway reached Taunton in 1842 and halved the time.[14]

The star turn of Knowles's early years of success, the design for Silverton Park (Pl. 2), said late in 1839 to be 'very recently begun on a magnificent scale', was probably prepared entirely in Gray's Inn.[15] From there Knowles exhibited two views of it in the Royal Academy Summer Exhibition of 1843, when building was still slowly going on. Its unbuildable predecessor, the Egremont Castle design, had been partly inspired by nothing less than the new Buckingham Palace of Lord Egremont's old Admiral of the

[14] Egremont Castle: drawing shown in my 'Silverton Park', *The Country Seat*, H. Colvin and J. Harris, eds. (1970), p. 235. For Silverton Park, n. 15 below. Blackborough House: photograph 1913 in E. S. Chalk, *Blackborough* (1934), also snapshots and comment from Howard Colvin, and on the church, Chalk in *Trans. Devon Assn.* (1910), p. 346 (both Chalk references from Dr. W. G. Hoskins). Rectories: Chalk 1934; Knowles to Earl 1842 on Rewe rectory as if he were contractor too, Wyndham Papers at Somerset RO, Taunton. Villa for Lord Monson: drawing published by John Harris in *British Drawings for Architecture in American Collections* (1971); on Lord Monson (1809–41), *Complete Peerage*, vol. 9; on 'Corsini Chapel' interior, Nairn and Pevsner, *Surrey* on Gatton Park. Dangstein (rebuilt 1933): tithe map 1839, electoral register 1842–3, sale particulars 1919, West Sussex RO; Lady Dorothy Nevill, *Reminiscences* (1906), p. 75, on living there ('a huge Grecian temple'); a James Lyon lived in Clapham (Batten's directory 1841, 1858). Travel London to Exeter, Cecil Torr, *Small Talk at Wreyland*, quoted in M. Robbins, *The Railway Age* (1965), p. 54.

[15] Silverton Park: *CBA for 1840*, p. 248; RA Summer Exhibition (1843) cat. nos. 1162, 1322; *CEAJ*, June 1843, p. 195; *Bldr*, 30 Sept., 16 Dec. 1843, pp. 406, 539; *Gardeners Magazine* (1843), p. 242. Now demolished (except stables), was a mile east of Silverton, 7 miles north of Exeter. See also *The Country Seat* as n. 14. An unsigned watercolour view is in the Mellon collection at Yale.

Fleet, the late King. The year of the new Queen's accession having seen also the new Earl's accession to his peerage, his prodigious family pride, combined with irritation at losing Petworth, apparently determined his choice of that model; or rather, a flattened version of it as engraved in 1838, with some extra influence from the new British Museum. But during 1838–9, while the difficulties of building on exposed heights were being demonstrated at Blackborough, the Earl shifted his attention to more sheltered property at Silverton for his principal house. His architect, having spent more time in London meanwhile, noticed that it was no longer fashionable to take the Greek Revival literally; so, gradually, he modulated the Castle design from long-strung-out Late Georgian Greek into a compacter Early Victorian Grecian. The result, by the time the Earl died in 1845, showed what could happen to such an architect moving into the swim, even if his client did not. There were colonnades on colonnades, Corinthian upon Ionic, and threaded through them the square piers and intermittent parapets of the well-thumbed monument to Thrasyllus that Greek Revivalists had made much of, but with recessions and projections of porticoes and pavilions forming a whole tissue of temples, or stage scenery, and studded with lion-mask gutter spouts taken, more likely, from Barry's new Reform Club than from some more classical model. Both the enriched Thrasyllan pedestals on the skyline and the lion-spouts were added after the exhibited design of 1843: designing here was a progressive affair. In total effect it was the fantasy of a client born in the eighteenth century and old enough to have served in Nelson's navy, interpreted by a bold young man unhampered by a careful education but, with a plumber-and-glazier's con-servatory-designing-and-landscaping eye, keen to stage a pictur-esque ensemble. There were to be some parallels in the younger Knowles's designing of Aldworth for Tennyson a generation later.

One feature at Silverton, the processional frieze around the upper storey, looked classical enough but represented the passage of the Israelites through the Red Sea: Knowles had probably been reading an almost Ruskinian appeal published in 1840 by Alfred Bartholomew (later, briefly, the first editor of the *Builder*) for sculpture in the spirit of Greek art but such as 'a Christian of the nineteenth century would, by the purity and dignity of his imagination, produce'. (That Bartholomew was talking about churches was one of those inconvenient facts that eclectic designers ignore.) Whatever the sculptural theme, the entire exterior was covered with, and all ornament executed in, a patent metallic-sand cement sent down in casks ready for mixing from Messrs. Benson Logan & Co. of New Broad Street, City. Its makers claimed that it would assume an agreeable stonelike colour and require no painting, that it would in fact be 'the most perfect substitute for stone ever yet introduced'; one can but observe that some specimens still around in this century tend to have a disagreeable greenish-brownish, unstonelike cast.[16]

Inside, a grandiose central hall (Pl. 2, as drawn for the Royal Academy exhibition probably, but doubtless never fully realized) was intended to combine certain features of Barry's two-storey hall at the Reform Club and a hall just added at Deepdene in Surrey, yet these models were treated with a difference. Through the centre arch of a triple arcade at one end was drawn the first flight of a staircase to the upper gallery, to which twin flights then proceeded at right angles to the first; and this idea of threading a T-shaped staircase through an arcade must have come from James Wyatt's stairs at Buckingham Palace as illustrated in Pyne's *Royal Residences* of 1819: one suspects that Pyne and Debrett were the Earl's favourite reading. By the 1840s stairs pouring through arches were motifs for painted scenery in theatres or at Vauxhall Gardens, just as Silverton's mixed colonnades outside had more than a whiff of the gin-palace 'fancy style' then enlivening London, not that the Earl or his architect would have admitted such a thing. For the scale of this house, two-hundred feet long, set it in a class by itself. At any rate, Knowles was to serve up his interpenetrating staircase again as late as 1860 in the Grosvenor Hotel, and a two-storey hall soon appeared *diminuendo* in his own house at Clapham Park.

He must have felt it something of a triumph to reach the Royal Academy in 1843 with two drawings that were no architect's dream but in course of erection under irreproachable auspices. Even though the exterior view was skied over a door, the cata-

[16] Alfred Bartholomew, *Specifications for Practical Architecture* (1840), section 681. On Benson Logan & Co.'s cement, *Bldr*, 16 Dec. 1843, p. 539, and London Architectural Society papers, MS. vol. 1 (1844) esp. p. 51 (RIBA Library); also Knowles's own paper 1850, n. 33 below.

logue entry was right at the top of the first page for the Architecture Room and, to arrive there at all, had been passed by the
architect R.A.s Smirke, Cockerell, and Barry, whose comments
one would like to have heard. The Latin tag on the catalogue title
page that year was from Quintilian: *Docti rationem Artis intelligunt,
indocti voluptatem*, or, something for everybody.

With the Earl's torch-lit funeral in April 1845, all work on
Silverton Park came to a stop, and the title died with him. The
mansion was dismantled in about 1892, when our photograph
was taken, and later demolished. A century after the Earl's death,
efforts to identify this photograph brought forth the following
memories:[17]

The lovely vanished house . . . [was] built by my grandfather's half-
brother the last Earl of Egremont. . . . As a small child I stayed there
frequently, with his widow, my great-aunt . . . who outlived her
husband many years. I can remember . . . playing in and out of the
colonnades as a child, and as a great treat the steward . . . used to
unlock the unfinished rooms for my nurse and myself to see . . . the
floors were unboarded and chimneypieces unfinished, and there were
large wooden cases, containing marbles and carvings, which Lord
Egremont had brought from Italy and Florence in his yacht. . . . My
great-aunt used to drive in a yellow coach from Orchard Wyndham
to Silverton and stay a few months in each place.

This reminiscence in 1945 was caught just in time, for the Countess
had died in 1876. It catches too the only hint of domestic life in
an extraordinary piece of stage scenery solidly stranded in Somerset for fifty years, relic of a European nineteenth-century mode of
seeing Hellenistic architecture that was to culminate in the
Victor Emmanuel monument in Rome.

So, in May 1843, Knowles could proudly mount the staircase
in Trafalgar Square on Private View day among the guests come
to gaze at the Landseers and Turners. Whatever the strains and
miseries of those years in England—when newspapers were
reporting 'exhaustion of the resources of all classes'—he had
successfully brought family and practice to the great centre of
things, or the suburbs thereof. We may guess that the 'Condition
of the People question', erupting in the bitter riots of 1839 and
1842, concerned him less than the effect on his clients of Peel's
approach to a free-trade policy: would that encourage a new set

[17] *CL*, 7, 21 Sept. 1945.

(merchants) to build more, or only offend the existing set (land-owners)? Perhaps he already sensed the impending shift in his clientele from the one to the other; yet merchants, in the old English way, tended to resemble landed gentry as fast as ever they could. The exodus from living over the warehouse in the City, often with a generation's stop in the suburbs on the way to the country, was already going on and almost any warehouse design might lead to a country-house commission. While Lord Egremont lived, there was still the example of Barry's lavish employment by the Duke of Sutherland. Nevertheless, in London was the place for an ambitious architect to be.

At first, several commissions in Surrey still took Knowles southward from Clapham, down the old Brighton road through Mitcham and Sutton to Reigate. Bypassed by the Brighton Railway and the new carriage road through Redhill, trade had slackened in Reigate, 'once the pride of the Brighton road—now occasionally re-echoing with the crack of a solitary whip!' as the *Illustrated London News* put it in 1844. It followed that City merchants began to find the neighbourhood suitable for country life. For one of these, Knowles built a house, probably not notable in itself except as his predictable next step from Greek to Italian, but leading to patronage even more fruitful than Lord Egremont's. In 1844 there stood 'on Reigate Heath, westward of the town . . . an Italian villa, lately erected from designs by Mr Knowles . . . the property and residence of Henry Lainson esq., brother of the late Alderman of that name, of London', John Lainson; since early in the century John and Henry Lainson had been in business as wholesale drapers and warehousemen at 53 Bread Street, City of London, and as retail linen drapers 'near the Platform, Rotherhithe' (also listed as 'next to the Angel' at No. 8 Rotherhithe Street), by the mid-1830s expanding their warehouse into Watling Street, and at Rotherhithe taking an Aldred as partner. There had been an Aldred, linen draper, at Reigate in the 1820s; and at the Knowles wedding in Rother-hithe church in 1831, an Ann Lainson was bridesmaid. Whether Knowles came in touch with the Lainsons via Aldred and the Browns of Rotherhithe, or in touch with Rotherhithe and his future wife via Aldred and Lainson, or whether he built for any of them in the City, or what the first Clapham connections were, one can only conjecture. Two of his chief clients were to be

William Cook, founder of a drapery dynasty in St. Paul's
Churchyard, who married John Lainson's daughter and lived for
a while in Clapham before moving to Kent, and their son Francis
Cook, eventually drapery tycoon, art collector, and baronet of
Richmond Hill and Cintra, who was born in Clapham. At any
rate Henry Lainson bought Colley Manor west of Reigate in
1842 and proceeded to build his villa, demolished in this century,
and part of this narrative only as a link in the Cook connection.[18]

The east side of the parish was livelier, where with new modes
of transport a new community was springing up under the old
local name of Redhill, an expansion requiring a new district
church. Dedicated to St. John the Evangelist, a nave, chancel,
and west tower were built in 1842–3 of white Suffolk brickwork
essentially to one of Knowles's unused designs for St. Peter's,
Williton, in Somerset; aisles were added later by Robert Hesketh,
and still later Knowles's portions were replaced by the great Late
Victorian architect John Loughborough Pearson. The site is on
high ground overlooking the blue distances of Earlswood
Common to the south, and overlooked by the wooded rising
ground of Redhill Common to the north. Earl Somers, em-
powered by custom as lord of the manor to grant away waste
land with the consent of the copyhold tenants, 'gave' a piece of
Earlswood Common for a new church and schools. Not a
'Commissioners Church', being apparently built entirely out of
private donations, headed by £1,000 from Lord Somers and a
gift for a font from his wife, St. John's was consecrated in the
autumn of 1843. At the Royal Academy in 1844 Knowles
exhibited a drawing, probably not now extant, of his (doubtless
plaster) fan-vaulted chancel. In surviving exterior views, the
church seems at first glance only a minimal Gothic box, meagrely
spired. But on second glance it must have been arresting. The
Westminster Review took the trouble to show an engraved view
of it in 1844 (Pl. 12) alongside an article that singled it out for
comment. An anonymous 'E' (possibly the youthful John T.
Emmett, an architect later known for outspoken journalism)
combined a long review of recent architectural books with a brief

---

[18] On buildings for the Cooks, n. 40 below, and chap. 4. Lainson's villa: E. W.
Brayley, *Surrey* vol. IV, part II, p. 236; Henry Lainson of Brixton, Lambeth, was
a Rotherhithe property owner e.g. in 1834 (electoral register, SRO); a Henry
Lainson Jr. of Reigate visited the Soane Museum in 1841 (visitors' book).

survey of the current state of the profession and remarks on new buildings. Aspersions upon churches led him to commend the church at Redhill for being 'almost as imposing as a cathedral' (Emmett's eye, if it was he, improved later on). Yet, while admiring the 'lofty open arches' upon which the tower stood, he thought the architect ought to have 'continued the lines of the whole of the piers upon which the tower rests to the ground, instead of allowing two of them, the piers at the back, to be lost in the body of the church' so that the tower scarcely seemed 'to stand upon all fours', reminding him of 'a stool with but two legs placed for support against a wall'.[19] There we have the touch of eccentricity without which no work of Knowles was complete, here born of a curious blend of imaginative pilfering out of recent architectural literature with practical thought about the site.

The site is part of what geologists call the Lower Greensand scarp-slope where sandstone overlies clays, a situation conducive to land-slips in wet weather in this area, the composition of which was known to the geologist Gideon Mantell in 1841 (then living in Clapham) when he contributed a geology section to Brayley's *Surrey*. Generations of local craftsmen will have known its habits: local familiarity, as with one's own skin, is sometimes neglected by historians. (The church at Williton, for which Knowles first made this design, stands on river-gravel.) Bartholomew in his *Specifications* of 1840, which seems to have been one of Knowles's bibles, pointed out the dangers for church towers standing on soft or rolling soils, and said that in open country even strong clay was apt to move. Hence the apparent virtue in lightening the load of the tower. Although the *Ecclesiologist* in 1843 found Knowles's tower 'totally unlike any ancient model', west towers with open ground floors were known in the middle ages (St. Peter Mancroft, Norwich) and after (St. Mary, Warwick), and eighteenth-century architects had noted with interest the opening up of Wren's St. Magnus tower for the widening of the London Bridge approach. Probably more influential here was the open-arched tower of Barry's first Gothic church near Manchester

---

[19] St. John's, Redhill: *Westminster Review* (1844), pp. 232–3; *Ecclesiologist*, Feb. 1843, p. 95; *ILN*, 28 Oct. 1843; Brayley (n. 18), p. 248; Church Commissioners file no. 5627; Knowles drawings (unused) for Williton church, Wyndham drawings, RIBA Drawings Collection.

(All Saints, Stand) although, as with those earlier examples, all four corner supports were visible. A more ambivalent treatment was to be found, however, in a Tudor-revival house in Cornwall, Pentillie, by William Wilkins (father or son), published by Britton and Brayley in 1831: Pentillie had a prominent carriage-porch merged with a keep-like tower interpenetrating the body of the house, two foreleg turrets standing out in the open while the bases of the hindleg turrets were 'lost' in the house. (One wonders if the Wilkinses took a good look at the Daniells' popular views of India, wherein similar building-formations occur, as well as at Tudor houses such as East Barsham; Knowles, at any rate, was to show a taste for Indian views later on.) For more intellectual architects, a theoretical basis for exploiting such ambivalence could have been offered by Professor Willis's paper on 'The Interpenetrations of the Flamboyant Style' (though that actually dealt with smaller elements such as mouldings), published in 1842 in a volume also containing Willis on fan-vaulting. Be that as it may, a clever eclectic merely leafing through such papers could absorb the hints he needed. An ounce of suggestion, all through this career, could be worth a pound of pedantry. The carriage-entrance towers of Knowles's Parliament design were earlier experiments of the sort. While the five-sided apse at St. John's may well have come from one of Pugin's recent books, Knowles's tower horrified the Ecclesiologists because he was ready to compile hints from so many contemporaries: intimations of Pugin, Barry, Willis, Bartholomew, Mantell, Wilkins, and the Daniells all in one box would be, the more we see of him, about par for the course.[20] Old photographs of Redhill church suggest that the result was, visually at least, somewhat unsettling. Pearson seems to have managed the foundations for his fine tower, fifty years later, perfectly well. Nothing of Knowles's church remains: it was unique in its way. And that is all we know of his early successes outside the metropolis. Still under 40, he had now, during a period of national stress, to consolidate his position in London.

[20] Site: Gideon Mantell in Brayley's *Surrey* I (1841), 154; Bartholomew (n. 16 above), sections 260–4. Pentillie: J. Britton and E. W. Brayley, *Cornwall Illustrated* (1831); *AR*, June 1968, p. 469; also G. Richardson, *New Vitruvius Britannicus* II (1808), on elder Wilkins's Donington Hall. Robert Willis, papers 1839–41, *Transactions RIBA* (1842).

CLAPHAM PARK AND THE WAY TO PROFESSIONAL STATUS

'Clapham . . . was for many years after its early
growth a district of large houses kept by well-to-do
people of the conservative sort. They helped to maintain its original rural atmosphere and to protect it, in
the eighties and nineties, from "development". . . .
Some of them even had meadows and cows.' Thomas
Burke, *London in My Time*, 1934, p. 213

Every Monday evening from October to May, during the 1840s–
50s, members of the Clapham Athenaeum walked across the
Common to the parish schoolroom behind Nelson Terrace to
hear a lecture, by one of themselves or a visitor, on the steam
engine perhaps, or on medieval brasses or the Acropolis, or on
Mesmerism or the new Menai Bridge. The society was founded
in 1841, and in November Knowles was recommended for
membership. The architect Edward I'Anson Jr. joined in 1843,
the building contractors Thomas Cubitt and William Herbert in
1844, Thomas Bosworth the publisher and bookseller, Thomas
Alers Hankey the banker, and George Grove the engineer and
future lexicographer of music in 1845; and in 1846, William Cook
of Clapham Rise, probably the eldest son of the drapery
merchant of St. Paul's Churchyard. Only once, 'in consequence of
the disturbed state of the Metropolis and its suburbs, there was no
meeting of the Clapham Athenaeum on Monday evening
April 10th 1848', the day of the Chartists' failed march on
London from Kennington Common, which was just up the road.

The founders of this 'first-class society, composed entirely of
gentry', included John Peter Gassiot, 'experimental philosopher',
member of the Royal Society, and wine merchant, active in
getting up exhibitions of The Electric Light in Clapham; and
Gideon Mantell the geologist, whose lectures 'peopled with
living sentient beings the flinty rocks, the beauteous marble, or
the long-concealed limestone'; and Dr. Charles Pritchard the
astronomer, who had founded the excellent local grammar
school. There also arose and flourished a Clapham Literary and
Scientific Institution, attended by some of the same people but
inclined to be less select. Both societies died out in the late 1860s
when community cultural life waned in the suburbs. By 1870
local concerts and lectures, compared with their earnest pre-

decessors, were said to 'lack a peculiar *animus* which those . . . possessed. There was less class distinction then than now'; and a local historian, lingering over the old minute-books of the Clapham Athenaeum in the mid-1880s, thought they gave 'a surprising insight into the great intellectual life which existed at that time in this parish' and sadly attributed the fact that it had 'completely died away' to the 'introduction of increased facilities by the railway for access to London'. As late as 1860 the *Clapham Gazette* coined 'Athenaeumania' to express 'that rage for scientific lecture-rooms, debating clubs, etc. which seems to be at fever heat in the scale of the progressive thermometer'. But in 1868 the Clapham Athenaeum was dissolved—and, in a sense, immediately reincarnated on a higher plane a few yards away, when the Metaphysical Society was founded at The Hollies.[21]

If Mr. Caudle complained to Mrs. Caudle in 1845 that 'retired wholesales never visit the retired retails at Clapham', this was partly because suburban social geology was a prime target of *Punch*, which in its first year in 1841 singled out the 'Clapham group' as next below the 'Russell-square group' in the Transition Class of Middle Life. *Punch* liked to guy earnest local societies as outposts of its favourite guy, the Society for the Confusion of Useless Knowledge. But the March of Mind did not mind, and the metropolis enriched suburban life before eventually impoverishing it. The Clapham that gratefully arranged an entertainment for its five hundred volunteer constables of 'the memorable 10th of April'—with dinner in a marquee set up in a field near the Common and the company promenading afterward to the music of a band, as reported and drawn in its other favourite periodical, the *Illustrated London News*—was no mean community. With a population by then almost three times that of Reigate, and grown from a village as ancient, though formerly much smaller than that market town, Clapham was poised in this period, for all the troubles of the 1840s but more confidently in the 1850s, at a singularly cohesive stage of its existence; no wonder those looking back from the Late Victorian decades thought it a golden time. The earlier burgeoning of the Clapham

[21] Minute-books Clapham Athenaeum at Minet; also *CG* reports at the time, and first leader on previous 17 years in *CG*, Nov. 1870; J. W. Grover, *Old Clapham* (1887), p. 54. Athenaeumania: *CG* leader, Jan. 1860, p. 25. Metaphysical Society, chap. 6, second half.

Sect involved a much smaller group of people (although its great outcome, the ending of slavery in British dominions, involved millions) and is outside the limits of this story. Yet Clapham thereby, and in other respects, had a history; it was not born in 1840. Macaulay, on weekly visits to his sister in the 1840s, 'continually [to] be seen crossing the Common on his walks from London', regarded himself as 'one of the aborigines returning to the haunts of his youth'. Long before, John Evelyn had been accustomed to visit Samuel Pepys at his 'very noble house and sweet place' here, near the end of their old age. By the 1830s Mr. Tag-rag the Oxford Street shopkeeper of the popular novel *Ten Thousand a-Year* lived in his Satin Lodge at Clapham, and multiplied, so that a generation later another novelist analysed the gentry of such a suburb as 'composed chiefly of those who had sufficient fortune to have left their old City employments and retire, or of those whose parents had made their fortune for them, and of a few families whose ancestors had lived there when scarcely three houses besides their own existed'.[22] In the 1840s–50s, with all the energies the more intelligent and ambitious residents were expending in the world outside, they had plenty left over for local use; social geology was characterized by expansion rather than stratification; and a high-minded regard for self-education prevailed.

Early in 1844, members of the Clapham Athenaeum were told that Mr. Knowles would deliver a series of lectures on The Rise, Progress, and Decline of Ancient Architecture—as befitted the architect of Silverton Park. On 4 March took place the first lecture, 'in which that gentleman remarked, at some length, upon the Pyramids, and other works, of the Egyptians, illustrating the subject by numerous Diagrams'. Two months later the second lecture dealt further with the works of the Egyptians, assisted by plans, elevations, and perspective views. But, although the Greeks were then promised for next time, the series never continued. Enough was perhaps mutually felt to be enough. And Knowles was still attending to Lord Egremont's houses in Devon. At any rate, books sold after Knowles's death seem to have included such indispensable lecture-sources as the *Encyclopaedia Britannica* (1841 edition) and Wilkinson's three-volume work of 1837 on the Egyptians, recommended by Professor Donaldson the architect

[22] Anna B. F. Leigh Spencer, *Scenes of Suburban Life* (1866), p. 30.

and scholar.[23] Indeed, a remark by Donaldson in his opening lecture of 1842 at University College, that a published list of Egyptian buildings would be most useful, was probably partly responsible for Knowles's lecture, reinforcing the latter's faith in his own powers—for had he not himself built a temple or two? But his self-confidence in the role of architectural historian was brief. In subsequent sessions the more articulate I'Anson often held forth on the Greeks and other subjects; Knowles in the latter 1840s was not necessarily the busier architect.

We know very little of what Knowles was up to professionally between Silverton Park and the Great Exhibition competition in 1850. There was apparently a trough between the waves of his success outside London and his first large City commission of 1852, a trough (to shift the metaphor) probably filled with lucrative bread-and-butter work unsuitable for a former Royal Academy exhibitor to declare: designing for speculating builders, perhaps. An application from him to the Metropolitan Building Office in 1846, for approval of overhanging eaves, probably concerned a semi-detached 'model villa' pair of houses on the south side of what is now called Durand Gardens, Lambeth.[24] When he took his sons into his office as articled pupils on their reaching the age of 15 in 1846 and 1848 (although with George this didn't last), the jobs on his drawing-board may have seemed dull to them. But he was biding his time. Immediately after Lord Egremont's death, and perhaps with the fees from that splendid connection, he undertook his own house.

During the first years in Clapham he leased No. 2 South Buildings, a neat but featureless stock-brick, three-storey-and-garret terrace house facing the Common. It still stands as No. 33 South Side, the second house west from Crescent (then Brixton) Lane, part of a row formed or extended in 1812, and of the sort more admired in 1945 than in 1845. The front windows look across the Common to the parish church, where the Rector from 1813 until 1847 was the very evangelical Dr. Dealtry. When the

[23] Assuming that the books sold in 1886 (chap. 1, n. 10) were his. On Donaldson, chap. 3.

[24] GLRO, MBO Special Register of Approvals, vol. 15, 1846, case 322, applicant Knowles, premises Grove Clapham Road (i.e. The Grove, Stockwell, now Durand Gardens), a pair of houses on the south side probably influenced by the suburban London work of J. B. Papworth (Summerson, *Architecture in Britain 1530–1830*, fig. 424).

census-taker came in June 1841, the five children were aged nine to three, and there were two maidservants. It was a lively household. Susannah Knowles was to be remembered in the family for her shrewd and witty tongue; a portrait painted of her in 1852 caught a look of benign, intelligent amusement, as if smothering a smile; brown-haired and blue-eyed, with a round, sensitive chin, and taller than her husband. James the eldest, the principal of this narrative, had his father's fair hair and slight stature, his mother's eyes and mobile mouth, and her vivacity, with an intense nervous energy compounded from both parents, and a piercing gaze all his own. George was to be taller, with a round, cheerful face, all his life delightfully eccentric, talented, and purposeless, perhaps from early habit as younger brother evading those more strenuous than himself. Isabella was to be tall and sensible, with presence and humour, spirited but plain, long-faced and narrow-eyed like her father. Julia was a retiring middle sister. For Emmeline the youngest we have a fuller impression; she was 'small, vivacious, and had a sense of humour almost uncontrollable. . . . She was extremely nervous; so quick and sudden in her thoughts, that it was breathless work at times to follow them. She jumped at conclusions, likes or dislikes. . . . She had a most original manner of expression almost fantastic, and she saw things in flashes . . . she never lost her youthful outlook, her repartee was as flashing as that of her brother James . . . whom she greatly resembled in character.' In the midst of them, their father was given to muttering that *all* he asked was to be let alone —a recurrent request that was still family lore for more than one set of great-grandchildren born a generation after his death, which suggests that he inspired a memorable fond irreverence at home.[25]

An architect risen from a background of centuries of tenantry, until his father's taste of freeholding, would as soon as possible make his own house. It was suitable, moreover, in the time remaining before he could become a member of his professional institute, to make his own statement in the latest Barryesque style

[25] Electoral register SRO and census 1841. Portraits of both parents, n. 36 below. Family memories from the late Miss Flint of Haslemere in 1968, the late Miss Skilbeck during 1964-9, and in *The Letters of Maurice Hewlett*, ed. L. Binyon (1926), with description of Emmeline by her daughter-in-law, pp. 19-20; also photographs seen at Miss Flint's and others obtained by Eric Smith, Clapham Antiquarian Society.

in this neighbourhood frequented by architects and the grander builders. A site with almost, but not too much, country-house privacy was available from Thomas Cubitt, who for some years had been developing Clapham Park, as well as much of London north of the river. This development, lying between the old village cluster around Clapham Common and the oak-forested, furze-grown commons of Tooting to southward, consisted mainly of well-spaced large houses in their own grounds. Cubitt had acquired most of this property in the 1820s from the Kymer family, who had bought it in 1798 from the Duke of Bedford. This irregularly shaped parcel in Streatham parish, divided into two or three fields and known as Friday Grove since at least the sixteenth century, lay east of Dragmire Lane (an old track from Clapham to Tooting, now part of Cavendish Road); south of it was Hyde Farm, belonging to Emmanuel College, Cambridge. Farm-paths gave the only access until Grove (now Weir) Road was begun as a private way to Knowles's new house and extended in the 1850s by Cubitt's trustees. When Cubitt bought Friday Grove, it was occupied by one farmer. Knowles first took two acres, in June 1845, on which to build his house, with four more purchases during the next twelve years: in 1849 to extend his garden, in 1853 to secure privacy on the opposite side of the road, where he eventually allowed or caused a church to be built, in 1856 farther westward where he erected some detached houses as an investment when Cubitt's trustees were building opposite, and in 1857 a final strip north of the road to keep the Cubitt houses at bay. The mansion that Knowles built and named Friday Grove was mainly completed by 1846, except for a wing probably added early in the 1850s, before the family began to be diminished by marriage. Its grounds in their maturity a generation later were surrounded only by the large gardens of other large houses, a country-style church, and an open field ('during the summer months not a house is visible'). Still in 1876 this was briefly considered a fit country house for a Lord Mayor, Polidore de Keyser the successful hotel-keeper. But by then a new neighbourhood of small houses was already gathering, and in 1895 when the covenants on Knowles's first purchase ran out the house was demolished for redevelopment.[26]

[26] Friday Grove: information kindly furnished by Hermione Hobhouse; abstract of title, St. Stephen's, Clapham Park (Church Commissioners as chap. 5,

In the 1840s, for a rising family, this was a different milieu from South Buildings, so near the shops and bustle of Clapham High Street. Most of the fellow-parishioners Knowles now met at Streatham church on Sunday mornings were rich City merchants, some of them future clients. That churchyard, a mile and a quarter south-east of Friday Grove, still had a village look above the High Road traffic although Streatham was already out-growing its village then. Beside the chancel arch a pathetic epitaph—*optimo et caro filio . . . in pugna Waterlooensi occiso . . . nox sequitur splendissimum diem*—reminded everyone of middle age in the congregation of that splendid day, then only day before yesterday. In 1845, Napoleon was as recent as Hitler was to the middle-aged of 1970, and remembrance of French wars was to recur in another generation in the 1880s when a Channel Tunnel was in question. Meanwhile unperturbed, this was a congregation of the comfortable, the cream of the southern suburbs.

In such a neighbourhood, Knowles formed his own house with care. Not like the more vertical mansions of Clapham Park, which followed a familiar Georgian formation once found singly in county towns but looking, after Cubitt's multiplication, like Outer Suburbia. Friday Grove was, rather, a middle-sized palazzo longer than it was tall, with the proportions appropriate to a country house, unaligned with any neighbour, aloof in its own 'home park' (Pl. 3). The main body of the house, with ground floor projecting at both ends, was probably modelled on Robert Banks's design, made in Barry's office in 1845, for No. 12 Kensington Palace Gardens, quarter-turned by Knowles to place his entrance at one end. Barry himself was to amplify this Genoese-palace formation at Cliveden, and Knowles was to extemporize on the theme in Kensington. Friday Grove was about one hundred feet long and undoubtedly covered with patent metallic-sand cement.

The most memorable room inside was the skylighted central hall inlaid with scagliola, mirrors, and plaster. The widely spaced Corinthian columns of a first-floor gallery rested on solid ground-floor walls that simulated an arcade with pilasters and recesses.

n. 39); Dom Anselm Hughes, 'The Manor of Tooting Bec', *SAC* vol. 59 (1962); OS 25″ map 1871; sale catalogue 1876 in BL Maps Surrey vol. III, 137.b.5(8). De Keyser's Catholicism may have led to a subsequent local illusion that Mrs. Knowles had been a Roman Catholic.

The walls behind the gallery, from which the bedrooms opened, were 'enriched with a representation in alto relievo of a Greek procession . . . also eight niches . . . with statues after the best models'. On plan this gallery seems to have been less than four feet deep, barely enough for the skirts of 1846, let alone those of 1860. The staircase had its separate compartment, the central hall not being on a scale to admit one. Altogether this was a bijou Reform Club *cortile* but for one freakish touch, the keystone-heads of the lower recesses, painted or fired in colour, and apparently culled from some appropriately mongrel Elizabethan hall-screen. A picturesque touch in the morning room, a window over the fireplace—bending technique to pictorial effect as recommended by Loudon in 1833—was also to be applied by young Knowles for Tennyson.[27]

Servants were accommodated under the low-pitched roof, their windows probably overlooking the hall skylight in a way Barry had adapted from Italian precedent at the Reform Club. There were four servants at first, a cook, two housemaids, and a boy footman, not one a Londoner: they came from Rugby, Exeter, Marlborough, and Charlbury—like their employers, part of the great migration up to Town. Later a coachman was added, a coach-house being built about 1853, with room for four carriages; and there were stables, fowl-houses, greenhouse, fruit trees, and kitchen garden. The auctioneer in 1876 described spreading lawns—the garden extended four hundred feet south-westward from the house and the average depth of garden from the road was two hundred feet—with shrubbery walks, filbert grove, chestnut, lilac, Portugal laurel, weeping lime, laburnam, and may. And of course the house was 'approached by a Carriage Drive, encircling a Bed of Rhododendrons .[28]

So by 1846, only ten years after they had moved out of the Bell Street craftsman's cottage, the Knowleses were at home in the most princely house in Clapham Park. Before smiling patronizingly at the thought of *nouvelles richesses* inside, we have to remember that the household tastes of Georgian upper craftsmen had been formed by the upper-class mansions they worked in, and

---

[27] Plan in sale catalogue (n. 26). Chimney-piece windows: at Aldworth (bedroom floor), also on top floor of young Knowles's clubhouse in St. James's Street; this trick was not peculiar to the Knowleses but to a whole generation.

[28] Sale catalogue (n. 26). Servants: 1851 and 1861 census.

with such antecedents an Early Victorian architect to peerage and gentry had more educated taste than, for example, a new-rich mine-owner might have—and not only for the household arts but for what constituted good company too. The Knowleses will have looked down their noses at vulgarity before they left Reigate. James Thomas and Susannah lived at Friday Grove for thirty years. Isabella married in 1858, Emmeline and James in 1860, poor Julia not until 1872, and George stayed home; on their mother's death in 1876, he and their father moving—as *Punch* could have predicted—to Russell Square. It was to Friday Grove that young James's first wife came in 1862 and 1863 to bear her children and died so young. Here Emmeline's son Maurice Hewlett the future novelist was brought as a child to visit; in a pot-boiling book *The Road in Tuscany*, he was to compare the Baths of Lucca and Clapham Park in their 'leafy amenity' and 'smug obtuseness'. (Yet his brother recalled that their grandmother Susannah Knowles 'was a great wit and had a very shrewd tongue, whose sharp thrusts . . . were keenly enjoyed by Maurice', and Uncle George's comical company was 'a source of great delight'—this was not a stuffy family.)[29] And to Friday Grove Sir Charles Barry came for dinner, whatever he may have thought of his sub-palatial offspring. A little bungalow-lined road, Radbourne Road, S.W.12, now crosses the site. In 1847, ready at last to join his colleagues at the Institute, Knowles had in London something to declare.

The Institute of British Architects had been calling itself Royal since 1837 (though not generally called so by the public) on the strength of its charter from William IV. In 1847 the number of Fellows was 108, and meetings were held in a Georgian house at No. 16 Grosvenor Street. At the opening meeting of the 1847–8 session on 1 November, a paper was read by Matthew Digby Wyatt on Mosaics, and Knowles's nomination as Fellow was approved by the Council. At the next fortnightly meeting, a plan of the Temple of Minerva was donated by a George Knowles: an occasional correspondent of the Institute and a Royal Academy exhibitor of views of Greek temples, he seems to have had no connection whatever with the Clapham Knowleses; his rumoured

[29] M. Hewlett, *The Road in Tuscany* (1904), i, 124. On the day of the 1861 census, the baby Maurice and his parents were visiting Friday Grove; and see his brother's introduction to *Letters* (n. 25 above).

interest in Greek politics was to make trouble for young James in Rome. At the 29 November meeting, William Tite discussed a note from Joseph Gwilt upon Pointed Architecture, and J. T. Knowles was elected. He was duly admitted at the next meeting on 13 December, when Edward I'Anson held forth upon the building of sewers.[30]

At short range, in that autumn of influenza and commercial distress, 1847 would seem to have been a bad year for architecture, with the *Illustrated London News* running leaders on The Crisis, The Panic, alarms of French invasion, scarcity of money, and the atmosphere of prevailing gloom. Yet real hope for architects was implied in the leading article of 20 November on the recently elected Parliament, which included men like Cubitt, Stephenson, and Peto: 'There are more Bankers, more Traders, Merchants, Railway Directors, and Newspaper Editors, in this Parliament, than ever before found entrance there. . . . Politicians by birth have had a long trial; let us now try the man of business . . . men who conduct establishments equal in importance to many kingdoms. . . . Knowing this energy and talent to exist among us, shall we despair?' These were the new patrons. Disraeli, as novelist, looking upon Buckingham Palace, the National Gallery, and the British Museum just then, thought architecture needed remedies more extreme than parliamentary government: 'Suppose an architect was hanged?' More indicative of healthy ferment were discussions in the professional journals. A random wander down the index to the 1847 volume of the *Builder* turns up: Architects, how Mr. D'Israeli would improve them; shall they be excluded from sewers commissions? shall they be Royal Academicians? shall they measure? shall they only copy? Architecture, degraded state of, inklings of future of, improvement of, professors of not consulted, and so on. In the social scheme of things, some architects were doing rather well. Not many so well as the remodeller of Trentham Hall in Staffordshire, where a family wedding party of about thirty people in the autumn of 1847 included five dukes and Mr. Charles Barry. However, in a procession to lay the first stone of a new Athenaeum and Mechanics Institution at Sheffield, for example, the 'Architect

---

[30] Although the epithet Royal was more securely added in 1866, the fact remains that all printed notices of meetings from November 1837 on called it so: bound vols. in RIBA Library, from which details of meetings here cited come.

with Plans', flanked by 'Managing Director with Trowel' and 'Secretary with Vase of Documents', marched just before the noble guest of honour and the mayor. And with similar panache, an architect of a new town (Kingston-on-Railway, or Surbiton) drove his four-in-hand smartly down to the site from London. Many buildings might have no (named) architects at all.[31]

Once among the elect, Knowles was not slow to show his energies. With Barry, Cockerell, Donaldson, Godwin, I'Anson, Kerr, Sydney Smirke, and others, he sat on the original committee for an Architectural Publication Society from 1848 until its reformation four years later. He was one of twenty directors of an Architects', Builders', and General Insurance Company founded in 1848 under the chairmanship of Sydney Smirke, with offices in Lombard Street. During 1852-4 he served on the Institute's Council.[32] And on 27 May 1850 he presented a paper before his colleagues on The Propriety of the Application of Cements or other Artificially Formed Materials to the Exteriors of Buildings. If his premise that this was defensible was felt in 1850 to be out of date, his casting of derogatory comment upon the Gothic style into this gentlemanly arena did raise some dust, long before the Battle of Styles raged publicly in the late 1850s. 'It is not often that the Institute of British Architects indulge in aesthetics,' observed the *Civil Engineer and Architect's Journal* afterwards. 'Generally . . . they avert the discussion to a matter-of-fact question respecting the economical use of slate, the number of feet and inches in a broken column.' Noting with 'surprise and gratification' that Knowles's paper led to 'an animated and interesting discussion', the journal remarked that to find 'the use of deceptive materials' in poor taste would be to condemn 'half the buildings erected by members of the Institute'; yet they were now

---

[31] *Tancred* (1847), opening of chap. x. On Barry, *ILN*, 16 Oct. 1847, p. 248. On Sheffield, *ILN*, 4 Sept. 1847, p. 149. On Surbiton, Rowley Richardson's history and VCH *Surrey*, iii, 494. In 1858 'out of some 1800 practising architects only 200 were members of the R.I.B.A.', J. A. Gotch, *The Growth and Work of the Royal Institute of British Architects* (1934), p. 110.

[32] First APS vol., *Essays and Illustrations 1848-52* (1853). Almanac issued by this insurance company 1849 (tiny pamphlet RIBA Library); the consultant physician Sir James Eyre of Lower Brook Street was later useful to young Knowles as source of introduction in Rome; cf. also *ILN*, 24 June 1848, p. 405, on Architects etc. Annuity & Reversionary Interest Co. RIBA Notes of Meetings, Council election May 1852 when George Godwin, editor of the *Bldr*, also joined the Council.

increasingly aware that this 'pernicious system' had for too long 'cramped the energy and spirit of modern architects'; emancipation could only come with 'the revived study of Pointed Architecture, a style which nobly evidences that in building as in morals, *it is good to be honest and true*'.[33] That was the background of changing opinion against which Knowles spoke. His son was never to be guilty of such poor timing, or hardly ever.

It must have been a long evening, for it began with presentation by the President, Earl de Grey, of the Royal Gold Medal to Charles Barry, with speeches by both. Knowles then read his paper, most of it a sober, practical, ponderously phrased defence of the latest cements properly applied, with examples from his own experience, and pointing out that the science of geology having revealed 'the nature and quality of the materials, which compose the crust of our planet', it was now possible, even where no building stone was available, to secure 'dry, healthful, warm and comfortable habitations' by knowledge of materials in relation to 'the vicissitudes of our climate'—even on that Devon height at Blackborough. There had been too much emphasis, he thought, on costly materials (that is, by people like Ruskin), an admiration 'vulgar and barbarous'. He himself believed 'the emanations of the mind to be above and beyond the mere vehicle in which they are embodied'; much better 'to have the emanations of deep thought . . . embodied in materials, which might endure for only half a century'—the leasehold mentality, in short—'than the eternal stereotypes we now see rising . . . perpetuated in stone, which would endure for countless ages'. (He could not, of course, mention his own design just then being considered for the Great Exhibition of 1851, of which no description survives.[34]) He then deplored the lack of originality or grandeur in recent buildings and 'the unaccountable apathy of the profession [that] allowed a small and non-professional party [the Cambridge Ecclesiologists]

[33] *CEAJ*, Oct. 1850, pp. 332–3 (their italic). Various bound volumes of Institute notices and papers contain text and discussion; paper also printed in *Bldr*, 8, 15 June 1850, and in *CEAJ* for July; and *Bldr* leader, 1 June, p. 253, was devoted to the occasion; see also comment *Bldr*, 6 July, p. 316. The lecturer showed views of buildings by himself, unspecified.
[34] On the *c.* 245 Great Exhibition designs submitted in 1850: *CEAJ*, May, p. 207, *ILN*, 8 June, p. 403, *Bldr*, 8 June, p. 265, *Journal of Design*, Mar.–Aug., iii, 141. Knowles's design was one of those selected for honourable mention, but not one of the 18 singled out for distinction. Paxton's eventual design must have interested him (quietly) as the apotheosis of glass structures once of close family concern.

to assume the direction of our art, and to introduce a movement of retrogression to the styles and fashions of a former age, which must, I fear, if not soon checked, prevent, for some long period, all progress and improvement'. That is, Knowles thought himself a functionalist and modernist. Without wishing to disparage those 'who have with so much care and skill, sought out, and given correct, and beautiful illustrations of the structures . . . of the middle ages', he suggested that 'the talents of those gifted individuals be directed to investigations, which may result in the production of novelty, beauty, fitness in design and of greater economy . . . in adapting to the wants of the existing generation those great discoveries in physical science, which may and ought to increase . . . the diffusion of comfort, and rational enjoyment amongst all classes of the community'. Some of this he had probably soaked up from Henry Roberts's paper on The Dwellings of the Labouring Classes read in that room four months earlier. As he made no mention of the *chef-d'œuvre* at Silverton, he sensed that its pretensions were no longer appreciated in informed quarters.

If only his theory of rational building had been offered without the two red rags—defence of a 'sham' material, and hard words on the Gothic Revival—it might have provoked friendlier rebuttals on this eve of Paxton's triumph. 'Mr Francis . . . proceeded, at some length, to vindicate architects of the present day from the charge of servilely copying the buildings of the middle ages . . . and observed, that the charge of want of novelty and of copyism applies to those who affect the classic styles, rather than to those who try to follow the spirit of Mediaeval architecture.' Messrs Francis were to be responsible for some fairly servile classicism of their own during the next twenty-five years. Meanwhile, 'Mr G. G. Scott thought . . . that we are acquainted with so many styles, that we do not know which to select. . . . The charge of copyism, he repudiated altogether; what they did attempt by the study of ancient examples was, to catch their spirit, and . . . the revival had given greater proofs of vitality, than Architecture of an exclusively classical character had given during three centuries.' To which Knowles replied, probably more warmly than usual with him, that he considered 'no mediaeval erections were . . . superior to the upper portion of the steeple of Bow Church, nor is there a structure in the world so

exquisite as the outline of St Paul's'. And 'an observation by Mr
Scott, that there is more copyism in the details of Sir Christopher
Wren's works, than in most Gothic buildings he was acquainted
with, called forth the expression of a directly contrary opinion
from Mr Billings'. Whereupon the President 'pleasantly wound
up the discussion by pointing out the good often produced by
collision of opinions'. The supreme eclectic, Charles Barry, sitting
there in the glow of his new gold medal, said never a word. A
few years later, Scott was to compose a more flexible prescription
for secular architecture in the spirit of Thomas Hope's much
earlier recipe for 'borrowing of every former style' in order to
create 'an architecture which, born in our country, grown in our
soil, and in harmony with our climate, institutions, and habits, at
once elegant, appropriate, and original, should truly deserve the
appellation of "Our Own" '.

Knowles appears to have had Hope's book on his shelf, and he
will have known Henry Noel Humphreys's comments published
by Loudon, along with large chunks from Hope, in the *Architectural Magazine*. Writing in the Queen's coronation year,
Humphreys had urged the cultivating of 'the true prinicples of
adaptation and combination, to lead to the formation of an
original style, fitted to the feelings and customs of our present
high state of civilization'—thereby anticipating the hopeful
epithet first applied only in the late 1850s to architecture:
Victorian.[35]

ARCHITECT TO THE MIDDLE STATION

> 'That Class which, of all others, should be the most
> proud of its "order" . . . in this emotional, eventful,
> Transition Century . . . comprises, or has supplied
> with scarcely an exception, the genius, the intel-
> ligence, the industry—in a word, the Mind of the
> Century.' Preface to 'Gold, or, the Half-Brothers, A
> Story of Life in the Middle Station', by Camilla
> Toulmin, *Illustrated London News*, 4 July 1846

[35] Early use of the term Victorian for architecture: *BN* leader-heading, 18
June 1858, p. 617, quoted at head of chap. 4 below. A copy of the 1840 edn. of
An Historical Essay on Architecture (1st edn. 1835) by Thomas Hope, d. 1831, was
in the 1886 book sale (chap. 1, n. 10). Scott's later prescription for secular buildings
is quoted (chap. 4, n. 4) below; for Humphreys's see chap. 3 section heading,
'A Search for a Motive' below.

The decade between the two Great Exhibitions of 1851 and 1862 was fruitful for Knowles's reputation. His clients were no longer peers, but City merchants and/or property speculators. In 1852 he had portraits painted of himself and Susannah in watercolour by Henry Tidey of Percy Street, who exhibited them in 1853 at the Royal Academy.[36] It was Knowles's only appearance in those galleries between 1844 and 1860; perhaps his clients preferred not to have their buildings shown there, however well publicized in periodicals; undoubtedly the architectural R.A.s had a vaster pool of contributions to choose from. James junior, early in 1854, went off on a six-month tour of the Continent; from 1855 he continued in the office at Gray's Inn, assisting his father until he had clients of his own.

Raymond Buildings is the plain brick four-storey terrace of chambers, built in 1825, that lies along the west side of Gray's Inn gardens, looking across that historic expanse of trees and lawn to Verulam Buildings on the east side. No. 1 staircase, flanked by three-window fronts, is at the north end nearest the gate into Theobalds (then King's) Road. The Inn's war-damaged records throw out one morsel of information, that Knowles was a sub-tenant at No. 1 South, floor unspecified, from 1834 until at least 1873, and that he was assigned a set of chambers at No. 1 North, first floor, from 1836 until 1869, his annual rent to the Benchers of the Inn being £100, according to his will drawn up in 1860. Probably for the greater period his office occupied the entire first floor, with the idea from the outset that his sons should join him there. (One other pupil is known, Henry Legg, later more active than distinguished in the Victoria Street area.)[37] There were not many architects in Gray's Inn, but it was convenient. Various services were available in the neighbourhood among all the hangers-on of the law—a map-and-plan engraver in Warwick Court, a drawings-colourist in Great James Street. One of

---

[36] Signed and dated, in family possession; in RA catalogue as James S. Knowles, perhaps confused with James Sheridan Knowles the playwright. Tidey's other sitters at the RA in 1853 included a brigadier-general and a captain in the Grenadier Guards. Other portraits of Knowles senior include photograph reproduced in this book, a later one in family possession, and a bust by Thomas Woolner (chap. 7, n. 26).

[37] 'An old fellow-pupil with me under my father years ago', Knowles to Hopgood, 6 Dec. 1888, letter-book at WPL. Gray's Inn records: Librarian, 25 Sept., 20 Nov. 1968. Will: probate copy kindly shown to me by Mr. Oliver Hopgood.

Knowles's best sites—for Hodgson the book-auctioneer—was only a short stroll down Chancery Lane; the daily drive from Clapham Park, probably by way of Waterloo Bridge, will have afforded opportunity to contemplate during traffic-delays that fine site at the corner of Fleet Street, as well as potential sites in the Strand, then full of jostling little old buildings. From the austere chambers in Raymond Buildings issued successive series of drawings that form in retrospect a surprising panorama. Knowles's main series in the 1850s included warehouse, office, residential, and hotel commissions. A number of these came about through social propinquity in Clapham. There, on the side, apart from the main series, Knowles deftly managed to produce a useful little building while cementing his local acquaintance. Clapham social life in the 1850s is reflected in surviving pocket diaries of Sir Charles Barry, who had moved his family to Elm House on the north side of the Common in 1852, the year of his knighthood: dinners, conversaziones, Clapham Athenaeum meetings, 'Knowles 7 dinner' (1853), 'Mrs Knowles 8 o'clock' (1854), 'Mrs Knowles' (1855), 'Mrs Knowles $\frac{1}{4}$ before 7' (1856), occasionally an appointment with Knowles by himself.[38] In May 1854, according to the *Clapham Gazette*, a dinner 'of a most recherché character', attended by Barry and the Rector and other first citizens, was held at the new General Dispensary in Manor Street to celebrate the opening of 'this noble building', and a toast was drunk to Knowles, who furnished the design, 'sedulously and earnestly overlooked the works in progress, and devoted a vast amount of care and attention to the details of the building (Cheers). He had refused all fee or reward.' The Rector had founded a dispensary in other premises during the 1848 cholera epidemic, and there exists an unused design by Knowles, probably for a prospectus to lure subscribers, for a larger and quite different building than the one built: of the Italian-villa persuasion with triple-arched loggia and odd hood-moulds of a sort published by the architect Waring in 1850, all intended no doubt to be covered in patent cement; the facilities were to include quarters for resident staff. As built, smaller and more up to date, the Dispensary (still now in use for other purposes) stands behind a boiled-down palazzo façade of grey brick dressed with red-brick and stucco trimmings. One detail, a set of bulky (neo-Wren?) keystones,

[38] Barry diaries, RIBA MSS. collection.

was to be drawn upon by young Knowles in St. James's Street. In its moderate pomp, and the context of Clapham Manor Street's two-storey Early Victorian houses, the Dispensary looks no more consequential than it should.[39] It was a footnote to its architect's chief work during 1852–4, on a prominent site by St. Paul's cathedral.

City of London dealers in 'Manchester wares', or cotton goods manufactured in Lancashire, were known as 'Manchester warehousemen' long before architects made Manchester's warehouses something for the City of London to emulate. Textile manufacture as part of the first wave of the Industrial Revolution had been followed by a new wave of urban wholesalers, channelling goods from the factories to the shops. The typical warehouseman and drapers' outfitter of the Cheapside–St. Paul's area occupied a complex of older premises taken over gradually as business expanded, until a fire or prosperity induced total or partial rebuilding. William Cook, who came to London to seek his fortune in 1806 and worked his way up in the drapery trade from Clerkenwell to Cheapside, set up opposite the south porch of St. Paul's in 1834. By 1847 Messrs. Cook, Sons & Co. occupied six adjoining buildings there between Black Swan Alley and King's Head Court, and paid higher rates than any neighbour. The whole row from St. Paul's Chain (Godliman Street) eastward to Watling Street, before the advent of Cannon Street, consisted of narrow four-storey structures dating from rebuilding after the Fire of 1666, some later raised to five or six floors and much extended at the back. By 1852 Messrs. Cook had acquired various small sites on courts and lanes behind the main premises: rebuilding probably began at the rear, so that business could be carried on there during rebuilding on the main site; a principal requirement of a City architect was the minimum interruption of business. Part of this rearward extension lay along Knowles Court, where it is not impossible that James Thomas Knowles arranged the demolition of Israel Knowles's own house.[40]

In the summer of 1852, the south arm of St. Paul's Churchyard

---

[39] Earlier design: extra-illustrated copy of Manning and Bray, *Surrey*, GLC Members' Library. *CG*, Apr., June, Dec. 1854.

[40] *Cook's of St Paul's*, commemorative pamphlet at GL; *DNB* on Francis Cook, d. 1901; Tallis view of St. Paul's Churchyard, part 16, 1847 (*John Tallis's London Street Views*, ed. P. Jackson, 1969); rate books, Castle Baynard Ward, G.L On Israel Knowles, chap. 1, no. 5 above.

became partly wilderness with Messrs. Cook's demolition works as well as the extension of Cannon Street into the east end. Crowds for the Duke of Wellington's funeral in November will have found that quarter of the cathedral precinct looking like a battlefield. 'Here, in streaming London's central roar. . . . Under the cross of gold/That shines over city and river. . . ./. . . in the vast cathedral leave him': the young architectural assistant on Cook's building-site, thirty-five years later, would be persuading Tennyson to read those rolling stanzas to a party beside St. James's Park.[41] During that summer of 1852 an archaeological find was 'exhumed during the excavations for Messrs. Cook's new warehouses . . . at a depth of about 25 feet': a limestone slab carved with a lively abstract monster in flat relief and inscribed with the name of Tuki. Now in the Museum of London, it is thought to be an Anglo-Danish tombstone, possibly for a member of Canute's court. In 1852 it was called Runic. In August young Knowles wrote to the *Illustrated London News* a careful description that suggests he had taken expert advice, and indeed he went into an energetic swirl of activity over it. To the annoyance of antiquaries who wanted it for the British Museum, the Cooks and the Knowleses, as late as February 1853, intended to build the slab into the wall of the chief warehouse room in course of erection over the spot where it was found, but other counsel prevailed and eventually it was deposited at Guildhall.[42] How typical these events of 1852 on St. Paul's hill—the great funeral, the exhumed slab—of that old compost-heap, the City. On this ground, doubtless after a concrete foundation was laid, the seven-storey building (Pl. 4) went up in 1853, 'ninety days only having elapsed from the time that the first brick was laid to the period that Messrs. Cook were enabled to resume their business' there— top speed in any age, although warehouse spaces need less finishing than other building-types. In height the drapers' cornice almost rivalled the cathedral's own, separated only by the width of a crowded thoroughfare; as early as 1827 James Elmes had urged the City Corporation to 'emancipate their fine cathedral from its monstrous thraldom' of surrounding roofs; nevertheless,

---

[41] According to Beatrice Knowles's note, Oct. 1887, chap. 8, n. 82 below.
[42] On Anglo-Danish tombstone (ill. Pevsner, *London One*, Bldgs. of England, fig. 3): *ILN*, 28 Aug., 2 Oct. 1852, pp. 157, 283; Knowles to Hewlett, 20 Sept. 1852 (*WPL*); *Archaeological J.*, X (1853), 82, XLII (1885), 251; and information 1965 from the then Guildhall Museum.

Cook's parapet was lower than that of St. Paul's as seen from a distance, and the great dome on its drum still rode the rooftops then.[43]

Large warehouses had been going up in the City for some time, but the latest models were in Manchester, where the Cooks had business connections; moreover, one architect active there, Edward Walters, was first cousin to Edward I'Anson of Clapham and had worked in the office of Lewis Vulliamy, also a resident of that energetic suburb; Knowles probably knew, especially, Walters' design for a warehouse in Portland Street, Manchester, and engravings of the huge Watts warehouse by other architects near by. In the 1850s warehouses were beginning to look like palaces: on a site beside St. Paul's, it seemed right to keep the horizontal dressings of palazzo prototypes; warehouses that looked like warehouses, with emphasis on the vertical, belonged in Thames Street. Nor did Cook's have the long ribbons of windows that earlier textile houses had; with its storeys of equal height it could have been an office building. A contemporary critic remarked on 'the danger from fire, through the non-compliance with the provisions of the Building Act', referring to its great undivided internal spaces. Messrs. Cook got round this, as appeared when Captain Shaw of the Fire Brigade brought the matter up in 1861 after his predecessor's death in the Tooley Street fire:

Within a stone's throw of St Paul's there are warehouses stored with goods of immense value . . . a vast mass of flames would be generated which would mock the efforts of all the fire-engines of the metropolis. The Act of 7 and 8 Victoria provides that the cubical contents of no warehouse shall exceed 216,000 feet, but the Manchester warehouse-men have completely evaded this enactment, under the plea that as they break bulk and sell by retail they are no longer warehouses. The cubical contents of the premises of Messrs. Cook . . . are said to be more than 1,000,000 feet.

Messrs. Cook were not alone in this, others near by including Wynn Ellis, Everington & Howell, and Pawson's, a greater pile of tinder around the cathedral than ever before. Nevertheless, Knowles's building outlasted the Second World War, equipped

[43] James Elmes, *Metropolitan Improvements* (1827), p. 6. Ninety days: *Bldr*, 3 June 1854, p. 287.

from the first with 'appliances for the discharge of water tantamount to seventeen fire-engines'. Other devices included a
'moving chamber traversing a perpendicular shaft' for lifting
goods, run by a small steam-engine; goods lifts, indeed, made tall
warehouses possible, and the old hoist outside the window was
not for handling delicate materials in bulk in this climate. The
internal spaces were lyrically described: 'there is in the centre of
the building a grand elliptic lantern, adorned with elegant
friezes at the several stories, which admits a flood of light from
the sky. . . . The galleries are supported by slender Doric columns;
and solid walls are superseded by lateral series of elegant arches,
which . . . present picturesque vistas suggestive of indefinite
space and distance . . . more like a Walhalla than a warehouse.'
Outside, the choice of white Suffolk bricks (laced with a little
red brick) to clothe a building in the smoky heart of London then
is a mystery. Knowles and the Cooks simply took the coming
coat of soot for granted. Wren's grimy masterpiece looming
above them we now see as the Victorians never did, and by the
time Cook's building was demolished in 1960 the air around it
had changed in quality.[44]

William Cook the first died in 1869 worth, it was said, more
than two million pounds. His eldest son having died, Francis
the second son became head of the firm (p. 144). At the time of
his death in 1901, Cook of St. Paul's had the 'largest concentration
of textiles in Britain's distributive trade'. The ground that lay
beside St. Paul's during Fire and Blitz and saw the comings and
goings of generations of tycoons, builders, and customers, the
ground that held Tuki's stone and the wealth that filled Doughty
House with Old Masters and recreated Vathek's villa at Cintra,
is now an open space at the head of a new processional way from
the river, intended to rescue the cathedral at last from monstrous
thraldom. It is difficult now to imagine that this strip of lawn
and paving ever held much of anything.

In the summer of 1854, while Knowles was busy with a new
building in Fleet Street and enjoying his successes in St. Paul's
Churchyard and Clapham Manor Street—with one son abroad
and the other quite useless in the office—there came a new com-

[44] *Bldr*, 19 Feb. 1853, p. 113; *CBA for 1854* (1853), p. 257; *ILN*, 25 Mar. 1854,
p. 270; also on fire danger, *Annual Retrospect of Engineering and Architecture*, ed.
G. R. Burnell (1861), p. 270, quoting Captain Shaw.

mission to design a large house in Kensington for George Moore, another textile magnate, partner in a great lace warehouse in Bow Churchyard. Moore was prominent in the City and later a considerable philanthropist, celebrated by Samuel Smiles. Because of its location, this house was more old-fashioned in design than Knowles's work in the City. The Crown property now called Kensington Palace Gardens was in 1854 administered by the Commissioners of Woods and Forests. As early as 1841 the Office of Woods, then combined with the Office of Works, had been making plans to lease the former kitchen garden of Kensington Palace for high-class residential development. Twenty of the plots were taken as a speculation by J. M. Blashfield the mosaic-and-terracotta manufacturer, whose career was only temporarily checked by the bankruptcy in 1847 that terminated his interest here. In general, development was hampered by the financial stresses of the time. When the Great Exhibition opened near by in 1851, about thirteen houses were occupied and others stood empty in carcass. By mid-1854 all but two of the ultimate twenty-nine houses in this enclave seem to have been built and occupied, or about to be occupied. London was slowly moving westward. Occupiers in 1854 included the contractors Samuel Morton Peto at No. 12 and at No. 19 his cousin and former partner Thomas Grissell, builder of both houses, Charles Lushington M.P. at No. 1, the bookseller and publisher Bevis Ellerby Green of Longman's etc. & Green at No. 5, Russell Gurney, Recorder of the City of London at No. 8, with a Spanish merchant at 8-A, and Lord Harrington at No. 13. Although so near to the old brick Palace, the houses here were required to be 'faced with Cement colored and jointed to imitate Stone, or with white or yellow Brick of the best quality and Stone dressings'—a pale Belgravian colouring typical of the 1840s. In the end, about sixteen different architects were concerned and the effect of twenty years' building was of two rows of single separate mansions, rather than the controlled variations of Nash's Park Village development that had been the original inspiration.[45]

At the south end of the estate's east row of houses was an un-

[45] As S of L *North Kensington* vol. was not ready when I prepared my original section on Moore's house, these paragraphs are based on research in the Crown Estate's files on Kensington Palace Gardens, on census returns and Office of Works plans and papers at the PRO, and on Westminster, Kensington, and Paddington rate books and directories in the relevant borough reference libraries.

developed plot lying just west of the royal stables and manure-
heaps, part of it marked for a possible side-road to the stables—
two reasons why no one originally cared to build there, in spite
of its untrammelled view over the grass of Palace Green, where
the ground falls away southward. Bullocks were pastured on the
empty plot until 1851 when a tea-trader moving into No. 14
next door was allowed a short lease on it to extend his garden.
Early in 1853 the offer of a Samuel Strickland to build on this
ground was accepted, but nothing happened for a year. When the
Crimean War began, the cautious Strickland—his handwriting
small and finicky, his tone anxious and smarmy—felt that times
were unpropitious, and asked Thomas Grissell to take the agreement off his hands. In July Grissell wrote to him—in a large
dashing hand that proclaimed the man of enterprise he was—
that was not inclined to 'build more' but had asked a friend if
he would like to build there. The friend was probably one of the
contractors, Messrs. Lucas, who did build the house; Grissell,
before moving to Kensington, had lived in Clapham not far from
one of the Lucas brothers, who may have brought Knowles and
George Moore together. Moore then lived in Oxford Terrace off
the Edgware Road, and doubtless knew of Knowles through the
drapers' grapevine. At any rate, Knowles submitted to the Crown
commissioners, for Moore as Strickland's nominee, a plan and
elevation of a single large house, instead of the semi-detached
pair proposed by Strickland. Between 8 August and 6 September,
Knowles prepared fifteen more drawings.[46] At the time, part of
Hodgson's old premises on Chancery Lane (below) had just been
pulled down and building begun, with demolition of the Fleet
Street portion due just as soon as book sales could be held in the
other; which is why, in mid-August when sudden illness struck
young James in Venice (p. 112), someone outside the family had
to be sent to fetch him.

Although Knowles's drawings for No. 15 Kensington Palace

[46] Knowles drawings not available since alterations for Sir Alfred Beit in 1930s.
Correspondence 1852-4, CEO file 11,110. The former coach-house and stables
now form No. 15-B as a separate household, while No. 15-A opposite has
always been another matter. Grissell (with his cousin Peto building-contractor
for Barry's Houses of Parliament and Reform Club) built four houses in
Kensington Palace Gardens to designs from Barry's office, and he and Peto
occupied two of them. On Lucases see also International Hotel scheme, n. 52
below.

Gardens are no longer available, the house stands, slightly altered for Sir Alfred Beit in the 1930s and more recently housing a Middle Eastern diplomat. Knowles's model for the west front was partly Banks's design for No. 12 (as with Friday Grove in 1845), partly Barry's early design for the Manchester Athenaeum as first planned with windows in the frieze, with the doorcase of the finished Athenaeum and windows as on Barry's Reform Club: old-fashioned features in 1854, to suit the conservative ground landlord. The rear, though few could see it, was quite different, symmetrical wings projecting from the main core at right angles, and within the inner angles two towers, as if a manor-house entrance courtyard were switched around to the rear. These towers, probably for secondary stairs and cisterns, were originally taller than now, the 1937 alterations including 'reduction in height of the two Towers on the East side'. Perhaps they were high enough to show above the front façade (like those at Castle Ashby behind Inigo Jones's range) and their top stages were probably belvederes with slotted sides as on Knowles's pair at Blackborough. At any rate, the vernacular Italian tower, once an asymmetrical feature, until merged in this designer's consciousness with the belvederes of Deepdene and the Villa Medici, and wings such as those on the Park Lane side of Vulliamy's new Dorchester House, were here adroitly fused with Banks's mildly Genoese palace-front on a traditional English plan in reverse. Since the house seems not to have been published, and the rear was shut off from public gaze by the Palace paddock and stables, this composition was savoured by few. And the full range of reference of a would-be creative eclectic, or latitudinarian, can only dimly be apprehended now. As a habit of thought and hand, it doubtless grew on a man, sounding more and more complicated overtones not fully overheard even by himself, much of his working life being concerned with plain matters, bricks and drains.

The client, George Moore (1806–76) was a remarkable man of irresistible energy who had come to London from Cumberland in 1825 to seek his fortune. An old Cumberland woman said of him later in life that 'his eye would fetch a duck off a pond', and his astonishing handwriting—thin, small, and flowing, interspersed with thick inch-long downstrokes like flag-staves—suggests a powerful, tense personality. According to Samuel

Smiles, Moore felt that such a house was wicked and aggrandizing, and only built it to please his wife, as they had no children; they furnished it partly with 'many superb articles' perhaps designed by Pugin, for these came from a great sale at Alton Towers in Staffordshire. In 1858 Mrs. Moore died; his memorial to her was the fountain in Wigton market-place designed by Knowles, with sculpture by Woolner, many years later. Moore married again in 1861, when Knowles designed a fernery for him. Smiles described big patriarchial parties given in Kensington for Moore's employees of Bow Churchyard, for London cabmen, for the clergy, as well as his charities to the poor huddled opposite Kensington Palace. Moore's will consisted of sixteen pages of charitable bequests.[47]

For men like William Cook from Norfolk and George Moore from Cumberland, arriving young out of the depths of the country, London was their America, their new-found land. Victorian London reaped the harvest as well as they, partly *was* the harvest, of that pre-Victorian influx of Dick Whittingtons. An architect self-made and newly arrived, like themselves, suited them very well. In London he too found all the stimulus and rewards he wanted. As a user of sources, Knowles was not the sort who went, notebook in hand, to the fountainheads of inspiration. His only visit abroad may have been a brief trip to Portugal on a specific commission. Almost every form he used could probably be traced to some English building or publication or pronouncement. Or to collections of ornament such as the Architectural Museum in Cannon Row and the Crystal Palace courts at Sydenham and the exhibitions of the Architectural Photographic Society. Or to engravings in books and periodicals. For a keen eclectic working in London in the 1850s, aids to design outside his own library and journal subscriptions, the Institute library in Grosvenor Street and bookshops such as Bosworth's in Regent Street, were his horse and carriage, the railways, and his own pillaging, roving eye. London and sometimes Manchester were fountainheads enough, now that he had within reach an ever enlarging ragbag of ideas to rummage in. And then there

---

[47] On Moore: *DNB*; biography 1878 by Samuel Smiles; will proved 15 Dec. 1876; David Owen, *English Philanthropy 1660–1960* (1965), p. 394. On Wigton fountain see end of chap. 4 below; and on rookeries swept away for young Knowles's house for Grant, and on Moore's part in Paris Food Fund, chap. 7.

was the stimulus of all the meetings and lectures that flourished. The Architectural Museum, founded in 1852 near the future site of Norman Shaw's Scotland Yard, was to be nostalgically recalled by Sir Gilbert Scott: 'the days when the Museum was housed in this picturesque cock-loft were, in fact, the days of the greatest and most earnest vitality of the institution. The lectures were crowded; the conversaziones overflowed with earnest visitors; and none of the early promotors of the undertaking can even now remember this "upper chamber" but with feelings of renewed and melancholy enthusiasm.'[48] There undoubtedly was something exciting about the 1850s in this profession, whether or not its older and younger members always agreed on what was exciting. For example, the elder Knowles's cast of mind was not receptive to Ruskin's prose, and young Knowles at first reflected this disparagement until, discovering poetry and art for himself, he was fired by Ruskin as other young men were.

Early in 1854, Edmund Hodgson, 'Auctioneer for Literary Property', and one or more of his neighbours arranged to rebuild their premises on a larger scale with space for letting. The building containing his 'Great Room' at No. 192 Fleet Street on the east corner of Chancery Lane had apparently been erected in or after 1828 when he became head of the firm, in which he was previously associated with another man near by. Hodgson's grandfather had come to London from Dent in Yorkshire in the eighteenth century and started a stationer's and bookseller's business with circulating library in Marylebone. By the 1850s, Edmund Hodgson was living on Brixton Hill, not far from Clapham Park. He and his descendants were notably active in the Stationers' Company and in promoting the well-being of the book trade. His auction room of *c.* 1829–54 was part of a five-storey building that included his arcaded shop-front on the Fleet Street side and, behind on Chancery Lane, the premises of a law-bookseller and a wine-and-spirits shop. Some decrepit houses north of this building were now acquired to add to the site. Building activity was already gradually impinging on the mouldering domains of the law: by 1852–3, when *Bleak House* in monthly parts was conveying its powerful sense of the courts and

48 Scott's guide to Architectural Museum (after removal to Tufton Street) bound with Arthur Cates's collection of Tracts on Architecture in RIBA Library. J. Summerson, *The Architectural Association 1847–1947* (1947), pp. 35–6.

alleys off Chancery Lane, Pennethorne's large building for the Public Records was under way. There was to be nothing of Dickens's world in the building journals' crisp wood-engravings of Knowles's design for Hodgson.

Knowles's drawing for the Chancery Lane front (Pl. 5), dated only '1854' and still in Hodgson family possession, shows a Florentine palazzo with the approximate cornice-height of the Palazzo Medici-Riccardi, but with four storeys and basement worked into it instead of the grandiose original three. The arcaded ground floor probably emulated John Gibson's Imperial Assurance Building of 1849 at Broad and Threadneedle Streets in the City, and openwork overdoor lunettes contained metal arabesques rather like those of Wyatt & Brandon's north gateway to Kensington Palace Gardens. Openwork insertions now became Knowles's pet motif (a bit of this had already appeared in the unused Dispensary design). In Hodgson's second-floor windows, of an Italian Gothic two-light type, he inserted some faintly Alhambresque tracery probably derived from Owen Jones's large folios of 1842-5 on the Alhambra in Spain (the Alhambra court at Sydenham having opened while the Hodgson site was being cleared). And the top windows introduced a first glance or *coup d'œil* of the 'eyelid' motif that was to be a Knowles trademark during the next ten years or so. Not that he was alone among architects then in developing the possibilities of window tracery—far from it—for this was an era of fringe, of ferns, of pierced screens, of network valences, culminating in stonework (real or simulated) in Henry Woodyer's chancel arch at Reading, half-filled with the Temple Veil. But the true Knowlesian product, developed in due course for the Grosvenor Hotel, began here in Fleet Street in 1854. To this modest beginning several folios in the RIBA library may have contributed: J. B. Waring's plates of 1852 on Burgos and Waring & Macquoid's plates of 1850 on moulded-brick tracery at Bologna, as well as Owen Jones's on the Alhambra. At any rate, a sort of cresting within the head of an arch, found in Spain and probably of Islamic origin, seems to have fused with Bolognese traceries to set Knowles off, out of elephantine volumes still on the Institute's shelves. One feels the intended ambivalence: any tracery in the head of an arch is bound to have English Gothic overtones too, and some subsequent designs by Knowles were undoubtedly so derived. The

cry for an English style, for a style of 'Our Own', fell on eager
ears; that was what all this selecting and merging of elements from
many styles was about. Foreign forms lodged themselves in a
family-consciousness of parish-church screens, piscina-and-sedilia
recesses, and window-tracery in Surrey. Fittingly enough, the
first book sale in the new quarters (in December 1854 before the
rest of the building was finished) disposed of publisher's unsold
stock of Owen Jones's large plates of the Alhambra.[49]

Hodgson's business palazzo was faced with Portland stone on
the ground floor, above with white Suffolk bricks. A great cornice
of Portland stone with the gutter hollowed in it 'projects 3 feet
8 inches from the face of the wall, and is corbelled back for a
counterpoise', the *Builder* reported, also that the roof was covered
with 'Italian tiling' from Surbiton. Hodgson's own premises,
including the new saleroom, occupied the lower half of the middle
third of the building (unloading books was easier from the side
street), part of the northern third was taken by a firm of legal
booksellers and publishers, and a stationer occupied the lower
floors at the Fleet Street end, with a separate entrance to chambers
above. In a public position as prominent as Cook's warehouse,
this building was called by the *Companion to the British Almanac*
critic 'one of the best works' of 1855 when it was completed.
Some unusual comment then appeared in the *Builder*, after the
usual factual description, in the form of an article signed by young
James Knowles, telling more of its author than of his father's
building, and beginning with an eclectic's declaration of inde-
pendence:[50]

In the design of this building, the architect has consulted but little that
antiquaries' Bible, the book of 'Styles'. He has endeavoured to produce
a building fit for its purpose and substantially beautiful, at the same
time a business pile, and not a palace. . . . We have surely had enough

---

[49] R. McLean, *Victorian Book Design* (1963), p. 69; *One Hundred Years of Book
Auctions 1807–1907*, pamphlet at GL; bound catalogues now at BL. Hodgson
family: Boase on Edmund Hodgson; information from the late Sidney Hodgson
and his son Mr. Wilfrid Hodgson; Edmund and his son Henry Hill Hodgson and
grandson Sidney were all Masters of the Stationers' Company. Site: rate books,
GL; Tallis views of Fleet Street *c.* 1839, 1847 (as n. 40); old views in family
possession. Books: Alhambra folios presented by Jones to Institute library; J. B.
Waring, *Archit.*, *Sculp. and Picturesque Studies in Burgos* (1852), and, with T. R.
Macquoid, *Examples of Architectural Art in Italy and Spain* (1850).
[50] *Bldr*, 18 Aug. 1855, p. 389, quoted further in chap. 3 section, 'Search for a
Motive' below.

of catchpenny advertisements done in stucco and paste. . . . A man will do his business with a healthier and clearer mind [here] than in such dens of darkness as line its next door—Chancery Lane.

Reactions against 'stucco and paste' had been absorbed. And young Knowles was a reader of Dickens.

This shared space did not fit Hodgson's volume of business for long. Eight years later the firm moved to its own newer building, tailored to its needs by the architect George Pownall, at No. 115 Chancery Lane where it continued until recent fusion with Sotheby's. The 1854–5 corner continued for about a century 'in energetic operation' by other owners, and was regarded even in our era as a building of character (although the twentieth-century romantic eclectic Clough Williams-Ellis was uncomplimentary on the 'Clark's College style', indicating a secretarial school housed there, the Mid-Victorians not being his cup of tea).[51] When Knowles's building was finally pulled down in the 1950s, Edmund Hodgson's grandson 'Mr Sidney', then still in charge opposite, observed with satisfaction that its demolishers found it a tough specimen: 'When the demolition firm got to work they found it so well built that they were not able to use pick-axes on the front, so resorted to drills, and the foundation was so solid that they gave it up & I believe went into liquidation!' And when Sidney Hodgson himself retired in 1967 aged over 90, he turned in one of the oldest season-tickets ever held by a British railway commuter. Even unto the third generation, Knowles's clients have been a hardy lot.

Early in 1858 Knowles made his first designs for an exotic house in Portugal—which, we shall find, was nevertheless British to the core—designs he was to develop further a year or so later, but which meanwhile brushed off a little on to another design. In April 1858 the *Illustrated London News* carried an engraving of an 'International Hotel' (Pl. 5) proposed for a prominent site in the Strand ('bran-new brobdignagian hotel' as Disraeli was to call the breed in general) with a most eccentric roofline.[52] Roofs were in the news. There were the Government Offices competition designs recently published, bristling with pavilion roofs. There were all the views of towns and buildings in India, of passionate

[51] Clough Williams-Ellis, *The Pleasures of Architecture* (1930).
[52] *ILN*, 3 Apr. 1858, pp. 349–50; *BN*, 5, 26 Mar. 1858, pp. 249, 320. On villa in Portugal, chap. 4.

concern just then. And still the largest hotel in London, as for the past five years, was the Great Western at Paddington, admired for its commercial success and for the convex–concave crowns on its towers. Further back, in the 1840s, the more eclectic architects had taken a great interest in seventeenth-century forms, as in Joseph Nash's romantic views of the *Mansions of England* and in John Clayton's careful drawings of Wren's churches. Of John Shaw's published design for Wellington College with its convex–concave roof forms, the *Illustrated London News* in 1855 observed that the architect had tried 'to make the building essentially English in character'. There was also, perhaps, the Londoner's memory of those pavilion roofs in Great Russell Street on the old British Museum and its gate lodges.[53] That is, never mind origins, these had been part of the English scene and could contribute to a new English style—washed with the orientalism of empire.

Knowles's heady roof design of 1858, a *mélange* of such influences, is hard to describe. There were to be five of these formations: a convexity surmounted by a concavity surmounted in turn by a vaguely orientalized lantern under a mushroom cupola carrying a ball-finial; and between the convexity and the concavity, where Hardwick at Paddington merely inserted a thin band, was to be a little arcade, perhaps partly a working-down of Pugin's clock-tower design at Westminster, partly a working-up of a conservatory dome in Loudon's *Encyclopaedia*—the borrowings, that is, of a William the Fourth man. The effect could also be described as Paddington tower roofs with park-bandstand fillips on top and no separate towers underneath. The façades below on four fronts were each to be almost two hundred feet long. Knowles was probably making his first design for Portugal at the same time. Out of those two dour exteriors, of No. 1 Raymond Buildings and of Knowles himself, such extraordinary things could come. The clients for this unrealized project were 'Messrs Hankey, Heath, Hope & Scott' (more likely Hope-Scott), probably a consortium of bankers and lawyers, as trustees *pro tem.* of a proposed joint-stock company. The contractors were to be Messrs. Lucas, then finishing Edward Barry's Covent Garden

[53] *ILN* vols. 1852–8 full of interesting skylines: e.g. Great Western Hotel, 18 Dec. 1852, p. 537; Wellington College, 4 Aug. 1855, opp. p. 150; Government Offices competition entries, 2nd 1857 vol.; many views of India, 2nd 1857–1st 1858 vols. The drawings in Clayton's folio of 1848 were later reduced for Wren Society vol. IX. The last vestiges of the old BM went *c.* 1849.

Opera House just up the road. The hotel project may have been cooked up in Clapham, especially if the banker Thomas Alers Hankey (Knowles's fellow-member of the Clapham Athenaeum) was the Hankey concerned. The proposed site was the entire block of land bounded by Wellington, Exeter, and Burleigh Streets and the Strand, containing among other buildings the Lyceum Theatre: after the Covent Garden Opera House burned down in 1856, its company performed at the Lyceum until the new opera house was ready in the spring of 1858; the latest Lyceum Management before that interregnum having ended in bankruptcy. The future scene of Irving's triumphs was about to be wiped out.

The International Hotel would have been well named. It was to be planned around a central courtyard as at the Hôtel du Louvre in Paris (Professor Donaldson having described that new hotel to the Institute three years before), but a grand central hall was to fill the ground floor of the courtyard—unlike the grand carriage entry in Paris—under a glass dome sixty feet in diameter. Above, where the bedrooms could look down upon it (like the servants above Friday Grove's hall skylight) and the first-floor *salle à manger* open on to it, 'a kind of hanging garden' was to surround the dome, somewhat like terraced palace gardens in Genoa and 'supplied with fresh flowers from the adjacent Coventgarden', according to the *Illustrated London News*. On the ground floor were to be a great coffee room and 'a grand American bar . . . where our Transatlantic visitors may refresh themselves after their manner, discussing telegrams flashed straight from Wallstreet to their rocking-chairs', also a hair-cutting saloon fifty feet long. London promoters were keen to outdo the New York hotels. Large rooms for billiards, chess, and smoking, moreover, were to 'give a "Palais Royal" flavour'. Some local flavour included an 'arcaded vestibule' entered from the Strand and 'somewhat recalling' the principal approach to Somerset House near by. This was a fine site for a hotel, facing the approach to Waterloo Bridge, although there was then no Aldwych to eastward, only the warrens of Holywell and Wych Streets crowding the north edge of the Strand—still then the main way, other than the river, from the City to Westminster.

This was the design of an Early Victorian with a Mid-Victorian inside struggling to get out. It was in some respects a prototype for the Grosvenor Hotel (a project perhaps then already in the wind), but in the Grosvenor design various influences that coalesced in 1859, and the idealistic intervention of young Knowles, were to produce something better. The Strand project came to nothing, and the Lyceum was saved for, eventually, Henry Irving and Ellen Terry—and a stage design by the editor of the *Nineteenth Century* for a play by the Poet Laureate.[54] In the spring of 1860, the elder Knowles submitted his Grosvenor design (Pl. 5) to the Royal Academy's summer exhibition.

Such buildings compiled by and for a robust generation of men were the outward and visible signs of their begetters' vigorous arrival at a 'Middle Station' in society. A process not new in this country, where merchants and their professional advisers have been arriving for centuries.

---

[54] On Tennyson's *The Cup*, chap. 8, n. 23. On Lyceum Theatre, R. Mander and J. Mitchison, *Theatres of London* (1961), p. 273; A. E. Wilson, *The Lyceum* (1952), p. 80.

3

Knowles the Younger: Learning About the World

'After all, the world was only created in 1830 or thereabouts, and we are all very new to it.' Draft c. 1892–3 for a reply by the Editor of the *Nineteenth Century* to a toast to Literature (Knowles papers, WPL)

IN THE SUMMER OF 1846 full-time schooling ended for James the eldest son. That autumn, just 15, he was articled to his father for seven years of pupilage in the chambers at Gray's Inn. Some autobiographical notes set down near the end of his life, and now lost, recalled 'dreary days and months' of sitting there under his father's eye.[1] The elder Knowles was no Pecksniff: dull the work might be, but it would be thorough. And during 1847–9 his son's office training was supplemented by attendance at evening lectures given twice a week during the academic year at University College in Gower Street by Thomas Leverton Donaldson, who in 1842 had started these courses for just such articled pupils pent up all day in offices.[2] The forming of an Architectural Association in 1847 by some older students made no impression on young Knowles at the time. But Donaldson did: he was not only involved in the larger professional issues of

[1] Short autobiographical MS. used by Sir Sidney Lee for his account of Knowles in *DNB*, and by Michael Goodwin in his introduction to the Penguin *Nineteenth Century Opinion* (1951), has since disappeared, but some direct quotation from it was given in 1951, as this (Goodwin, p. 9). On the chapter-head quotation, chap. 9, n. 16 below.
[2] Prospectus for the lecture course, printed at end of Donaldson's preliminary discourse at University College, 1842, pamphlet in RIBA Library. On him, n. 5 below.

the day, but was probably the first teacher the boy encountered who tried to convey the excitement he felt in his subject.

This need not have been the case in Clapham between 1834 and 1862, for boys from 11 to 15 who were lucky enough, as young Knowles was not, to be sent to the grammar school run by the Revd. Charles Pritchard, later Savilian Professor of Astronomy at Oxford. The unusual stimulus of Pritchard's educational ideas was recognized beyond the boundaries of Clapham. Darwin and Herschel sent sons there. So did Barry (before he moved his household to Clapham) and Brunel and Cubitt. George Grove and his friend George Bradley the future Dean of Westminster, son of a Clapham parson, were among Pritchard's earliest pupils. Knowles much later, in 1884, commissioned Dean Bradley to describe his early school days in the pages of the *Nineteenth Century*, in an article that is worth quoting on Pritchard's methods, for Knowles was to meet these in an extracurricular way.[3] Pritchard was

full of fire, enthusiasm, and original ability . . . [flinging] our Latin Syntax to the winds, and substituting a few, a very few, rules that he gave us on a blackboard, which now for the first time became one of the instruments of our education . . . he taught us something, at the same time, of the beauty and charm of literature, old and new . . . [and] no week passed . . . in which we did not receive and eagerly look forward to at least one lesson in natural science. . . . It became impossible for any one of us to look henceforth on science as a foe.

It is hard to forgive the elder Knowles for not sending his sons to that school in the High Street. James might have found himself sooner. George might have found himself. Perhaps Friday Grove was the price of their education. Presumably they went to the parish school in Clapham, having been introduced to letters and numbers in Reigate. (And in these schools James learned old-fashioned spelling, with the -or rather than -our suffix, that he used with a few lapses all his life.) Determined though their father was to rise in the professional world, and confirmed as he was in self-esteem by self-made success, he apparently could not see what difference schooling of the quality then provided at the Clapham Grammar School might make in stirring the subsoil of a

---

[3] On Pritchard, G. G. Bradley, 'My Schooldays from 1830 to 1840', *NC*, Mar. 1884, pp. 460–2; Charles Pritchard, *Annals of Our School Life* (1886); Ada Pritchard, ed., *Charles Pritchard . . . Memoirs of His Life* (1897).

boy's mind, or how different his boys were from himself. For him common sense and professional expertise were enough; he reckoned without the imagination they had from their mother. It was only after school days were over, probably in 1852, that young James by his own inquiring eagerness won the friendship of Pritchard, the very man to see how well worth fostering this eagerness was. Knowles in later life when writing journalistically referred to him as 'my old schoolmaster', but he told Pritchard's daughter that 'I was never his school pupil (I wish I had been)'; nor did a list of Old Boys compiled in 1886 include him.[4]

EARLY INFLUENCES

> 'Geology's a noble thing/To teach in Alma Mater,/ So straight I will proceed to sing/The earth and all its strata./ Of peat and chalk I've much to say/ Of limestone, sand, and gypsum;/'Twill teach the student made of clay/*Cognoscere se ipsum.*'
>
> *Punch* X (1846), 240

Professor Donaldson was no cloistered teacher either, but the genial moving spirit of the Institute of British Architects and, now and then, a practising architect. His University College evening course was in two parts, stressing a duality of which, as a pedagogical device, he was fond. On Tuesday nights he dealt with architecture as a fine art, on Thursday nights with architecture as a science. This evening instruction was, in a way, an ancestor of Birkbeck College, and also, in a way, of the Bartlett School of Architecture, in the present University of London. Donaldson defined his subject thus: 'Architecture has this distinctive feature from any other department of knowledge, that it is essentially composed of two divisions—Imagination and Reason.' One student remembered him 'tabulating, as was the habit of the eclectic school, century by century, the progress of architecture style by style' and marking his own generation '*Chaos*'; and that he 'was never weary of declaring in the very plainest of language how "the authority of antiquity" was something very much of the supernatural, if not even the divine'.

---

[4] Pritchard, *Memoirs*, p. 76, quoting letter from Knowles, and lists in *Annals* (n. 3 above). Further on Pritchard, this chapter on 1852, and chap. 6 on Metaphysical Society. The -or spelling continued in Mid-Victorian England, e.g. inscription under dome of 1862 Exhibition.

Donaldson cared very much about the practice and reputation of architecture as a profession, and 'the duty of the Professional Man'; most of all he cared about fostering that 'complex and laborious process' the study of architecture: 'The imagination must be aroused and cultivated to its utmost power, and then sobered down by considerations of economy and practical utility.' For young James 'the harangues of my old Architectural Professor' were to shape modes of expression later on.[5]

In June 1849 James won a prize and first certificate in construction, for which the examination questions happen to survive. Eleven questions concerned geology, for example 'Of what does the crust of the globe consist?' and 'Describe the constituent parts respectively of granite, statuary marble, sandstone, limestone, Portland, Bath.' Then followed thirty-two questions on masonry, materials, structure, etc., such as 'Describe the causes of settlement in the French Pantheon, Paris' and 'Enumerate the different sorts of bricks used in London, and describe the purposes to which they are applied.'[6] The constituent parts of marble columns for a great house in Kensington, and the different sorts of bricks needed at Battersea, were to plague him professionally. Here, and at Mantell's Clapham Athenaeum lectures, began a burning interest in the then popular science of geology, the first science to touch on evolution and raise questions about creation. It was in May 1850, perhaps in Bosworth's bookshop in Regent Street, that young Knowles made first a geological and then a poetical discovery—'From scarped cliff and quarried stone' meant something, and led on to the rest of *In Memoriam*, as he later recalled:[7]

I came by chance on a copy of 'In Memoriam', then just published anonymously. I was quite entirely ignorant and indifferent in those

[5] On Donaldson (1795–1885), longest surviving founder of RIBA, S. Blutman, 'The Father of the Profession', *JRIBA*, Dec. 1967, obituaries *Bldr*, 8 Aug., and *BN*, 7 Aug. 1885, and Robert Kerr's recollections in 1891 edn. of James Fergusson's *History of Modern Architecture*, ii. 121–2, 131; preliminary discourse 1842 (n. 2 above), and young Knowles in retrospect at head of 'Grand Tour' section below. As a practising architect Donaldson designed e.g. for University College from 1848 onwards a library, a sculpture gallery, and on Gordon Square a hall, later Dr. Williams' Library.

[6] *Bldr*, 14 July 1849, p. 334, and examination paper in RIBA Library's old bound pamphlets, vol. 30.

[7] Knowles, 'Tennyson and Aldworth', posthumously published in *Tennyson and His Friends* by 2nd Lord Tennyson (1911), p. 245. *In Memoriam* was published anonymously in May 1850, the author being known by June.

days about all poetry . . . but, opening it haphazard at the Geological Stanzas, was so impressed and riveted by them—for I was a student of Geology at the time—that I could not put the book down until I had read it all through. . . . It made an epoch in my life. . . . I soon came to know my Tennyson almost by heart, and was taunted by my friends for my worship of the 'divine Alfred', as I reverently called him.

From that worship much was to come about.

THE CLAPHAM MAGAZINE, 1850

> '. . . a vehicle for free discussion . . . for which purpose
> the Editors pledge themselves to afford a fair field.'
> *Clapham Magazine*, November 1850

Knowles's discovery of poetry may in part have prompted an attempt at high-minded journalism in company with his friends Henry Hewlett and John Hopgood.[8] Both were solicitors' sons, and Hopgood was later James's solicitor. Hewlett, just entering his father's office in Gray's Inn after several years at Harrow where his uncle was the school doctor, became Knowles's closest friend and, eventually, doubly a brother-in-law: tall and thin, black-haired, of scholarly intellect and romantic temperament, as emotional as Knowles but more reserved, and without his flashing humour. The Hewletts lived in Acre Lane near Clapham Park Road, and Mr. Hewlett's office was at No. 3 Raymond Buildings. A parcel of letters, written by Knowles to Hewlett in the 1850s when one or the other was on holiday, starts off with the adventure of founding a local magazine.[9] The first stage in Knowles's editorial career, twenty years before he was to take on the *Contemporary Review*, was anonymous, inglorious, and short. It might have lasted a bit longer if he had met Pritchard first.

The first letters in July and August 1850 were anxiously concerned with the printing and distribution of a prospectus to lure subscribers and to cost all of £2. 10s.: 'Now as my "Governor"

---

[8] John Hopgood (d. 1902) became partner to his much older brother James (Cubitt's solicitor) in 1854, according to John's grandson Oliver Hopgood; both brothers were solid handsome vigorous men, in surviving photographs almost stepping from the frames. Henry Gay Hewlett (1832–97), Keeper of Her Majesty's Land Revenue Records, is in Boase, and the *Letters* (1926) of his son Maurice (chap. 2, n. 25 above), introduction by his son Edward.

[9] Thirteen letters, Knowles to Hewlett during summers 1850–3, in family possession until deposited at WPL in 1973: all quoting from Knowles to Hewlett in this section comes from this packet of letters.

has been liberal enough to place a sovereign at my disposal to meet expenses of this nature . . . I shall have the greatest pleasure in contributing my share of the sum—which otherwise I should have had some difficulty (as you know) in doing' (23 July). An articled pupil had no earnings. Plans for the magazine itself brought on the discovery that publishing and printing were not the same thing (3 August):

We have decided upon Jarrett as the Publisher but have not yet settled the Printer—for I have discovered what before I was ignorant of— that the two offices are by no means coincident. . . .
    Our Prospecti were to have been ready this morning—and therefore *were not* . . . the thousand printed on one page only (which is all our composition covers)—the paper being of the best make; for it would indeed be intolerable to have thin flimsy stuff instead of cream-laid & hot-pressed—the only admissible thing in these days—Render your 'Lawyer's' mind easy . . . we are not going to be sold!
    . . . We shall rely entirely on you for light articles, Tales, & Poetry . . . [for] Tales especially your assistance will be invaluable. . . .
    We shall proceed at once to arrange our first number . . . inasmuch as when one element of the number is decided the rest must be 'complementary'—to use an optical term.

Twenty-five years later, arranging the elements of a number that included contributions by Cardinal Manning and Mr. Gladstone was to be a delicate complementary exercise. Meanwhile, Brickhill the printer's production of the prospectus, probably in a tiny type-size with no space between lines, was a nasty surprise (6 August):

Your surprise and indignation will equal if not exceed my own at beholding the cunning manner in which that cheating rascal Brickhill has sold us—You will perceive that the Prospecti are actually consisting of but half a page each! For me, the idea never enterred my head to tell him each must be a whole sheet—It is so entirely a matter of course —that I have not the smallest hesitation in ascribing the mode in which Mr Brickhill has executed our order to *pure knavery*—our only consolation must be 'experience' . . . P. S. Brickhill shall have nothing more to do with us whilst I am an 'Editor'.

That printers as well as builders require precise specifications was a lesson: 'how truly amazing it is that they cannot print straight and right—only imagine . . . what *my* difficulties are as an architect in getting my ideas realized!' Knowles was to say to Tennyson in 1872.[10] Meanwhile the bustle continued and Jarrett 'received strict orders to preserve an "incognito" as to all parties concerned —if this be not observed, we are done for!'—that is, among the general public of Clapham for Knowles wrote forty letters in two days to potential contributors, remarking to Hewlett: 'Time sometimes travels by Express Train'—that recently new metaphor of the 1840s.

As a local periodical, the *Clapham Magazine* lacked local character. Three years later a monthly *Clapham Gazette* was to be launched by a printer and stationer in the High Street; to its successful life of almost twenty years we may think of the *Magazine* as a precocious, doomed predecessor.[11] A chief difference between them, aside from editorial expertise, was to be the *Gazette's* emphasis on news, with a large view of Clapham's 'estate in the Metropolis' and a nice sense of local interests. The *Magazine's* aims were idealistic and didactic, without local colour, chiefly concerned with literature and science, 'relieved by poetry, tales and humour only as collateral assistants'—it was the product of three 18-year-olds (Knowles was 19 in October, the other two younger). It ran for three monthly issues, from November 1850 to January 1851, of which copies were duly deposited in the British Museum Library at the time. It had a buff paper cover, in eight-by-five-inch format, with advertisements on the back cover of the first two issues, which contained 24 pages each (28 in the third), and the price was sixpence. It was published by W. Jarrett, bookseller of Crescent Place, Clapham Common, a modest shopping terrace still extant near the entrance to Crescent Grove.

Said the opening leader put together by the three editors, though mostly by Knowles: 'Now a local magazine affords in a peculiar degree that *concentration of interest and equalization of advantage* [their italic] so conducive to mutual instruction.' This extra stimulus 'to all parties concerned in its production and perusal' would provide 'a direct incentive' that would fill 'a too frequent void in the grand labor of "self-education" ' in a neighbourhood which, 'we are proud to say, can boast of many

---

[10] Knowles to Tennyson, 25 Dec. 1872 (TRC). Jarrett and Brickhill were local printers, the former also a bookseller.

[11] *Clapham Magazine*: the three issues are in both BL and Minet. *Clapham Gazette*: Minet has probably the nearest complete run, 1853–71.

possessing intellects far above mediocrity'. Presciently the leader-writers wondered 'whether the lot of the present generation be but cast in the advancing phase of another of those great waves which from the dawn of history have periodically influenced the human race'—in this probably reflecting Donaldson's romantic philosophy of the cycles of history and of architectural styles. Less presciently, in view of the magazine's fate, but of interest for Knowles's later principles, the leader continued: as the magazine had been founded for mutual instruction, '*a freedom of expression therefore to diverse or opposite opinions* [their italic] is the fundamental element of its constitution . . . to afford a vehicle for free discussion and the temperate advocacy of varying sentiments and views, for which purpose the Editors pledge themselves to afford a fair field, refusing only statements and opinions opposed to strict morality, good feeling, and universal Charity' and 'Theology and politics controversially treated'. 'Free discussion' on a 'fair field', utilitarian principles of the 1820s, suggest that the Knowleses and Hewletts had been regular readers of the *Westminster Review*.[12] Here already is the notion of a periodical as platform for all sides, not just one side, of a discussion—the character of the *Contemporary Review* that was to emerge under Knowles's hand in the 1870s and then more fully in the *Nineteenth Century*. Local incubators of this notion—since Knowles's schooling had apparently not been of the sort to foster his taste for it—will have been the meetings of the Clapham Athenaeum and the Literary and Scientific Institution where, he said later, he began 'to dare to think about thinking'.[13]

In the November number an opening article on 'Ethnology', citing Humboldt's *Cosmos* and 'Meyer on the Geography of Plants', decided that racial traits were really only regional differences conditioned by climate and geography, and concluded in the usual pre-Darwinian manner that this leads us to see the general scheme of creation as 'an original intention'. Then came a poetical piece on music as the 'mutual joy of angels and men', probably by Hewlett, followed by 'Hospital Reminiscences', probably by Hopgood and not at all poetical. 'Confessions of [the] M.P. . . . for Bubbleditch' sounds rather sub-Samuel Warren (whose *Ten Thousand a Year* was still selling). There was

12 See chap. 2, n. 11 above.
13 Goodwin (as n. 1), p. 9.

also the first instalment of 'Fossil-Nations', intended to epitomize existing knowledge of ancient Egypt, Assyria, and Etruria, and metaphorically equate their buried architecture and sculpture with geological fossils; young Knowles's quickness with a timely metaphor and the family interest in such remains suggest the authorship of that. Also in this number, a notice of the opening meeting of the 1850-1 session of the Clapham Athenaeum was prophetic of Knowles's combined operations with the Metaphysical Society and the *Contemporary Review*, as well as the *Nineteenth*'s notices on 'Recent Science': the editors hoped 'to be enabled, through the kindness of the lecturers and the committee, to present our readers with abstracts of many of the papers . . . and thus to form a more accessible and enduring record of the many highly interesting and valuable statements and observations, emanating from the "rostrum" of the Clapham Athenaeum, than is now enjoyed': this they were at least once able to do. On the back cover were advertisements for a 'New Patent Elastic Calisthenic Chest Expander', a carver and gilder, the bookseller's 'Crescent Library', and an insurance company for which Jarrett was local agent; also, on the second number, the advertisement of a plumber, painter, and glazier. By 1850, a Knowles need not withdraw the hem of his garment from that.

The December issue was the best, and the worst, of the three. The opening article, rather a scoop for the young editors, was obtained from that somewhat tetchy co-founder of the Clapham Athenaeum, Dr. Gideon Mantell: it was, in fact, the paper he had read before that body on 4 November 'On the Connection between Archaeology and Geology'.[14] But with 'Virginie', a most intemperate tale, came catastrophe. It was a torrid story of a French girl visiting Rome, who falls in love with the Apollo Belvedere in the Vatican Museum, swoons at the statue's feet, and is awakened by a priest to whom she addresses a 'glowing torrent of accusation':

Who are ye, false prophets and deceiving wolves, who in your knowledge of the iniquities whereby ye stand—of the vile superstitions and abject ignorance wherein ye chain a wretched people, dare to condemn

[14] *The Journal of Gideon Mantell, Surgeon and Geologist*, ed. E. C. Curwen (1940), p. 261, mentions giving the paper but not its local publication; Mantell published a book, *On the Remains of Man*, in 1850; he is characterized in C. C. Gillispie, *Genesis and Geology* (1959 edn.), pp. 137–9; see also chap. 2, n. 20.

the veneration of that supernal power wherein is God? . . . what
mean your images, pictures, and relics to the multitude. . . . Can they
discern the knife-edge doctrines whereon ye build your justification?
. . . The smoke of your iniquity as of a furnace ascends before the
Throne of Infinite Justice. . . .

and much more, before she rushes off to die at the feet of Apollo.[15]
Hysteria about Rome was all too common in 1850, in that very
month of Cardinal Wiseman's enthronement in Pugin's chancel
three miles away in Southwark, when 'papal aggression' meetings
vented the feelings of many an outraged Anglican parish. Even
as fiction this story hardly suited the judicious tone of the
Magazine's stated policy, or good sense in a neighbourhood
where a Roman Catholic house of worship had been building—
a hundred yards from Jarrett's shop—for the past year. The elders
of Clapham must have liked such hysteria no more than they did
the parading and burning in effigy 'of a Cardinal, with scarlet hat
and robe mounted on a donkey' on Clapham Common that
'Guy Vaux' day: 'all this foolery in 1850', wrote Dr. Mantell in
his journal on 5 November.

So the third number arrived in January with a valediction (and
no advertisements whatever): 'We regret the causes that have
induced the abrupt termination of our enterprise, and freely take
such blame upon ourselves as may be deserve for a *miscalculation.*'
Nevertheless, they were not going to lie down under criticism,
but expressed disappointment in the lack of 'that kind and
neighbourly encouragement we had led ourselves to expect'. A
note inside the back cover pointed out that the incident of
'Virginie' had really happened in the Louvre in the seventeenth
century—removing any reference to Rome—and had formed
the subject of a poem by Barry Cornwall. (The Roman incident
appears, without harangue, in Mrs. Charlotte Eaton's *Rome in the
Nineteenth Century* which had gone through several editions since
1820—and of course all parties will have been reading the fourth
canto of *Childe Harold.*) The editors then bravely declared that,
'fully immersed in professional occupations' as they were, they
could not proceed without local co-operation but hoped someone else would take up the idea and improve upon 'this abortive
attempt to establish a scientific and literary journal in Clapham'.
It had been valuable to their own knowledge of 'the conduct of

[15] *Clapham Magazine*, Dec. 1850, pp. 35–42, unsigned.

life', they would look back upon its threefold issue as a *memento mori*—for when readers and advertisers took flight in December, the editors were left with a deficit of fourteen pounds and the January number probably already set up. In it, Diogenes Smith on the coming Exhibition of 1851 defended progress against fogies. The concluding instalment of Mantell's article discussed the occurrence of human remains and artifacts in geological strata and the remains of animals in more ancient strata, 'even of that race which approaches nearest to man in its physical organization', and found that 'the facts at present known afford us no . . . evidence . . . by which the existence of the human race . . . can be traced back to those remote ages of the earth's physical history', and called in the support of Professor Whewell to say that we must be content 'to close the volume of the earth's physical history, and open that Divine record [on] the moral and religious nature of man': the toe was dipped in, and briskly withdrawn. No earnest journal in 1850 could avoid theological worries of some sort; nor, in the end, did this one avoid politics. The final article—published because 'the excellence of this paper, joined to the conclusion of our scheme, have induced us to waive . . . anti-political feelings'—dealt unsigned, in an unfeeling and illiberal manner, with the 'Jewish Disabilities' question, that is, the obstacles of the Christian oaths required of Members of Parliament. None of the contents of the *Clapham Magazine*, by the way, appears to have been inspired by the early works of Mr. Ruskin. And of course the editors were quite unaware of that other young men's magazine of 1850, *The Germ* of the Pre-Raphaelite Brotherhood.

FAITH, FOSSILS, ART, AND COMETS

> '. . . what sixteen to twenty-four is talking about, twenty-four to sixty-four will usually write or think or do.' G. M. Young, 'The Victorian Noon-Time', *Victorian Essays* (1962), p. 134

For several years there flourished a young men's society, instigated by Knowles 'to meet at each other's houses and discuss music, art, philosophy—in fact, everything'—a sort of junior Clapham Athenaeum. They met once a month at the full moon 'for the sake of our gas-less neighbourhood'—in the late 1840s–early

1850s Clapham Park had no street lamps—and called themselves, at one stage, 'the Lunatics'. For hours, as well, Knowles and Hewlett alone would discuss their pet theories, mostly Knowles's, 'poor Henry sitting and listening with infinite friendship', and drew up summaries of potential scientific lectures.[16] Architecture, it seems, was but daily bread.

Knowles later recalled how these occasions made him feel his lack of education; and of one fellow-lunatic, a university man, he observed to Hewlett at the time that 'our poor polished friend . . . does humbug me rather too much even for my verdure'. Hewlett, moreover, was becoming a convert to religious free thinking. Feeling too ignorant to challenge this, Knowles with his 'inherited evangelical conscience' could only 'guide and strengthen myself by perpetual prayers that my faith might not be undermined'. The elder Knowles certainly bore marks of a 'serious' upbringing, and Clapham parish church, which they attended *c.* 1839–46, was the old home of Evangelical conscience. To modern seekers after Victorian Thought who ask whether the founder of the Metaphysical Society was 'religious': the only period for which only a simple evangelical answer to that over-simplified question could be given may be that covered by this chapter. Personally devout Knowles continued to maintain that he was all his life ('I should be more than satisfied with Theism', he informed Gladstone after Mill's 'Essay on Theism' came out), with a faith that widened to embrace an Hellenic idealism, first stirred by Donaldson's reverence for antiquity, and an aesthetic sense of beauty in art and poetry and the natural world, first stirred by Tennyson and Dr. Pritchard, the art galleries of London, and dormant impressions of the Surrey countryside.[17] However, it was not to be religious fervour but sheer intellectual and social opportunism, handled with a deft catalytic talent for bringing men and ideas together, that founded the Metaphysical Society.

Eighteen-fifty-one was a startling year, 'the happiest of my hitherto life', an enviable year in which to reach 20. G. M. Young reminded biographers that a birth-year only matters in directing us to the state of a man's world when he was 20. These young men were the quintessential Victorians, born in the 1830s and

[16] Goodwin, p. 10, quoting Knowles as n. 1 above.
[17] On Hewlett, Goodwin, pp. 9–11, quoting Knowles. Knowles to Gladstone, 14 May 1876 (BL, as chap. 7, n. 50).

gone before the First World War. To members of that generation untouched by poverty, the 1850s were a decade of discovery. Knowles later recalled that the contents of the Crystal Palace gave him a great shock of excitement, but no letters were needed when he and Henry explored it together. In July the Knowles family took its first seaside holiday: the cost of Friday Grove had apparently prevented that before, although the holiday habit was not new in Clapham, for according to *Punch* ('The Geology of Society') in 1841, the second layer of the Clapham Group in the Transition Class of the Middle Stratum always went to Ramsgate for three weeks in the dog-days. Wherever it was the family went in 1851 (the year the painter Frith began his 'Ramsgate Sands') young James's next few years were filled with a romantic nostalgia mingling the new sight and sound of the sea with the pain of falling hopelessly in love: 'She' came from Clapham too, and spurned him after a short acquaintance, and that is all we know of it.

Meanwhile, back at home in August, quoting *Dombey* and discovering Sir Walter Scott, he wrote to Hewlett in answer to an invitation to visit in the country that he would have accepted 'had I felt more equal to "the effort" as Mrs Chick says . . . [but have] rusticated at home for a couple of days, reading the Waverly Novels, and otherwise idling my time! and I still feel rather "Cousin Feenix-y" in the legs', and warning Hewlett against women, testifying as a victim reduced to 'a wretched relic' while able to report on 'some stunning girls and a glorious dance . . . at Gassiot's on Thursday'. Under the same date (5 August 1851) are seven sheets of criticism of nineteen poems (now fortunately missing) by Hewlett. Since 'thorough and true criticism on my part . . . would but consist in a recapitulation of "Paley's Evidences" . . . I therefore have thrown aside all other considerations than those of a *technical nature* . . . and, so far as I can judge of it, their adequacy to represent the ideas *you* wish to convey—albeit I esteem those ideas erroneous and hurtful'. One critical excerpt is telling enough: ' "The Prophet" rather too excessive in language. . . . Heavy language built up of violent terms savours of green-ness . . . equally intense feelings might be embodied with equal power in a composition lacking so much of "groans", "yells", "shrieking", "damned", "wolfish lust", etc. etc.' So, it was bound to have been Hewlett who wrote the tale that sank the *Magazine*. At any rate, his friend's critical powers had shed some 'green-ness' in the meantime.[18]

In June 1852 young Knowles received from the Institute of British Architects a medal of merit for a public-baths-and-laundry design. During that summer the supervising of demolitions and excavations for Messrs. Cook's new warehouse in St. Paul's Churchyard apparently forbade any holiday for its architect and his assistants that year. It was in August that the carved slab was dug up and energetically adopted as a subject for research by young James, relieving the tedium of endless working-drawings for warehouse construction. His description of the slab published in the *Illustrated London News* for 28 August was businesslike and informative, which suggests that he had expert advice as well as his father's training in the precise approach to a practical problem.[19] Theories about inscriptions, theories about machines, and heaven knows what about the habits of comets, helped him to bear personal woes (20 September 1852 to Hewlett):

I have been very indolent indeed at business since—you know when & why. . . . It sounds ridiculous . . . being very well in health—Sleeping sound at night—eating great big dinners. . . . I have told you before I am an idolator—I must see what I worship—know what I work for . . . well, well don't laugh at me—tho' I deserve it—remember many a Pantaloon has at home empty cupboards— & dark rooms. . . .

As to my Comets—I have told Bosworth the notion. . . . He tells me that he thinks I must be very near the Truth.

Thomas Bosworth, a neighbour, and a member of their discussion society though older than Knowles and Hewlett, was one of the last of the scholarly bookseller-publishers; he published for the Irvingite sect, and carried on his business at No. 215 Regent Street (west side between Conduit and Maddox Streets), once

---

[18] Pencilled at foot of Knowles's last sheet: 'A very kind criticism of some sad stuff/HGH Oct. 1853.' 'Paley's Evidences' was of course Archdeacon William Paley's *Natural Theology; or, Evidences of the Existence and Attributes of the Deity collected from the Appearances of Nature* (1802 and other edn.) on the utilitarian basis of nature's purposeful and benevolent contrivances. Even Pritchard read Paley with his boys, according to Bradley, p. 462 (as cited n. 3 above).

[19] RIBA *Proceedings*, 1851-2 session; public baths and wash-houses having become subjects for architectural concern during London's first sanitary crisis (e.g. article by Ashpitel and Whichcord in first APS vol. 1848–52, for which Knowles senior sat on committee). On Anglo-Danish slab from Cook site, chap. 2, n. 42 above.

the premises of *Fraser's Magazine*, from 1847 until 1869.[20] The letter goes on:

The 'Athenaeum'[21] gives me a notice amongst their correspondents this week—They 'refer their correspondent to Herschel'. As if I hadn't looked there first of all!... Altogether I begin to think it really is *new*.... Did you ever dear friend meet with a much more conceited fellow? With regard to my Museum researches—they came to but little good —I have decided that my inscription is beyond doubt Runic.... Have had another letter from a gentleman about it—begging a rubbing. So that you see what with comets and Runic letters I am on the fair high road to an imperishable glory—without calling up my reserve of Cranks and Cones for organs—Water Meters—or other shadowy & more grand theories—too splendid to be named.

A wretched letter followed a week later, he could not 'forget', he was determined 'to write to the Cape . . . [yet] I must not sneak away as if into an ashamed oblivion'. There were difficulties:

But as in doing this I shall be acting quite in opposition to the advice of my kind old friend at Ashby—and I have already three or four times done so—I have decided that I will go down personally to tell him my reason—So that under plea of geologic excursion (I shall hate the Coal fossils soon) I have told my father that I mean to ask for a day or two in Leicestershire after the 13th of next month [his 21st birthday]—and said that therefore I hardly supposed he would allow me to accept your invitation. To these observations also my father replied 'not a word'—'Vir sapis est etc' you know.

His father's reaction to shadowy theories, as to pleas for a holiday, was nil. Tennyson and Gladstone, both over twenty years older than young Knowles, were to be father-figures who never, or hardly ever, met his outpourings with silence. The kind old friend at Ashby, perhaps a fellow holiday geologist and adviser on romantic problems at the seaside in 1851, was apparently one of those sympathetic older men whom Knowles loved to consult and admire all his life until he stepped into that role himself. Meanwhile, life was hard. 'I really don't know why I do these things—for I am sure they are useless—Last night I went to Clapham Church—"She" was in a seat near me—with Fan—who instantly with "her" left the seat—and I fancy the church too—

[20] Boase; and *A Visit to Regent Street* (c. 1861).
[21] The periodical, not the Clapham society of course.

Pleasant wasn't it.' Two days later he was writing again, that he had sent his 'Comets' to another periodical, and the *Builder* had published a letter from him: 'Do you wonder dear friend why I have so betaken me to write to papers & scribble my name so as to see it "in print".... I have a purpose and a farther one ... one ever-widening, deepening motive which secretly decides—or should decide all that I do.' Whatever that precisely was, he mourned that he was growing dull, 'and deserve to do so—"What a man soweth that shall he also reap"—There is a comfort tho' I have found in discomfort—that God is glorified in justice—and that much more than I suffer would be just.' Emigration to Cape Colony, if that was what he meant by writing 'to the Cape', was then at its height: 1852 was the year Ford Madox Brown painted 'The Last of England'. It was probably in this autumn of 1852 in Clapham that Knowles came to know Dr. Pritchard, a welcoming mind more stimulating than a temporary friendship on 'geologic excursion': 'I shall hate the Coal fossils soon' was a sort of farewell to geology. And the grammar-school chapel, open to the neighbours, was an asylum from painful meetings at evening service in Clapham church; morning service with the family being enough for Streatham church. Some forty years later, Knowles described to Pritchard's daughter how it had seemed:[22]

When I was 'little more than a boy', your father admitted me to his friendship. . . . I came to know him from attending that pretty little school chapel which he had built . . . and out of that pastoral relation-ship grew my acquaintance with him in his observatory and garden, and ultimately my friendship with him of so many years' duration.

The chapel, the garden and the observatory . . . he made 'full of voices', which I have never forgotten to be grateful for. . . . He had a marvellously strong and embodying imagination, which made the Bible stories actual facts. . . . Then again, I remember how he would pace for hours up and down the walks of his garden, bordered on each side by all sorts and kinds of plants and flowers, whose names and qualities and virtues he made texts for endless illustrations of mental and moral questions . . . especially, I recall the nights in his observatory when he brought all the wonders of his material heaven into one's mind and heart as well as to one's eyes, his enthusiasm carrying one, as in a chariot of fire, up to and beyond the highest.

[22] Letter of 1894 quoted in Pritchard, *Memoirs*, cited nn. 3, 4 above.

There was a sense of power in Pritchard's common-sense sincerity, and the spell of 'that deep, soft, emphatic voice of his' was recalled by many people. He was both man of science and theologian, deeply concerned about the reconciliation of science with the Bible while recognizing that Genesis was irreconcilable with what he knew of Nature, and therefore regarding the sacred story as a vision vouchsafed to some ancient seer, 'a divine intimation of as much knowledge as man then needed', not intended to anticipate the 'discoveries which lie within the reach of man'. The very person to reassure a young man worried about faith and comets. Elements of that 'sort of triangular duel' between Pritchard and Tennyson and Knowles at The Hollies beside Clapham Common in 1868, from which the Metaphysical Society sprang, began to come together half a generation before.[23]

Appreciation of art, apart from architectural embellishment and instruction in sketching, such a young man had to cultivate mostly for himself, but there was considerable opportunity for it. Clapham had its private collectors, such as John Allnutt the retired City wine merchant who had bought pictures from Constable and Turner, and in the 1830s added to his mansion by the Common a 'picture saloon' designed by Papworth; his collection made £19,000 at Christie's after his death in 1863. Another Clapham collector was the retired builder William Herbert, whose son Knowles knew. Francis Cook of the drapery warehouse, later to form at Doughty House in Richmond one of the world's great collections of Old Masters, was buying pictures by the early 1850s; the elder Knowles probably designed his first art gallery. 'Whosoever would wish to see the rich resources of this country in works of art, must pierce into private houses,' Waagen the German historian of English collections had observed in the 1840s. Friday Grove no doubt contained, besides its plaster copies of ancient sculpture, architectural engravings, mezzotints by John Martin, and copies of paintings Raphaelite and post-Raphaelite: 'the Cenci is perfect & gives the Governor great satisfaction' (Knowles to Hewlett in October 1859 of a reproduction of Guido Reni's painting). When young James began to collect and George to call himself 'artist' (to the census-taker in 1861), an impression arose in the neighbourhood that the central

[23] Pritchard, *Memoirs*, pp. 14–18, 97–8, 188–94. On Metaphysical Society, chap. 6 below.

hall of Friday Grove was an art gallery, a notion lingering long after the house was pulled down. As for public and quasi-public collections in London then, besides the National Gallery and the British Museum, on certain days the Soane Museum, the Dulwich Gallery, and the Painted Hall at Greenwich were open. A young Englishman confronting 'the celebrated tapestries' in the Vatican could loftily observe, with Knowles in 1854, that they did not do justice to Raphael's original cartoons, then on view at Hampton Court. And, not the least of art's attractions in Mid-Victorian England, an interest in it was something of a social leveller too.[24]

In the summer of 1852, in the midst of theories and miseries and warehouse drawings, Knowles was mulling over the Turners exhibited at Marlborough House (where some thirty-odd years later he was to be such a welcome caller). Wondering how best to look at these half-understood works, he wrote to the *Builder* with his solution, and the signed letter was published on 25 September headed 'The Genius of Turner':[25]

In common with many, it was long before I could distinguish, in the works of our great artist, Turner, anything besides confusion. . . . At last . . . as I stood for the twentieth time before the 'Golden Bough' . . . I raised my hand as a tube to one eye, closing the other, the only fair mode of viewing any drawing (except scene-painting). The effect was 'Turner' as I had heard of him from his devotees. . . . I felt that the great Humboldt had not over-rated the high position of the landscape painter. . . . Why had I never before seen Turner? . . . Wheatstone's stereoscope had just come out, and seemed to suggest the proper answer.

We see all real objects in a compound perspective. . . . But all representations of objects on plane surfaces are drawn to *one* point of sight; from one point of sight then only should we view them. Yet how is it that I see other paintings fall into their proper arrangement whilst looking with both eyes—and can never see Turners but with one?

[24] On art as social leveller, T. H. S. Escott, *England* (1885 edn.), p. 503. Allnutt sale, *CG*, July 1863, and *Art J.*, Aug. 1863, p. 160; gallery, Colvin on Papworth. On Cook's gallery, chap. 4, section on 'Cook's Villa' below. Waagen as quoted by *ILN*, 23 June 1849, p. 427. William Herbert (d. 1863), retired building contractor who 'realized an ample fortune' from the West Strand and Cranbourn St. improvements, became 'a considerable buyer of pictures and sculpture' for his house at Clapham Common, and sat on the Art Union council for many years (*Bldr*, 26 Sept. 1863, p. 682). On 'Cenci' reproduction, Knowles to Hewlett in Oct. 1859 (WPL).

[25] *Bldr*, 25 Sept. 1852. The publisher John Weale in the early 1840s had advertised *An Essay on Single Vision* by John Thomas Woodhouse (not at BL or RIBA).

Because no man besides him has so exactly carried out in its intricate niceties that *monocular perspective* upon which all *drawings* must be based. He is *so* exact that only by becoming his one point of vision can you discern him. . . . *He* knew the full value of the Greek optical corrections, and of all artists has alone followed their scrupulous example.

The Greek optical corrections, of course, had rather to do with architecture. What Ruskin had said on the matter was that 'it is in Turner only that we see a bold and decisive choice of the distance and middle distance, as his great objects of attention; and by him only that the foreground is united and adapted to it . . . by the most precise and beautiful indication or suggestion of just so much of even the minutest forms as the eye can see when its focus is not adapted to them'.[26] But young Knowles's awareness of Ruskin at the time seems to have been entirely and derisively second-hand. One day, Ruskin was to present him with two Turner drawings.

The works of Alexander von Humboldt may have come to his notice through Dr. Pritchard or through Bosworth: the *Cosmos* had been available in cheap translation for several years, and the Knowles library appears to have contained a copy in an 1850 edition, as well as 'Humboldt's Personal Narrative & Views of Nature, 1850–2'. A year or so after Humboldt's death in 1859, an approximation of his likeness was to join those of the Queen and Palmerston and others on the Grosvenor Hotel frieze beside Victoria Station.[27]

On the occasion of the Institute's award of its Royal Gold Medal to Sir Robert Smirke in April 1853, a medal of merit was awarded to young Knowles for an essay on architectural education. That summer Bosworth published it as a pamphlet, and then the *Builder* printed it on 27 August. Here already Knowles was showing a gift for picking up an issue just as it was becoming one, that is, when the larger professional body was beginning to take note of what the young men of the Architectural Association had been saying for the past six years. And he managed to single out the principles at stake with a lighter touch than his father's

[26] *Modern Painters*, vol. I, part II, section ii, chap. iv, section 7.
[27] Baron Alexander von Humboldt (1769–1859) summarized in his *Kosmos* the history and physical state of the universe, trying to show unity in nature, as a seeker after synthesis well suited to appear on the Grosvenor Hotel, chap. 4, n. 9 below. *ILN*, 22 Sept. 1849, p. 205, mentions two cheap translations of *Kosmos* having 'a very extensive sale' in London.

portentousness in defence of cement, while deploying the large antitheses of Donaldson's lecture tactics:[28]

Art has been forgotten for generations whilst men have pursued science. . . . But in the vibrations of the great pendulum of thought, art seems now about to fill the ascending sweep. And is it not time that the fine art of England became something better than a lie?—her towns and cities than old curiosity shops? . . .

. . . For of all things that art—and architecture especially—requires, public attention, sympathy, or even blame, is in our time the most needed. Neglect is the *Grotto del Cane* [doghouse] of fine art. . . .

The name of 'Architect', which should be the signal of respect, the manifestation of competent ability and of gentlemanly uprightness, is assumable and assumed by men remarkable for ignorance and vulgarity of conduct and mind.

Vulgarity was always to worry him, with the dread of the idealist newly arrived socially, and the intolerance of an intensely, self-consciously discriminating man. The crudity of some newly risen architects, whose forebears had *not* soaked up several generations of clients' discriminations, must already have struck him; for it was not the thought of having risen recently—about which both father and son must have been quietly practical—that was painful, but the awfulness of some of the others. Here, along with the sweeping statements, was not so much maturity of thought as an ear for what the mature were saying: English towns as old curiosity shops, blame better than neglect, standards in danger in a profession anyone could join.

The catalogue of excellencies insisted upon by the arch-architect Vitruvius describes not only the most perfect of artists, but almost the completest of men. . . . Yet we shall find in society not a few people totally unacquainted with the *meaning* of an 'Architect'. We shall be told, 'That he is a sort of builder—differing somewhat—rather superior, it is believed, but pretty much the same'. The title of architect is not, as it should be, like that of a barrister or physician, a certificate and diploma of honour . . . we have heard it said that an architect does not always talk good grammar!

He therefore proposed 'formal and public examinations of all candidates for entry into the Profession':

[28] *Bldr*, 27 Aug. 1853, p. 547, and bound pamphlet in vol. 11 (RIBA Library) with Knowles's letter of presentation; printed introductory letter dated July 1853; pamphlet also at BL. On the medal, RIBA *Proceedings*, 1852–3 session.

[This is not] adverse to the freely competitive spirit characterising our age. . . . It protects the many from the few . . . the effect of a wise protection to a learned Profession [is] the benefit and protection of the Public . . . and if there be quacks in medicine and book-making, what shall be said of house or Church-making? If anybody doubts, let him walk round the suburbs of London!

An Act of Parliament should 'confer upon the Royal Institute of Architects powers analogous to those placed in the hands of the Inns of Law, and of the College of Physicians', 'with a legal power of examination so that any young man entering an architect's office as a pupil 'would feel assured that he must do something more than tattoo the desks, fight the clerks, snub the visitors, or scribble for magazines'. He mentioned the need to separate the surveyors from the architects and to prevent the latter from measuring for builders, although he thought that an architect might certainly 'design for a builder as an Architect without the danger even of imputation' of impropriety. (There is reason to think that both he and his father quietly did a bit of that, without imputing it to themselves publicly.[29]) Finally, he thought, 'we should find an Architectural College associated with, and growing out of the Institute', conferring upon the community 'the leaven of a highly educated class of men, and the advantage of a *Living Architecture* to ennoble, embody, and perpetuate its epoch'. This reflected his own longing for education, as well as that consciousness Victorians had, more than any predecessors, of living in an 'epoch'. It reflected too their concern for status: clearly, his profession meant more to him than daily bread.

The question of an architect's education had been much in the air, in and out of the *Builder*'s columns, even before the founding of the Architectural Association in 1847. Knowles may have been brooding over a volume from his father's office shelves: the late Alfred Bartholomew, briefly editor of the *Builder* in 1843-4, had said in 1839 that he had thought out as early as 1831 and put in writing about 1835, 'Proposals for the Foundation of a Great National College for the Study and Regulation of Architecture throughout the British Dominions, for the Examination of Students and Professors of Architecture, and Artificers in Building,

---

[29] For example, Knowles Sr. in Durand Gardens, Lambeth (chap. 2, n. 24), possibly Knowles Jr. in Victoria Street, corner of Strutton Ground; for both, the client-developer was probably the builder.

for granting Honorary Degrees to Proficients therein of various Stages of Maturity, and [hear this] for the Conservation of Public Buildings.'[30] The profession which occasionally remembers to pay its respects to its founders might spare a few for Bartholomew. Yet the immediate impetus for young Knowles's essay will have been a discussion at the Architectural Association in October 1852, duly reported in the professional journals, in which William Tite described the German examination system for the licensing of architects to practise. At any rate, young James joined the A.A. in 1853, taking a burning interest in it for a little while before more articulate talkers put him off and before travel deflected his thoughts to the nature of architecture itself. In 1855 at the A.A. a qualifying diploma was to be recommended for discussion at the Institute and the long, still continuing, process of thinking out the education of architects began. In 1853 Knowles's essay, highly theoretical though it was, played a small part in stimulating that process: besides its appearance in the *Builder*, Bosworth sold seventy copies of the pamphlet in deepest August.[31]

In this August of 1853 the family took its holiday at, for the first time, Broadstairs. That little resort, from the early days of *Punch* in 1842 ('colonized by genteel emigrants from Ramsgate') to the Bank Holidays of the Pooters in 1892 ('Good old Broadstairs'), was for those who found Margate raffish; it still is. In 1853 Professor Donaldson published an article on the vernacular architecture of Broadstairs in the Architectural Publication Society's first volume (prepared when Knowles senior was sitting with Donaldson on the society's committee), so doubtless recommending this watering-place to the Knowleses more than any word of Dickens might do. For at least a generation already, Chandos Place on the front had been recommended (for example, in *The Thanet Itinerary or Steam Yacht Companion* of 1823) as an elevated spot, with an extensive prospect, in which to take a lodging; it was later replaced by the Mid-Victorian Chandos Square. And so, at No. 6 Chandos Place young Knowles sketched

---

[30] Bartholomew, *Specifications* (chap. 2, n. 16 above), preface of 1839 and chap. cxiv.

[31] On Tite's lecture, *Bldr*, 9 Oct. 1852. Membership of A.A., Summerson (chap. 2, n. 48 above), p. 9, from minute-books. On sale of pamphlet, Knowles to Hewlett, 8 Sept. 1853 (WPL).

the prospect (Pl. 4) and wrote to Hewlett on 10 August, enclosing a copy of Bosworth's pamphlet:[32]

I find myself seated by candle light in my bed room writing to you— whilst the musical monotone of the perpetual surf sounds hushingly from the ebbing tide. This is a capital place—we all like it immensely— it's quiet but by no means dull—very pretty— & very breezy. . . . I have but to turn my head from this paper—to see from my castle window the far off light on the Goodwin Sands . . . how many a head at this moment is 'tossed with tangle & with shells'!

To me dear friend at this time the sea—always mournful—becomes more so still—The last time that I listened to it there was but one name that its waves for ever sounded on the hollow shore . . . the year 1851 —a *past year*— & the happiest of my hitherto life . . . is sung out with every tide. . . .

We had a most pretty railway ride thro' Kent. Many a scene we passed worthy the divine Alfred's words, 'a haunt of ancient peace', and the old Cathedral of Canterbury from the W looks really more like some piece of nature which had grown like a forest where it stood than been reared by hands—So truly has it been placed in the bond & family of brotherhood with nature by following her modes— & ful- filling her dicta of harmony—This naturalness I take it is always the character of the most glorious art works—only think of how the Parthenon must have fitted into that picture of rock & sea & blue sky —whose harmonies it essenced & centred—only think how the minarets & cupolas of Mecca must harmonize with the desert. . . .

I'm reading Bulwer's 'Pelham' & am much pleased & interested with it. . . . I really fear I shall do very little here . . . in the 'paper' line —'Instinct & reason' I fear must keep the world waiting for a season.

By the bye—just send me down the no. of 'the Times' which will have the Leader in it about my Essay—in case I should overlook it.

If the Editor of *The Times* took no notice in 1853, James Knowles was to invite him to dinner with Gladstone in 1875, when the Editor of *The Times* was still Delane.[33] As for the 'pretty railway ride', although the masses went to Margate by boat ('the migratory hordes', *Punch* called them), a family like the Knowleses went to Broadstairs by the South Eastern Railway, probably driving over in dignity to Croydon to board the train from

---

[32] Sketch-book (in family possession) inscribed 'a Present from his Mamma' for James's 13th birthday in Oct. 1844. Letters to Hewlett at WPL. Donaldson advocated the 'lost picturesqueness' of certain brick gables at Broadstairs in the 1851–2 section of the preliminary *APS* vol (1853).

[33] Knowles to Thomas (later Earl) Brassey, 10 Apr. 1875 (chap. 7, n. 62 below).

London Bridge. The words 'A haunt of ancient peace' are from that Royal-Academy-Summer-Exhibition-in-verse 'The Palace of Art', although Knowles may have meant to recall the image of East Kent ('a land of peace') near the end of 'The Princess'. Already the image of Canterbury was in his mind for later use to describe the growth 'round some early shrine' of *The Idylls of the King*.[34] A sense of harmony-with-setting was part of an inherited sense of the Picturesque that Knowles glaziers working with garden and conservatory designers had, enhanced by theories from Humboldt on landscape painters joining 'the loftiest poets in inspiring a fervid love and reverence for the "Aspects of Nature"' (young Knowles on Turner), along with snatches from Kata Phusin (young Ruskin) noticed in old issues of Loudon's *Architectural Magazine* on the shelves at Raymond Buildings. As for landscape poetry, even if 'all poetry' only reached James after he discovered Tennyson, men like his father may have been occasional readers of Thomson's *Seasons* and Cowper's *Task*; John Martin's dark-engraved panoramas of *Paradise Lost* made Milton visible; and even indolent brother George, later in life, was said to know Shakespeare by heart. Meanwhile, the reading of novels, not always the latest (*Pelham* having been out since 1828), will have been well served by the circulating library at this watering-place (a boy sailing a boat in Knowles's sketchbook is labelled 'A Pelhamite') and Dickens on Broadstairs in *Household Words* for 2 August 1851 went on circulating there too.

When, in his letter to Hewlett, Knowles also remarked how sailing ships harmonized with the sea as 'those horrid steamboats' did not, this suggested to him the 'antagonism of Science & Art' —so echoing Donaldson's 'Throughout the whole history of our art, there seems to have reigned an antagonism of two principles: the useful and the decorative', in his article on the picturesque gables of Broadstairs—or, indeed, in the dialectical imagination-and-reason of his University College lectures. Three weeks later, Knowles wrote again from Chandos Place (31 August 1853):

This visit which was to be the Hegira of a new Scientific Life, has degenerated into a mere indolent Carnival—I have done nothing but read novels (no end)—play billiards & idle about with a pack of young

[34] Knowles to *Spectator*, 1 Jan. 1870 (chap. 7, n. 37 below).

ne'er-do-wells whose cheerful and chaffing acquaintance I have made—
& what with sailing & idling & larking with these fellows that
monster eel Time has slipped thro' my fingers and left nothing but
slime! Ah well—I must hope for the reaction—

By the bye if you want to know Broadstairs read 'Our watering
place' in No. 71 of Household Words—tho' that is certainly drawn too
dull.

Have you seen the Comet? I did on Sunday evening after church—it
was the first time of making personal acquaintance with these wild
giants whom my daring fancy has tried to tame. . . .

Congratulate me old fellow that 'the Builder' at any rate has
behaved like a gentleman & printed both my letter to itself & *all
my Essay*—this of course will give it wider circulation than anything
else could have done. . . . I shall wait till I come home about the Prince
—but *he* ought to be poked too.

As for 'poking' Prince Albert—whose zeal for the arts occasionally
extended to architecture, and whose interest in cultural centres
and in vocational training was already shaping South Kensington
—it was only thirty years later, on other subjects, that Knowles's
opinion was sought in royal circles.

He next wrote from Clapham Park (8 September 1853)
thanking Hewlett for an invitation to join him on holiday in the
country, which 'I, freshly returned from furlough am quite
unable to accept—I assure you . . . that I should of all things enjoy
a few days with you in the Country—Metaphysics fit so well into
Physics where 'η φυσις surrounds us . . . (is my Greek article right?)
and you and I could scarcely I think be together for an hour
without trying to mount on each other's shoulders and overlook
the boundary wall of visible Nature.' Thus, metaphysics of a sort
entered Knowles's vocabulary much sooner than Tennyson was
to imagine.[35] Knowles also reported Bosworth's sale of seventy
copies of his essay on architectural education ('who on earth can
have bought them?') and that, having shown his 'Instinct and
Reason' paper to a 'vastly clever' clergyman at Broadstairs, 'we
had together a most agreeable hour or so of metaphysical talk—
the only one I've been able to get since I saw you—I declare it's
quite unfortunate our holidays coming "end on" in this way'.
This dwelling on the perennial romantic-classical antitheses of
Donaldson's teaching methods foreshadowed Knowles's con-

---

[35] See chap. 6, n. 30 below.

tinuing concern for possible syntheses: in the 1850s of the Gothic
and Classic styles in architecture, in the 1860s of religion and
science—powerful issues of the mid-century.

The letters of 1853 have a more adult ring than those written
earlier, as in this from Raymond Buildings on 20 September:

Hurrying like a pickpocket among the jostling hours in the streets of
'today'—I seem to notice Messrs 12 and 1—so fully occupied that I
can filch from their tail pockets a few stray minutes which I proceed to
enclose to you—who as receiver of stolen goods cannot grumble at the
theft! . . . I am now in high business upon . . . a competition-design for
a town hall at Pontypool in Monmouthshire . . . which (as I work after
office hours) I shall have enough to accomplish. . . .

I don't know what to make of the table speaking you mention—I
mean as to the actuality of the occurrence—'au reste' I see no difficulty
—we have but to suppose that somebody there knew the proper
answers . . . and that *their knowledge* acted decisively in directing a
motion to take place where no other motive directive influence
could have existed. . . .

How does your Poem progress? Among the pine woods is the place
to write one—They are vestibules to the grave of joy—and melancholy
must ever be the loftiest strain of man on the demon-haunted earth—
Shall I say that a pine wood looks like a deserted Pandemonium?
(I mean as Milton describes it) with the lamps gone out and silence
slumbering soundly whilst she may—too soon to be waked by the
returning fiends.

On 'table speaking' this was an early ripple of his later theory of
'brain waves'.[36] And always the journalist's liking for figures of
speech—time as express train, as monster eel, as stolen goods. In
range of reference and feeling these were not letters that just any
ill-educated 18 to 22-year-old in 1850–3 might write. For this one,
truly, these were charging years, although in 1853 the charging
process was far from complete. Curiosity, a strong conscience,
and a thin skin were to make him restlessly aware of unused
powers for some time yet.

Late in 1853, seven years after entering his father's office, young
James became an Associate of the RIBA. Faced with the prospect
this presented, he found he could not settle down in Raymond

---

[36] Chap. 6, n. 31 below on *Spectator* letter of 1869, and chap. 6, n. 18 below on
'trying to move a table mesmerically' in 1868; for 'table-speaking' OED only has
table-rapping 1858. A Pontypool Town Hall competition was not prominent in
the building journals and no more is heard of Knowles's entry.

Buildings in a state of unsatisfied wonder about the rest of the world. 'I felt', he said later, 'more and more that my abominably neglected schooling must be repaired or supplemented by something, as I was not to to go Oxford or Cambridge, and at last I made up my mind that I must and would go abroad and see the world. I was ashamed wherever I went, finding I had no foundation, as it were, to stand upon, knew nothing, had done nothing, and seen nothing. I could bear it no more.' And so it was arranged that he should go for six months to Italy and Sicily, on two hundred pounds provided by his father, accompanied as far as Naples by Hewlett, who had less money to spend.

Before they started off in March 1854, each addressed a meeting of the Clapham Athenaeum: on 13 February, Knowles discoursed upon 'The Distinctive Attributes of Man'; and Hewlett, the following week, upon 'Recent News from Utopia', both lectures as reported in the new *Clapham Gazette* consisting largely of moral reflections. More particular marvels were to fill their talk when they came home again.

The long-expected war with Russia was declared three weeks after their departure. While they were embarking from one of the Kent ports, the newspapers were full of the embarkation of troops from Portsmouth, Southampton, and Plymouth. But no well-insulated young civilian, early in 1854, was going to be deterred from travel by news from the Crimea.

GRAND TOUR, 1854

> 'How many lessons of Livy—dry enough to hear at the time, and how many harangues of my old Architectural Professor came to my mind at this hour of compensation, while I looked delighted on the strange and antique pile?' Notes on the so-called Tomb of the Horatii and Curiatii near Albano, for a lecture to the Clapham Literary and Scientific Institution by J. T. Knowles Jr. in January 1856

The flavour of the tour emerges from surviving travel journals, letters, and later lecture notes that remind one of Richard Doyle's contemporary drawings of *The Foreign Tour of Messrs Brown, Jones and Robinson*: Hewlett could be the tall, thin one with air of aloofness, Knowles the small engaging one with sketchbook. In

the beginning, at Clapham Park, a bad cold and worry over the
expense of Paris induced Knowles to delay their start, telling
Hewlett that 'yielding to advice from all sides, and specially
from Edward Barry last night—I have decided to recommend
strongly to you to delay . . . our departure . . . If we spend the
time we have intended in Paris—it will certainly make a great
hole in our finances. . . . Edward says he doesn't think we could
manage under a guinea a day.' (The opinion of the Barry boys
carried weight; Edward, only a year older than Knowles, was to
design the new Covent Garden Opera House two years later.)
In Rome they were to join another young Clapham acquaintance,
a future Anglican clergyman George Herbert, son of the retired
successful builder of the West Strand and other London improvements, William Herbert.[37]

The first month went something like this: a week or less in
Paris, then probably by the new railway line to Marseilles via
Lyon and Avignon, probably by boat via Nice to Genoa, unless
they took the slower Mt. Cenis road to Turin first, or else by rail
from Genoa to Turin and back, then via Pisa to Leghorn where
they embarked for the port of Rome, where the journal begins.
One's first day in Rome is a special day: 'Many of us, young or
middle-aged [Thackeray was writing in *The Newcomes* just then],
have felt that delightful shock which the first sight of the great
city inspires'—and written it all down in a ruled exercise book.
And so Knowles landed at Civita Vecchia in April 1854, aged 22,
with Murray's *Central Italy* and all his English prejudices in hand.
Yet, while carefully noting the name, owner, and horse-power of
the steamer that brought them overnight from Leghorn (the
Neapolitan Steam Navigation Company's *Calabrese*, 300 h.p.),
he was probably unaware that she had quite likely been built in
the Thames.[38] On the quay with 'whole herds of rascals who were
banded into concert with the officers of the Douane for purposes
of robbery,' the angry passengers 'were mulcted of pauls upon

[37] This section is based on 180 pp. of travel journals (6–22 Apr. and 10 May–
7 June 1854; others presumably lost), three letters to Hewlett of February, June,
and July 1854, and a later lecture-script delivered 1856 and quoted at head of this
section (all in family possession until 1973, now at WPL). On Herbert's father, n.
24 above.
[38] *ILN*, 28 Nov. 1846, p. 348, on Thames-built steamers *Capri* and *Vesuvio* for
that company. Murray's *Central Italy* was in its 3rd edn. by 1853. Clive Newcome
reached Rome in Thackeray's chap. xxxv. Unspecified quotations that follow
are from Knowles's travel journal (n. 37).

pauls [small coins] by the dozen'. The scene 'with its attendant rows and shoutings and crowds was bewildering to the last degree' until, sorted out at last in 'a caravanserai of 3 diligences', they set off on the eight-hour dusty ride along the old Aurelian Way. As they jolted along, noting ruins and wild flowers with equal excitement, 'a very interesting and long conversation with a Russian noble, an owner of 6000 serfs, upon the condition of his country, which I enjoyed in the diligence' caused Knowles to reflect on the 'great advantage of travelling that one meets with so many things & persons to modify & moderate previously formed and prejudiced views'. Finally they saw from miles away the cupola of St. Peter's rise 'like a small hill' above the Campagna:

At length with head uncovered, from involuntary reverence, I was driven under the Aurelian gate, and beneath the very walls of St Peter's into the Eternal City. . . . I took a rapid rush down into the Piazza San Pietro, saw the Cathedral and the colonnades by moonlight, was disappointed, and nearly lost my diligence which I had to chase down the middle of the street at full galop in mortal fright of losing my place, my luggage, my passport, and I don't know what more. . . . We went to the hotel d'Angleterre, found it quite full so, leaving Hewlett in the position of watch dog to the luggage—valises and carpet bags—I made vain attempts for lodging for the night at 3 or 4 more hotels. I began to think we must spend our first night in Rome in the streets—at last I took a vettura and drove in desperation to Herbert's address of which I seemed to have a fragmentary recollection. I found a card from him giving me the address of rooms he had taken for us [at 12 via de' Due Macelli, off the Piazza di Spagna] and in the end made a settlement and finish of a hard day's work by dinner & bed.

John Evelyn, aged 24, had written in *his* diary in 1644: 'we began to enter the plains of Rome; at which sight my thoughts were strangely elevated . . . and [arrived] by the Vatican (for at that gate we entered) . . . about five at night; and being perplexed for a convenient lodging, wandered up and down on horseback, till at last one conducted us to [a house] near the Piazza Spagnola.' Horace Walpole at 23 in 1740, wearing a more worldly-wise air than Carolean or Victorian, was 'persuaded that in an hundred years Rome will not be worth seeing'.[39]

The Victorian visitors set out next day, to be struck by 'the extreme beauty of Rome as she lies along the Tiber's banks', the

[39] Evelyn's Diary for 4 Nov. 1644. Walpole to West, 7 May 1740.

piles of roofs and towers 'mingled with the green of gardens', and over all the sense of 'Rome' enveloping the scene: 'all this produces on the mind a feeling which becomes a little choky in the throat & a little misty in the eyes—at least for a moment, till one thinks one ought to be ashamed of it'. The picturesque Rome they saw was to vanish after 1870, and Knowles was to have it nostalgically recalled in 1889: 'If a traveller who had known Rome twenty years ago were to go there now. . . . Instead of that picturesque confusion of broken, irregular roofs, of towers and loggias surrounded by dense masses of foliage which he remembered . . . he would see a big modern city', one of his authors was to write for him in the *Nineteenth Century*.[40] Meanwhile, for an English architectural student in 1854, 'St Peter's itself disappointed even me who was most prepared for disappointment'. ('St Peter's I expected to be *disappointed* in. I was *disgusted*': Ruskin in Rome, aged 21.[41]) Young Knowles took particular exception to the shape of the dome: as a Londoner he missed Wren's soaring equation of drum, dome, and lantern:

I was quite riled & sad—I said it is too bad—St Peter's is a dead swindle—I said it & I think it. . . . So is the dome . . . it does not grow —it doesn't carry itself—it is hoisted up there & there it stays but it hugs the earth. . . . A really grand & noble cupola is built for the air . . . I wouldn't exchange the peristyle & dome of St Paul's in London for all the scot & lot of St Peter's, inside, outside & underneath, bones of Saints included. . . . I said to Hewlett, do let us go & see the Transfiguration now & look at something which cannot disappoint us, which must be truly great. So we went out of St Peter's, & admired far more than it, the true Cinque-cento masses of the Vatican palace rising high above the colonnades—Every day I see greater, more simple noble & majestic beauties in this genuine style of mediaeval Italy.

The ideal of Cinquecento Rome set by Barry in Pall Mall in the 1830s was still in force in circles that knew little of genuine styles of medieval Italy, although the English palazzo ideal of the 1850s was moving in search of variety toward, for example, Quattrocento Florence which Knowles senior was then invoking in Chancery Lane. The tastes of architects like this became pre-

[40] Mrs. Henry Ady (Julia Cartwright) in *NC*, Oct. 1889, pp. 593–4.
[41] Quoted by Kenneth Clark from a letter of 31 Dec. 1840, *Ruskin Today* (Penguin edn. 1967), p. 31.

Raphaelite in their own profession long before they warmed to
the Quattrocento in painting. At sight of Raphael's 'Transfiguration', 'we were ourselves transfixed . . . the language of
Scripture itself is the only parallel to its sublime & awe-full
beauty. . . . The Mecca of my Pilgrimage is reached—& its
Cuaba has been seen' (two pages of this). Mecca and the Ka'ba
were in use as metaphors already.

Next morning after breakfasting at the Caffè Greco and trying
unsuccessfully to obtain *cartes de séjour* from an obstructive
Bureau of Police, they found their first view of the Forum less
crowded than in engravings and paintings, and paused to meditate
on Greatness. Then 'by toilsome stages' they climbed the tower
of the Senators' Palace and 'at length sat down in a shady Storey
just below the Summit—& with the help of lorgnette & maps
retraced as well as we were able the scenes so familiarly sounding
to the ear that the eye itself seemed almost old acquaintance with
them', noting that they 'would earnestly advise every traveller
to carry a good double barrelled glass' and that the heat was
'completely exhaustive'. Next day, after breakfast at Nazzarri's
in the Piazza di Spagna, they were again 'made savage' by the
police and their own 'passportless' status. Then back to St. Peter's,
discussing as they walked along the 'limitation of Art's proper
sphere to natural and abstract religion— & the just position which
she thus may take in a Christian Society, without degenerating
into either a sentimentalism or idolatry, displacing true religion
as she has done in the Church of Rome, by usurping the Gospel
offices of direct moral teaching', when it ought to demonstrate
'like Science the harmony between natural & revealed religion',
until they reached the Scala Regia—'the most effective Staircase
I have ever seen'—for Knowles was fond of 'an architectural
vista'. Then came the Sistine Chapel. Craning at the tremendous
ceiling, they deplored at length Michelangelo's earthiness and
Power without Beauty: oh, that Raphael had lived to 'paint
another over it'. But after this 'earthly host', they 'revelled in the
charming decorations of vines & roses climbing over light
bamboo trellises' on the walls and ceilings of the Vatican loggias:
these 'speaking tendrils & leaves & their wild roses talking so
purely of the country, & growing quite naturally in these city
domes & vaults . . . from the indescribably fascinating soul of art
which has made these children of nature's own wild bosom so

much missionaries of the Poet's human preaching & lesson—as human forms could be—or the man-created language of the Architect'. If, as will shortly appear, he was not yet taking Ruskin seriously, the disposition to do so was growing.

They then copied down Raphael's epitaph in the Pantheon, stared at a 'shuddery' monkish funeral processing down the Corso, and called on 'Mr. Chomley the banker, Sir James Eyre's friend'—Eyre having been consultant physician to the Architects', Builders', and General Insurance Company of which Knowles Sr. was for a while a director; it was a proud thing that the network of one's acquaintance might reach to Rome.[42] Early next morning, Palm Sunday, 'got up in full evening dress' they drove off to St. Peter's to join the thousands waiting in the nave.

The whole thing was dreadfully long . . . but [I] was determined to see the complete operation if possible at any rate for once. So I read Kugler[43] during the everlasting part recitatives of the lessons—and was glad I stopped because towards the end the only grand spectacle took place, when at the elevation of the host, the vast multitude was prostrate on the ground, and all the huge quadrangle of soldiers fell onto the pavement with their arms—in moments of a dead Silence— After that some beautiful singing . . . & the nave filled with people, sunlight, the waving palms & music, was theatrically & considerably imposing.

But this praise was accompanied by ruder reflections: 'Ugh it was disgraceful to see scores & scores of great big priests & soldiers in full uniform sprawling like frogs on the ground & kissing a fat commonplace old gentleman's rather gouty foot.' Three days later, 'I had no idea till I came to Rome of the gigantic humbug & miserable blasphemous tomfoolery of her everlasting services'; but a year or so after, he inserted in his lecture script: 'We witness these things against the Church of Rome—but what other church could occupy her position without sharing her guilt?'—in the climate of Clapham, unwilling to tolerate religious intolerance after the affairs of 1850. And this was to be his attitude (lion-hunting aside) to the Cardinal Archbishop of Westminster later on.

That Sunday evening Knowles made up a party for the

---

[42] On Eyre, chap. 2, n. 32 above.

[43] Probably Eastlake's edn. (introduced by him but translated by a Mrs. Hutton) of Kugler's *Schools of Italian Painting* (2nd edn. 1851).

indispensable ruin-experience by moonlight (one's Roman tour had then to be arranged with due regard for the phases of the moon), first 'beneath the awful vaults of Constantine's basilica':

> Thro' a rent in the central vault edged with a profuse vegetation of hanging & creeping plants the moon was pouring down a flood of light upon the huge Cassoons.[44] . . . By Jove! they *were* giants these old Romans—& if Architecture went to sleep soon after these vast works she reared herself in them a worthy and an awful pillow of repose. . . . Cannot all the wisdom of our day nurture some new young goddess? . . . what sort of food is needful to rear as vast a strength from out ourselves? From her death trance what food is poison to High Art? The Death & the food lie here side by side.

A Victorian ruminating here was bound to wonder what his own age might make 'from out ourselves'. And so to the Colosseum 'with minds full of Manfred's soliloquy':

> Thro' the broken arches, the moonlight streamed till the building looked like a great gaunt honeycombed Skeleton. We revived betwixt us all the Tales of horror and dismay told of this fearful slaughter house. . . . From the highest precinctio—the view down into the gulf of seats & parapets . . . is the most tremendous. . . . I got into a solitary place—& sitting down, thought Byron & history intently—'From afar' I heard the watch dogs 'bay beyond the Tiber'—and from the herbage at my feet the quiet mournful chirps of grass-hoppers alone broke the silence. . . . [I sat there] thinking—unutterable things—mournful yet deeply full of pleasure . . . a delight which ranks with my recollections of the Primroses & foxgloves, hay fields—and Park-hills of which my earliest impressions & happiest are composed.

Echoes of *Manfred* and *Childe Harold* merged with the self-conscious particular childhood memory of Reigate. Afterward, 'Herbert and a Mr Wood, a young sculptor, came in to our rooms to have a little refreshment—Wood & myself fell into a long enthusiastic & interesting talk about the common principles of our respective Arts—where with much gratification I found his practice (that is to be) exactly what my theory of Art, costing me some meditation of late, required'. But he was not yet ready, apparently, to set down any theories in writing. The sculptor was probably Shakspere Wood, a native of Manchester who lived

---

[44] Old-fashioned word for coffers as sunk panels in ceilings (*OED*: 1799); Knowles in the Farnese Palace noted 'splendidly cassooned & carved cedar ceilings': his training was, or rather his trainers were, partly pre-Victorian.

in Rome from about 1851 and became a connoisseur of its antiquities.[45]

Next day at the Borghese gallery there were raptures over Correggio's 'Danae' ('tho disgustingly immoral in its tendency exhibits the most ecstatic animal beauty') and a little architectural discovery:

I observed a charming 'dodge' in the Borghese. At the end of a long vista of rooms a fountain is seen dashing—from out a window—seeming to lead into the garden where it is placed—but when you reach this window you find that all the charming effect is produced by an aperture cut thro' a blind wall within 15 feet of the window—& which else would have shut the place up in a kind of prison yard—An aperture of same size as the window—& exactly on the axial line of the vista of doorways is cut thro' the dead wall—which is very thick—& a few jets of water play in this aperture—falling over rocky pebbles and creepers—This wrinkle might be very useful for London Houses—& might be combined with what Dr Ward hinted to me concerning his closed cases—& their application to buildings.

That is, the inventor of the Wardian case, who had retired to Clapham.[46] The possibility of developing the glazed enclosure for plants into one for people, 'a climate within a climate, a little world within a world', had influenced Paxton (in his proposal for a glass sanatorium at Victoria Park) and must have appealed to the glaziers' descendant in 1854—with no effect on Knowles's work that we know of, yet it was a 'wrinkle', it was news.

In the Vatican Museum, the Apollo Belvedere was 'the divinest thing' (Hewlett and Knowles doubtless exchanging wry glances): 'I certainly did not believe until the last few days how greatly important mere material is to [the quality of] Sculpture', for in architecture had not his father found it better to embody the 'emanations of deep thought' in short-lived cement than to perpetuate 'eternal stereotypes' in stone? The contrast between 'the flaky opaque heavy white' of plaster casts and 'the lambent play of life' in marble opened eyes accustomed to the sculpture-gallery of Friday Grove. From the Vatican Museum's 'hall of animals . . . full of wonderful Landseer sculptures' (a wonderfully

[45] Shakspere Wood (1827–86) is in *DNB* and Boase.
[46] Nathaniel B. Ward (1791–1868), doctor and botanist, author of *On the Growth of Plants in Closely Glazed Cases* (1842, 1852), whose work had just been expounded at the Royal Institution in March 1854 by his son, and by Faraday there in 1838.

parochial remark), they came to the Library, where Knowles noted fine 'early Italian paintings principally on wood'—noticed more as curiosities perhaps than as art, but still, noticed (the National Gallery had its first 'gold-backs' in 1848)—and the ancient fresco of the 'Aldobrandini Wedding' was full of the 'freedom power & ideal nature' of the antique, an ideal he was to cherish all his life. Then, at Herbert's rooms, they inspected some newly purchased photographs—the new treasures for tourists— 'one especially lovely of Raphael's Sybils, which I fear I must buy' (to one of these figures in S. Maria della Pace was related a Raphaelesque drawing that Knowles did, a dozen years later at Sotheby's, buy from the Wellesley Collection).

On Wednesday in Easter week, Knowles and Hewlett stationed themselves in the Sistine Chapel among the crowd for Tenebrae, aghast at human smells and the length of the service ('all nonsense to talk about Covenanters' sermons and their lengths') until the Miserere came and was worth the suffering. 'It rose like a far-off evening wind over the sea, & swelled imperceptibly into a wail of song. . . . I was reminded of the girls' "soft music" raised to the highest pitch of Art'—his sisters singing at the piano in Clapham Park. On Holy Thursday the nave of St. Peter's, lighted only by a few tapers, 'looked the St Peter's of which one had dreamed', but the long service left him divided between an aversion to Juggernaut and a sense of the ridiculous—which was no help to a new acquaintance, Hemans, 'Son of the Poetess' and a Catholic, who tried energetically to convert him.[47] A Good Friday tour of the basilicas included the old sweeping view still then to be seen from the Lateran steps, of 'the great Claudian aqueduct stepping silently over the hot plain' of the Campagna. That night with George Herbert they talked art, morals, manners, and theology until two in the morning, Herbert's recent Oxford degree and plans for the clergy giving him a certain ascendancy.

Saturday brought glorious discoveries. First, in the Palazzo Barberini, that Victorian favourite, Guido Reni's painting of Beatrice Cenci: 'the Cenci, what am I to say—I had never believed in it—hundreds & almost thousands of copies & engravings I have seen. . . . Shelley has failed to tell half that his picture does' (more than a page of this). The other glory was the

---

[47] Apparently C. I. Hemans (1817–76), youngest son of Mrs. Felicia Hemans; he founded the first English newspaper in Rome in 1846 (Boase).

Palazzo Farnese with the 'nervous curves of the consoles in [under] the lower windows, & the great energy of compressed spring in the Sima curve of the lowest plinth . . . crowned at the top with a very diadem of a Cornice.'⁴⁸ The palace seemed 'to stand so firm as a mountain built upon the ground—rather growing from the ground'—although of course he disapproved of Michelangelo's top storey in the courtyard. But there was no building anywhere 'to beat this noble & palatial pile'; and the stucco clothing its façade must also have been of interest.

Easter Sunday in St. Peter's brought the thrilling sound of the 'celebrated silver trumpets' circling round and round the vaults, and then the excitement of the benediction scene in the great square afterward, among 'dense multitudes of sight-seers'—a fairly new word then.⁴⁹ At the culminating illuminations in the evening, first the 'silver illumination' outlining the huge building from colonnades to dome-ribs with hundreds of candles in paper lanterns, then the 'golden' one with 'great lumps of resin soaked tow or shavings on the ends of sticks', the 'vast pile' was made gorgeous: 'a little too Vauxhall-like in the 2nd Act', Knowles thought. He was not sorry when Holy Week was over. 'It's a great deal more bother than profit— & yet one is obliged to *do* the whole thing—or what would become of one in argument about it?' Although visual-minded by inheritance and training, to him the importance of experience lay much in talking about it afterward; more than most architects, he verbalized and dramatized everything.

Visiting sculptors' studios was also the done thing—long before *Roderick Hudson*—so they went the rounds, calling on B. E. Spence (whose 'Highland Mary' is at Osborne) and H. M. Imhoff whose well-draped Flora was found to be 'charming for a drawing-room'; and at Pietro Tenerani's Knowles 'worked a human skeleton about . . . and marvellously admired the surprising & complex simplicity of the sublime mechanism'; while Lawrence Macdonald was observed to model his drapery from 'a

---

⁴⁸ The old English usage of 'nervous' (as sinewy, strong) in architectural description was still in old-fashioned service in the mid-twentieth century.

⁴⁹ *OED*: 1847. He also in retrospect (lecture script) was more pretentious, as at Catania 'we employed a day or two in getting up its lions', and found Messina 'with no remarkable "menagerie"—such a relief'. Another such expression appeared for Florence (letter to Hewlett), 'the dear grand old Town—which I expect to "spoon" for some time', and at Naples where he 'spooned about'.

sort of Cachemere'. Yet Knowles observed more than details, finding that modern sculpture lacked life and complaining as a true Victorian that it seldom had a story to tell or a lesson to preach, though he admired his friend Wood's 'Evangeline' (a fairly recent subject, Longfellow's poem having been published in 1847). Another morning he went with Wood to the studio of John Gibson 'the famous sculptor . . . an iron grey haired man of about 40 I should think [Gibson was 64] & with a singularly dry quiet manner. . . . He took us to see his great figure of the Queen preparing for . . . the palace of Westminster' (a murmured 'friend of the Barry family' will not have gone amiss here): 'The whole group is to be colored on the Gibsonian School of sculpture— which as its author told me is by no means meant to imitate nature but to assist the ideality of the work.' The seated figure of the Queen (now without attendant figures) in the Prince's Chamber behind the Throne in the House of Lords was disliked by Barry for injuring the delicate detail of its surroundings. It was never coloured, but if Knowles recalled the talk correctly, his journal shows that Gibson still had other intentions in the spring of 1854. The work he showed them next, later called 'Tinted Venus' (a private commission not publicly shown until 1862), was already 'celebrated as the embodiment of his views' and Knowles attentively noted its connection with a very contemporary controversy: 'Gibson condemns Jones's doings at Sydenham —but makes only a difference of degree in his own practice— & to my taste is himself less condemnable only in degree.' Owen Jones's decorations of the Greek Court at the Sydenham Crystal Palace (not open until June, but known to those in the know) were, like the Tinted Venus, a product of the 1850s and of the running argument since the 1830s, on 'the vexed question respecting the colouring' of Greek temples and statues, a topic that was to interest Knowles at Girgenti and in vigorous recollection later.[50]

[50] John Gibson R.A. (1790–1866): in Gunnis, Boase. *ILN*, 7 Mar. 1857, p. 206, on statue *in situ* mentions only touches of gilding. On Barry's dislike, the *Life* by his son Alfred (1867), p. 261. *ILN*, 24 June 1854, p. 600, reviewed Crystal Palace handbooks including *The Greek Court* by George Scharf and *An Apology for the Colouring of the Same* by Owen Jones, on 'the vexed question respecting the colouring' of Greek temples and statues, with chemical analyses of matter 'picked off' originals by Faraday; wrangling over this question went back to the 1830s, e.g. in RIBA's first vol. of *Transactions* (1837) with an early chromo-litho colour-plate and observations by Donaldson and others.

They continued to 'do' picture galleries filled with Guidos, Dolcis, and Gaspar Poussins, 'about a cloud in one of which Herbert & I had a fight' (since Herbert's father not only collected pictures but sat on the council of the Art-Union of London). Again they inspected St. Peter's, 'Murray in hand', though most of the monuments were 'in Bernini's worst style'. Then to a concert, where 'some poor creatures' throats were nearly rent to pieces by the shrieks of that wretch Verdi—He ought to be restrained from injuring his fellow creatures in the way he does'. And 'the overture to Tell was played on 2 pianos one of which had several loose strings'. Knowles was to publish an article on Verdi by the composer Grieg in 1901.

Once again they asked at the Bureau of Police for their papers and were dismayed by 'a man who told us it was very awkward that we had no receipt for our passports & billets. . . . So I went— rather frightened to Chomley's—who said the Consul will make any row all right', and the banker kindly invited Knowles and Herbert to dinner 'off stunning beef & champagne'. When they went, like most tourists then, to MacPherson's to buy photographs,[51] that connoisseur of the Roman scene told Knowles 'that a man named *George* Knowles—an architect & a late traveller was a marked man of the police—having mixed himself with Greek politics— & that probably the reason of my getting no letters is connected with the identity of names—This is particularly hard upon me because I don't care 2 straws about the whole politics of Europe—so long as they leave me to travel in peace.' This may have been the George Knowles who in the 1840s had sent views of Greek temples to the Royal Academy and reconstructions of the Acropolis to the RIBA.[52] Very likely the whole confusion arose from innocently chaffing letters to James from his own brother George in Clapham Park. The uneasiness of both Greek

[51] Robert MacPherson (d. 1872), originally an Edinburgh surgeon, in the early 1840s settled in Rome as painter-connoisseur-dealer and friend of artists and writers, taking up photography in 1851, and his splendid views of Rome were soon in demand by tourists (Helmut Gernsheim, *History of Photography*, 1955, pp. 221–3). The 1858 catalogue of the Architectural Photographic Assn. (later Society) in London lists 120 views of Rome by him.

[52] George Knowles, painter, exhibited views of Greek temples at the Royal Academy 1845–8 (Graves), sent plans of the Acropolis to the RIBA in 1846–7 (RIBA *Proceedings*), and Burford's Panorama in Leicester Square advertised a view of Athens taken from drawings by him as 'most intellectual' (*ILN*, 19 July 1845, p. 39).

and Italian politics then was part of the general unease of south-eastern Europe during the Crimean War. The travel documents materialized next day, after two weeks of anxiety, but no letters, 'thanks to that meddling ass whose name I bear'. Nothing of the republican struggles of five years before, or to come, seemed to penetrate the tourist orbit in Rome in 1854; and it was many years before Mazzini became one of Knowles's authors, and 'the whole politics of Europe' entered his professional range.

Ancient architecture continued to absorb him, as at Nero's Golden House: the division of the plan into '2 suits' of rooms on either side of a central corridor, with a north or summer aspect and a south or winter aspect, was to occur to him in planning 'Baron' Grant's house in Kensington twenty years later. Next they 'enjoyed a most delightful scramble' at the Baths of Caracalla, as the last generation of travellers to revel in Roman ruins unstripped, unmended, and unsafe:

The mixture of gigantic vaults & lofty walls fragments of rich architecture & groves of wild flowers & shrubs growing upon the summits of arches 100 feet above the ground was absolutely unique . . . wandering along upon the giddy heights formed by the crowns of the ruined vaults, one comes unexpectedly to gulfs and rents looking down on to the strewn masses of wall or roof or pavement far below and looks thro' fissures out away over the purple Campagna smooth & flat as the sea. . . . It was one of the greatest treats I have had, wandering about there picking violets & wall-flowers . . . and gathering small specimens of mosaic pavement from the floors of rooms above—lava or tufa or pumice from the vaults (used largely for the sake of light construction) & small bits of marble ornaments from the piled heaps of ruin.

A generation earlier, Shelley had been writing *Prometheus Unbound* while seated aloft upon these 'mountainous ruins . . . among the flowery glades and thickets of odoriferous blossoming trees which extend in ever-winding labyrinths upon its immense platforms and dizzy arches' (preface to the poem). A generation after delightful scrambles in the 1850s, such ruins were to rise 'bare and gaunt against the sky' (Mrs. Ady in 1889), with all the virtues of cleaned teeth as now so sensibly understood.

Knowles and Hewlett, with two young men, Sawyer and an American 'Romanist' introduced by Hemans, then went for a three-day 'round of the environs', to Albano, Frascati, and Tivoli.

On donkey-back they rode through a countryside thick with wild flowers ('greenhouse & garden plants in England') among the odours of narcissus and violets, laughing and 'racing each other & chaffing to the last degree', and revelling in views 'just as Turner has so often painted' (in, for instance, Mr. Allnutt's view of Tivoli in his private gallery by Clapham Common). In the hotel at Frascati, 'I sit writing in about the finest "Salle a manger" I ever occupied—a segment of 12 Doric cols mounted on a surface of about 2 ft 6 ins in height & with a chord or diameter of about 55 feet and a versed sine of about 22 feet' (with sketch-plan). Several pages of rhapsody follow, on the 'ruins rocks and waters' of Tivoli, yet even among its cascades he thought it shared the faults of 'all Continental scenes—where ruins enter into the composition—namely, that there is not enough water' (ah, the appeal of Claude's sea-coast scenes to the island English). But looking down into the long waterfall to the Grotto of Sirens he thought of Milton's description of the fall of the rebel angels. Of the villa of Maecenas, 'I had no idea of how exquisitely perfect were the domestic buildings of the Romans'— his father's colonnades having so magnified classical domestic scale. The visit ended ebulliently: 'We enterred Rome—after a glorious ride across the plain . . . and after dining at Lepri's together, separated with mutual expressions of satisfaction and goodwill—having all 4 of us enjoyed each other's company in the most delightful—poetical—classical and beautiful excursion— that it was ever the good fortune of travellers to make.' Never mind that Knowles and Sawyer weren't speaking when their paths crossed again at Naples; such is travel. Hewlett and Knowles still had a fortnight in Rome, covered by a journal now missing. From Rome on 8 May they left by road for Naples, where early on their first morning they set off 'for a day's sight seeing of the environs'.

First to the long grotto of Posilippo, 'and noticed very Turner-like effects of light and dust and darkness' (as, on night drives in Sicily, 'flaring resinous cressetts lighting the markets' recalled Rembrandt). Then to Pozzuoli, observing 'in the stucco of the vaults division lines to imitate large layers of stone—a thing to make Ruskin crazy—if he were not so already' (in this rude reference to 'The Lamp of Truth' forgetting how Donaldson had censured the imitative scoring of stucco). The most fascinating of the waterside ruins of Pozzuoli were, of course, the shellfish-eaten columns of the so-called Temple of Jupiter Serapis, already known to Knowles in the engraved frontispiece to Lyell's *Principles of Geology* carried in his carpet-bag.[53] 'The very name makes the heart of a geologist bound with excitement—so intimately is its witness connected with the establishment of his Science upon rational principles'; that is, it was evidence of more than one catastrophe in the world's history, of the former submersion of this temple in the sea and therefore of the rise and fall of the Neapolitan coast, still in action in our day. 'It is a shameful thing to allow piece of the cols to be sold—but one bit *was* offered to me for sale which I couldn't resist buying & which makes the most intensely interesting specimen which a geological collection could possess.'

Exploring more ruins at Baiae and eating their packed lunch on the terrace of a 'miserable little hostelry'—where 'a pretty little French girl upon whom I instantly became spoony should not be omitted from the memories of the place'—they discussed how 'the proud bad city is sinking inch by inch into the waves . . . and the unstayable purpose of God is working out before our eyes—and yet men say that the wonderful things of old have stopped in our day! & the catastrophes of Nature which the earth commemorates too great to be the result of a scheme of forces like that which now prevails!' Whether the 'catastrophist' view of Nature prevailed or not, for them as for most romantic tourists ruins under the sea were the most romantic of all. Next day, feeling 'unwell with effect of Naples water, of which I must drink no more', Knowles 'spooned about, changing money . . . and trying at no end of shops for [an] india-rubber swimming-band [what was that?] and buying colored shirts', before embarking for Sicily with Herbert and a new friend Coles, while Hewlett returned northward. As the ship headed into the open sea past Capri, sickness was averted 'by dint of lying on a couch

[53] Travel journal: their luggage consisted of 'valises and carpet bags' (first night in Rome) and he 'read Lyell diligently' (on the way to Girgenti). Lyell's *Principles* in 9th edn. by 1853. Ruskin, *Seven Lamps* (1st edn. 1849), 'Lamp of Truth', section xv; and editorial introduction to Cook and Wedderburn eds., p. xxxix, on architects denouncing Ruskin as mad. But Donaldson also, discussing Knowles Sr.'s paper on cements at RIBA in 1850, had said that imitation jointing gave 'a false appearance' and *CEAJ* (Oct. 1850, p. 333) felt that the whole question of whether stucco was a sham could be left to 'this single issue' of the scored lines (chap. 2, n. 33 above): neither Knowles had waked up to that yet.

with corpse like rigidity & speaking little', and reading the odes of Horace. Perhaps the 'Exegi monumentum', 'I have made a monument', which he was to confess to Gladstone in 1894 was one of the few he remembered.[54]

Sicily, they thought at first at Palermo, was not at all 'the Sicily of dreams': 'The view from our windows is . . . much like an English watering-place—especially the rain—and we walked down a mile of street today . . . reminding me much of Manor Street, Clapham. Resemblance is much more prevalent than variety to my mind in all I have yet seen abroad compared with Home (dear Home!)', he thought. Before they left home, he must have spent many hours in modest, stuccoed Manor Street while his father's Dispensary was building there. The 'quiet gentlemanly air' of Palermo was a relief 'after that bad boisterous dirty Naples' (yet so far there had been 'no city to equal Genoa in general aspect of magnificent beauty', then a favourite model for architects of the City of London). Sunday service at the English consulate was held in 'a large room decorated with a painted ceiling representing the Apotheosis of some Caesar' and the hymns were accompanied on 'a harmonium played by a lady'; the sermon on faith and works 'made me think of what we are living for and doing—what?' On a rainy Sunday, after two months of sightseeing, melancholy was breaking in.

The fascinations of sightseeing were revived next day by 'the quaint rich style of Saraceno-Gothic' of churches, that of the Martorana 'being the first real edifice in that style which I have ever seen. I was proportionally delighted—for it has all that dreamy fantastic elegance and daring which makes Arab architecture more like an illusion than a fact'. That spring Knowles's father was making tentative use of Arab-derived ornament, out of books, and here was the real thing. 'The historical nature of Architecture is nowhere more beautifully exhibited' than in the 'mixed style', he told Hewlett later. 'Mixed styles' were one Victorian answer to the problem of what to do next. Sicilian baroque churches, on the other hand, were dismissed as 'Rococo upholstery style . . . covered with elaborate bad taste', one high altar being 'so decorated in ballet fashion . . . that we should hardly have been surprised to see 2 figurantes dance into position

[54] Presumably 'and reading Carmine' in 1854 meant Horace. Knowles to Gladstone, 13 Mar. 1894, Gladstone Papers, as chap. 7, n. 50.

from the side scenes'. The English watering-place feeling was quite routed by bursts of military band music in the cathedral square and by a drive through glorious views framed in the ochre of rocks and the green of orange and fig trees to Monreale. Of its 'queer & interesting & ugly old mosaics' the colossal Christ of the apse was 'greatly solemn and noble', while the paired colonnettes of the cloister 'would send Ruskin wild with joy by their full storied bad proportions—He would as usual forget the Art & rave about the intention.' The Saracenic elements were 'richly & delightfully good', the Byzantine elements were barbaric, 'transitional chaos'.

After exploring the horrifyingly corpse-packed catacombs of the Cappaccini convent ('Salvator or Fuseli would have studied them with joy'), they found an Arabian Nights paradise of a garden near by, full of semitropical fruits and flowers 'such as no English garden knows' and all 'in such a maze of brilliant sunlight shade & beauty, that . . . we walked about more like men in a dream than awake', these were '*the* gardens of the world', summoning up not only the Arabian Nights but the lustrous woodlands and heavy blossoms of Tennyson's garden descriptions. The ride back to their hotel was a very Brown-Jones-and-Robinson affair:

In Palermo it is forbidden to wear beards or wide awake hats—or to carry roses in public, and . . . there came an order from the Police commanding every man to cut off his Imperial—When therefore returning from the gardens in an open carriage we traversed—all innocently—the whole length of the Toledo (the Regent St of Palermo) loaded with roses, surmounted by wide awakes and exhibiting every possible variety of beard moustache and imperial—we created a 'genuine sensation'—Every body stopped to stare and wonder at us—and we left a wake of pity whitening behind us on the crowd of coward faces—One old priest moved to charity by our rashness repeated in an earnest voice 'beware beware' as we passed by.

The repression of revolutionary symbols in the wake of 1848 was mere light opera to him then. This account was worked up in retrospect for his lecture on Sicily; the travel journal simply recorded of that day: 'writing a diary is the most infernal of all possible bores.'

Palermo's principal production appeared to be 'infamously bad statues and crowds of curiously latticed balconies', with a little

sketch of those billowing upper balconies, 'the Mania of Palermo
. . . bristling along the perspective of a street'. At the hotel he
came across a fellow-observer of such things, a French architect
from Tours. M. Vestier being pleased to join them in an excursion
to 'the interior' it was agreed 'with the government for a rotten
old posting carriage the body of which stands about 6 ft above
the ground, which is to convey us . . . to Catania via Girgenti for
100 dollars paid "en avance"'. So off they went through 'one
vast confusion of hills tossed into every form & group by
volcanic force'; and at posting stops Knowles 'read Lyell diligently' and made sage comment on 'argillaceous tertiary schists'.
Groves of prickly pear and great aloes 'tell very powerfully of
more than 1000 miles from home', so too did wretched huts and
their wretched occupants: 'it is mournful, truly, to see the
degradation of the Maker's image in these places to a point below
brutality', though there were pretty girls to be sketched at posting
stops, where gaping crowds collected round the carriage to watch
the performance. The inns and beds at Caltanissetta and Agrigento
filled the visitors with horror: 'I verily believe that the vermin
are doing injury to my blood. . . . Oh how delightful it will be
one day to have again a clean bed in England!' They liked their
'gentlemanly quietly chatty French companion', who was 'one
of the old school of France— & I'm sure hates England at heart'.
And 'I never knew till I talked with him of what the French
language was capable.' This 'cheerful old gentlemanly bird' ('a
man of at least 50', Knowles thought) 'seemed to feel a sort of
Professional paternity' towards the chatty young architect from
Clapham.

The goal of their drive across Sicily was the ancient site at
Girgenti, for the ruins of Magna Graecia were necessary goals to
architects unable to afford travel as far as Greece itself. A day of
scrambling about the temples started in the branches of an
almond tree, to sketch the site, followed by botanizing and
'geologizing after our fashion' in a luxuriantly overgrown ravine
on the way to the Temple of Castor and Pollux. There Knowles
carefully noted that an original covering of 'thin hard and
glistening white stucco' bore no traces of colour, and that red
discolouring of the stone itself was the same as that of the natural
rock below. (Here, says the lecture-script, 'Exhibit specimens'.)
At the Temple of Jupiter he busily measured the huge scattered

remains: even the guttae, smallest elements of the Doric order but here each five inches across, will have made the Euston gateway seem tame. Sketching a prostrate giant atlas-figure 'as well as I could in the great heat— & nearly driven crazy by clouds of buzzing tormenting insects', he noted 'a lesson in the sublime possible application of the human figure in architecture'. (But the nearest he ever came to supporting architecture upon human figures was to be with Baron Grant's parvenu caryatids at Kensington.) Meanwhile, as a well-prepared visitor he imagined this 'mighty range of temples' as dazzling new buildings 'which saluted the arriving stranger with the aspect of grandeur & of religion', yet with overtones of Milton on the palace of Pandemonium rising 'like an exhalation'. Then back to 'some odious wine . . . [and] the hole we stay in . . . alive with vermin & we are nearly dead with irritation & suffering . . . very shocking that such disgusting drawbacks should accompany such splendid pleasures as today's'. Teasing 'the Harpy' who ran the hotel, they thought 'Dickens would make a fortune out of her'.

The departure of their old posting carriage from a town was 'a thing to see':

The horses are slowly brought out amid a chorus of 'lestos' & 'subitos' from ourselves & with the help of half a dozen stable men & boys . . . all the travelling being done with 3 horses abreast—and at the expense of an immense quantity of argument vociferation and abuse on all sides are at length harnessed—Meanwhile about 30 or 40 idle men & women have gathered round the carriage to watch & discuss the 'forestieri' & at least half a dozen beggars with every sort & kind of whine howl & deformity are besieging our ears & eyes . . . a substratum of filthy children completes the crowd & puts a climax to the noise—at last all is ready—the postillion from the last stage comes for his buono mano & . . . is profuse with blessings, thanks & bows—and after one more combined entreaty to the driver to mount—at last we start—And then oh heavens the yell that rises from all sides—the myriad-voiced driver swearing screeching & shouting—thrashing his horses & wildly waving & cracking his whip—one mighty groan from the beggars— an involuntary cheer from the small boys & the idlers—a last shout of thanks from the postillion—the slamming of the horses' feet upon the stones . . . accompany the heave forward & round of the carriage & the complicated jolt which announces the start. Then rush dash clatter bang fly away we go amidst a cataract of bristly pigs & barking dogs— and calves & goats— & children snatched by parents from the horses feet—We whirl out of town & gallop madly on—now catching some poor mule upon his rump & leaving him spinning round & round in the road—now frightening another into a gallop which overthrows his rider—on and forward at a swaying pace.

The pace, in piled-up description, of a reader of Dickens. As a modern young man addressing his lecture-audience in Clapham, Knowles added sedately that 'the travelling in Sicily is quite what one reads of in books but which rail-roads are rapidly banishing from Europe'.

Then came 'one of the adventures of my life', the climbing of Mt. Etna. He had watched it looming up as they crossed the centre of the island: 'All the scenery of Sicily is a preparation and a vestibule for Etna. . . . There is always in the aspect of great majesty a simplicity which strikes deeper than any multiplication of elements—It is so in Architecture & all the Arts. . . . It is so in real life of men when in a royal procession after the heralds the trumpets the blaze and the glory the Sovereign's self appears, grand in unexpected plainness' (a clear-eyed Londoner's view of the Queen).[55] With guides and mules, Knowles, Coles, Herbert, and a Dutchman set off to the sound of a medley in which each joined with the 'noise that suited him best': 'one member of the troupe shrieking like a scalped Indian, gobbling like a turkey, & imitating a railway whistle with his hands—to which variable accompaniment one of the guides & myself sang airs from Norma . . . and another droned a dead-alive endless moaning of a mule-teer's song'.[56] Coming to the snow, they left the mules and set forth wearing 'thick worsted gaiters' and feeling violent sensations of altitude, as the 'glistening white desert' behind them fell away 'into a gulf of mist and darkness' while 'the starry heavens rose in a majesty of brilliance and a luxuriance of light . . . such as one never sees on lower ground', and the planet Jupiter 'hung like a burning lamp from the dark sky'. Through his exhaustion Knowles noticed the geological composition of the cone as he

---

[55] Possibly his first view of Queen Victoria was on the particularly grand City occasion in October 1844 when she went to open the new Royal Exchange.

[56] Bellini's *Norma*: since 1847 Italian opera could be heard in London at what was then called the Royal Italian Opera House, Covent Garden (refs. cited S of L XXXV 80). Scalped Indians will have been familiar from the Leatherstocking Tales of James Fenimore Cooper (d. 1851), said to be the first American novelist famed abroad (Benet).

struggled behind the others until, greatly cheered by seeing
'poor Coles . . . striving up and down over a little bit of smooth
mud like the spider in Bruce's prison. . . . I fairly lay along my
own slipping couch of ashes & ice and laughed till I found myself
tumbling.' 'Steeper than the roof of Westminster Abbey', it was.
At the crater, 'I looked over its lip into the great mouth of the
volcano—fatigue departed completely—at the arrival of so much
horror and surprise—and despite the clouds of filthy sulphur
smoke which drove suffocatingly over us I made a hasty outline
of the scene, for the guide would let me do no more. . . . A yellow
narrow ledge of yielding sulphur was the walk along this horrible
hole.' In a partly sheltered place they awaited the rising of the sun:
'Below us stretched away like a darkly coloured map the island
of Sicily . . . the sea . . . looked like some variegated dark stone
which has been polished . . . and no more like water than those
masses in the moon which astronomers tell us have no waters
tho' they call them seas . . . at length above Calabria this golden
shield was lifted by the God of day.' Half-suffocated by fumes,
like being on 'top of the Pottery chimney by Vauxhall Bridge',
they gathered souvenir bits of lava and gazed terrified 'into the
hell of vapors' before starting back in a freezing gale of snow.
Cherished notions of 'standing on the Summit of Etna & commanding on the one hand Scylla & Charybdis, on the other etc.
etc.' were very different from 'the choking shivering truth'.
('Sometimes I thought I could see the coast of Apulia . . . but by
reason of the terrific cold, I was unable to bring sufficient attention
to bear on the task'—thus Richard Payne Knight, watching the
sun rise from Mt. Etna on 27 May 1777.) On 27 May 1854, 'I
tried to sing God Save the Queen, but my voice "haesit in
faucis" '.[57]

The long way back afforded several pages of natural history in
comfortable retrospect. The descent, he told Hewlett, was 'an
epitome of the earth'; the snow having turned to rain, 'under an
umbrella I rode . . . on the back of my mule down the steep
ravines learning with interest the natural lessons which the
mountain teaches. . . . Several different sorts of singing birds too
we heard among the groves—and the dear old Cuckoo which

[57] Knowles to Hewlett, 13 June 1854, from Florence (WPL), Hewlett having
already returned home. Excerpts from Payne Knight's Sicilian diary are printed
as appendix to Pevsner's article on him, *Art Bulletin*, Dec. 1949.

sang as Coles said "in plain English"—tho' a German artist to whom he told it said *he* thought in "plain German".'

The drive along the coast road to Messina, where they were to embark for Naples, revealed 'delicious headlands buried in trees & flowers & crowned with ruins' jutting out 'into the limpid sea', while in the distance 'Calabria rises veiled in that purple bloom which spreads itself so generally over distances in the South'. (Or, as Payne Knight had put it, 'that same pearly tone which imparts such distinction to the paintings of Claude Lorraine and is quite peculiar to this delectable climate'.[58]) At Messina there was only time to detest the hotel and hastily to admire the cathedral's 'Gothic flat enrichments to doorways'—that is, Trecento coiling grape-vines in flat relief, seen with the new Victorian eye for foliage. At the pier there was 'no end of pass-port business with hot and angry officials . . . in the dreadfully sultry air it was hard work.' Yet 'the aspect of Sicily as we retired from it shows Messina is the most exquisitely placed town . . . backed & sheltered by a chain of the wildest and grandest hills which rise in a noble succession of buttresses to Etna. . . . With a sublime regularity and yet with the wildest diversity.' Sublime regularity coupled with wildest diversity: that, apparently, was 'what my theory of Art, costing me some meditation of late', required; or, in retrospect, the Victorian fusion of the Sublime with the Picturesque.

Other reflections struck them during the slow voyage from Messina to Naples in 'that rocking old tub the Polyfemo', calling at various Calabrian ports. Disembarking briefly at Reggio for a stroll, they entered a church where the corpse of a young girl rested in an open coffin: 'How terribly *real* it was this presence of Death by the side of all our travelling turmoils and anxieties—and how fearfully in earnest the set close features looked. . . . But Wisdom higher than man's has known and provided for all this'—and he quoted *In Memoriam* to himself, that one must remember the dead as the living, else the Earth would be all a grave, 'and dust and ashes all that is'. 'A dead girl—and a living noble palm tree—the highest we have seen abroad—these were the strangely coupled sights which Reggio offered—whose juxtaposition in memory is happy. Who will not remember the vision of the dead

---

[58] Payne Knight in Apr. 1777, p. 311 (as n. 57 above).

that carried Palms in their hands & sang the song of the Lamb?'
He was to need this faith nine years later.

The voyage was beguiled by 'a most agreeable and lady-like
widow' and her unmarried daughter, whom they had met at
Catania; the widow had a Russian son-in-law and spoke 'as
highly of the Emperor as the lady whom we met at Lyons did'.
(The Crimean War, then two months old, enters into the journal
hardly at all; such passing references to the enemy were the
nearest he came to mentioning what faced other Englishmen on
troopships heading eastward through the Mediterranean just
then.) This lady also communicated 'facts of high life in Palermo
more than disgraceful and the same as one hears of everywhere
on the Continent'. One can hear Clapham clucking. To the
daughter Knowles gave lessons in astronomy on deck until one
in the morning, ' & chaffing about the inferior moral standards of
girls—who conduct their life by the rule of 3 whilst men live by
the rules of honor & enthusiasm'. There was also much argument
on board—'all the classical knowledge in the boat was at issue'—
as to which was Scylla and which Charybdis.

At the Hotel de Russie in Naples on the first of June, summer
heat after the rigours of Sicily and the thought of rigours to come
seemed overpowering:[59]

I heartily wish I was somewhere in the cool—that that abominable
Paestum trip was done—Paestum is the devil's own hole for malaria . . .
a man here has had 15 days' fever dreadfully bad from a visit—Besides
all which the vipers there are affreux—Oh Lord I wish it was done—it
is so beastly hot—that everything's a bore—and I long to be North again
—in Munich or somewhere up there [except] if that ass the King of
Prussia has turned out to the Czar as they say here which will keep me
from his dominions of course.

At the theatre he was unimpressed by the Neapolitan 'sort of
stupid Pantaloon . . . a very different notion to our brave rascally
English Punch'. Naples was 'unpleasant and disgusting', the
diarist had a 'dreadful cold'. Yet the pages for the Paestum tour
are headed *dies memorabilis mihi eheu!*

Still worrying about malaria, Coles and Knowles carried 'mild

---

[59] In Italy in 1854 tourists entered four separate dominions, of Piedmont
(Cavour's republic), Rome (the French), Naples and Sicily (King of the Two
Sicilies), and Venice (Austria). In April the King of Prussia had formed an alliance
with Austria against Russia, whatever rumour said.

Cigars' which they were 'obliged ultimately to present to the Coachman, their odour & taste being affreux', and camphor for protection 'against the fearful foe whom we knew to be awaiting us in every hedge & ditch & breath of air'. Herds of 'little black savage buffaloes' bathing in dirty pools were 'quite a wild "down western" sight'. Once arrived at the ruins, there was matter for five pages of attentive rapture, first on the Great Temple of Neptune:

There is about the conception of a Greek Doric temple a marvellous harmony of form & expression—which invests the Stones with a Poetry greater far than any that can speak from the complicated Stones of Venice . . . the architecture of Greece stands a wonderful monument to the mode in which the mind can minister to the Spirit in the priesthood of Nature . . . [but] when a Ruskin comes it is necessary to have ladders & scaffolds & climbing & running about like a lizard up top all the walls & among the roof timbers & behind the statues to ferret & find out if something hasn't been left somewhere which might state emphatically what the total conception was unable to do. . . . When Architecture itself [should be] equal to conveying without a borrowed aid from other art-language . . . what it wants to tell.

The rudeness to Ruskin at Pozzuoli, Monreale, and Paestum suggests that one new architect had bogged down in the first volume of the *Stones*, so long on pedagogy, so short on poetry. At the so-called basilica he sketched the 'profile of the anta cap . . . quite Gothic with a roll and hollow', and at the Temple of Ceres found 'the little row of necking leaves under the Echinus of the caps very pretty'—both examples of the peculiar Paestum capitals that were bound to take a Victorian eye. There is not one word about the heat, it was all too interesting, Such buildings witnessed to the means whereby Beauty might teach 'the universal truths of natural religion'.

The last journal-entry leaves them driving off in the evening light for Amalfi. For the rest of that excursion there is Knowles's description of it to Hewlett as 'the most Italian thing I've done at all': 'joining ourselves in the Tarantella' at Capri, and doing Pompeii, and running up Vesuvius 'like a couple of cats, laughing at the profferred help of ropes & chairs, the thing being a mere joke after Etna'. We find him next in Florence, writing to Hewlett from the Hotel d'York that already he was 'enchanted with the dear grand old Town—which I expect to "spoon" for some time'. While 'your absence has been & will remain a considerable diminution of my pleasure in travelling—Herbert and I got on together better than I thought we should, but . . . he wouldn't do at all for a lunatic [club member], he can't differ without difference of temper', a tendency that 'already needs repressing rather than encouraging in my own case'.[60] Knowles was to have similar difficulty late in life with contentious contributors such as Canon MacColl. After an excursion to the Baths of Lucca 'amongst Derbyshire scenery by day—and a fiery firmament of fire flies by night. . . . I completed my Florentine pleasures by making the acquaintance of Mrs Somerville and Mr & Mrs Browning.' Mrs. Somerville, 'the most exquisite old lady, quite up to and even beyond my ideal of herself', was then well known as a writer on science. The Brownings—to whom he may have been introduced by friends in South London or on the way—delighted him 'with both themselves & their beautiful little boy', and pressed him to come often. Fourteen years later, Browning was to become one of Knowles's lions at The Hollies, Clapham Common. Meanwhile, 'after luxuriating in Florence . . . I left the most fascinating spot in Italy for Bologna . . . [by way of] the Appennines via Pistoia—very glorious the descent on the N side is it not and quite a lecture on the upheaval of rocks.'[61] By mid-July he was in Milan on his own, with the Lakes and Venice still to come, and planning to be 'once more in dear old Clapham Park by about the end of August'. A hotel bill survives from a short sortie over the St. Gotthard Pass: total four francs for three meals and *logement* at 'La Croix blanche et du bateau a vapeur', an inn at the little port of Fluëlen on Lake Lucerne.[62] Toward the end of July, apparently, he arrived in Venice.

No word survived the time in Venice, except the denouement reflected in an anniversary letter to Hewlett in August 1855 that begins: 'I indeed thank God—that I am sitting here writing to

[60] Knowles to Hewlett, as n. 57.

[61] Knowles to Hewlett, 15 July 1854, from Milan (WPL), also mentions meeting on the road Mrs. Somerville's son Woronzow Greig, 'Clerk of Peace for Surrey', and his wife, 'who know a great deal about pictures & buy them too', and he spent a day at Parma sightseeing with them. It was for Mrs. Somerville (d. 1872) that the Oxford college was named.

[62] Knowles scribbled on the bill (with journals, WPL): '. . . a curiosity for cheapness . . . no charge for wax lights'.

you today—A year ago—and now: of these elements memory makes a striking picture—Then—half conscious that messages were brought to me from time to time, which I scarcely comprehended . . . only knowing that they gave me the hope of once again seeing home-faces'; and ends: 'the 23rd (today) had been decided—after careful revision of dates, to be the day of the month on which, last year, you left England to come to me in Venice'.[63] Whatever the fever that struck him down—brought on by vermin or the stenches of Venice—it could not be taken lightly in August 1854, when cholera was sweeping across Europe. His family's state of mind at the news, probably from the British consul, can be imagined as one leafs through the *Illustrated London News* for those weeks: cholera in London by the first week in August, panic in the south of France late in August, a reported exodus from Rome, and thousands reported dead at Messina.

But he survived, and these letters and journals survived, minor documents of what it was like to be young at home and abroad in the 1850s. If they say little of what it was like to be an articled pupil in an architect's office (they might have said far more if the head of the office had been no relation), they do forcibly convey the difference between that pupilage—driving daily from Friday Grove to Gray's Inn—and his father's apprenticeship in the old Bell Street workshop beside the stream. His father's Grand Tour had been over the hill to London.

SEARCHING FOR A MOTIVE

> 'Rich foliage, which occupies a part of the opening . . . forms a good example of the only manner in which an effect similar to Gothic tracery could be introduced in the windows of buildings in the Roman style . . . to lead to the formation of an original style, fitted to . . . our present high state of civilisation.' Henry Noel Humphreys in the *Architectural Magazine*, January 1839

> 'The Anglo-Classic style . . . awaits but an infusion into our architects of . . . the fire and the energy

[63] Knowles to Hewlett, 23 Aug. 1855 (WPL). Austrian political rumblings probably contributed to the family alarm. On cholera, *ILN*, July–Sept. 1854.

that animated the Gothic builders . . . to make it vie with that style in life, and . . . the profoundest sympathy with the beauty and fulness of the material creation.' Samuel Huggins in the *Builder*, 10 September 1853

'I believe the fact is that I want some great direct incentive.' Knowles to Hewlett, 23 August 1855

Through young Knowles's next five years ran an intermittent search for some personal reason for being. Also, like others in his profession, for a motive (in another sense) that would fuse the old styles into a new English architecture. For him these processes, personal and professional, crystallized out only in 1860. His generation, coming of age with Paxton's glass Palace, expressed voluminously, if not always very well, the searchings and questionings of many adult Englishmen, neither too poor nor too rich, in the latter 1850s—even if some of the largest themes of the day (Darwin, Drainage) are missing from the random private writings that, in this case, remain.

Hewlett and a servant having fetched the patient home from Venice, the autumn of 1854 will have been spent in anxiously tended convalescence. By the New Year, Knowles was staging 'some farces' at home for the entertainment of neighbours including the Barry family, and earnestly reading Gibbon and Carlyle while polishing his French with the *Revue des deux mondes*.[64] He and Hewlett were reading 'Strachy's book', possibly Sir Edward Strachey's *Miracles and Science* (1854), one of many works by would-be reconcilers of the mid-century. And Knowles spent some time at 'old Ward's', probably chatting on the new indoor climates for people in glass houses, conjectured upon in Rome. During 1855 'the Governor' had large works proceeding in Kensington Palace Gardens and Chancery Lane, also probably in Kent, all past the working-drawings stage but requiring site supervision; and impending designs for some dignified speculative house-building next door to Friday Grove were probably on his drawing-board. A separate practice for the new ARIBA could not be created immediately.

The summer of 1855 was a time of germinating thoughts and dissatisfactions. He wrote from Raymond Buildings on 23

---

[64] Knowles to Hewlett, 9, 14 Feb. 1855 (WPL), and Barry diary (RIBA MSS.).

August—anniversary of Hewlett's departure to rescue him in Venice—gratefully painting, as we have seen, 'a striking picture' of the situation. 'And now—when God has given me a twelve-month's more of home blessing and kindness . . . being grateful for all his goodness of God has grown into a kind of everyday habit. . . . I only hope if another year is given me—I may multiply the talent better than I have done this last one—which was given to me, as it were, out of the grave'—a foretaste of his thankful epitaph in 1908. The letter to Hewlett, away on holiday, continued:[65]

> You ask after my goings-on—They are but slight. . . . I perceive in myself a general disgust at my powers as compared with my ambitions —By this you guess that the design does not 'march' better than it should do—that the review hangs heavy on hands and that the essay is in abeyance—Old boy, I believe the fact is that I want some great direct incentive—some visible fruit to be gathered or at least reached after. . . .
>
> Only consider how much I have speculated & theorized and attempted and hoped—and then consider the results—what they are— 2 or 3 bundles of paper written over & forgotten by all but their author—8 or 9 bundles of drawings—d⁰—one or two leaves and a portrait case d⁰! . . .
>
> I believe old fellow that this . . . worse than distrust of my own nature power or use—must be as I say—the sign that manhood coming on— demands from the fruit of its labors . . . tangible facts—not words and dreams—which are but wind & ghosts—Translated into plain language this means, I want some real practice to do in my profession—*and*— *or*—some girl to be in love with—
>
> I begin to despise myself so heartily, for being nearly 25 years of age —and doing nothing but talk—talk—talk—However all this rave will be rather boring to you—and was quite unintended to be expressed 5 minutes ago—Allons donc out of this subjective region of complaint & groaning—
>
> The Govr has I am glad to say found some shooting whi promises to be very good—It is at Fleet Pond—near Aldershott—Some 700 acres with great lake and old farm house, where for the rest of the Autumn one or another of us in turn will I expect be rusticating.

He was not quite 24, but 'nearly 25' seems rather to echo 'Ah, what shall I be at fifty/Should Nature keep me alive,/ If I find the world so bitter/When I am but twenty-five. . . . And ah for a man to arise in me,/ That the man I am may cease to be!' Tennyson's *Maud*, most unsettling, had just come out in July.[66] Knowles's forefathers were all married and starting families at or about his age—his father and *his* father for seven generations back. Before them, the James Knowles born in 1600 had to wait until he was 29, probably for lack of means to set up for himself, but after him came those seven cycles of fixed social habit. Their Victorian descendant had to wait till he too was 29 and for the same reason: the horizon of means required to set up a household and a livelihood had drawn farther off. To put it another way, the elder James Thomas had levered up the threshold of expectations for his sons. Meanwhile, for his first son, to have some second career dimly in view—'in my professions' is written clearly in the plural—supplied something an architectural career lacked, for him, while increasing his uncertainty.

Fragmentary notes of July or August, probably for the essay 'in abeyance' (the 'design' and 'review' are unexplained), may partly reflect another publication in July 1855, the second edition of Ruskin s *Seven Lamps of Architecture* with its new preface. Among Knowles's papers, pencilled on a scrap of notepaper with the beginning of a letter dated in that month and year, a scribbled fragment of what Loudon would have called 'architectural metaphysics' is headed 'Phil of Arch':[67]

Tastes of the English—love of flowers & domestic life—Something in arch[itecture] which introduces these feelings—buildings with a sympathy & a life in them. This reason preference of Gothic with its crisp vigorous leaves crockets heads etc over the more abstract sympathyless features of Classic such as balustrades dentils etc.
  In an arch[itecture] for our own day we may take dignity—repose — & calmness, sufficient power, catholicity etc from the Classic—but over this a sweet & wooing growth of life must run—the flowers must love & clasp it— & sympathies & affections must cling round it for enrichments—at the least symbols & not abstract forms—'Pure classic' is not companionable nor *alive* enough—for the English people. A [middle way] must be sought between it & the exclusive bigotry of Gothic—from the one we shall take that symbolism of sympathy &

[66] *Maud* I: VI, v; X. vi.
[67] Pencilled on notepaper with unfinished letter on verso dated Thursday, 5 July (i.e. 1855), inserted in lecture script (WPL).

affection with which to a Xion & domestic nation life is barren—that more near employment of Nature as we know & love her—from the other that calm wise great serenity which speaks of the abstract powers of mind as the first of the concrete.

Upon a basis of forms sympathetic with cosmopolitanism & catholicity we must train a growth of objects (as enrichment) dear to the affection & life. In this way we may extract from all preceding archtrs an excellence fitted for ourselves whilst a pure science of symbolic forms guides us to our selections & discoveries.

A classic bldg to an Englishman will be *cold*—as a Gothic bldg to a cosmopolite is narrow—let us throw away the coldness from the one (by covering it with absolute meanings & sympathies for enrichments) & the narrowness from the other.

In other words, some new equilibrium between the perpetual classic–romantic poles of art was a congenial concept for Donaldson's pupil. Knowles's solution was not Ruskinian, but the synthesizing of the Humphreys–Huggins school quoted at the head of this section: here young Knowles was his father's own son. But Ruskin's poetical language, like Tennyson's, 'set many dreamy people dreaming like himself'. Though the *Stones* fell on barren ground at first, the returned traveller now had time to meditate on all he had seen, and to prick up his ears at the stirring of Ruskin's words among the rising young generation of the 1850s. The inborn feeling for the English countryside that inspired untold numbers of watercolourists and amateur geologists was stimulated in sensitive young architects by Ruskin's call for buildings carved with sculpture displaying 'the beauty of every flower and herb of the English fields . . . doing as much for every tree that roots itself in our rocks . . . as our ancestors did for the oak, the ivy, and the rose': Knowles's musings may well have followed a reading of the lines in the 1855 preface to the *Seven Lamps* that echoed the final paragraph of the *Stones of Venice*. He had seen clasping leaves carved on the portals of Messina Cathedral and painted on the loggias of the Vatican; and the views of 'cosmopolites' will have echoed the opinions of M. Vestier, aired on those long drives across Sicily. In 1856 Tennyson himself was carving ivy leaves to decorate cottages on the Farringford estate, and incorporating in 'Enid' some earlier lines in which 'monstrous ivy-stems/Claspt the grey walls with hairy-fibred arms'. And three years later the first *Idylls of the King* were to come out at a time of much debate about the place of the natural world in art.[68] Another scribbled fragment remains on the back of a Broadstairs hotel bill (under £3.0.0 for a week's stay with meals at the Albion in July 1855). Here he sketched a theory that 'the genius and character of a people' invariably expresses itself in that people's arts, that there is a connection 'between an age in its social & political or religious aspects & the fine arts of that age', a theory he proposed to pursue in regard to architecture: 'If then I can find in the histys of other nations a correlation between their characters & arts which my Science of form will meet—then I have but to know the character of my own age & fearlessly apply my science.' This verged on the theories of hereditary and environmental influences subsequently expressed by Taine, here more likely a fusion of Donaldson's art-and-science teachings with a Picturesque, associative sense of the special genius of places and peoples, the sense of an evolving world derived from geology, and the words of young Ruskin (masked as Kata Phusin) considering 'the Architecture of the Nations of Europe . . . in its Association with natural Scenery and national Character' in old copies of the *Architectural Magazine*.[69] When Knowles eventually edited his own review, 'then I have but to know the character of my own age & fearlessly apply my science' could well have been his motto. Meanwhile, little came of these meditations, surviving as scraps among the pages of the lecture-script he was composing at the time, until some of them took shape at the Grosvenor Hotel. A more finished piece of rhetoric, filled with 'the spirit of his

[68] The line on 'the oak, the ivy, and the rose' occurs both in the final paragraph of *The Stones* (1853) and in the 1855 preface to *The Lamps*; we refer to it again in chap. 4. Ruskin's influence: Kerr in 1891 edn. of Fergusson (as n. 5 above), chap. vi, also Kerr, 'Ruskin and Emotional Architecture', *RIBAJ*. 10 Mar. 1900; and C. L. Eastlake, *History of the Gothic Revival* (1872), p. 278, on Ruskin's attraction for young architects. Tennyson's woodcarving: Usher Art Gallery, Lincoln, catalogue (1963), no. 320, running-vine relief 1856 for casting in plaster to mould brick (cf. cat. no. 159, correspondence 1855 with Ruskin on Farringford clay); the lines quoted, inspired by Tintern Abbey, were first intended for 'The Princess' (Ricks, pp. 1525, 1535).

[69] This associative sense was not Victorian in origin but dates from the early days of romantic neoclassicism (e.g. Joseph Warton's essay on Pope, 1756, on Theocritus: 'We can never . . . understand any author . . . except we constantly keep in our eye his climate, his country, and his age'). Knowles's theories, pencilled on back of bill dated 28 July 1855, Albion Hotel, Broadstairs (apartments 2/6 per night, dinner 3/6, repairing trousers 6d, total £2. 18s. 8d. for the week), with lecture script WPL.

age', was the article accepted by the *Builder* in August to embellish the announcement and engraved view of his father's neo-Florentine palazzo of offices and chambers for Hodgson the book-auctioneer.[70] Unusual though it was for a member of an architect's family to be allowed to puff his work, the editor's excuse will have been that the article had almost nothing specifically to do with the building in question. This was, rather, a fanfare for Mid-Victorian commercial architecture in general:

Fleet Street and the Strand, transformed into a succession of such edifices might become a worthy Corso for the trading Rome, and make a grand connecting artery between the region of docks and warehouses at one end, of mansions and palaces at the other. . . .

. . . and for learning the character of our own day, where shall we find a better school than the streets and shops? We *are* a commercial people, a common-sense trading race, a nation of shopkeepers. But are these epithets then, so damnatory? . . . [we] can find . . . brotherhood with the great republics of mediaeval Italy. . . . It is not by forgetting but remembering our commercial real street life, that we shall become a people great in wisdom as in wealth. . . . From counting-houses, offices, warehouses, and chambers, come the schemes for baths and washhouses, and model dwellings, ragged schools, and reformatory asylums. . . . Let us . . . perceive that it is in these very streets that the way is opened for us to commence our stone daguerreotypes of the 19th century.

We architects are the limners of the future. To us is, perhaps, entrusted the verdict which remotest time will form . . . architecture, that substitute for nature, is nourished by Time, as the fossil history of mankind; and as the shells which the nautilus and ammonite of the primaeval world have formed become to us the sure records and interpreters of their far-departed times, so these shells, under which humanity has dwelt . . . will become, may be, to future races, the . . . fossil records when the 'epoch of man' shall be clearly read.

For us, then, who have to mould these latest 'medals of creation', there is the responsibility that we rightly represent our race, our age.

Architects had been admonished to pay more attention to 'street architecture' ever since Loudon in 1834 had founded his *Architectural Magazine* partly to tell them they had better, 'since it is

---

[70] *Bldr*, 18 Aug. 1855, p. 389. On 'street architecture', J. C. Loudon, *Architectural Magazine*, Apr. 1834, p. 90; also Scott's *Remarks on Secular and Domestic Architecture* (published 1858 but parts given as lectures 1855), and trenchant comment *passim* in *CBA*.

likely soon to constitute a principal part of their employment'; the professional journals and annuals of the 1850s constantly referred to street architecture; Gilbert Scott was lecturing on the subject in 1855, partly to justify his Sanctuary Buildings beside the Abbey; and City money was now the senior Knowles's chief source of income. Young Knowles as usual picked timely figures of speech, modernizing his father's 'eternal stereotypes' remark of 1850 into 'stone daguerreotypes', and refurbishing his own 'fossil nations' metaphor from the defunct *Clapham Magazine*. Geology did give, as no other science then could, a sense of time to a young man knowing little world-history outside architecture and the classics and only just becoming aware of Gibbon and Carlyle (although no resident of Clapham can have been unaware of Macaulay). And, over this article lay the brooding shadow of Ruskin's concluding sentence to *The Stones of Venice*, '. . . the London of the nineteenth century may yet become as Venice without her despotism, and as Florence without her dispeace'. Behind Knowles's *pastiche* lay some brave idealism that appealed to readers of architectural journals in 1855, and that survived in many architects of his generation until the late 1860s and foundered among uncomfortable realities thereafter.

While preparing his lecture on the Sicilian tour, Knowles thought over the vexed question of colour in classical architecture and sculpture. How well he knew more learned pronouncements is doubtful, but just as he had tried out his comet theory on a bookseller friend and the question-column of the *Athenaeum*, he treated this matter as of general rather than specialist interest. Constantly in the nineteenth century there was this attitude of anyone-can-play, this inheritance of Brougham's March of Mind and the spirit of self-help combining with the more aristocratic Renaissance ideal of universal man: for example in 1880, the artist Henry Holiday investigating the Afghan situation while Mr. Gladstone investigated the genuineness of Italian ivories (although of each of those individuals it could be said, he would). This Anglo-Saxon attitude was to be a source of strength to Knowles as an editor—and yet, eventually, he helped to kill it by providing a platform for specialists, from which practitioners of 'Victorian studies' now feel their way earnestly back. Knowles's thoughts on colour reflected the worries and catch-phrases of 1855: 'When Art is imitative it is mechanical and base—The Spirit of Man is more than a photographic apparatus!'—and ended with impatient Clapham common sense: 'If then the Greeks did color their temples and the statues of the immortal Gods—the only conclusion is they ought to have been ashamed of themselves—and we who inherit 2 thousand years of additional wisdom—will not obey a mistaken example—Example is the bane of Art—its ruin in our day—It is necessary as Bernini said to transgress the rules.' Latitudinarians of the world unite, even with Bernini, a rare preceptor for a Victorian.[71]

One letter remains from the summer of 1856, replying to Hewlett's description of hearing Handel's *Creation* sung in Gloucester Cathedral, that his own experience of that work must have been superior, though only in Exeter Hall, because it had included Jenny Lind: 'There is a point attainable as I think in my art— & clearly so in music—where the surroundings are of no importance—all the senses being flooded by the intensity of the tide that pours thro' anyone.' In 'my art', did he mean that the old picturesque feeling for setting was gone, or that it was still possible to produce what his father called 'emanations of deep thought' in the dull office at Gray's Inn? He was reading Scott's life of Napoleon, and had the wit to see that 'the author's partialities are so evident that they don't get much in the way— & the book is sufficiently extensive to throw some light upon my ignorance of contemporary history'—Napoleon I, in the 1850s, being still 'contemporary history'. The Surrey shooting holiday was about to be repeated (the Kent coast resorts, perhaps, were by then somewhat low-caste for professional men): 'We propose all going down posting in open carriage across the country to Chiddingfold on Thursday next—the Govr has taken an empty house & had it furnished from Guilford.' A sequel was that Isabella the eldest sister married a young gentleman-farmer of the Chiddingfold neighbourhood two years later. Meanwhile, it appears that Knowles and his father were competing jointly in an important competition:

[71] Notes at end of lecture script for Clapham Literary and Scientific Institution, Jan. 1856 (n. 37 above). Vexed question of Greek colour, n. 50 above. On both Gladstone and Holiday, the latter's *Reminiscences* (1914), pp. 269–70. On Knowles's lecture, *CG*, Feb. 1856, p. 44: 'It was delivered hardly as a lecture, but in the far more agreeable form of a reading, Mr Knowles taking his seat and becoming as it were one of a large party of friends.'

This evening I have to go down with the Govr to Liverpool—The Committee of our affair down there has adopted a clever course. They invite the competing architects themselves to come and decide (paying the railway fares for them). It is to be managed by each man giving in a report of what *3 designs he considers next best to his own*—neat idea isn't it of getting over the responsibility & putting it on the shoulders of ourselves? However there's nothing for it but to go—and . . . get a peep at L'pool for nothing.

This was the notorious competition for the Brown Library, an issue much debated in the columns of the *Builder* during 1856. The winning design was to be modified by the Borough Surveyor; ambitious architects were well out of it.[72]

Early in 1857 Ruskin, with his usual incandescent vagueness, electrified the young men of the Architectural Association with an address on imagination in architecture. He asked them where they thought their search for a new style would lead them: 'you shall wreathe your streets with ductile leafage, and roof them with variegated crystal—you shall put, if you will, all London under one blazing dome of many colours that shall light the clouds round it with its flashing'—but 'what after this? . . . if you cannot rest content with Palladio, neither will you with Paxton'. What good was all this style-changing? 'Whatever is easy you call architecture'—how superior its practitioners must have felt at that—and 'whatever is difficult you call sculpture': in separating 'building' from 'sculpture' they had 'taken away the power of both'. And so on until, most powerfully, 'Do but build large enough, and carve boldly enough, and all the world will hear you; they cannot choose but look.' This was a trumpet-call for many, ready for a more aggressive scale than that of Barry's generation—however bored by Ruskin's final demand that they love one another. 'All this style-changing' exercised architects

[72] Knowles to Hewlett, 15 Sept. 1856 (WPL). 'Scott's life of Napoleon 9 v. 1827' was one lot in the 1886 book sale (chap. 1, n. 10). Isabella Knowles married James J. Russell Stilwell of Killinghurst, Surrey, at Streatham church in April 1858; according to the 1861 census her father-in-law was a 'landed proprietor' and her husband farmed 175 acres; Killinghurst House is a large Georgian brick house near Chiddingfold where a photograph *c.* 1860 in family possession shows the family ranged like a frieze across the lawn, with monkey puzzle; on the Stilwells as local link with Tennyson, chap. 6, n. 3 below; a century later, a collateral descendant's immediate reaction to mention of Isabella, 'oh yes she married beneath her', was just London superiority. On Brown Library competition, *Bldr* 1856, pp. 521, 536, 553, 568, 582, 690.

very much in this year of the Government Offices competition.[73] The only letter surviving from 1857, in September, is entirely concerned with brotherly advice to Hewlett on the strategy and tactics of courting James's youngest sister.[74] Of himself he only said he was 'continually interrupted and in much haste': possibly this was the time of his father's professional visit to Portugal. And no letter remains from 1858, when the first floor of No. 1 Raymond Buildings was certainly busy. There was the International Hotel scheme publicized in the spring, for it seems to have matured as far as the drawings required for contractors' estimate. At some time in 1858, supposedly after the journey to Portugal with Francis Cook, Knowles senior produced a preliminary pair of designs in considerable ornamental detail for the rebuilding of the ruined Villa Monserrate at Cintra. In July a railway terminus with proposed hotel (architect unknown) was authorized for the Grosvenor Basin site, and then separate plans arose for a rival hotel alongside the station and the Knowleses' long series of drawings for that will have got under way. During 1859, young Knowles probably contributed a good deal of the imagination, the striking scale, and the industry there.

He continued to try his hand at competitions, submitting two designs for the Manchester Assize Courts in 1859, one Gothic and one irritably described by *Building News* in April as a combination of Newgate Prison and St. George's Hall, Liverpool, with towers: in plan 'very satisfactory', but with that 'our approval ceases', though the tinting of the drawing was commended. (On which young James hastily wrote in, perhaps with a faint tinge of notice-hunting or only in excess of conscience, to say that Mr. Rowe Clark of Great James Street should have credit for the tinting.) The *Builder*, mistaking the author of this design for his father, thought it 'incomprehensible as a design from his hand, so bald and ugly is it in what is hardly to be called the *decorative* part , but grudgingly finding in the 'internal arrangement . . . features deserving of notice'.[75] This sounds like an attempt at a bold scale

---

[73] Ruskin's lecture of 23 Jan. 1857 in Lyons Inn hall was published in *The Two Paths* (Cook and Wedderburn eds., XVI, 346); Summerson, *Architectural Association* (1947), p. 12.

[74] Knowles to Hewlett, 4 Sept. 1857 (WPL). There is also one note for 1859, just after their return from, apparently, the Continent in October.

[75] *BN*, 29 Apr., 6 May 1859, pp. 394, 434; *Bldr*, 7 May 1859, p. 308. Knowles's early drawings (e.g. for Thatched House Club) used the Early Victorian delicate

not practised by his father since those (how different) great Greek houses of the 1830s. A neat touch on an assize-courts design was the pseudonym under which, according to the journals, it was originally submitted: 'For he beareth not the sword in vain', from St. Paul's chapter on magistrates, Romans 13:4. Arthurian though it also sounds, it was not a line from Tennyson. The Laureate later gave the phrase a despairing turn—'And have but stricken with the sword in vain'—a line added to 'The Passing of Arthur' about 1872 (when Knowles was closest to the continuing composition of the *Idylls*—though Tennyson was too steeped in biblical phrasing to need a suggestion of this sort).[76]

In March 1859 the Clapham Athenaeum was lectured by young Knowles on Art Criticism (duly followed in April by Hewlett on Literary Forgeries). Art was synthesis, science was analysis, and mental growth alternated between them, Knowles informed his neighbours: this over-simplifying dogma still ran in his mind and was to emerge, somewhat matured, in print ten years later. As useful arts, fine arts, and high arts minister respectively to man's animal, human, and spiritual needs, the lecturer dealt with questions of economy and fitness for use, the possibility of a purely physical constitution of beauty, and the Greek versus the Gothic notions of the sublime, all illustrated by architectural drawings, engravings of paintings, and casts of sculpture—also some examples of 'bad Art' unspecified in the *Gazette* but very likely derived from over-ornamented 'abominations' illustrated as warnings in lectures delivered by Ralph Wornum at Marlborough House.[77] Victorian taste was not a monolithic affair.

The Clapham Athenaeum then heard, in May, a paper by Edward Barry on the works of Christopher Wren, an occasion to gratify the elder Knowles who as we know preferred Bow Church and St. Paul's to anything medieval. An interest in the Wren period was never quite out of fashion among the 'verna-

---

technique of his father's drawings, which probably sat ill with the concept described.

[76] Date of added line from Kathleen Tillotson, 'Tennyson's Serial Poem', *Mid-Victorian Studies* (1965), p. 109.

[77] Wornum's lectures published later as *Analysis of Ornament* included some 'abominations' (p. 9, 9th edn. of 1884). On Knowles's lecture, *CG*, Apr. 1859, p. 67.

cular classic' men.[78] Wren's fusion of Classic and Gothic elements appealed to many architects in the 1850s; they thought of it as his Englishness; and the shaped panels of carved foliage in his buildings did not escape them. Although there have been few periods in the whole history of English building when some sort of realistic plant-life found no root-hold at least in interior ornament, the early nineteenth century had not been fertile in such design; and so the reaction found stimulus in plant-ornament of the seventeenth century, as well as that of the thirteenth. The philosophy of 'crisp vigorous leaves' in art was mooted more than ever in 1859. Whether to 'fall back upon the conventional foliage of the thirteenth century, on account of its wonderful strength and vigour' or to work out 'such as we require fresh for ourselves' —'the range of natural objects brought under out notice being in these days greatly extended'—were the alternatives posed by Gilbert Scott, and now persuasively weighted in favour of the latter course by Ruskin on behalf of the new Oxford Museum, 'which has fearlessly put to new trial this old faith in nature' in the O'Shea carvings from actual plants bent to architectural uses. Also to strike a medium between 'Nature, red in tooth and claw' and a 'more near employment of Nature as we know and love her' (Tennyson and young Knowles respectively) was part of the mid-century search for a new balance, with the sense that thirteenth-century carved foliage had achieved 'something deeper too than a balance of nature and style or of the imitative and the decorative . . . perhaps also a balance of God and the World, the invisible and the visible' (Pevsner in our century on the leaves of Southwell)—the great antitheses, in fact.[79]

[78] On Early Victorian appreciation of seventeenth century, cf. chap. 2, n. 53. On use of term 'vernacular' for these men, see also p. 155 below. *Bldr*, 21 May 1859, p. 340, E. M. Barry's 'Wren and His Times' lecture on 9 May to Clapham Athenaeum; also that year at RIBA, George Wightwick's paper on Wren (Sessional Papers, 1858–9). Knowles Sr. expressed his preference for Wren in the discussion after his paper in 1850 (chap. 2, n. 33 above). All will have heard Cockerell's R.A. lectures (1841–56), more influential than I have space to show.

[79] Foliage-furore 1858–9: *Art J.* series 1857–8 by Christopher Dresser on 'Botany as adapted to the Arts and Art-Manufacture'; *BN*, Feb.–Mar. 1858 published J. K. Colling to RIBA on architectural foliage, J. P. Seddon to Architectural Museum contradicting Colling, Gilbert Scott on thirteenth century to Royal Academy and Architectural Museum, and on 16 April a leader on architectural foliage; the next spring Ruskin's book on the Oxford Museum came out (April 1859, Cook and Wedderburn, vol. XVI), Colling lectured the Architectural Association on architectural botany in May, and in December came Scott

And Gothic was English; the way to a new national style might lie that way. A new English style was thought to be just around the corner in 1859: 'no doubt, a century or two hence', prophesied the *Builder* in September, 'it will be as easy to recognize the architecture of Queen Victoria's reign as it is now to distinguish that of Queen Elizabeth'. A great English style, was it too much to hope for 'in a country which has produced Shakespeare and Milton . . . Watt and Stephenson . . . Reynolds and Turner . . .? Who can say how soon the Shakespeare or the Newton of architecture may arise?'[80] Hope was high in the profession in 1859. In December the members of the Institute were forcibly reminded that glorious medieval work stood in the midst of London, ignored by students of the stones of Venice (though not by Ruskin). The occasion was a paper on Westminster Abbey given by Gilbert Scott as architect to the Dean and Chapter, a lecture later expanded into a book, *Gleanings from Westminster Abbey*. Scott's ringing peroration will not have fallen on deaf ears so far as the architects for a prominent site at the other end of Victoria Street were concerned:[81]

I will only add, that I recommend all students of Gothic Architecture residing in London to devote to it every extra hour they have at their command. London has been pretty well denuded of its medieval remains, but like the Sybil's books those which remain are worth as much almost as the whole, and to live in a city which, amidst its gloomy wilderness of brick and compo, contains so glorious and exquisite a work of original art as this, is a privilege which few other cities could offer us. *Let us make use of it.*

Whatever the elder Knowles's opinion of the Gothic revival, this offered a supremely English source of enrichment such as his son had been feeling for—if indeed they hadn't been ransacking the Abbey for sympathetic motives already. Unaware, perhaps, that vigorous plant-carvings just sprung from the bud around 1200

---

on the Abbey (n. 81): only a sample of papers thick as leaves in Vallombrosa on the subject.

[80] *Bldr*, 10 Sept. 1859, p. 603.

[81] The original RIBA paper was delivered in two instalments on 5 and 19 Dec. 1859 at 9 Conduit Street, to which the Institute had moved; Scott gave a condensed version before the London and Middlesex Archaeological Society in October 1860; 1861 edn. of his *Gleanings from Westminster Abbey* has sharper reproduction of Orlando Jewett's engravings, but 1863 edn. has added papers by Burges and others; engravings of Abbey's carved foliage, pp. 29, 33, 44, 54, 66.

on the nave capitals of Reigate parish church—seen Sunday after Sunday—had prepared their way to them.

In March 1860 a perspective view for a new Grosvenor Hotel, signed by Knowles senior and complete in exterior detail save for later modification of the roof, will have been ready to send in for the Royal Academy's summer exhibition. Construction was already under way. In March as well, initial drawings for the pair of monster terraces inaugurating the speculative Cedars estate development at Clapham Common, signed by Knowles junior, were approved by the developer and building begun. None of these drawings for either enterprise remain, only engravings from them in periodicals—and the buildings themselves.

In April 1860 Henry Gay Hewlett married Emmeline Mary Knowles at Streatham church. Letters from them on their wedding tour provoked an envious reply from her brother on 9 May, 'feeling something like the "dogs beneath the table" towards you sitting at a banquet of happiness . . . not expecting more than a crumb of attention. . . . It makes me quite long to be married myself to hear of your golden time.' He had been 'intensely busy . . . but altogether in my profession—I haven't touched one of my books—tho' Bosworth is really beginning to get rampagious— Tonight I am going to hear a lecture about King Arthur— & perhaps that by great good luck may set me going.' This is the first sign of a notion for an Arthurian book, probably initially impelled by the publication of the first *Idylls of the King* the previous summer. Hewlett was ahead of him (with *The Heroes of Europe* published in 1860, and the next year a volume of poems, *Shakespeare's Curse*) and Knowles felt 'still so far down the ladder', with 'too much going out . . . and one way and another . . . "muddling" my life away'. He talked of starting an Excursion Society, and reported on a reading-room he was running for working-men's classes in Acre Lane: at the end of session he had given the prizes after 'a wretchedly small examn—only 5 went in but of these 2 answered splendidly. We keep the lending library open "till further notice"—and propose to re-open the reading room in Novr—but it has cost a "mort" of money—as old Peggotty says.' The weather of that notoriously cold spring was reported on ('everybody has had the most horrid colds and been generally mopy and low'), but 'Ah well—perhaps Sir the time will come when *I* shall have *whitebait breakfasts* in the middle of the day—and spend £50 in a fortnight in "guzzling and muzzling" with *my* wife!!' With that, 'a wretched plasterer has claimed my brain', and the letter ends.[82] Soon James was engaged to the daughter of the parson of St. Mary's, Tothill Fields (Vincent Square), Westminster; a Bible owned by their descendants is inscribed 'Jane Emma Borradaile from her ever most affectionate James, July 9, 1860'. The Borradailes were a numerous South London clan originally from Cumberland and active in Surrey, the City, the Church, and the Colonies. George Herbert, Knowles's lively contentious travelling companion in Rome and Sicily, was Abraham Borradaile's curate at St. Mary's from 1856 until 1860 when he was translated to the district of St. Peter's, a church then about to be built on part of the old Vauxhall Gardens ground. On 27 June, a large company including the Revd. Mr. Borradaile and the Revd. Mr. Herbert—and perhaps Miss Borradaile and her betrothed—met near the church site for the young Prince of Wales's first-ever stone-laying ceremony, for a drawing school for local artisans (designed, like the church, by J. L. Pearson). The *Builder* had just published on 16 June the design by James Knowles Jr. for new terraces of large houses on the Cedars estate at Clapham Common, with a flourishing announcement of their important situation, probably in the architect's own words. It was his first signed and published commission for works actually to be erected, and the engagement to marry may have coincided with its publication.[83]

Jane Borradaile was barely 18 when her father married them in his church near Victoria Street on 13 October 1860, James's 29th birthday. They settled down on the north side of Clapham Common in the centre house of Nelson Terrace, an early nineteenth-century row of houses still facing the parish church and

[82] Hewlett–Knowles marriage, *CG*, May 1860, p. 84. Knowles to Hewlett, 9 May 1860 (WPL). On Knowles's book, chap. 5, 'Malory Modernized', below. [83] Bible in family possession. The church of St. Mary the Virgin, 'small and very unpretending' by Blore (*CBA for 1838*, Colvin), stood on the south-east side of Vincent Square. A. F. Borradaile, *Sketch of the Borradailes of Cumberland* (1881): the parents of Jane's father were first cousins; the brothers who were his grandfathers were partners of Lanark Twist Mills and lived in Streatham, one an M.P. and chairman of the Hudson Bay Company, the other High Sheriff of Surrey. On stone-laying for drawing school, *Bldr*, 30 June, 4 Aug. 1860, pp. 413, 497, and *ILN*, 7 July 1860. On consecration of St. Peter's, Vauxhall, *CG*, July 1864; also chap. 7, n. 2 below on later buildings there by Knowles. Cedars estate design: *Bldr*, 16 June 1860, p. 380.

the Common, and then with a view from upper back windows toward the pastures of Battersea Fields. Knowles's working hours continued to be spent on the Grosvenor or Cedars building sites and in the office at Gray's Inn, apparently with plenty of spare hours to devote to a book adapting Malory's *Morte d'Arthur* for the young. And so it was to seem natural, when a son was born, to ignore precedent in this family and name the child Arthur.[84]

[84] *CG*, Nov. 1860, p. 12; 1861 census. While Arthur had already become a favoured name after the Duke of Wellington, and the Tennysonian influence usually came later (Tillotson, p. 85, n. 3, as cited n. 76 above), there is no question here.

4

The Grosvenor Style:
a Mid-Victorian Synthesis

'Englishmen are the most eclectic of the human race
. . . in their architecture . . . they receive elements
from foreign sources . . . purifying them down into a
homogeneous, compact, and national compound, as
enduring, as distinct, and as capable of giving out
clear fresh harmonies as bronze.' *Building News* on
'Victorian Architecture', 18 June 1858

DURING 1859, AND PERHAPS THE FIRST MONTHS OF
1860, the Knowleses gradually worked up a style all their
own. Many Mid-Victorians sought some reconciliation
between life's great antitheses, and the reconcilers included
architects who believed that a new English style might emerge
from judicious blending of old styles. Such men were respected
members of their profession, talking less than the extreme Goths
and Classicists of the Battle of Styles, and working harder than
the 'anything goes' style-mixers. A judicious eclecticism implied
more discrimination than the loose tolerance of the mechanical
mixers, and even a certain creativity theoretically unknown to the
purists, although in practice the best purists exercised both choice
and creativity; it was all a matter of degree. The forging of a new
'national compound' was urgent for men who had just begun to
call their architecture 'Victorian'. Comparisons with Victorian
attempts to reconcile faith and knowledge, instinct and reason,
art and science, are all too easy.

The case of fusion then occurring on the elder Knowles's
drawing-board was worked up, with young James's aid, for the
Grosvenor Hotel at the new Victoria Station in London. The

Grosvenor (Pl. 6) is an interesting, neglected specimen of reconciliation, admired in its day for a form of professional design-
expertise that a decade later was as dead as the dodo, and then not
for a century recognized for what it had tried to do. Such
recognition requires the sort of detective work that biography
requires, into modes of thought and sight and available stimuli.
Biographically speaking, this high point in the older man's
working life was only a prophetic incident in his son's—yet a
meaningful one. Architecturally speaking, the Grosvenor was
one answer to the Battle of the Styles, for it embodied not so
much a style as a Truce of the Styles.

Hotels in the 1860s succeeded clubhouses as the new urban
palaces. With the new crowds of visitors flocking into London by
railway, to transact business and see the sights, came flocks of
investors too.

THE GROSVENOR HOTEL AT VICTORIA STATION

> 'It would be well for us . . . to take hints from
> [Italian] palaces . . . working them up for ourselves,
> with details of our own.' Gilbert Scott, *Remarks on
> Secular . . . Architecture* (1858), p. 195

> 'And ... to display in them the beauty of every flower
> and herb of the English fields, each by each; doing as
> much for every tree that roots itself in our rocks, and
> every blossom that drinks our summer rains, as our
> ancestors did for the oak, the ivy, and the rose.'
> John Ruskin, *The Stones of Venice*, vol. 3 (1853),
> concluding paragraph

As it rose beside a former inlet of the Thames during 1860–2, the
Grosvenor's carcass assumed at first something of the lonely bulk
of a great steamship hull, like that of the *Great Eastern* rising a few
years before at Millwall. In spite of prompt estate development
by the Marquis of Westminster near by, the hotel was to hold its
local dominance until the end of the century. Today the Grosvenor's double lanterns mounted on their domelike mansards are
still landmarks, and still the carved heads on its lofty frieze lean
from their roundels like passengers peering from portholes,
serenely surveying the scurrying street-life alongside their great
vessel. It stands on a long, narrow site parallel to Victoria Station's

platforms and to Buckingham Palace Road, its north end overlooking the narrow way, choked with buses and taxis, from
Grosvenor Gardens into the station yard, its south end abutting
on a goods entrance and the cab entry for the Brighton trains.
The hotel's main door is on Buckingham Palace Road where
that thoroughfare meets Grosvenor Gardens. There is a back door
on the station concourse, but in spite of infill between hotel and
station, the hotel was and is an entirely separate structure.

A hotel was meant to be part of a proposed railway terminus
there at least as early as the summer of 1857. The Grosvenor
Basin—the Chelsea Water-works' old domain then edged with
wharves and yards let to builders and coal-merchants—was to be
filled in for the station site and most of the canal linking it to the
Thames filled in for railway lines that were to be brought over a
new Thames bridge. The promoters also had to secure some forty
acres of ground around the basin, then a busy backwater similar
in character to the remains of Paddington Basin today and
dependent on what was then, as for centuries, a chief carrier of
London building materials, the Thames barge. A prospectus in
promoters' prose claimed that the train-shed would enclose a
great space roofed 'like the Crystal Palace' and terminating in a
'huge quadrangle' formed by a 'noble range of buildings'.

The style will be Gothic, and the front elevation in its general features
. . . not unlike the terrace front of the new Houses of Parliament,
though, of course, less florid and expensive in detail. This portion will
be expressly built for an extensive hotel—an hotel sufficient, if need be,
to shelter all the multitudinous visitors who daily flock up to London
from the south of England. . . . Into the [quadrangle] passengers will
drive on coming to start per train.[1]

A new version, in short, of the old coaching inn yard, and based
partly on the Hôtel du Louvre built two years before in Paris.
At this stage, the hotel in the front range, as at New Street in
Birmingham, but unlike the Great Western Hotel at Paddington,
was intended to be part of the station like the coaching inn, as the
future terminus hotels at Charing Cross, Cannon Street, and St.
Pancras were to be.

Although a hotel was not precisely specified in the Victoria
Station and Pimlico Railway Act of 1858, one was clearly

---

[1] *The Times*, 27 Aug. 1857.

intended. Yet, according to announcements in *The Times*'s 'Money Market and City Intelligence' column during October 1858, the Victoria Station and Pimlico Railway Company had a rival in the hotel business: 'The prospectus has been issued of the Grosvenor and West-end Railway Terminus Hotel Company . . . to supply accommodation at the Victoria and Pimlico terminus . . . to contain 174 sleeping and dressing rooms . . . [and] to be an imitation of the Great Western Hotel at Paddington, which, owing to its large profits, is uniformly quoted by joint-stock hotel promoters.' Thereupon the secretary of the Victoria Station Company begged to say 'that the plans of this company . . . have always embraced the construction of an extensive hotel, to be called the "Victoria", attached to the station—which the Grosvenor will not be—and intended to be conducted on a popular scale. The plans are prepared, and arrangements are in progress for the building, so that it may be opened simultaneously with the station and the railway.' But by January the hotel site 'could not be determined at present', there was no further mention of a Victoria Hotel during 1859, and by August the station works were affected by the building strike. In February 1860 it was announced that the lines and bridge, though not the permanent station, would be finished that year and then, after amalgamation with the London Brighton and South Coast Railway Company, the Victoria Station Company would be dissolved.[2] Meanwhile, foundations for the Grosvenor Hotel were being laid.

In the Royal Academy's summer exhibition for 1860, opened in May, there was shown a perspective drawing for 'The Grosvenor Hotel, now in course of erection, at the Victoria Station, Pimlico', by J. T. Knowles of Gray's Inn. The contractor was John Kelk, whose firm built the bridge and the station. When the Victoria Hotel scheme faded—for a complexity of reasons, including rows among the railway companies—and as soon as the builders' strike allowed, the Grosvenor Company had the

___

[2] *The Times*, 18 and 21 Oct. 1858; 15 Jan., 11 Aug. 1859; 28 Feb. 1860. In 1900 the London Brighton & South Coast Railway Co., freeholders of both station and hotel, having taken over the Grosvenor & West End Railway Terminus Hotel Co.'s lease and being about to rebuild the station with an annexe to add 100 rooms to the hotel, leased the hotel to Gordon Hotels Ltd. who were to close it for two years for repair and redecoration by the architectural firm of Alfred Waterhouse (deed of covenants between Brighton Co. and Gordon Hotels, 3 Jan. 1900, kindly shown by manager in 1978 during restoration by British Transport Hotels, the present owners).

field to itself, and construction began early in 1860. Its site beside
the station had contained a row of modest buildings fronting on
what was then Lower Belgrave Place with wharves and outbuildings behind them on the Grosvenor Basin's north-west bank,
a place of 'quicksands, mudbanks, and old peat-bogs' above the
London clay, that required the laying of a concrete bed ten feet
thick. By September the hotel had reached its second storey, yet
in June 1861 interior work had still not begun, 'retarded by the
unfortunate differences between masters and men'. By the time
the 1862 Exhibition opened the following spring, the hotel was in
business.[3]

The first proposed design of 1858 seems not to have survived.
Its promoters may have been impressed by, may even have
themselves at first promoted, Knowles's raffish unbuilt design of
early 1858 for an International Hotel in the Strand, which as we
have seen was much influenced by the Great Western Hotel at
Paddington, parent of most railway hotels in London, with its
unprecedented size, prominent roofs, and profitable returns. For
the Grosvenor, during 1859, the ill-digested elements Knowles
had set out for the Strand were fused into something approxi-
mating the 'national compound' the critics were waiting for. And
indeed, every element of the Grosvenor design not due to habits
and admirations of the senior Knowles's youth is traceable to
English designs or English pronouncements or English enthusiasms
that were in the news during the 1850s. His nose for the news
that London's professional air was thick with was not for
truffling up treasures abroad all by himself: his Portuguese villa,
we shall find, was worked out in the office at Gray's Inn. The
Grosvenor Hotel is an entirely English building.

Gilbert Scott, a prime eclectic for all his Gothic pronouncements, in 1858 pronounced upon urban architectural design in
words that the Knowleses took to heart in their own way:

It would be well for us . . . to take hints from such palaces as the
Ricardi, the Strozzi . . . and working them up for ourselves, with
details of our own . . . we should adopt the horizontal cornice, and
give it considerable importance, though designing it with Gothic

---

[3] RA catalogue (1860), no. 660. *CEAJ*, July 1860, p. 189. *ILN*, 7 July 1860, p.
13. *Bldr*, 24 Nov. 1860, 1 June 1861. Rate books at WPL: first assessment for half-
year Mar.–Sept. 1862. In spite of the concrete platform, the great Thames flood of
1928 brought basement flooding, with fish (local memory in 1965).

rather than classic details. We should have uniform ranges of arched windows . . . the tracery, if any, being of the boldest and simplest form. . . . The details I would not make in any degree like Italian. . . . This would be copyism rather than development.

Development: that was the process these men groped for. Scott went on:

The mouldings should be founded rather on Northern than on Southern Gothic. . . . The capitals . . . should be founded on natural foliage of familiar types . . . all should be fresh and genuine. . . . A lofty roof rising boldly from behind a parapet . . . will give individuality to our building. . . . Few features tend more to give a palatial air to a building than a noble cornice . . . a feature, however, which we should do well to work out for ourselves.

Scott's words could almost be the textbook for development, in the evolutionary or musical sense, at the Grosvenor.[4]

The long, narrow site was suited to a ground plan of central space linked to end-pavilions on the same axis, the old villa-skeleton Knowles was used to. On it he could pile five main storeys and basement, plus two storeys in the roofs, and at the ends an extra storey tucked behind the cornice. It was the management of the terminal wings, with more wall-space, depth of frieze, and roof display than the main range, that gave the Grosvenor its quality. Externally its materials are a once-golden Bath stone (ground floor), a once moon-white Portland stone for parapets, medallions, and cornice, and Knowles's usual off-white Suffolk bricks for walls above the ground floor—materials all emerging from cleaning, in 1978, in light tawny tones. The Portland cement for the large oak leaves on the deep frieze-panels (probably cast in sections from huge matrices at the sculptors' yard) was said to have been stained to match the stone-work while the cement was setting, or 'green' in the cement-worker's sense, presumably to match the white stone of the 'portrait' medallions embedded in the leaves.[5] A modest strati-fication of stone-colours was the nearest an architect of Greek Revival background generally came toward 'structural poly-chromy'. As with Cook's warehouse a few years before, we may

---

[4] G. G. Scott, *Remarks on Secular and Domestic Architecture* (1858), pp. 195–8.
[5] Long description, *BN*, 20 Mar. 1863, pp. 210–11, 218–19.

wonder that a practical London architect with experience of
materials, or any canny clients in the year of coal-smoke 1860,
should have selected such light-toned brick and Bath stone,
materials with an especial affinity for soot, in central London
beside a railway station. But the clients were keen for quick
returns on their investment, Knowles was keen for the verdict of
here-and-now, and both knew the smoke must fall on the just as
on the unjust.

The building's surfaces were one of its newest features, that is,
the vigorous ornament with which these were worked. At the
ends and centre of the ground floor are those carved garlands so
proudly called 'the largest swags in London', depending from
keystones carved with lion-masks, a combination suggesting
engravings of Baalbek—upon which a lecturer had recently discoursed to the earnest members of the RIBA. Lion-heads were
more 'English' than the ox-skulls or human masks more often
hung with garlands by classical revivalists. Each of the 'festoons
of flowers such as the rose, lily, peony, and ranunculus' (*Building
News*, but described by a ruder contemporary as 'diseased
efflorescence') is looped under one of the bold leaf-lipped cantilevers of the first-floor balcony. Balcony balustrades of cement-
work set in patterns of running ivy leaves and stems are repeated
on the roof parapet and also indoors in the main hall, all suggesting
Ruskin's precept in 'The Lamp of Power' to lay a few leaves on
white paper and make figures that 'cut boldly through a slab of
marble, would be worth more traceries than an architect could
draw'. These must stem from young Knowles's discovery of
Ruskin in 1855—a source less appreciated by his father's generation
until Ruskin was seen to be 'news'. There was a personal element
in this too, as well as the generation gap, the older man having
little poetry in him, while young James had been prepared for
Ruskin by first discovering Tennyson—yet father and son had in
common a sort of news-conscious literalness, a half-innocent eye.
And so the long ribbons or hedges of parapets were seen, by eyes
sympathetic to Wren's carvers and to *The Seven Lamps*, as
suitable fields for naturalistic ornament.[6]

[6] 'Largest swags', *Bldr* 1860 (as n. 3), p. 755. Sir Thomas Deane read a paper on
Baalbek at the RIBA (*Bldr*, 25 Jan. 1851, p. 60). 'Diseased' comment by F. T.
Palgrave, *Essays on Art* (1866), p. 310, a reference kindly given by Peter Howell.
Ruskin, *Seven Lamps*, 'The Lamp of Power', section xxiv.

The Grosvenor's window-tracery (Pl. 6), now almost entirely gone, was something else again. Such arbitrarily shaped fields as window-heads afforded were thought to demand forms more abstract. We can still see Knowlesian tracery surviving on the great twin terraces designed at the same time by young Knowles for the north side of Clapham Common (Pl. 7). Each storey of the hotel had a different set of it, mostly shaken off in the Blitz but originally an important part of the full optical effect, giving the openings a lidded look. One historian likes to call these devices 'cataracts', but 'eyelids' may say it better: the windows have a staring gaze without them. Two sorts of tracery were manipulated, a slightly Arabic type that Knowles Sr. had started using in Chancery Lane the year Owen Jones's Alhambra court opened at Sydenham, and a slightly Bolognese type adapted from terracotta tracery illustrated by the Architectural Publication Society when Knowles was sitting on its committee. The top-floor window tracery, making a two-light opening with a bold flower-form between—not merely an eyelid but a pupil too—was a deft *coup d'œil* to finish off such a façade below such a head-piece of roof. The critic James Fergusson can never have complained, as he did of Munich railway station, that the Grosvenor 'wanted eyebrows'. If the optical metaphors seem mixed, mixed metaphor may be the only instrument for describing such a building.[7]

The aim of all this window-tracery on the Grosvenor was of course to re-create, or develop, English Gothic tracery, impelled by young Knowles's browsings in Ruskin but translated, as a modern creation, into cement and ironwork. Ruskin would have especially detested the fact that such materials were painted stone-colour. Window-glass was set well behind it in the deep opening, as recommended in 'The Lamp of Power'; from inside, the tracery appeared black against light, as a permanent valence until curtain styles thickened. (The ground-floor glazing-bars have been altered since.) Some first-floor tracery survived over the main entrance, protected for many years by a conservatory. Ruskin may never have noticed any traces of his principles upon the Grosvenor, as his arrivals for Metaphysical Society meetings

---

[7] Engravings of window-tracery in *BN*, 1863 (as n. 5), and photograph in *Round London* (1896). On Munich station (1857), Fergusson, *Modern Architecture* (1873 edn.).

were to occur mostly after dark.[8] But there was more to it than this. The wings at first and fourth-floor levels are emphasized by the deep friezes or 'ground-cover' of leaves into which window-heads rise, flanked by stone roundels containing carved heads, echoed by more heads ranged across the whole building. Those at first-floor level were said to represent 'various eminent persons, including the Queen, the late Prince Consort, Lords Palmerston, Derby, Russell, and others', even the great German synthesizer of knowledge, Alexander von Humboldt, who died in 1859 and whose works young Knowles had been reading; but the like-nesses were more journalistic than recognizable. The upper row of heads, so far from the spectator, were vaguely allegorical. (How odd that on these supposedly expressive façades there seem to be no symbols of the river on a former branch of which the hotel stands: evoking the Thames though, then, was unnecessary anywhere within smelling-distance.) It was more fun to borrow ideas of carved capitals from the Florentine Bargello or, rather, from Woodward's Crown Insurance building's borrowings from the Bargello, by carving extended capitals (or impost mouldings) with plants in the manner of English stiff-leaf work, 'the ivy, the oak, the horse chestnut, the hop, and the convolvulus . . . the vine, the strawberry, the rose, the maple , as young Knowles (it would appear) told *Building News*, complete with comment inspired by Owen Jones's popular *Grammar of Ornament*: 'Though the closest imitation of nature has here been attempted . . . the com-pact grouping of the leaves and severe outlines within which they are confined have entirely prevented the weak and spiritless effect which is often too apparent in naturalistic designs.'[9]

Under all the vegetation were elements of the classical Renais-sance. It was from palatial houses of the 1840s in Grosvenor

[8] Although *Bldr* in 1860 spoke of plans for 'pierced and foliated Bath stone hoods' and some simple top-floor tracery on the station side seems to be of stone, the careful description of 1863 (n. 5) suggests that some of the tracery was of iron. though much of it, like that at Clapham (chap. 5), was probably of painted cement. Ruskin on deep-set glass: 'The Lamp of Power', section xix. He attended about 13 Metaphysical Society meetings there between 1870 and 1877 (Brown, as chap. 6, n. 11 below).

[9] On portrait heads, *Bldr*, 1 June 1861, *CBA for 1862* (1861), p. 277; *BN* 1863 (as n. 5) noted that likenesses were not good. On foliage ornament, 1863 article referred to Jones's 'Proposition 13', that natural objects must be conventionalized (*Grammar of Ornament*, 1856).

Place (Nos. 18–20) and at Albert Gate that the Grosvenor's storey proportions, bold cantilevers, and some other features derive.[10] Yet the elder Knowles's hotel design for the Strand had been drawn with small-scale ornament: there he was fumbling, an Early Victorian in at the (apparent) death of the classical tradition and unsure where to head for next; it was the new sense of scale sought by his son's generation that informed the grand end-wings at the Grosvenor. But it was in the (for all we know) joint manipulation, within the classical outlines of the building, of its strange vegetation that the deftest reconciling was done. Drawing on new awareness of leaf-carved spandrel panels all the way from Westminster Abbey to Wren's churches, these two scene-setters pulled the old classical frieze down around the windows—instead of filling the spandrels with figures as Scott was to do on the Home Office—and left only a narrow rose border above in the old frieze position (Pl. 7). (Although sinking a deep frieze part way down a window-arcade in this way, complete with range of ornamental roundels, will have reminded learned architects of Alberti's sidewall system at Rimini, there were eminently stealable sources nearer at hand, such as the Palace of Industry at the Paris Exhibition of 1855, illustrated in English journals at the time.) One wonders whether Louis Sullivan recalled old illustrations of the Grosvenor's bands of closely scattered oak leaves, thirty years later, when he was designing the great frieze on the Wainwright Building at St. Louis, Missouri. As for the Grosvenor's running rose border above, that may have been translated from some small-scale Decorated Gothic moulding. And just above the cornice runs the smoke-stained parapet of ivy leaves. Oak leaves,[11] rose spray, and ivy carefully composed together: 'as our ancestors did for the oak, the ivy, and the rose', Ruskin had said. Here was literal translation for you.

Rearing up from this stony verdure, the consoles of the great cornice half-reveal the windows of the extra garret there—an old palace servant-loft dodge. The tall consoles above the rows of busts suggest some ransacking of Italian palace views (for instance

[10] Nos. 18–20 Grosvenor Place were by Thomas Cundy, the Albert Gate pair by Thomas Cubitt.

[11] That the leaf-cover on the Grosvenor's deep frieze was meant as oak leaves (although *BN* description called them vine leaves) seems more probable since Owen Jones's *Grammar* plates xliv, no. 2, and xlv, no. 3 of oak leaves look as if they were the models used.

of the Spannocchi at Siena, where heads peer out between the consoles) or else of some nasty variations published by the English architect J. B. Waring some years before. At any rate, this cornice would be one of the more impressive left in London even if there were not also its great headpiece of roof. There Knowles was able to resolve his Strand design's ridiculous rendering of Hardwick's Paddington roofs into the larger, simpler lines of, perhaps, certain domes suggested by Sir Charles Barry for Whitehall (on paper only) during the Government Offices competition, wherein so many of the entrants itched to outdo the pavilion roofs of the New Louvre. And Knowles's arcaded band linking his twinned cupolas above may have been partly a working-up of the 'smoking storey' Barry added in the 1840s to his Travellers' Club, and partly a trick picked up from glasshouse designs new in the 1830s, with a dash of Quattrocento hybrid façades in North Italy savoured in engravings. Moreover, in this Francophile period there was the RIBA copy of the Grand Marot folio of engravings of French architecture, full of *château* roofs, in the Institute's library since 1848, whether the Knowleses ever looked at it or only took in the conversation and sketches of those who had. An ounce of suggestion could indeed be worth a pound of pedantry to them. And this far from complete analysis of a battered building is provided not for pedantry but suggestion —as to how a clever journalist's mind might work when his time came.[12]

Inside, the Grosvenor was and is a working hotel, where commuters and shoppers recuperate with tea or gin before joining the surge to their trains, children from schools in southern counties are met by their parents, and travellers off the boat train or the local from Purley or, increasingly, tourists spewed from motor coaches, stop for the night. Stock-jobbers, such as Cobbett sneered at for hurrying back and forth to Brighton, come and go. During the American Civil War, when the hotel first opened, Confederate agents were said to frequent it on business connected with blockade-running. Before the First World War, Julian Field the swindler lived here, presumably as a disarmingly

[12] J. B. Waring, *Thirty Designs Adapted for Civil Architecture* (1850). Barry's design (1857) for Government offices inserted in back cover of his son's biography of him (1867). The Institute bought its Grand Marot in 1848 (note inside front cover). Restoration (up to a point, no new window-tracery) and interior improvements are now going on (1978).

dignified address. During the Second World War, this is said to have been a Free French headquarters. We may also imagine, ascending the grand staircase to a private parlour in the 1870s, Mr. Gladstone, Mr. Huxley, Mr. Tennyson, Mr. Ruskin, Dean Stanley, Cardinal Manning, and the rest, summoned—as we shall hear—by young Mr. Knowles and their own active consciences to discuss their doubts about prayer and miracles and whether frogs have souls.

The form of this lofty entrance hall began life in its architect's elastic mind in the 1830s: one can perceive overtones of Buckingham Palace (staircase threaded through an arcade), Silverton Park, Friday Grove. It remained Early Victorian, even partly Late Georgian, in decoration until after the last war: columns and pilasters cased in white scagliola veined with black, mouldings probably once gilded, and under the modern carpet a floor of plain white marble squares with black insets. At the half-landing, where a door was made in this century, there will have been a niche, with statuary as in the United Services Club or a mirror as in the Reform Club. The present stair-balustrade of podgy marble balusters, put in by the Waterhouse firm in 1900, will have replaced an ivy-leaf balustrade in keeping with and continuing that of the gallery, and like the leafy ones Knowles was designing for a villa in Portugal. Also replaced were diapered panels 'in Keene's and Martin's cements' on the walls of the main rooms, in keeping with various diapers that remain on the ceilings.[13] Those emulating Gothic fields of foliage would have been finished in a stone-coloured or marbled cement that could be polished, those of Victorian–Islamic origin picked out in gilding and colour. The drum of the entrance-hall skylight (with a now-obscured deep light-well over it) is surrounded with figures in relief that may recall Della Robbia's foundlings or the garland-swinging children on Renaissance friezes, combined in scenic function with Soane's caryatids at the Bank of England—here in cement with a stone-coloured, gilt-edged finish, no doubt. The mahogany chimney-piece in the dining room, incorporating a mirrored niche below an open pediment, is on precisely the large

---

[13] On 'diapered work' *Bldr* 1860 (as n. 3). Waterhouse tiles: *BN*, 7 Mar. 1902, p. xxviii, by Leeds firm of Alfred Whitehead (Bodleian copy bound with advertisements, per Peter Howell); and other redecoration by Waterhouse (Stuart Allen Smith, D. B. Waterhouse).

simple lines of those in the Reform Club and not one moment later. In 1900 Waterhouse clothed the main corridor walls with faience tiles in tones of buff and cream, later painted over. Any views of Grosvenor interiors as originally furnished have yet to be found. When the hotel opened, just in time for the invasion of visitors to the International Exhibition of 1862, probably there was neither time nor money for elaborate decoration. So, except for dignified fixtures and fittings designed by the architect, the original furnishings will have been more hardy than memorable. Promoters hoping for returns from a large building programme hampered by strikes were unlikely to provide the marbles and lapis lazuli, the ottomans and cut-glass chandeliers, the frescoes and gilt-framed portraits of Pall Mall clubs.

For modernity there was from the start a 'lifting room', to rival the 'ascending room' at the Westminster Palace Hotel. Suites were provided on first and second floors, an idea from the Great Western Hotel, where it had been called a 'Continental arrangement not common here' in 1852. Above, there were originally only two bathrooms to each bedroom floor and an only slightly larger number of water closets. Such paucity of plumbing seems odd, considering the amount that architects like Knowles were ready to put in as early as the 1830s and the lavishness of New York hotels published in the 1850s in London journals, but the scarcity in London hotels before the Savoy can probably be blamed partly on the conservatism of company directors or, at this time of sanitary crisis before the Main Drainage was done, on a general distrust of drains and reluctance to multiply them. The passages were heated by hot-water pipes, the rooms by fireplaces.[14]

In 1862, except among purists, the Grosvenor was well received: 'the most splendid of its class yet erected in this country', said the often critical *Companion to the British Almanac*.[15] It held its own with newer railway hotels of the 1860s, until it was somewhat thrown in the shade in the 1880s by the Savoy and the Cecil in the Strand and the Metropole and the Grand in the new Northumberland Avenue. But, until 1898, Victoria Station had no other demonstrative architecture, only a group of low buildings without distinction, the Grosvenor alone lending artistic verisimi-

[14] *ILN*, 7 July 1860, p. 14; *Bldr*, 24 Nov. 1860, o. 755.
[15] *CBA for 1862*, p. 277, 'executed with admirable skill and spirit'.

litude to an otherwise bald and unconvincing terminus. By the
1920s, of course, the firm of the hotel's sculptor, John Daymond
& Son, while boasting of their work on the rebuilding of Regent
Street and on the first Lyons Corner House, were silent about
Daymond's work on the Grosvenor.[16] Those laurels in its
window-boxes (until recently) had a faintly suburban air,
reminding us that its architect and his clients lived in Italianate
palazzos in new London suburbs thickening with newly planted
laurels. The Grosvenor became a sort of apotheosis of the way
they lived then.

'It is designed in a large, liberal spirit', said *Building News* in
1860, 'There is no littleness or affectation about it.'[17] No one
could have said that of Knowles's first design of 1858 for the
Strand. Somehow during 1859 he shifted his repertory about,
renewing here, enlarging there, drawing on young James's
enthusiasms and on all the public talk of a new Gothic flora,
suited to the year of publication of *The Idylls of the King*. The final
design may be a measure of young James's catalytic powers;
even such an unbending parent was quick to take a hint. The
elder Knowles owed much to veneration for his Clapham
neighbour Sir Charles Barry, yet Barry, who died as the hotel
was begun, would have disowned the large scale of the ornament.
In fusion of forms Classic and Picturesque, and of theories
picturesque and sublime, the Grosvenor was in more ways than
one the end of the road from the Houses of Parliament at the
other end of Westminster. For, in a sense, the Grosvenor mixture
of regularity and irregularity is a late expression of Barry's
Anglo–Italian spirit, however differently derived and newly
stimulated by Gilbert Scott: a late product of the romantic-
classicist striving for a synthesis of the picturesque and the logical,
the old styles and the new science, instinct and reason, fit scene for
the unresolved debates of the Metaphysical Society.

In 1860 an English style of architecture was thought to be just
around the corner. To it the Knowleses contributed this carpet-

---

[16] Daymond's name reported at first to the building journals as Dayman
(young Knowles in a rush probably confusing with name of South London
magistrate constantly appearing in *CG* police reports), but by 1864 correctly
reported by *BN* on Thatched House Club (chap. 5 below). Daymond had his yard
off Vincent Square: directories, Gunnis, pamphlet history *Build With Beauty* . . .
(1925), in V and A Library.

[17] *BN*, 28 Sept. 1860, p. 748.

gardening in stone and cement and brick and iron—Gothic-derived, yet without a pointed arch on the premises—as an improvement on the tired old Renaissance surfaces. (For us the hotel could be a splendid foil to any stark curtain-walling British Rail may install at the railway station.) The spacious character of the Grosvenor's carved and cast vegetation, where one leaf seldom overlies another, attained a sort of 'Early English' equipoise between abstract and real that was just pre-full-bloom Mid-Victorian, whereas bushy branches young Knowles was about to compress into panels in St. James's Street were to be full-grown, past-first-bloom Mid-Victorian; and his father, left to himself as a designer after 1860, allowed such ornament to shrivel. The brief equilibrium of the Grosvenor synthesis was held by two hands: neither Knowles was ever quite the same again. Meanwhile, the Grosvenor style was planted in Clapham. And there was a strange delayed flowering in Portugal.

COOK'S VILLA AT CINTRA

'Lo! Cintra's glorious Eden intervenes
In variegated maze of mount and glen. . . .
There thou too, Vathek! England's wealthiest son,
Once form'd thy Paradise. . . .
But now, as if a thing unblest by Man,
Thy fairy dwelling is as lone as thou!
Here giant weeds a passage scarce allow
To halls deserted, portals gaping wide.'
Childe Harold, I. xviii, xxii–xxiii

For many years English visitors to Portugal have found at Sintra (modern spelling) that Englishmen have been there before them: Byron in 1809, Southey in 1796 and 1800, Beckford in 1787 and 1793–5. Esteem for its scenery, as for port wine, appreciated during the French wars. 'Cintra rose . . . strange and beautiful . . . dear, dear Cintra . . . a spot the most delightful I have ever known. . . . Cintra is too good for the Portuguese. It is only fit for us Goths,' Southey wrote in his journal. With its rocky scenery, its fireflies and evergreens—cork, olive, and lemon trees, pines and laurel—its garden tanks and running brooks and wild flowers, it was worth the numerous presence of one's fellow English. Tennyson in 1859, calling it 'that Cintra which Byron and Beckford have made so famous', reported that it was said to be 'Lisbon's Richmond and rather cockney tho' high and cool', 'a mountain of green pines rising out of an everywhere arid and tawny country', but 'crammed with Lisbon fashionables', and 'an Englishman keeps the hotel'. Other Mid-Victorians might have called it Lisbon's Bagni di Lucca, and Late Victorians might have compared it with Simla. But 'Lisbon's Richmond' suited a Mid-Victorian who was reviving Beckford's villa at Cintra as well as a Georgian mansion on Richmond Hill in Surrey, and who then for almost forty years divided his time and his art collections between them. This was Francis Cook, who in 1869 succeeded his father as head of the wholesale drapery establishment in St. Paul's Churchyard. While continuing to be very much in control there, as a man of organizing power and tact, until within a few days of his death in 1901, he was able, as the second generation of success, to devote more of his intelligence to the enhancement of life. He appears to have been one of those Victorians who were somewhat larger than life.[18]

From 1852 or before, Knowles senior was devoting a good deal of professional attention to the Cook family's architectural arrangements, commercial and domestic: besides the rebuilding of the warehouse by St. Paul's on a palatial scale, he also probably added various outbuildings to a Tudor house in Kent, Roydon Hall, the country house of William Cook, who had taken it over in lieu of an unpaid mortagage in 1837, with major alterations to come in 1869 for the younger son, Edwin Cook; and at some time in the 1850s Knowles seems to have made for Francis Cook alterations and additions to the mid-Georgian Doughty House at the upper end of the Terrace, Richmond Hill: cement dressings on the front including a main doorcase in the manner of Barry's Reform Club side entrance, and behind the house the art gallery, forming a long wing (with later colonnade) on one side of the garden.[19] In the 1850s, for newly arrived solid citizens the private

---

[18] Robert Southey, *Journal of a Residence in Portugal*, ed. A. Cabral (1960). William Beckford, *Italy with Sketches of Spain and Portugal* and *Recollections of an Excursion* . . . in various edn. Byron's first canto of *Childe Harold* came out in 1812. Tennyson's letter-diary, August 1859, and letter to Duke of Argyll, October 1859 (*Memoir*, i. 439–40, 442, 456). DNB on Francis Cook, and bust in Cook family possession.

[19] Francis Cook was living at Doughty House by 1855 (directories). On St. Paul's warehouse, chap. 2 above. On Roydon Hall: A. R. Cook, *A Manor*

art gallery was very much the done thing (even by such as Surtees's Mr. Jawleyford, displaying his new 'pictures, busts, marbles, antiques', and leaks from the skylights to Mr. Sponge). The Old Masters assembled at Doughty House have been a worldwide legend among connoisseurs ever since.

In the 1840s Francis Cook had travelled in Portugal, and married the daughter of an English merchant there. In 1856 he acquired, apparently at first, the leasehold of the Monserrate estate at Cintra, about fifteen miles out of Lisbon, with its ruined villa, three-foot walls still intact, and a tree growing up through the floor—Beckford's 'fairy dwelling' where Byron saw giant weeds and gaping portals in 1809. Now, there survives an engraving dated 1841 showing the main elevation and ground plan of a *Casa de campo de Monserrate, de Devisme* with the battlements, pointed windows, and round towers of Georgian builders'-gothic, on an axial plan with octagonal hall linked to end-pavilions. In its title, style, and tidiness this view suggests that the engraver of 1841 copied an engraving fifty years older, when the original villa was newly built for the first owner, one Devisme. For, toward the end of the eighteenth century in Lisbon, a Gerard Devisme (or de Visme, perhaps of Huguenot origin) was an English dealer in brazilwood, the shrub valued as a source of red dye. In 1791 he is said to have had a country villa built at Cintra, bringing a builder from England for the purpose: 'a carpenter of Falmouth', complained Beckford, who had to make repairs. Devisme is said to have retired to England in 1794 after losing his brazilwood contract (and indeed a house was built in 1792 for someone of that name at Wimbledon Common). William Beckford, on his second visit to Portugal, is supposed to have leased Devisme's country villa from the autumn of 1794 until the autumn of 1795. And this is what Byron said he found deserted in 1809.[20]

About 1857 or 1858, Cook is said to have taken Knowles out to Cintra with him to look at the ruins on the hilltop. Two

through Four Centuries (1938), pp. 176–9; A. Oswald in *CL*, 24 Feb. 1940, p. 198; pamphlet history, *Cook's of St Paul's*; N. Lloyd, *English Brickwork* (1925), p. 153.
[20] J.-A. França, *A arte em Portugal no Seculo XIX* (1966), i. 172–4, 474, ii. 388. Boyd Alexander, *England's Wealthiest Son* (1962), pp. 135, 280. Falmouth was the port whence English packets sailed to Portugal. Wimbledon Lodge for Devisme by Aaron Hurst (Colvin) was quite unlike Devisme's houses in Portugal (ill. in D. Hughson, *London*, v. 393).

elaborate preliminary drawings for a reconstituted house, an elevation and a section, one signed by Knowles and dated simply 1858 (Pl. 8), are in the possession of descendants of his client.[21] These show, under the skin of ornament, the thick walls and arched openings of Devisme's house: Knowles's house was to rise within that shell. For one reason or another, actual building operations only began in 1863, when (once again) an English builder, a James Samuel Bennett, was brought out to act as contractor: his name appears on contract drawings known to have existed in Portugal up to the Second World War.[22] Whether Knowles went there again is doubtful, but the design seems to have been worked out more fully in or soon after 1859 in the wake of his design for the Grosvenor Hotel. Already in the 1858 drawings appeared the window tracery and the eyelid insertions Knowles was then experimenting with, topped off by cupolas of a bandstand orientalism that may reflect the pages of illustrated periodicals during this time of awakened interest in India and, among architects, the books of James Fergusson, the first Victorian writer to take oriental architecture seriously. Also, for a London architect, just down at Brighton was the stone latticework John Nash had added to the Pavilion, filling the heads of arches and casting patterned shadows on the walls behind. For Monserrate was to become in the 1860s a Brighton Pavilion-once-removed, imbued with an English watering-place romanticism in partial translation. At first Knowles did not quite let himself go, for the 1858 drawings proposed wall-facings in brickwork of all too stolid Englishness, instead of the rough-textured pinkish-tawny cement with off-white stone dressings as built. Meanwhile, little happened at the site between 1858 and 1863 except legal delays. Cook may have been willing to wait for the Grosvenor Hotel, also conceived in 1858, to be delivered. Distress in the Lancashire cotton mills early in the American Civil War, and readjustments of trade in India after the Mutiny, may have affected the turnover

---

[21] As I have never been to Sintra, my descriptions are based on material shown me in 1965 by the late Sir Francis F. M. Cook, Bart., at his house on Jersey: the two Knowles drawings, seven photographs c. 1870 (n. 25 below), albums of sumptuous Edwardian photographs, Victorian watercolour views by William Stockdale who went out to take charge of the gardens, as well as much family information and kindly assistance in working out the plan of the house.

[22] Information by letter from Dr. França (n. 20) who was most helpful, he thinks Cook's purchase was not completed until 1863.

of cotton goods at the Cook warehouse. By 1862, Knowles had other solid commissions on his hands and probably did not go to Portugal to launch construction there. But the working drawings for Cintra—vast numbers there must have been—will have been made as soon as those for the Grosvenor were done, while the Grosvenor style was still fresh.

There is nothing small about this villa, the dimensions inherited from 1791 running about 250 by 70 feet along an eminence overlooking the countryside. Excavations were made for a basement kitchen, lighted by skylights in the front terrace ('tons of light', says its last private owner). Knowles gave the central and east pavilions a second upper storey with windows in the bracketed frieze, inserted in the west pavilion an interior dome for a circular music room there, and for arcaded corridors between the pavilions provided the series of skylit compartments he had been unable to realize, so long before, for Egremont Castle. From the east entrance one looked along a procession of arches, toplighted and flanked by niches, to a fountain—splashing out the southern sound of dripping water—in the centre of the main octagon, and on through another forest of arches, as of a rococo Cordoba, to the traceried end-window of the music room, eighty yards away —the very apotheosis of a picturesque indoor vista as recommended by Loudon in the 1830s. The relentless profusion of intricate carved detail inside and out, with the use of much local red, white, and tawny stone, suggest the wealth of local employment afforded by Francis Cook's house and explain the two years the contractor needed to complete it. Above the tawny skin added to the old walls are red-tiled roofs and three coppery green, mushroom-shaped, leaf-capped lantern cupolas, while the chimneys are Victorian-Mughal microcosms that Loudon might have liked. And lighting the garrets are little dormers of a type then to be found on Hardwick's railway hotel at Paddington.

Indoors the main staircase, with a broad handrail of dark-red marble, had a white marble balustrade carved in an openwork pattern of giant vine leaves, ending in a newel scroll like Chinese carving-within-carving—a more expensive version of the once ivy-clad original balustrade, in Portland cement, at the Grosvenor Hotel. 'Having marble at his command . . . the southern architect was able to carve the intermediate spaces with exquisite leafage', as Ruskin put it in *The Seven Lamps*. The internal dome of the music room may reflect Fergusson's remarks in his *Handbook of Architecture* of 1855 on the Portuguese dome intended at Batalha, as well as Sidney Smirke's Reading Room dome of 1857 realized at the British Museum. Below, walls faced with blank arcading and 'eyelids' of relief ornament filling the pointed arch-heads, and spandrels containing medallions with busts, half recall the round nave of the Temple Church in London, under much-discussed restoration in the 1840s. At the other end of the house in the entrance lobby, a picturesque ambiguity of overlapping wall-planes and receding traceries shows the sleight-of-hand of which Knowles was sometimes capable (egged on, no doubt, by his son) when there was plenty of time and money and a sympathetic client. Carved stiff-leaf capitals are as English as can be, perhaps inspired by O'Shea's carvings in the Oxford Museum, alongside flat conventionalized Owen Jones Alhambra capitals, and walls with glazed skirting-tiles that are perfectly Portuguese. The wondrous interlaced mixture attained in the twin corridors was described in 1869 by a poetical English neighbour, after exhausting more fulsome adjectives, as 'Knowlesian': no one outside the family had a hand in the final design here. Yet some actual work from India was also incorporated: the upper balcony parapet surrounding the central octagon is made of pierced-marble panels said to have come from Delhi—pieces of Indian palaces have floated westward with the spoils of empire for years. These panels may have reached Cintra via England and, with the writings of Fergusson and old engravings of drawings by the Daniells, helped to inspire Knowles with visions of the pavilions of Shah Akbar and Shah Jehan. But not unalloyed visions. In this octagonal hall, rising the full height of the house, light filters in through triple-arcaded windows in the dome's octagonal drum: it would be amusing to think that engravings, which Knowles doubtless knew, of Wyatt's Fonthill octagon for Beckford in Wiltshire contributed to this re-creation of Beckford's villa. Beckford, doing the sights in Portugal, had been much taken with the long corridor vistas seen from such vantage points.[23]

---

[23] On inlaid marbles from Agra for sale at East India Docks, *ILN*, 28 Oct. 1843, p. 288; on pieces thereof donated to RIBA, Notes of Meetings, 20 Apr. 1846; Fergusson, *Handbook of Architecture* (1855), p. 447 on 'the spoiling hand of the English', and p. 835 on Batalha. The polygonal hall or tribune rising the full height of the house and surrounded by 12 arches, had been used by Dance at Cole Orton, Soane at Tyringham, and Holland at Benham and Carlton House (D.

For Monserrate's Victorian incarnation there was little of the ransacking of rich local sources of Manueline ornament around Lisbon that one might expect: it is just possible that Knowles never left England at all, bodily anyway, and that a local surveyor measured the ruins for him. But the Cook family legend that Knowles was taken out there need not be discounted, for he undoubtedly would have gone equipped with his own brand of Victorian imperviousness. (And the most noticeable 'Victorian' building erected by the Portuguese at Cintra, the Palacio de Pena on its crag, is a sort of Balmoral, not especially Manueline either.) At any rate, a recent historian of Portuguese taste finds Monserrate Anglo–Indian—another way of saying that it was a Brighton Pavilion-once-removed (and he slips in a pert local saying that Cintra was the Brighton of Portuguese gentlemen).[24] There was, indeed, an Indo–Portuguese tradition that a merchant in the textiles trade might be expected to appreciate. Of Cook's predecessors, Devisme's money had come from Anglo–Portuguese trade, Beckford's from West Indies trade (without measuring the wilder shores of his imagination). No purely local form was likely to come of placing a ruin with such a background in the hands of an architect like Knowles, out to 'catch the spirit' of an exotic semitropical villa and, as always when he essayed the picturesque, remorselessly regularizing it. The evoking of the spirit of Byron and Beckford was finally done in the office at Gray's Inn. To anticipate with a comparison to his son's career, Monserrate was in a sense the elder Knowles's Aldworth. No subsequent description quite comes up to that first eulogy of 1870:[25]

> Moorish chiefly its design,/. . . it doth well combine
> With the stately Gothic's flight/Of lofty decoration. . . .
> Yet another order, bright/ With fancy's pure mysterious light,
> Sparkleth throughout our chosen fane,/Order all original,

Stroud, *George Dance*, 1971, p. 198), and cf. Beckford, *Italy . . . and Portugal* (1834 edn.), ii. 141, on corridor views in Convent at Mafra.

[24] França (1966), i. 373, ii. 406, n. 400.

[25] *Fairylife and Fairyland, A Lyric Poem Communicated by Titania through . . . Thomas . . . the Rhymer* (London 1870, published by Lionel Booth, 307 Regent Street), long poem on Cintra apparently by an English resident inspired by Byron's 'fairy dwelling' line; on Monserrate, pp. 196 ff., esp. pp. 202–7. Special edition of 25 copies of which present baronet has No. 1 is in larger format with more photographs (interesting for their date) than copy at BL.

Mingling there. . . ./ 'Knowlesian architecture'—all
From that gifted mind unfolded,/Mind by thought and fancy
   moulded. . . .
Calling from dark nonentity/Things which be not—and they be!

Even Knowles in his starchy self-esteem must have smiled. As for
his sympathetic client, Cook's enthusiasm in restoring the house
and forming its famous gardens, his acquisition of much land
hereabouts and benevolence to the local poor, rescuing the
prosperity of a countryside in decay, led the King of Portugal to
make him Viscount Monserrate in 1864. An English baronetcy
for benefactions in London was to be conferred in 1886. [26]

Anti-Victorians of the early twentieth century looked askance
at Monserrate; Rose Macaulay in 1946 thought it barbarous.[27]
What if it does lack a certain Sitwellian elegance? It is a Mid-
Victorian folly—if anything so large and so comfortable can be
a folly—perfectly adapted to its milieu (Pl. 8). Now it belongs to
the Portuguese government and its gardens are open to the public.
Although emptied of family treasures and family life, a bygone
by-product of empire and trade and the long Continental holiday
in one's own house, they say it still sparkles.

THE END OF A STYLE

> 'Never before were there so many new buildings
> erected in the same period . . . of so expensive a
> description. . . . The period of which we are in the
> midst, will leave for centuries its mark on the land.'
> *CBA for 1868* (1869), p. 214

The Grosvenor Style petered out in the mid-1860s, although the
elder Knowles continued to be called upon for large works until
the end of the decade. Possibly his last commercial work was a
building completed in 1863 at Elephant and Castle, the busiest
traffic junction in South London, on the Newington Causeway
side where the Department of Health and Social Security now
stands: this was a big multi-storey shop for the retail draper

---

[26] In the 1880s Cook married as his second wife the extraordinary American,
Tennessee Claflin, sister of (the even more so) Victoria Woodhull. Lady Cook's
receptions in the 1890s to preach family planning blocked Richmond Hill with
carriages.
[27] Rose Macaulay: 'barbarous orientalism . . . constructed in a Moorish
delirium' (*They Went to Portugal*, 1946, p. 137).

William Tarn. (The younger Tarns and the elder Knowleses were neighbours in Clapham Park.) Although it was intended to surpass anything in the West End 'in magnificence and capacity', available views show little that was bold except a central window 'composed of a single sheet of glass no less than 16 feet high' surmounted by a pair of recumbent figures representing Commerce and Manufacture, worked up (by Daymond, no doubt) from Paris models on the New Louvre. Otherwise the outside was busy with all-over low-key ornament. not at all bold—genteel, rather, and in general effect dignified second-rate Second Empire. Which, with up-to-date technical equipment inside, was doubtless what Tarn wanted. Occupied from 1900 by the drapery establishment of Isaac Walton, the building was bombed in the last war.[28]

Meanwhile, returning to the domestic practice in which he had first made his reputation, Knowles during 1862–7 was altering and enlarging a Georgian villa in open country south of Tooting Common, in Streatham parish a short drive from Friday Grove. The client was Philip William Flower, an Australian merchant in his 50s with a large family, a large fortune, and a new wife; he was to be young Knowles's client in Westminster and Battersea. Furzedown—still standing as a teachers' college—had been built around 1800 on the brow of a slope commanding a southward view over Mitcham Common and the valley of the Wandle toward the North Downs. Much of Knowles's work there was in keeping with the existing villa, but he also designed a stately conservatory, not glass-walled but glass-windowed, an 1862 Exhibition sort of conservatory rather than a Crystal Palace one. The only truly 'Knowlesian' bit at Furzedown is a little one-storey gate lodge north of the house beside the former entrance drive, near Tooting Common. Here on a small scale a deep, curving frieze or cove is clothed with plaster leaves in relief, partly bijou offshoots from the Grosvenor frieze, partly copying (to the extent of curving the decorated surface) a lodge of Nesfield's at Kew that was an opening gun for the impending Queen Anne Revival. Little balustrades resembling the tiny spindle gallery surrounding an autioneer's rostrum, and simulated

[28] William Tarn of Brixton Hill, 1860, William Tarn Jr. of Elmwood, Clapham Park, 1868 (*CG*). On the new building, *CG*, Nov. 1863, p. 8. Views, Southwark Reference Library, Walworth Road.

extra chimneys of brick-and-a-half verticals symmetrically disposed, like a model-maker's reductions, are amusing evidence of
Knowles's way with a small building. As a disciple of Loudon he
knew all about The Picturesque, but nothing of 'Queen Anne'
playfulness.[29]
    The Grosvenor Style had its last innings during 1865–8 at
Hedsor (Pl. 13), a country house standing on high ground above
a beautiful reach of the Thames opposite Cookham and upriver
from Cliveden, in the Chiltern Hundreds of Buckinghamshire.
George Ives Irby, fourth Baron Boston, after marrying a new
wife in his 60th year, decided to demolish his eighteenth-century
house, by then regarded as hideous, and to have a new one by
Knowles. Possibly, like Knowles's earliest commissions, this one
came through the country-house network of naval acquaintances,
either through the Irby family or the Saumarez family of the
new Lady Boston, yet Knowles by now was well known anyway
as a safe man for symmetrical well-drained work on a large scale.
Hedsor's four-square plan with pavilion roofs suggests fashionable
French *château* models, though Knowles may have thought to
condense the ground plan of Mentmore in the same county
or that of Bylaugh Hall in Norfolk, both recommended in Robert
Kerr's *The Gentleman's House* of 1864 as good model 'classical'
plans for country houses. And crowning the corner pavilions with
Grosvenor Hotel roofs was doubtless regarded by both client and
architect as the *dernier cri* in English design. Window openings
were given 'eyelid' insertions, not with the vigour and variety of
the Grosvenor ornament but a 'refeened' lacework tracery:
Knowles was reverting to the scale of Barry's ornament; perhaps,
if it had not been for young Knowles, he would never have left it.
Other exterior embellishments included coats of arms carved in
stone but no friezes. The finely executed white-Suffolk brickwork
of the walls presents a surface almost like masonry—a meticulous-
ness of bricklaying among London craftsmen that was post-Main
Drainage.[30]

[29] Furzedown was sold in 1811 by Henry Baring (*Morning Chronicle*, 3 July
1811, cutting kindly shown to me by Miss Eddowes of the history dept. there).
Flower's account book (Park Town papers as chap. 5, n. 32 below), ff. 31–3, and
a contemporary photograph of the conservatory in a family scrapbook were both
kindly shown to me by Col. P. H. Flower.
[30] Hedsor: information from MS. family history (*c.* 1899) quoted to me by
eighth Baron in letter April 1967, and from John Harris, biographer of Chambers

Despite subsequent failures in the interior finishing, whether attributable to contractor or decorator, Knowles seems to have been proud of the house, preserving a photograph taken shortly after it was built. It was, after all, neighbour to Barry's Cliveden. In the 1880s, when the sixth Lord Boston was Lord-in-Waiting at Court, Queen Victoria came from Cliveden to call. Hedsor's Victorian decoration was wiped out in the 1920s, and during the Second World War the house was occupied by U.S. Strategic Air Command; more recently it has sheltered a computer company. Knowles's client the fourth Baron died in 1869, survived until 1927 by his widow; her sister who married his elder son the fifth Baron (d. 1877) survived until 1929. And outwardly Hedsor is a well-preserved dowager of a house.

Knowles was busy in his last years of practice, for there were also these solid works going on: the continuing of Broomfield at Stanmore Hill, on the London–Watford road, as (then) a rather plain mansion entered through a conservatory leading to an inner hall with a glass dome; alterations at Roydon Hall in Kent, probably by him, filling in a courtyard and interfering with Tudor brickwork on the north front, for Edwin Cook; probably (according to Knowles family hearsay) additions to the seventeenth- and eighteenth-century Walton Grove at Walton-on-Thames for a Paul Cababe, including a new top storey and balcony ironwork incorporating the initials P.C. and the Lion of Judah bearing the Star of David; and other possibilities, including perhaps Nos. 14–25 Oakley Street in Chelsea, a stuccoed terrace of *c.* 1862 with medallioned busts, bearded-head keystones, and vaguely Islamic ornament (Strickland the timid speculator of Kensington Palace Gardens lived opposite the site in the late 1850s); perhaps the dignified plain stone building with great keystone heads at No. 119 Cannon Street (now a library), built about 1866 for the wholesale grocers Joseph Travers & Sons, for part of that family lived in Clapham Park. The network of connections wore very well. Knowles senior seems to have ended

who designed the first house; photograph kept in Knowles family (via Mr. Eric Smith); also Burke and *Complete Peerage*, and information from Mr. Brian Maskell. Influence of brickwork, new Outfall Sewer 'laid with a degree of care and finish that a few years ago would have been thought unnecessary on the exterior of a mansion', *CBA for 1863* (1862), pp. 238–9.

active practice in 1869; at least, the lease of the northern (chillier) half of the first floor at No. 1 Raymond Buildings, which he had kept up since 1836, was terminated then. The other lease on No. 1 South was kept on until young Knowles moved to Albert Mansions in 1872.[31]

There was still one suitable last work for the elder man, undertaken for his old client George Moore the textile millionaire, a public fountain for Wigton market-place in Cumberland, erected 1872–3 as a memorial to the first Mrs. Moore (d. 1858), with four bronze reliefs by Thomas Woolner. Woolner had already been dining at the younger Knowles's house with Tennyson, and was to ennoble the elder Knowles in marble in 1873. In the 1850s Moore, the one-time draper's apprentice at Wigton, having married the daughter of his first London employer, a Cumberland man, and established himself so richly in London, bought Whitehall near Wigton as a country estate. (Here the architect Salvin was brought in to enlarge the house only a few years after Knowles's mansion for Moore in Kensington was finished, because, it has been said, Salvin was socially so desirable to employ, yet during the period in question, 1858–61, Knowles undoubtedly had his hands full.) The fountain being intended to honour Mrs. Moore's bounty to the poor, Woolner's plaques set in Knowles's granite pedestal celebrated her acts of mercy in generalized classical terms. On top Knowles put an elongated pyramid or squat obelisk faced by flat panels of foliage —perhaps he remembered the Maseres tomb placed in Reigate churchyard when he was 19, its stubby truncated obelisk faced with panels of leaves in flat relief. He crowned the Wigton monument with a bulbous finial sprouting a cross; below, his classically moulded pedestal sits oddly under most unclassical little pediments stuffed with naturalistic leaves mantling busts in roundels; in the end, his mixture did not fuse, and the calm beauty

[31] Broomfield: sale catalogue 1869, BL Maps Middlesex 137.a.11(7), better mapped in Bentley Priory catalogue, same lot (ref. from Sandra Milliken). Roydon Hall, n. 19 above. Walton Grove: VCH *Surrey* III (1910), 469, information from local historian Mr. Greenwood, and family lore. Attributions of Oakley Street terrace (dated by rate books, Chelsea Reference Library) and Travers building are guesswork. Elliott Terrace on Plymouth Hoe was apparently imitation-Knowles by local builder-and-developer John Pethick's tame architect Alfred Norman: letter from Plymouth City Librarian. On possible house for Alfred Jones, chap. 5, n. 15 below. On Gray's Inn leases, chap. 2, n. 37.

of Woolner's work is the praiseworthy part of this memorial.[32]
  The Grosvenor Style was paid the compliment of a bit of
imitation abroad, little recognized as such, in the form of squashed
versions of the Grosvenor–Hedsor domes on the Indianapolis
State Capitol in the 1880s. Be that as it may. Meanwhile, a
Building News leader in April 1875 on Darwinism in Architecture
or the survival of styles, referring to the mixers of styles named
the Barrys and Knowles as 'some of our best architects', a surprising accolade in a journal already publishing the work of
Norman Shaw. But when Knowles died nine years later, such
was the progress of fashion, there was no such accolade. And
when in the 1890s Professor Kerr used the term 'vernacular
European' of the hybrid-*palazzo* men, long after Butterfield and
Webb had rediscovered the English vernacular, Kerr in his old
age was talking of a generation in its prime when he was young.[33]
'Vernacular' can be one of those words that means just what one
chooses it to mean.

[32] Wigton's historian Mr. T. W. Carrick kindly sent me a photograph and
description of the fountain. Woolner's panel (at RA 1872, no. 1468) illus. in
Pevsner, *Cumberland and Westmorland* (1967), pl. 66. On George Moore, chap. 2,
n. 47 above. Woolner bust of Knowles Sr., chap. 7, n. 26.
  [33] Robert Kerr's edn. of Fergusson's *Modern Architecture* (1891) on the Battle of
the Styles. *BN* leader, 2 Apr. 1875. On Knowles Sr.'s last years, pp. 296–8, below.

II

JAMES KNOWLES AFTER 1860

Pencil sketch by Tennyson, drawn for Beatrice Knowles, aged 6, on 28 October 1872 at The Hollies, Clapham Common (Knowles papers, TRC).

5

King Arthur and Bread & Cheese

'Godliness is the security of England . . . yet how
many there are who set up an idol in their hearts.
Sometimes it is Gold, sometimes Honour, and sometimes men deify Reason. Perhaps the last is the most
dangerous of the three.' Suburban sermon, preached
at St. Stephen's, Clapham Park, 20 June 1869

YOUNG KNOWLES'S WORKING LIFE in the 1860s was'
on the surface, mainly architectural and fairly successful.
Designs for three housing estates, four churches, a
clubhouse, a bank, a large block of flats, and finally a renowned
private house, probably with other designs built or unbuilt,
occupied him during those years. In those years also he published
a book of Arthurian legends, sought out the friendship of
Tennyson and Dean Stanley, was elected to the Reform Club,
collected works of art in a modest way, contributed anonymously
to periodicals, and eventually founded almost single-handed a
distinguished debating society. As we shall hear, after less than
three years of marriage Jane Knowles died, and a year and a half
later he remarried. By the spring of 1870, in his 39th year and
about to take on the *Contemporary Review*, he was to know more
of life than the young man who wondered, in the spring of 1860,
if he were muddling it away. The quarter-century of his architectural practice was to contain increasing non-architectural
activity, until the success of a new profession allowed the gradual
dropping of the first. Nearness to intellectual life was a necessity
to him, but the paths of the shapers of an expanding London in
the 1860s did not lie among thinkers. There, once the possibilities
in a piece of land were seen and a design made, doing was all,
there were no ideas to express, the conversation was not very good.

For a man with a sense of theatre, most of the architectural commissions available to him lacked drama. All of Knowles's working life, until his death at 76, was to be conducted with strenuous nervous energy in waves of intensity, from which art and friendship were some respite, and with brief plunges into exhaustion, but usually buoyed up by a sense of mission, of causes to be organized, minds consulted, influences engineered. Once the layout and drawings for his first successful commission in 1860 were done, it cannot have been burdensome. Nelson Terrace, where he and Jane went to live, was not far from the Cedars ground, convenient for taking sardonic note of the builder's slow progress and certifying his right to his leases. Until another client materialized late in 1861, Knowles presumably continued to help his father with site supervision at the Grosvenor and with the Monserrate working-drawings. In general in London then, the fabric of daily life was assailed by ugliness and clamour: between the two green havens of Clapham Common and Gray's Inn, miles of streets shook and clanged with ever-thickening traffic and with vast burrowing for the new Underground Railway, the new sewers, and a new railway invasion. Especially during the Exhibition year of 1862, foreign visitors complained of the *tumulte formidable* of central London's crowded streets.[1] Perhaps an accelerating enthusiasm for Arthurian romance in widening circles of book-readers should be seen against those passages of discomfort in Londoners' daily lives.

LITERARY INTERLUDE: MALORY MODERNIZED

> 'Puseyites and Pre-Raffaelites . . . have a holy horror
> of the practical turn of this epoch of the march of
> intellect . . . the Mort Arthur is a Norman romance
> . . . it cannot be considered a subject so acclimated as
> to be popularly accepted, but as exotic even among
> scholars.' *Building News*, 'Oxford and Wall Painting',
> 1 January 1858

Early in 1861, reassured by married life and still unbesieged by clients, Knowles started the Arthurian book he had talked of to Hewlett the year before. When Tennyson's first *Idylls of the King*

---

[1] H.-A. Esquiros in *Revue des Deux Mondes*, 1 Oct. 1862, quoted by Charles Knight, 'London in 1862', *CBA for 1863* (1862), p. 6.

were published in 1859, Knowles's quick mind noted among the enthusiastic reviews some ignorance about the subject-matter. By 1866, however, Du Maurier's 'Camelot' series in *Punch*, for example, presupposed the wider popular acquaintance to which Knowles contributed. He found in Southey's introduction to the 1817 edition of Caxton's Malory the precise incitement he needed: 'were it modernised and published as a book for boys it could hardly fail of regaining its popularity.'[2] Knowles's preface to the first edition of *The Story of King Arthur and His Knights of the Round Table*,[3] began thus:

The story of King Arthur will never die while there are English men to study and English boys to devour its tales of adventure and daring and magic and conquest.

King Arthur was to our forefathers what and more than what 'Robinson Crusoe' and 'The Arabian Nights' are to the present generation . . . [but,] since the days of cheap books, it has never been modernised or adapted for general circulation. . . .

The author of the following compilation has done little but abridge and simplify Sir Thomas Mallory's Collection of the Legends as printed by Caxton—adding from Geoffrey of Monmouth and other sources where it was desirable, and arranging the many tales into a somewhat clearer and more consecutive story than appears heretofore to have been formed from them. He has modernised the style only so much as seemed indispensable. . . .

He has endeavoured, nevertheless, at however great a distance, to follow the rule laid down in the 'Idylls of the King'; and has suppressed and modified where changed manners and morals have made it absolutely necessary to do so for the preservation of a lofty original ideal.

That is, Lamb's Tales with a tinge of Dr. Bowdler—although Guinevere's guilt is not ignored. He was surprisingly successful: the book remained in print until about 1970. His way with the

[2] As quoted in Knowles's preface 1861. On 'some ignorance as well as distaste for Arthurian story . . . outside the circle of scholars and of Pre-Raphaelite poets and painters' when the first *Idylls* came out in 1859, Kathleen Tillotson, 'Tennyson's Serial Poem', *Mid-Victorian Studies* (1965), p. 94.

[3] BL has: first edn. of 1862 (but with BM date-stamp 26 Dec. 1861, and reviewed in *ILN*, 30 Nov. 1861, p. 561), published by Griffith and Farran with 15 chapters; third edn. of 1868 (see chap. 6 below) published by Strahan with 12 chapters retitled *The Legends* . . .; and ninth edn. of 1912 (which says eighth edn. of 1896 was first in author's full name) published by Warne with 14 chapters. Warne kept it in print, illustrated by Lancelot Speed and with original dedication page, until *c.* 1970.

ancient manner was just right. This is how it begins, no beating
about the 'once upon a time' bush: 'King Vortigern the usurper
sat upon his throne in London, when, suddenly, upon a certain
day, ran a breathless messenger, and cried aloud . . .' And the
book ends:

> With that the barge put from the land, and when Sir Bedivere saw it
> departing, he cried with a bitter cry, 'Alas! my lord King Arthur,
> what shall become of me now that ye have gone from me?'
>   'Comfort ye', said King Arthur, 'and be strong, for I may no more
> help ye. I go to the Vale of Avilion to heal me of my grievous wound,
> and if ye see me no more, pray for my soul.'
>   Then the three queens kneeled down around the king and sorely
> wept and wailed, and the barge went forth to sea, and departed slowly
> out of Sir Bedivere's sight.

A nearer rendering of Malory (by Thomas Wright) then recently
published[4] shows how much Knowles did with it:

> And so they rowed from the land, and Sir Bedivere beheld al those
> ladies goe from him; then Sir Bedivere cried, 'Ah! my lord Arthur,
> what shall become of mee now ye goe from me, and leave me here
> alone among mine enemies?' 'Comfort thy selfe,' said King Arthur,
> 'and do as well as thou maiest, for in me is no trust for to trust in; for
> I wil into the vale of Avilion for to heale me of my grievous wound;
> and if thou never heere more of me, pray for my soule.' But evermore
> the queens and the ladies wept and shriked that it was pittie for to
> heare them. And as soone as Sir Bedivere had lost the sight, hee wept
> and wailed.

Perhaps we can say that the latter rendering comes closer to the
antiquarian Arthurian style that Morris and Burne-Jones were
attempting to realize on the walls of the Oxford Union; the
former to the 'modernism' of Dyce's Arthurian frescoes on the
walls of the Robing Room at Westminster. As for Tennyson's
incantatory rendering in his early 'Morte d'Arthur'—'And
slowly answered Arthur from the barge: "The old order changeth,
yielding place to new"'—Knowles will have known it by heart.
But he was not one to let it blind him. Revering the 'divine

---

[4] Thomas Wright, *The History of King Arthur . . . compiled by Sir Thomas
Malory* (1858). Knowles's, as his preface said, was mainly but not entirely out of
Malory; e.g. Wright did not use Knowles's opening episode with King
Vortigern.

Alfred' as much as ever, he decided to be daring: he would ask if he might dedicate the book to Tennyson.[5]

1 Raymond Buildings
Grays Inn
August 13th 1861

Sir

I venture with very great respect to lay before you the accompanying proof sheets of part of a book about to be published as 'the Story of King Arthur and his Knights'—and which I have the strongest desire to be permitted to dedicate to yourself.

It would not become me—either as a stranger or in any way—to try and further my request by any other reason than the subject of the book.

I may only say besides—that if on looking through these sheets you can consider them at all sufficient to aim at becoming a popular re-introduction to the Arthur legends—an 'Argument' as it were for the great unlettered public to 'the Idylls of the King'—and if looked at in such a light you can think the book worthy to be offered and received as a tribute of the sincerest and warmest respect to your name—I shall feel that I have indulged a right impulse of homage in making my request and justified in taking a step which you Sir—(even if refusing me) will be too generous to think impertinent or vulgar.

The book has been written for Mr Bosworth the publisher of Regent Street—and will be anonymous—both as a first work—and because, being fully occupied in another profession, I am not anxious to appear publicly as a writer.

The publisher anticipates a considerable sale in Australia and America. I trouble you with these details in case you should give me leave to dedicate my book to you—and heartily hoping that it may be so I am Sir,

Your most obedient Ser^t
James Knowles Jr.

Already English publishers—even, it seems, Thomas Bosworth, Knowles's scholarly friend from debating-society days—were seeking a market in 'the great unlettered public' of Australia and America. Knowles's 'argument' introduced many more of Malory's tales than Tennyson himself had so far made use of. And so it was as a published expert on Malory that Knowles was later able to urge the poet to go further.

[5] Knowles to Tennyson, 13 Aug. 1861 (TRC), and draft in Knowles's papers (now TRC).

Meanwhile, in August and September 1861, the Tennysons were travelling in France and the Pyrenees; Knowles had to wait until October for a reply from Farringford. This was favourable (only the envelope remains, and the letter has not returned to the fold).[6] A dedication page was accordingly inserted: 'To Alfred Tennyson, D.C.L. Poet Laureate this attempt at a popular version of the Arthur legends is by his permission dedicated as a tribute of the sincerest and warmest respect'. A bound copy was ready to send to Tennyson on 7 November, with the following letter:[7]

Sir

I waited before acknowledging and sincerely thanking you for your letter accepting the dedication of my 'King Arthur' till I could send you a copy of the book.

This I do by today's Book post—and shall be most anxious to know your judgment on it—if you think it at all worth your criticism.

I greatly regret that at the last moment before publication the book should have been sold by Mr Bosworth—it was done against my wish —and without my knowledge.

I also much regret the childish prints which have been bound with it, and have ordered a copy bound without them to be forwarded to yourself. I aimed at compiling a book which grown up readers might consult as a fair abridgement of the Legends—while children yet might read it for the mild stories only.

They were none of my desiring or approving and I have constantly requested an issue of some copies purged of them. Mr Bosworth tells me in reply that he has sold only the first edition of the work—and that if others should be wanted my wishes may be gratified.

Again assuring you Sir of my great & lively satisfaction in having been allowed to dedicate my book to you,

I have the honor to be
your obed[t] Ser[t]
James T. Knowles Jr.

Bosworth at the last minute, perhaps unsure whether the book was in his own publishing line, off-loaded the first edition on to Griffith & Farran of St. Paul's Churchyard, who specialized in children's books. In fifteen chapters 'compiled and arranged by J.T.K.' and bound in gilt-stamped blue cloth, this edition was

---

[6] Professor Lang, when preparing Tennyson's letters for publication, had not seen this letter: envelope postmarked Yarmouth and Southampton, 9 Oct. 1861.
[7] From draft 7 Nov. 1861 in Knowles papers, now TRC.

ready for the 1861 Christmas trade although dated 1862. Compated with other black-and-white work of the early 1860s, the illustrations were indeed poor.[8] Knowles had to wait again for an answer from Farringford, for Tennyson was in London seeing his doctor during much of November, but the book was appreciated in his absence by his children: Mrs. Tennyson recorded, then or later, in the family journal that she was reading them 'Mr Knowles's King Arthur Stories in the evening which delight them greatly'. On 10 December the author was addressed at last:[9]

Sir,
    I was from home and ill when your double gift arrived. Accept my thanks now. Your task seems to be admirably done. My boys of 9 and 7 could think of little else but King Arthur and his Knights while reading your book and I doubt not it will be hailed with delight by numbers [of] men no less than boys. My wife sends a petition for a Layamon's Brut from you now, that the old Legends of our Country may all be made familiar among us.

I have the honour to be

Sir

Your obedient servant

A. Tennyson

The Layamon's Brut idea was to be a useful excuse for a meeting five years later. Meanwhile, Knowles wrote his thanks for these thanks from Gray's Inn on 28 December, reporting that the book was said to be selling well and that it had had 'some very complimentary notices in the journals'.[10] In fact, the *Illustrated London News* for 30 November had pronounced it to be 'admirably compiled and arranged' and that it 'would do a great deal' toward perpetuation of the Arthur legend if that were in any danger of 'sinking into oblivion'. The dedication to Tennyson undoubtedly added interest, and still stands in the edition most recently available, which also cites Knowles's recollection in 1896

---

[8] The illustrator G. H. Thomas was somewhat more at home in his own time, judging by a lively if uninspired picture of Rotten Row at the RA that year (*ILN*, 17 May 1862).

[9] Tennyson to Knowles, 10 Dec. 1861, in Knowles papers, now TRC. The Tennyson family journal (TRC) suffered much from family revision.

[10] Knowles to Tennyson, 28 Dec. 1861 (TRC) and draft in Knowles papers, now TRC; the 17-day delay in Knowles's reply probably due to proper funereal delicacy after Prince Consort's death on the 14th.

that Tennyson had declared—perhaps in the lost letter of October 1861—that 'it ought to go through forty editions'.[11]

At the end of 1861 Tennyson was composing his own dedicatory lines for a new edition of his first four *Idylls* in memory of the Prince Consort, who had died just before Christmas. In January a copy of Knowles's book was ordered from Bosworth (as bookseller) to be sent to Buckingham Palace for young Prince Arthur to give to his younger brother Prince Leopold at Cannes: 'your book is appreciated in some good quarters', wrote Bosworth to Knowles, enclosing as a memento the black-bordered note from the equerry at Osborne.[12] A paperback edition retitled *The Legends of King Arthur and His Knights* was to be published in 1868 by Alexander Strahan—the forerunner of an uneasy partnership.

THE JONES, WOODGATE, AND FLOWER DEVELOPMENTS

> 'It is to be doubted whether there is a successful
> tradesman amongst us who does not look forward to
> purchasing a freehold. . . . [Owing to] this English
> fondness for the acquisition of the soil of our country
> . . . there is always going on amongst us [this] process
> of transmutation of real property.' *Illustrated London
> News*, 22 February 1862, on 'The Title and Transfer
> of Land'
>
> 'Safe as houses' (saying)

During those first experiences with publishers, Knowles was busy with a more down-to-earth breed of speculator. Within less than two years, through neighbourhood acquaintance in South London and Gray's Inn, he became architect to three London developers. There was Alexander Jones, ground landlord and shadowy figure behind the contractor who built the Cedars estate on the north rim of Clapham Common: a solid, undisastrous development completed within ten years and inhabited for almost a century by solid and, for the most part, undisastrous people. Next there was William Woodgate, neither solid nor undisastrous, for whom Knowles designed buildings in St. James's

---

[11] Quoted by Knowles in a letter to an unknown correspondent in July 1896, quoted by his widow in preface to 1912 edn. of Knowles's book.

[12] Major Elphinstone to Bosworth, 15 Jan. 1862, with Bosworth's note to Knowles (Knowles papers, now TRC). Ricks says Tennyson's dedication was written about Christmas time.

Street, Westminster, and Lower Sydenham, South London—a connection that can be said to have flourished only during 1861-3. A more considerable client than these was the Australia merchant Philip Flower, developer of part of the new Victoria Street, Westminster, and part of Queen's Road, Battersea, as the Park Town estate. Knowles's connection in Battersea was to continue until surprisingly late in his career. In the 1860s also he designed four churches. There is biographical value in understanding these contributions to London's expanding web, for his heart was in them at first—or as much of it as he could spare for the then intensely conscientious practice of his profession.[13]

The Cedars property, a long, narrow piece of some seventeen acres less than a mile south of the Thames, extended downhill from Clapham Common to what is now Wandsworth Road continued as Lavender Hill, the old turnpike to Kingston. Beyond it, the meadows of a great dairy farm still in the early 1860s lay between the upper ground of Clapham and the riverside Battersea Fields area where the new Chelsea Bridge and the new Battersea Park were opened in 1858. Until 1860 The Cedars consisted of one Early Georgian mansion in its gardens facing the Common, with a quarter-mile or so of grass sloping down behind it. This and other Georgian tycoons' estates east of it were said to have been carved out of the Hewer estate where Samuel Pepys had spent his last years. By the early nineteenth century an irregular row of comfortable houses ranged along the north side of the Common included The Hollies, which we shall meet again, and The Elms, or Elm House, by 1853 occupied by Sir Charles Barry. About 1853 the Barry family developed a new road northward, now Victoria Rise, alongside the east margin of the Cedars property, and proceeded to build houses on speculation there. Except for a lane along the west margin of The Cedars and a private road east of The Elms, the only other way northward from the Common lay considerably farther eastward. Some parish talk in 1853 of acquiring part of the Cedars land for a new burial ground came to nothing, for it was recognized that 'in this parish a considerable increase of houses and population must be expected' and that any open sites were becoming too valuable for such uses 'with the

---

[13] This section summarizes much material setting these developments more thickly into their Victorian context. References to the Cedars estate are in my *Victorian London* (1972), pp. 52-4 and 94-6. On Park Town estate, n. 32 below.

increased demand for building ground in the vicinity of London'. In 1853 a private purchaser acquired the Cedars land which then lay fallow, while its value ripened, until 1860.[14] The new non-resident owner was Alexander Jones, a native of Whitechapel according to the census; in business south of the river by 1830, as a clothing salesman at Newington Butts and then until 1846 as a tailor in the Old Kent Road, he was out of the Post Office directory entirely during 1847–9 (Australia? California?), returning as 'bill broker' in 1850 when he lived in Union Crescent, New Kent Road, moving across to the grander Paragon in 1851, thereafter dropping out of the commercial directories altogether and into the Court Guide for 1852 as 'esquire', a neat example of ascent traceable in the public records. It is just possible, a long guess, that the elder Knowles had been architect to another member of the same Jones family, with connections in the City and in Clapham, so that young Knowles's first commission may have arrived via that grapevine.[15] The speculating contractor who built the Cedars houses and took the first leases was a local builder of some repute who had been active in Clapham Park, Henry Harris—with increasingly active financial support in Cedars Road from his lawyer. The initial agreement between Jones and Harris was reached in March 1860, from which Harris's leases were to be dated. The *Builder* in June, reporting that 'the whole scheme is the property and speculation of Mr Harris' (that is, the risks and the leases were to be his) and that the designs were by young Knowles, rather implied that Harris was Knowles's client.[16] But the standard lease for the estate stipulated that work was to be completed 'to the satisfaction of the surveyor of the lessor' (Jones's surveyor) and that will have been Knowles's position. In conveying the news with his drawing to the press, he was at first less expert in conveying the nuances of leasehold reality than he later perforce became. In 1957 the vendors of most of the surviving Cedars Road houses to the then

[14] For Cedars Road houses acquired in this century by the LCC, original title deeds seen at County Hall, and deed for one of the terrace houses kindly shown to me by Mrs. Cristea, to whom I am obliged for permission to see over the house. On parish projects, *CG*, Feb. 1854, pp. 40–1.

[15] No. 117 Harley Street (formerly 45-A Upper Harley Street) at north-west corner of Devonshire Street with pertinent ornament, occupied from *c.* 1863 by an Alfred Jones, possibly one with City and Clapham connections noted in directories. But the Jones–Knowles link may have been Harris.

[16] *Bldr*, 16 June 1860, p. 380.

London County Council were still trustees of the Alexander Jones estate. If this seems a lowly start for the decade that was to end with Aldworth, there was nothing lowly about Knowles's designs, vigorous applications of the Grosvenor style to a twin set of terrace houses of dramatic size facing the Common and to two rows of solid detached villas (scaled down two years and eleven villas later) along the new road behind. All were faced with the pale Suffolk brick, dressed with cement, that his father favoured. By 1862 young Knowles's High Victorian roofs at the Common will have been visible from Chelsea Bridge—where by turning one's head one could then also see the newly risen roofs of the Grosvenor Hotel—although the way between Common and Bridge was yet to be made.

The twin terraces, now Nos. 43–52 Clapham Common North Side, are still the largest and most spirited examples south of the river of a type of grandiose Victorian row-housing then spreading through Belgravia, Pimlico, and around Hyde Park. Knowles seems to have seized upon the twenty-year-old image of Lewis Cubitt's terrace of five houses at the foot of Lowndes Square, pumped up their scale and applied his new window tracery, and steep French roofs on the end-houses. The vigorous window-tracery (Pl. 7), suggesting what the Grosvenor's was once like, looks in close-up more rubbery than Ruskinian, but is still effective from inside when unobscured by curtains. By so marking the entrance to a road that might 'become at no distant date [part of] the channel of direct communication, by means of Chelsea Suspension-bridge, between Pimlico, Belgravia, and Kensington on the one side, and Battersea-park, Clapham, Wandsworth, Tooting, Brixton, on the other side of the Thames', as he told the *Builder*, Knowles was adapting the gateway effect of Thomas Cubitt's great pair of houses of the 1840s at Albert Gate, sometimes compared with Gibraltar and the Pillars of Hercules. As usual in a large Knowles private house, plumbing was plentiful, with either a bathroom or a water closet on each landing, so that slops were no longer to be carried down the long flights of stairs. But coals were still to be taken up and ashes down: indeed, between basement and garret, the end-houses had seven storeys for servants to traverse. (Knowles like many other architects never chose to live in such mountainous houses himself; in fact, apart from his father's Friday Grove—in many respects

Late Georgian in character—he never lived in a Victorian-designed house in his life: a Victorian comment upon the ideal London house.)

Some of the Cedars terrace houses still have original interior fixtures: the iron stair-balustrade of bars that become ivy-stems, with junctions concealed by square ornaments with rosettes (as advocated by William Burges when contemplating medieval grille-work at Westminster Abbey) may or may not have been designed by the architect, for such ironwork may have been obtainable from some up-to-date firm's stock by Jaques the Clapham ironmonger who took several of Harris's building leases in Cedars Road. And the cast-iron double-vine cresting along one garden wall was a popular 'line' around the time of the 1862 Exhibition, for it can be seen here and there all over London. Marble chimney-pieces and gilt-framed chimney glasses, of the sort drawn by Tenniel for Alice entering Looking-glass House, and by Millais for Trollope novels in the *Cornhill* at the time, were conservative, generally available designs.

For the Cedars Road villas behind the terraces, the costliness of window-tracery was avoided by following Gilbert Scott's advice that on 'ordinary private residences' an arched window with 'the tympanum unpierced' was quite enough.[17] The ornament was of the Grosvenor character, with vaguely classical relief panels of oak leaves at window openings, vaguely gothic leaf-corbels on porches, and stiff-leaf storey-courses possibly adapted from leafy mouldings admired at Paestum. Other touches were less individual: quarter-turning classical dentils to make a course of diagonal headers giving a jagged Italian Romanesque look was common by 1860, and brick cross-ornament on chimney-stacks was a trick probably borrowed from the work of Soane. Otherwise, these villas were the familiar Early Victorian suburban three-storey, hip-roofed type with emphatic eaves-cornice all round, long garden behind, and enough space in front for a diminutive carriage-sweep. The houses became less spacious and closer together as Harris proceeded down the hill and after a church was fitted in among them. Although it was certain by 1863 that Queen's Road was to continue the way north across Longhedge Farm to the river, it was not until 1866 that the Heathwall open sewer along the farm's south rim was sealed in as part of the new

---

[17] Scott, *Remarks* (chap. 4, n. 4 above), p. 37.

main drainage. Until that was done, the new villas and their new drains up the hill must have contributed to the medieval ditch as that did to every wind that blew. Life was still raw at the edge of Battersea Fields.

Nevertheless, Cedars Road became on its slope a pleasant tree-lined avenue, and its well-bred Gothic church was a landmark until the 1940s.[18] The estate was inhabited at first especially by well-off young couples with City connections, interspersed with a few retired people and comfortable widows. There was Henry Doxat, who had an observatory in his garden, and published an annual weather almanac; John Humphery, son of the M.P., City alderman, wharf-owner and railway director of that name; Henry Dumas, of a local family active in the City and the Law (his brother, much later, married Julia Knowles; according to her brother James aged 18, Henry knew 'a great deal of the world'); George Parker Bidder Jr., the barrister and son of the engineer; Barnard Hodgson, the book auctioneer's son who married a Thornton and left the book business; also one or two retired officials of the East India Company, and Mrs. Allnutt, widow of the merchant-collector. And George Cattermole the artist is said to have committed suicide at No. 4. Forty-two villas were finished and most of them occupied by 1869. Today all but five (not in private domestic use) have been replaced by humanely scaled public-authority housing to the same roof-height as the old villas and with added approach roads separated from the traffic as modern equivalents of the former carriage sweeps.[19]

At the head of the road the great terraces still confidently stand, shorn of some of their ornament but part of the backdrop to the Common, and rock-like landmarks on the horizon as seen from Battersea down the hill, still forming a gateway where main roads meet, with all the panache of a young man's design. What Tennyson thought of them while pacing the Common before them in the 1870s, we never hear.

Knowles's next professional connection was less fortunate.[20]

[18] For St. Saviour's, n. 38 below.
[19] On first residents, directories and *CG* birth, marriage, and death announcements.
[20] The Woodgate episodes come mainly, on Lower Sydenham, from files of the Church Commissioners (former Ecclesiastical Commissioners) and, on St. James's Street, from files in the Crown Estate Office (successor to the Office of Woods and Forests); and on Woodgate in Battersea, n. 32 below.

Office propinquity may have brought it about, or furthered it. From around 1859, William Woodgate, solicitor, had an office on the Knowleses' staircase at No. 1 Raymond Buildings. For some years Woodgate had been a member of a firm in Lincoln's Inn Fields, where conveyancers of property were thick, before branching out in property speculation on his own. In the 1850s, he had a country house in Kent, Swaylands, which suggests he was in funds, and by 1860 his town house was in the very new Prince's Square, Bayswater, which suggests he may have had a hand in that development. He wrote his letters in a bold, sanguine hand. We find him in 1861 purchasing 'an Estate at Sydenham called the Champion Hall Estate as a Building Speculation'. In November an application to the Metropolitan Board of Works by 'Mr James T. Knowles Jnr. for the approval of the Board of a Plan for the formation of a road at Champion's Park, Lower Sydenham' was granted, that is, for the present Champion Road S.E.26. Champion Crescent, which defines the churchyard on the west side of that road, was not formed until after 1870, when it was reported that 'the Speculation failed and up to the present time the land surrounding the Church Site has not been built upon'.[21] A photograph taken about 1864 shows a chapel with open country beyond it to the north and west. A sketch-design for a chapel—the core of Woodgate's intentions, perhaps under pressure from his architect—will have been part of the scheme of November 1861.

St. Michael and All Angels, Lower Sydenham, built in 1862–3, was completely destroyed in the Blitz of 1940. In the beginning, alone in the rolling countryside north-east of the Crystal Palace, it was a miniature version in white brick of one or two recent works by Gilbert Scott well engraved in the press: of Exeter College chapel at Oxford, or of Wellington College chapel in Berkshire, the latter opportunely illustrated by the *Builder* in early November 1861. It may also be remarked that the church-building firm of Myers were the contractors both for the Wellington College chapel and for Knowles's St. Saviour's, Cedars Road—and quite possibly for Knowles's St. Michael's,

---

[21] Solicitors' recapitulating letters 1870, ChCom files 26473, 29243; and MBW *Minutes*, 22 Nov. 1861, p. 848, no. 55. Directories on Woodgate's addresses (long before Swaylands was Tudorized in the 1880s).

builder unrecorded.[22] The house-types intended to surround St. Michael's can only be conjectured, perhaps little semi-detached villas in white brick; not, at any rate, the crowded row of red-brick houses built there after 1870 by another hand. The chapel, at any rate, was produced (at the outset anyway) in the spirit of Knowles's *Story of King Arthur*, in a glow of ardour to reinterpret an age of chivalry for modern use.

Woodgate's ardour was all to secure some terrestrial return on his investment. The opening of the Crystal Palace on its permanent site in 1854 had, as it were, fertilized all the surrounding property. Lower Sydenham railway station had recently opened and much building in the neighbourhood was expected. Woodgate agreed in April 1862 with the parson at the district church of St. Bartholomew, in the parish of Lewisham, that the chapel site would be given to the Ecclesiastical Commissioners and the chapel built for four hundred persons at a cost to Woodgate of £4,000. In return he expected out of pew rents—after deduction of an annual £130 for the curate and with a fourth of the sittings to be free, for the pew-holders' servants—the eventual sum of £2,000 plus five per cent interest, presumably encouraged by his young architect in this ingenious and sanguine arrangement.[23] Reluctance among the church authorities to sanction such a mortgage on pew-rents was overcome, subject to approval of the structure, which was hurriedly begun in September 1862 'before even the formal Agreement was signed'. In July 1863 the building was reported to be structurally respectable, but the Commissioners' architect objected to the seating plan: benches for eight, right up to the wall at one end, were too long for convenience and the single aisle's width of three feet three inches was too narrow. A plan of 1864[24] shows what Woodgate made his architect do about *that*: each bench to seat nine, and the aisle narrowed to three feet; each bench a foot deep, the benches eighteen inches apart, and each sitter expected to be eighteen inches, or less, wide. That in

[22] *Bldr*, 9 Nov. 1861, p. 773, plate of Scott's Wellington College chapel. Much sod-turning last week of September 1862, for St. Saviour's on 25th, St. Michael's on 29th.

[23] Woodgate's agreement, with solicitor's letter to Eccles. Com. 5 Apr. 1862, and signed seating plan of 1864 (n. 24), in addition to Knowles's application to MBW (n. 21) make it clear that he was the architect. Mr. Gordon Barnes kindly told me about this.

[24] Knowles's seating plan with solicitor's letter to Eccles. Com. 1 Aug. 1864.

the years when no pew-holders' wives and daughters would
have been caught dead only eighteen inches wide, when *Punch*
published a Hints-to-Architects drawing showing the lower half
of a church doorway extra-chamfered for wide skirts. And
presumably only thin men were to kneel. But few can have
attended the chapel while Champion Park remained undeveloped,
and Woodgate in the time remaining to him paid little attention
to it. No villas, no pew-rents. The villas-in-reduced-circumstances
eventually erected there made it possible for a separate church
district finally to be formed in 1878; it was found in 1901 that
pew-rents the year before had totalled £9.[25] Knowles never
claimed authorship of this building, as he did for his other three
churches (although the surviving Church Commissioners' file
for 1862–4 makes it quite clear that he was the architect here):
the whole episode, culminating at a time of personal woe in
1863, was too painful; he may have urged Woodgate on too
enthusiastically at first; his original ideas for the interior were
undoubtedly never realized; quite likely his fee was never paid.

Concurrently, Woodgate was launching a scheme for the
building that for most of its existence has been known as the
Thatched House Club (Pl. 9), near the south end of St. James's
Street, Westminster, on the west side at Nos. 85–6 between the
Conservative Club of 1844 by Smirke and Basevi, and Norman
Shaw's Alliance Assurance building of 1905.[26] The Thatched
House Tavern (on part of the site since 1842 when displaced from
next door by the Conservative Club) had long been a meeting-
place for clubs: the Society of Dilettanti still kept its pictures
there in 1861; an Architects' Club founded in 1791 had met at the
original tavern. From 1770 the tavern had been managed by the
Willis family, whose rooms in King Street were to be a favourite
Victorian meeting-place. The former coffee-house at No. 85,
into which the tavern moved in 1842, was chiefly distinguishable
by its tall front window meagrely modelled on Boodle's.
Woodgate was not ostensibly on the scene at first, but a solicitor
named Haynes had obtained leases from the Crown owners of
the site, the Office of Woods and Forests, informing them in
December 1861 of a proposal to build either 'a Club House and

[25] By 1870 the estate surveyor was Octavius Hansard (ChCom file 29243).
[26] On Nos. 85–6 St. James's Street, Crown Estate files 11707 and 11706 (in that
order); also S of L vol. XXX, *St James's South of Piccadilly*, pp. 466–9, 478–86, 488.

Chambers or a Private Hotel with Shops or Offices under'—that is, purely on speculation and not for any particular club's premises. Knowles seems to have been on hand from the first, preparing sketch plans for such a building while corresponding with Tennyson and laying out Champion Park. In February Haynes formally assigned his leases to Woodgate and Knowles ordered demolition of the existing buildings. In the summer of 1862 he submitted finished drawings for Crown approval and building began in the autumn, proceeding to the stage when the builders, George Smith & Co., expected their first payment. And Woodgate, involved by then with builders at Sydenham and in costly wheeling and dealing with two railway companies at Battersea—where he was also then committed—began to drag his feet, so that much letter-writing among solicitors ensued. By the end of 1864 most of 'the difficulties occasioned by Mr Woodgate and his Incumbrances' were removed and the building completed enough for the Office of Woods to hand over the lease to George Smith's lawyers as security. Meanwhile, in January 1864, Woodgate having decided that chambers for letting would be more lucrative than a clubhouse, Knowles was required to subdivide the large rooms on ground and first floors, a contingency he had arranged for from the start, no doubt with the same distaste he felt for the benches of St. Michael's.[27]

But Knowles was lucky that, on Crown property, penny-pinching was not allowed to deprive such a prominent building of its stone façade—even though Bath stone becomes drab all too quickly in London. The tall front has the indispensable clubhouse feature of a bay-window—in a Forsyte word, the Iseeum motif—treated as a two-storey oriel, in position similar to the tall window on the little building just demolished. A basic town-house model for Knowles's front will have been the Russell house then standing in Park Lane, by Gilbert Scott's former partner Moffett and somewhat Tudor in flavour with its centred 'noble oriel' on a carved corbel. Knowles's roof is French in flavour with a dash of attention to Waterhouse's new striped chimneys on an Italianate insurance building in Manchester (opportunely illustrated by

[27] Eight sheets of drawings on fragile tracing paper, countersigned by James Pennethorne the Crown architect in Aug. 1862 and found in a file for alterations of the 1930s, augmented by two printed plans for alterations submitted in Jan. 1864; all now at the PRO, photographs at NMR.

Building News in early August 1862). As usual, whatever the models, the actual flavour of the club front is Knowlesian, with its foliage-panels carved by Daymond, like carpet-bedding or topiary work (Pl. 9)—yet, compared to the Grosvenor (Pl. 7), with a difference. According to the building press at the time, young Knowles's flair for the apropos was operating. 'The architect has . . . carried into effect one of Mr Ruskin's concepts, and instead of conventional ornaments has represented in panels the birds and foliage natural to the site when its ancient name of "The Thatched House" was still appropriate.'[28] The wood-pigeons among oak branches carved beside the front door may be based, rather, on a relief in one of the ambulatory chapels at Westminster Abbey, pointed out by Scott in lectures to the RIBA and the Royal Academy,[29] although the Victorian vegetation has thickened—as indeed it did in successive engravings of the Abbey carving in Scott's books of 1863 and 1878—thickened with the change in vision brought about by improvements in technique, thickened like the onset of Victorian shrubbery in Virginia Woolf's *Orlando*. Just at this time, in and around 1862, the elder Knowles at Hedsor and on Tarn's shop was resorting to an arid small-scale ornament with no juice of its own. That, just after the distinctive Grosvenor ornament was designed over his signature—at a time when his son was there to help before starting his own practice. How these buildings do demonstrate that the brief equilibrium of the Grosvenor synthesis was held by two hands, and at a particular unrepeatable moment of extreme brevity, knife-edged between the 1850s and the 1860s. A generation later, in the 1890s, Heathcote Statham the editor of the *Builder* singled out the clubhouse front as a design completely lacking in 'style' (that is, quality of completeness) like the poetry of Alfred Austin—which was rather hard on its architect as an admirer of the previous Poet Laureate. That pronouncement was an obituary for all mid-century attempts to make a national style: 'the moment free choice comes in . . . personal taste comes in, architecture becomes a personal art . . . [and] a spontaneously

---

[28] *BN*, 9 Sept. 1864, p. 681, saying also that the carving was by 'Mr Daymond, of Regent-place, Westminster'.

[29] Scott's *Gleanings from Westminster Abbey* (1863 edn., p. 29) and *Medieval Architecture* (1878, i. 178), engravings of carved spandrel in chapel of St. John the Baptist.

practised national style . . . is for us a mere chimera'.[30] Yet Statham's own buildings at the corner of Catherine and Tavistock Streets, Covent Garden, designed a few years after he said that, have very much the quality of their own time and nationality.

On Knowles's original plans, two interior features of the club-house were notable: the passenger lift and the lavish number of water-closets (one for each of the twenty-seven bedrooms as proposed); in the end, the former was installed, the latter but few as usual. The building was opened early in 1865 as Thatched House Chambers, but reverted in 1866 to the original intention as the Civil Service Club, which about 1870 changed its name to Thatched House Club, with members 'mainly recruited from the Civil Service of the Crown, including county magistrates, ex-high sheriffs and deputy-lieutenants', and the club continued there until 1949, with ground and first floors long since opened up again; and other clubs have occupied it since.[31] Woodgate apparently managed to pay off the contractor before he died in 1866. For all his encumbrances and all his shortcomings in South London, he did provide the architectural museum that is St. James's Street with an interesting specimen for its collection. A commonplace, easy-going architect would have cost him less. One ironic circumstance was that George Salting, to whose father Philip Flower turned for partnership in developing part of Battersea, after Woodgate failed him there, and who himself became a joint proprietor of the Battersea estate, lived in chambers upstairs over the club—quite likely at Knowles's suggestion—from 1865 until his death in 1909, crowded into two rooms with his swelling art collection and watching over his investments.[32]

The full story of Knowles's twenty-five years as architect and surveyor to a private housing estate in Battersea, South London, has been published in another place; those seventy acres of Longhedge Farm, and the people concerned in their development, form a previously unsuspected background to his other doings between 1862 and 1887, as witnessed by papers preserved in the

---

[30] H. Heathcote Statham, *Modern Architecture, A Book for Architects and the Public* (1897), pp. 23–6.

[31] From 1949 the Union Club, then Constitutional and Savage Clubs together, and from 1978 Markmasons' Hall.

[32] On George Salting, *DNB* and Metcalf, *The Park Town Estate and the Battersea Tangle* (London Topographical Society, 1978, based on private estate papers), pp. 39–40.

office run till 1978 for descendants of the Australia merchant, Philip Flower. Matters went like this. Although Battersea Park at the river's edge and Chelsea Bridge beside the park were opened in 1858, Clapham's inland community up the hill from Battersea Fields was cut off from them by old farmland and by new railway lines that threatened to strangle any attempt at a road leading across the farm to the bridge. Years of local agitation and Flower's (partly) public-spirited intervention in 1862, piloted by the Knowleses, thereafter brought about the construction of what is now called Queenstown Road to connect the bridge-approach made by the government with the new Cedars Road to Clapham Common—so that the crucial portion of one of London's main thoroughfares was made by private enterprise. In the beginning, in 1862, the senior Knowles was busy with Flower's house at Furzedown, Streatham, young Knowles was still trustfully busy with Woodgate's affairs, and Woodgate was still avid for more: it would appear that the elder Knowles brought his son and Flower together and the younger Knowles then brought Flower and Woodgate together. All plotted the course of a private Bill that it was necessary to take through Parliament during 1862–3 in order to get back farmland needed for the road from two increasingly arrogant railway companies then scheming their own invasion of London (in a convolution of railways north-east of Clapham Junction, still known among railwaymen as 'the Battersea Tangle'). In the summer of 1863, with a Queen's Road Battersea Act safely passed, and with his own private woe to bear, young Knowles sorrowfully laid out the road across the meadows of Longhedge Farm and plotted the estate of little houses that were, some day, to pay for the road, while Flower noted laconically in his private account-book: 'Battersea lands . . . all of which was taken over by myself August 1863 Mr W. being unable to fulfil his engagements.' Fees and expenses totalling £700 owed by Woodgate to Knowles in this connection were paid by Flower, two years later. Flower meanwhile turned for support to an old friend, Severin Salting—they had grown rich in Australia together—and a brief partnership lasted until Salting's death in 1865, after which Flower proceeded alone until his own death in 1872, thereafter succeeded in the slow development of Park Town by a consortium of young Flowers and Saltings. There, rows of grey brick houses scaled down from Knowles's Cedars Road style represent the building programme of the 1860s; several sets of red brick houses, many but not all designed by Knowles, came later; surviving correspondence shows that he was still much concerned here in the 1870s–80s. From 1871 until 1882, incidentally, Alfred Tennyson owned the freehold of twenty-seven houses at the north end of the estate, Knowles doubtless having acted as investment counsellor in the first instance.[33]

Philip Flower was a thoroughly sound man, son of a City merchant of Norfolk origin, and himself established as a merchant in Sydney by the late 1830s. There in 1842 the partnership of Flower, Salting & Co. was formed. Salting was a Dane who had gone out to Australia in 1834 and set up a ship-chandler's firm, dealing in marine equipment while investing in sheep stations and sugar plantations and becoming a bank and insurance director. As soon as the partnership was formed, Flower made London his headquarters at the other end of the firm's shipping routes, and Australian wool, tallow, and gold came to his wharves on the Thames, from which heavy industrial equipment went out in return. The discovery of gold in 1851 enhanced every canny investment in Australia, and the price of wool was to figure in later Park Town correspondence alongside the price of bricks and mortgages. His London property included Colliers Quay and other wharves, as well as two urban office-blocks built in the 1850s, and lands in Surrey and Westminster. The chief requirements of him at Battersea in the last decade of his life, besides money and the energetic surveyor he had in Knowles, were dogged tenacity and common sense, although he probably had more cultivated traits: his elder brother John Wickham Flower, partner in the firm of Flower & Nussey, solicitors, was a Fellow of the Geological Society interested also in archaeology and author of two religious books; their younger brother Horace, a merchant in Australia, was 'loved for his hospitality, humour and wit, and admired for his classical learning and unbending honour'. Philip's sons Cyril and Arthur, with their cousin Wickham and Salting's two sons as co-proprietors at Battersea, were to demand a good deal of Knowles's time after he became a busy editor.

By 1867 Philip Flower was also investing in Victoria Street,

[33] *Park Town Estate* (n. 32), p. 27 on Flower, p. 35 on Tennyson.

Westminster, then one of London's arrested developments.
Perhaps his architect was already a frequenter of the Deanery at
Westminster Abbey, as he had been of the Borradaile parsonage
in Tothill Fields, not to mention the palatial hotel looming over
Victoria Station, and had drawn Flower's attention to the reviving
possibilities in the neighbourhood.[34] Victoria Street had been
conceived in the 1830s and authorized in the 1840s as a route
between Parliament and Buckingham Palace, and by 1851 had
been carved through 'a wilderness of purlieus' (as Baedeker was
to put it) from Broad Sanctuary before the Abbey to the banks of
the Grosvenor Basin, that is, to the future forecourt of the railway
terminus. Building by the first developers of the new street had
then begun with two blocks 'on the Scotch principle', that is, of
flats, one for middle-class occupation on the south side near the
west end, with arcaded shop-fronts, while a model lodging-house
for the working class went up behind it on Ashley Place. Development thereafter was slow, so that much of the length of the street
still lay between empty sites and hoardings in the 1860s. But after
Victoria Station and the Grosvenor Hotel were built, and the
Metropolitan Underground Railway was taken under the
street's west end, and development began on the Grosvenor
estate near by, building picked up; although some sites waited
even until the 1890s. The first blocks established a norm of five
or six storeys and something of the relentless quality of Hauss-
mann's new Paris boulevards. No great architects distinguished
themselves here, and when Bentley built his cathedral for the
Catholic diocese it was hidden, except for its slender tower, on a
side street. Victoria Street was a speculators' street, much of it
nearer to the anarchic meanness of Charing Cross Road and
Shaftesbury Avenue than to the controlled urbanity of the old
Regent's Street—yet, in height and storey levels controlled, for
a while. Opposite the new blocks at the western end from about
1861 there stood for four years or so an elaborate, domed
'Oriental Baths', an Irish enterprise ('the Turkish bath . . . [having]
made such rapid progress in Ireland') rich in marble, stucco, and
stained glass; and not only did it have facilities for ladies and

[34] This section is based on maps, rate books, views, and directories at WPL, also
H.-R. Hitchcock, *Early Victorian Architecture* (1954), i. 475–9, the building
journals, *ILN*, and *CBA*; e.g. *ILN*, 18 Nov. 1854, p. 504, shows empty site of
future Albert Mansions. On this neighbourhood in 1880s, chap. 8, 'At Home in
Westminster', and J. S. Cooper letter-books in Park Town papers (n. 32 above).

gentlemen, it had horse-baths. Decorative insertions over the windows suggest imitation of the Grosvenor Hotel: at any rate, neither Knowles seems to have claimed its design. With Irish improvidence, and two basements of furnaces and waterworks, it stood squarely in the path of the impending Underground Railway—now part of the Circle and District lines. So, in 1865, the Oriental Baths were liquidated and the Underground Railway was inserted on its way from Westminster to Kensington and covered in. In 1867 the site of the baths with the rest of a long frontage formerly belonging to Watney's brewery behind it was conveyed to Flower, who then took sundry partners.[35]

This long piece of ground, partly now swallowed up in an approach-road of the 1960s, lay along the north side of Victoria Street with the Standard public house and music hall (on the site of the Victoria Palace Theatre) at its west end. The portion west of Palace Street, where Knowles's Albert Mansions were soon to go up, was only ninety feet deep with no room along the brewery wall for a mews. Behind part of the eastern piece running to the present Buckingham Gate, however, there was room for stables and it was there, in the summer of 1867, that building began: very few managers of the new blocks of flats in this street were to be able to offer stables as one of their amenities, since most speculators were too keen for multi-storey returns. In the spring of 1868 a short approach road made from Victoria Street directly to these stables was named Spenser Street (Spenser so spelt suggesting that that poet was in Flower's architect's mind at the time of the stone-laying at Aldworth). Flower next chose to develop his land nearer the west end of Victoria Street, probably because the ground in front of the stables lay opposite Vickers' Distillery (later Army and Navy Stores), whereas the preferred site, however close to a brewery behind, lay opposite the street's first blocks of flats and nearer to the more eligible Grosvenor estate, then going up. At any rate, Knowles's application of September 1867 for Metropolitan Board of Works approval of 'bay-windows and balconies to houses in Victoria Street' seems to relate to the long block of flats and chambers subsequently called Albert Mansions, designed either in March, when purchase of the

³⁵ Oriental Baths, *ILN*, 21 June 1862, pp. 635, 641, and *CBA for 1862* (1861), p. 278. Albert Mansions, schedule of deeds 1863–93 relating to mortgage, Park Town papers.

ground was completed, or only after the flurry of designing
Aldworth in June and July had subsided.[36]

Aldworth and Albert Mansions had little in common—aside
from harbouring the Poet Laureate—except a studied picturesqueness of outline, dulled by multiplication in Victoria Street. To the
almost unrelieved flatness of the block of 1852 opposite Knowles
did pose a certain variety of plan and elevation, more obvious in
old photographs taken before shop-fronts replaced his open
basement areas in the 1890s and top storeys filled out his separate
roofs in 1910. Albert Mansions' length of just under 500 feet was
composed of nineteen 'houses', the middle three and both end
threes emphasized by forward projection further accented by
canted bays, plans unrecorded, each floor of each house containing
a separate flat. This treatment as separate houses, each with staircase, was already old-fashioned; those over the way had already
introduced 'a sort of stair-tower' leading to flats on both sides (on
the legal chambers plan of, say, Raymond Buildings, Gray's Inn),
yet Knowles had apparently provided for conversion to that
principle which younger proprietors at Albert Mansions were
to adopt in the late 1870s. He drew on his clubhouse for a unit of
façade design, narrowed and then multiplied by nineteen: one
'house' is left at the far west end, now No. 124, in 1870 containing
a bank, an office, an artist's flat, and briefly Cyril Flower's own
flat before he moved farther off from the music hall. So far as one
can tell, the ground floors were not designed as shops and most
were let as flats at first. Eminent occupiers at Albert Mansions in
the 1870s included John Stuart Mill and Arthur Sullivan. At first,
only the houses No. 1, No. 2, and No. 16 were occupied, and
Mrs. Tennyson's cab-driver had trouble finding the place in the
summer of 1870, when Tennyson took chambers at No. 16.
(There were at first service kitchens at No. 16: Lady Emily Pepys
complains in June 1871 that she 'could not get her tea served last
evening' and the managers 'are continually changing'.)

So far as the outside was concerned, more trained sensibility
went into the Albert Mansions design than into most of Victoria
Street. A reshuffling of repertory to meet a new use, attended by
an eye for the picturesque-where-possible, or pragmatic-pictur-

[36] MBW *Minutes*, and Cases 9879 (1867) and 11402 (1868) with drawings and
letters from Knowles at GLRO. Spenser Street not to be confused with Spencer
Place behind Army and Navy Stores.

esque, was Knowles's method. When the cement facing was newly painted and each section of area-railing had its gas-lamp, the full extent of it must have resembled (and been meant to resemble) the side of a London square, with projecting end and centre features to mitigate the street's cliff-effect. When Tennyson looked out of his window one foggy morning and told Knowles that Victoria Street looked 'like a street in Hell', it was the block opposite, through the brewers' and railways' smoke, that he saw. Now, opposite the former site of his chambers, the new forecourt of Westminster Cathedral has been opened—today's only re-mission in a newly rebuilt and still relentless street.[37]

Meanwhile, during 1862–7, Knowles designed three more churches. While his first unacknowledged St. Michael's still stood forlornly in open country, these were set in suburbs already partly completed (Cedars estate, Park Town estate) or long since built up (Clapham Park). Of picturesque rural type in Kentish ragstone, with substantial towers, they were safe, conservative, efficiently assembled designs agreeable to the donors and deferring to the works of Gilbert Scott. Each had its little history. St. Saviour's, Cedars Road (Pl. 12) was built as chapel-of-ease to Holy Trinity, Clapham Common, and its interior resembled Scott's at St. Giles, Camberwell. In the spring of 1864 while St. Saviour's was still going up, the rector's wife Mrs. Bowyer, who with him had taken much interest in it, died leaving a large family. Among those who attended the funeral at Norwood were Myers's masons and carpenters, for she had shown them much kindness. After they had finished the church, however, the Bishop of Winchester, in whose diocese this was, refused to consecrate. The sorrowing rector had placed a large table-tomb bearing his wife's recumbent effigy at the crossing under the tower directly before the altar rails, as if the whole building were a chantry, perhaps even encouraged by Knowles, whose own loss had

[37] Tennyson's chambers were on the top floor (let as 'third' but, with entresol, fourth, or American fifth), presumably chosen for light and air; and there Lord Stratford de Redcliffe at over 80 'gallantly breasted the staircase' when the poet was confined with gout (*Memoir*, ii. 79). Pepys letter in Knowles papers (WPL). *British Architect*, 2 Sept. 1881, p. 437, said that in general flats with a common kitchen were not working well and the system was not being used in new blocks in Victoria Street. Tennyson on hellish aspect: removed by Knowles, along with the Ammergau poem Tennyson made there, from surviving proof-sheet for Jan. 1893 *NC* article (now TRC, p. 11 in proof, cut occurs at p. 174 as printed), but included in privately printed leaflet on *Idylls* (chap. 8, n. 88 below).

occurred the year before. Two successive bishops, first Sumner and then Wilberforce, insisted that the tomb be moved, but the rector was obdurate. It was generally thought that he had paid for the church out of his own pocket, so services were held without the sacraments until he died in 1872. His trustees then preparing to sell the church, were stopped by a parishioner, Miss Harrison: for she had advanced the money in the first place and, just before the rector died, had released him from repayment on condition that the building be conveyed to the Ecclesiastical Commissioners and consecrated. Nothing was said directly about the tomb, but it was moved forthwith to the north transept and, nine years after building had finished, St. Saviour's was consecrated by Wilberforce's successor—a triumph for Miss Harrison. The church was destroyed by enemy action in 1944.[38]

St. Stephen's, Clapham Park, built 1866-7, was also said to have been the beneficiary of a rich spinster, supposed to have been in love with the incumbent. The lady has sometimes been named, apparently quite wrongly, as Julia Knowles—because her brother provided the design and her father provided the site, at a low purchase price, opposite Friday Grove, and because her own wedding in 1872 took place elsewhere (in Eaton Square, doubtless for social reasons). The likelier story is that the lady was a Miss Thorowgood, who lived in a large house in Acre Lane. The gossip may be embroidery, that her father—probably William Thorowgood the type-founder of Goswell Street and Acre Lane—disliked the clergyman George Eastman so much that she was to lose her fortune if she married him, yet it may have been true that after her father's death she gave Eastman the money to build St. Stephen's; somebody did. He was a man who wrote in a powerful hand the sort of letter that began, 'Sir, I have built the above church', and according to various records was self-made: the son of a butcher of Bethnal Green, he was a curate at Brixton (at the other end of Acre Lane from Clapham Park) during the 1850s while studying for a Cambridge degree as a 'ten-year man' (receiving his B.D. in 1862 after twelve years at the age of 40). The prosperous type-founder—whose type specimens have been

---

[38] St. Saviour's: ChCom file 48042; GLC deeds, Cedars Road, conveyance to Eccles Com November 1873 by Bowyer's trustees; CG Oct., Nov. 1862, p. 135, p. 6, Oct. 1863, p. 146, June 1864, p. 93, Jan. 1865, p. 30; *CBA for 1865* (1864), p. 142.

called vile examples of deterioration in design—may well have despised the butcher's son as a curate on the make, but type-founding money may have made St. Stephen's. Built by Edward Muspratt, a local builder, to young Knowles's design in a mixture of Gothic styles, it had a west tower and a south aisle, with a west wall for an unbuilt north aisle standing like a film set for many years. At its consecration on 22 June 1867, if its architect was there at all, it was in bodily presence only, with his mind a whirl of house designs for Mr. Tennyson, whom he had momentously encountered at Haslemere the week before and was to meet again next day, the 23rd. During Eastman's incumbency, Clapham Park lost caste socially with the building of smaller houses and emptying of large ones, though enough of a congregation continued after his day for the north aisle to be added in 1909. Thereafter, St. Stephen's emptied slowly until, soon after the end of its first century, it was rebuilt on a smaller scale.[39]

Meanwhile, Bishop Wilberforce 'heartily approved' of St. Philip's, Battersea, built by the old City firm of Colls between 1867 and 1870 on the Park Town estate in a square beside the present Queenstown Road. It stood in what was from the first a mainly poor area and so had the aspect of a mission church, ministering to the 'increase in the railway population' employed in the railway repair shops near by, although churchwardens and sidesmen lived up the hill in middlebrow Clapham, outside Battersea parish. A district was formed in 1871, a year after the church was consecrated and only after considerable in-fighting with neighbouring incumbents over boundaries and fees, in-evitable in an area flooded with new housing for a population that could pay no pew-rents and put little in the collection on Sundays. A suburban curate like Mr. Eastman in Clapham Park, cushioned by admirers in a district with 'no poor', led a very different life from Mr. Hall at St. Philip's with its district of '6000 souls' about to be augmented by still more housing estates, 'the inhabitants of which will be of the poor class . . . [and] of a very migratory character', as Mr. Hall dolefully reported. Aid in securing a permanent vicarage and starting a school had to come

[39] St. Stephen's: ChCom file 37493, and records at GLRO; *CG* July 1867, p. 108; on Eastman, Venn's *Alumni Cantibrigianae*, London directories 1837–57, S of L vol. 26, *St Mary Lambeth, Part Two*, p. 112, D. B. Updike, *Printing Types* (1937), ii. 196, and photocopies at Vicarage of correspondence 1926–8.

from benevolent outsiders; before the London School Board's programme got under way here, six thousand children in Battersea (Mr. Hall liked that particular round number) were said to have no school, and Knowles was asked to provide a drawing (never used) for a modest one-storey school in a minimally medieval style. A fund was then started for St. Philip's Schools, with Nassau Senior the economist's son as treasurer; his wife and Miss Thornton, probably E. M. Forster's Aunt Marianne, sat on the committee which late in 1871 hoped for a piece of ground cheap from the estate proprietor. But by then Philip Flower was ill and tired; he had given the church and maintained the parson and given an otherwise lettable house for the parsonage while delays in forming the district went on; the long campaign to make Queen's Road, and to found the housing estate that some day would pay for it, had been expensive and exhausting, he had had enough. In 1872 he died, and his young son Cyril declined—in large flowing handwriting of princely carelessness—to help in any way. The new buildings of the London School Board soon rose above their pupils' modest homes. St. Philip's had been meant to lord it over them all with a tower carrying 'a lofty spire, with flying buttresses', that is, with corner pinnacles linked to the spire, but there was doubt that an alluvial soil subject to flooding would support it: according to one local historian, a committee of six, including the architects Street and Scott, was consulted, and the tower stands unspired. Still today among Park Town's rows of little houses, the church of St. Philip's is visible across the new Battersea Fields, where motorways threaten to multiply like railways and tower blocks rise near by like a new workmen's city.[40]

Whatever the social and structural strains these churches were subject to, together they ministered to a representative cross-section of South London during a century of stress; and St. Philip's, at least, survives intact. For all the earnest mulling over Godliness and Reason at meetings of the Metaphysical Society in the 1870s, it may be noted that Knowles was the only member who had ever designed a church—a practical rather than a moral exercise though that was for him.

[40] St. Philip's: ChCom file 40160; estate layouts in MBW files at GLRO and BRL; Park Town papers (n. 32 above): churchwardens' minutes and Knowles school drawing at Vicarage; *CG* Mar. 1867, p. 56, Aug. 1870, p. 116; *CBA for 1871* (1870), p. 189; J. G. Taylor, *Our Lady of Batersey* (1925), p. 293.

LIFE AND ART 1862–8

> 'I can only say that . . . if faith mean anything at all
> it is trusting to those instincts, or feelings, or what-
> ever they may be called, which assure us of some life
> after this.' Tennyson to 'a stranger who questioned
> him as to his belief in a hereafter' (1863), *Memoir*,
> i. 495

> 'A. is fond of the Abbey and of strolling about it by
> himself' (1866); 'we wandered about the Abbey for
> a long time . . . my father suddenly said: "It is
> beautiful, but what empty and awful mockery if
> there were no God!" ' (1883), *Memoir*, ii. 33, 275

In July 1862, Jane and James Knowles named their first-born Arthur James. Life was busy and full of hope. Two churches and the club building were begun, Harris's villas went ahead, *The Story of King Arthur* was selling, 'the Governor' was receiving congratulations on the newly opened Grosvenor Hotel and importantly engaged on other large works, the chess game with the railways in Battersea Fields was about to be played out before parliamentary committees in the coming session, Clapham was a pleasant place to live. Soon a second child was on the way, to be born at Friday Grove as Arthur had been; that house, for a while, assumed a dynastic character. But in July 1863, Jane died there in childbirth, not yet 21.[41] James returned to his parents' house to live, with the babies Arthur and Millicent for his mother and sister to care for. Life was suddenly dust and ashes. The Queen's Road Extension Act had just become law in June and seventy acres of pasture and meadow, partially entangled with railway lines, were to be laid out; during the year 1863–4, young Knowles had to be as much land surveyor as architect, staking out the old Longhedge farmland among the railway embankments. Hard work will have been a blessing. In August, Woodgate backed out there, but that was not the end of him, for during 1863–4 his architect was still cumbered with his business elsewhere. Unable to avoid the man on the staircase at Raymond Buildings, Knowles must have loathed the sight of him, a feeling perhaps cordially returned.

[41] *CG*, Aug. 1863, p. 122.

We hear nothing directly about this dark time, no family memory of it survived, and no letters such as Knowles later wrote to Gladstone and Tennyson about the death of his mother remain. Yet one agonized appeal was apparently made to Tennyson in 1863 by 'a stranger who questioned him as to his belief in a hereafter': Tennyson's reply (as reflected in the *Memoir* and quoted at the head of this section) may well have gone to Knowles. It would have been characteristic of Knowles to seek this comfort, having introduced himself by post in the autumn of 1861.[42]

By the end of 1864, hope was filtering back. Professionally, hard work was being rewarded with some recognition for colleagues and clients to notice. In September, *Building News* gave two full-page plates to Thatched House Chambers, and then James Thorne's annual commentary on the architectural scene, for the *Companion to the British Almanac* that came out before Christmas, considered no fewer than three works by Knowles Jr.: the layout for Park Town as 'one of the largest projects for supplying in part the destruction amongst the smaller houses in London' by railways and city improvements; St. Saviour's, Cedars Road, with engraving, as a 'simple, regular, stately, substantial' example of a suburban church; and Thatched House Chambers, as 'a costly and handsome structure'.[43] Architects on their way up doubtless took care to supply Thorne with his material.

Personally, balance was restored to Knowles's life by his engagement to marry Hewlett's sister Isabel; from what one can gather, she had loved him before he ever met Jane Borradaile. They were married by Jane's father at Streatham church in February 1865, bringing the families already linked by Emmeline Knowles's marriage to Henry Hewlett even closer.[44] From 1865 until 1884 James and Isabel lived at The Hollies (Pl. 16), a late eighteenth-century house in an irregular row beside The Elms where Sir Charles Barry had lived. Now part of a nursing home, The Hollies then had a very large garden behind it and the Common's grassy distance before it. Neither James nor his

[42] Prof. Lang, to whom I mentioned this conjecture while he was preparing his edition of Tennyson's letters, thinks it very likely.

[43] *BN*, 9 Sept. 1864, p. 681; *CBA for 1865* (1864), pp. 139, 142, 167, and on p. 166 would mention Tarn's shop 'had we space'—a back seat for Knowles Sr.

[44] *CG*, Mar. 1865, p. 60. The chancel of Streatham church had then recently been altered to designs by a fellow-parishioner, the painter William Dyce.

father, once away from the Bell Street view of Reigate Priory wall and houses opposite, ever lived in a house facing a mere row of other houses, the elder proceeding from prospects of woods on Cockshut Hill to a view of Clapham Common, and thereafter to the private grounds of Friday Grove, and eventually to Russell Square; while his son, after Friday Grove, proceeded from Clapham Common to St. James's Park, and finally to a view of the sea at Brighton. It was one of the more civilized Victorian snobberies—of Regency origin, no doubt. Even brother George in bachelor quarters late in life continued the *rus in urbe* tradition as best he could in Soho Square and Colville Gardens.

In March 1866 to James and Isabel a daughter Beatrice was born, and in May he took his family to Brighton, writing to Hewlett on the 12th from the Bedford Hotel. It was the week of panic in the City following the Overend–Gurney crash:

I was in Town yesterday—and shall never forget Lombard St. at $\frac{1}{2}$ past 3 o'clock. It was filled with excited crowds—especially opposite Barclays & other great Banks—while cab after cab drove up in hot haste to the doors & 'men pale & trembly' with nervousness rushed out & up into the Houses—One old gentleman I saw come out of Barclays—who would have made an ideal of fright and greediness—clutching his money in one hand & a little bag to put it in with the other—Up & down among the crowd walked those native wits who are always turning up to the surface in a multitude—carrying little empty money bags stuck in their hot hands and making gestures of insolvency and irony as they walked about—The contrast of expression in the face of the Bank officials was admirable. One of them I saw come to the door of a Bank with an impassive sort of amused contempt straight at the nervous excited mob in a way that was worthy of the stage.

This fascinated observer of the stage of London life added that 'even if I were inclined (which I am not) to draw my money out of the L.J.B. I could not do so without professional risk of loss—as the Bank are my clients & I have only just been building for them in Chancery Lane'. Then there is a jaunty note on 'my good sporting chances for the Derby—To my surprise—when I went to the Club yesterday—I found that my name had drawn "Lord Lyon" (the first favorite)—in a guinea sweepstake of which the first prize will be over £100. If the favorite does win on

Wednesday we shall have made a cheap holiday of Brighton'—
and Lord Lyon did win the Derby.[45]

This letter indicates some work on the former London Joint-
stock Bank, now Midland Bank, at Nos. 123–4 Chancery Lane
(now altered at roof level after war damage, modernized since at
ground level).[46] The work of 1866 seems to have been mainly a
refacing of upper floors with rebuilding at ground level (that
recurrent process), two Georgian houses having apparently been
merged at some previous time. The façade fuses various Knowlesian devices with certain elements of the Waterhouse insurance
building at Manchester illustrated four years before in the building
journals. With touches of polychromatic inlay, of red brick and
white stone on the yellow-brick front. Knowles was keeping up
to date; yet his grafting of 'structural colour' on to Renaissance
window-forms, though neatly done, is uncomfortable. His
father's building of 1854 for Hodgson stood opposite: if that was
the first attempt at a family brand of fusion in central London,
this bank was one of the last. By 1866 such synthesizing works,
which many architects were turning out, were evidence not so
much of a search for a new style as of the practical opportunist's
drawing upon his funds of form, reliable bank deposits, as it were.
For young Knowles the idealism of 1859–62 as a basis of architectural style had gone. Architecture was 'bread & cheese getting',
as he described his life to Hewlett around 1866.[47] One's profession
was to be conscientiously practised—although for architects of the
second rank in the 1870s a thick skin might be more useful than
conscience. Yet a disciplined professionalism was better training
for one of his nervous intensity than universities in the 1850s
had provided.

In October 1866 he called on Tennyson at Farringford. Since
the desperate questioning letter of, probably, late 1863—if that
was his—Knowles had written others. A gift of a 'Photograph

[45] Knowles to Hewlett, 12 May 1866 (WPL); *Annual Register* on Derby winner;
on Overend–Gurney, e.g. F. Sheppard, *London 1808–1870* (1971), pp. 77–80.

[46] The Midland Bank have no record of the 1866 work, and I have not seen
the rate books, but directories show that a confectioner on the ground floor was
replaced by London Joint-stock Bank in 1867, while the same lot of solicitors,
engravers, and stationers' offices continued upstairs; the disposition of windows
and storeys behind Knowles's refacing are still those of Georgian houses; until
ground-floor work in the 1960s, the bank front had Italianate pilasters of the
1860s. NMR has photo of war-damage to roof.

[47] Knowles to Hewlett, undated, one of four letters *c.* 1865–7 (WPL).

from Raffaele' obliged Tennyson to reply on 31 January 1866 that he was very grateful, 'but yet—fie upon "but yet"—says Cleopatra in Shakespeare—I would request you not to send me any other present. You are laying a heap of obligations upon me which I cannot return & as I am not your enemy "the coals of fire" can be no object to you.'[48] It was not then clear, before they met, that Knowles was not just one more tiresome celebrity-haunting member of the vast letter-writing public. But in October he went to the Isle of Wight to see Dr. Pritchard, and there took his courage 'in both hands'. There are two accounts in Mrs. Tennyson's journal, both in the same hand with the first crossed out (the corporate self-consciousness of that journal, with its use of the present tense and successive family revisions, somewhat blurs its value as a record): '16th Mr Knowles calls to return Layamon's Brut. He is at the Hotel & came the other day introducing himself to borrow it owing to our having written in acknowledgement of his gift to A. of his pretty book for children from the Morte d'Arthur that we wished he could make a similar one from the Layamon's Brut.' The recast version adds, ' & so began our personal acquaintance'.[49]

Knowles's version was written many years later and probably recast even oftener.[50] The call he had felt he must make to offer his respects had been put off through shyness, but at last he found himself there:

I was shown upstairs to the top of the house and into an attic which was the Poet's own study, and presently, with my heart in my mouth, I heard his great steps as he climbed up the little wooden stairs. His bodily presence seemed as kingly as I felt it ought to be, though a little grim and awful at first; but he made me very welcome, and then groped about for and lighted a pipe, and sat down and began to speak of King Arthur as being a subject of common interest and sympathy.

This soon thawed the chill of my spirits and I began to feel more at home, until I felt I could make the request I was longing to do—would

---

[48] From transcript of a letter owned by Dr. Gordon Ray, to be published in full by Prof. Lang, to both of whom I am grateful.

[49] TRC, Lincoln.

[50] Published posthumously as 'Tennyson and Aldworth' in *Tennyson and His Friends* (1911), ed. 2nd Lord Tennyson, pp. 246–7; date of writing uncertain, but in the late 1890s, probably after the *Memoir* came out, Knowles was planning a memoir of his own, according to J. G. Millais (*Life of Sir J. E. Millais*, 1899, ii. 142 n.).

he read me one of his Poems, as I desired earnestly to hear from his own lips what I already knew and loved? . . . it was . . . intoning on a note, almost chanting, which I heard, and which brought the instant conviction that this was the proper vehicle for poetry. . . . I was so enchanted that I begged for more and more; and then I suppose may have begun a personal sympathy which grew and lasted . . . until his death. For when I made to go he took me all about the house, showing me the pictures and drawings with which his walls were lined. . . . I having been all my life interested in art and in a small way a collector of drawings and pictures.

They were to meet again eight months later.

Knowles's election to the Reform Club in 1865[51] suggests an expanded acquaintance; his father had been content to use its façade as an architectural source. After Lord Lyon won the Derby, the winning sum from the club draw may have been spent partly at Sotheby's a month later at the Wellesley sale (of Old Master drawings collected by Dr. Henry Wellesley, late of Oxford). Knowles owned a number of Wellesley's drawings by 1868 when he loaned six to an exhibition at Leeds, catalogued then as: a Farinati once in the Lely and Reynolds collections, two Corregios, a Guido Reni, a Rubens once in Lely's collection, and a Raphael Sybil. Another of Knowles's drawings, attributed in 1868 and 1908 to Michelangelo and thought to relate to the Medici tomb-figure of Dawn, came from the Woodburn collection dispersed at Christie's in 1860, and may previously have been in Sir Thomas Lawrence's collection. Of other drawings by Michelangelo (or called so) in the Woodburn sale, the British Museum was able to buy eight for £314, and one dealer bought five of which the most expensive cost him £45: in the middle of the last century the buying of Old Master drawings was a game collectors could play without high stakes, because comparatively few did. The National Exhibition of Works of Art held at Leeds in 1868 was intended to emulate the success of the great art exhibition held in 1857 at Manchester, with the additional (unsuccessful) aim of paying for the new Infirmary, by Gilbert Scott, in which it was held. Building and exhibition were opened by the Prince of Wales on 19 May. About 270 Old Master drawings, as well as paintings, were loaned by a distinguished list of owners, the Duke of Devonshire, John Malcolm,

---

[51] From Nov. 1865 (club secretary); records of proposers lost in the last war.

the Bodleian, Christ Church, and Ashmolean at Oxford, the Royal Academy, Messrs. Agnew, and a few other private owners including James T. Knowles Jr., who loaned eleven drawings and five paintings. Another lender was Francis Cook, that splendid client of Knowles Sr. at St. Paul's Churchyard, Richmond Hill, and Cintra. Young Knowles's paintings shown at Leeds, as then attributed, were a Salvator Rosa, a Correggio, a Greuze portrait, and two landscapes by Jacob van Ruysdael, one a 'Haarlem Bleaching Grounds', bought in 1867 for 13 guineas, that went for 920 guineas in 1908. It seems that he had a collector's eye not entirely influenced by fashion. 'My few things', as he offhandedly called his collection later on, were to take three days to disperse after his death.[52]

The Derby win in 1866 may rather have had a more pious use. From that year and during the next thirty years, Knowles gave in memory of Jane a set of stained-glass windows by Clayton & Bell to her father's church of St. Mary, Vincent Square (transferred to St. Matthew's, Wandsworth Bridge Road, Fulham, in 1925 when St. Mary's went the way of unwanted churches).[53] About this time occurred the death of Mrs. Borradaile, Jane's mother. Knowles described the midnight scene at the parsonage to Hewlett:[54]

Hoping for the reply she got—she said to Mr Borradaile very shortly before she died—'Do you think I shall live through tonight?'—When he told her 'No'—'Then' she said 'I shall rest in Heaven'—
    This from Mrs Borradaile meant so very much—seeing she never indulged in any word or thought of fancy—no *figure* of speech or of mind—It was the sublime unconscious acme of Faith.

Such evidence for life hereafter—'He thinks he was not made to die'—helped to confirm the answer Tennyson had sent three years before. When James himself died, forty-three years after his second marriage, Isabel was heard to murmur, 'Jane's got him at last.'

[52] *National Exhibition of Works of Art at Leeds 1868, Official Catalogue* (1869), and *Art Journal* for 1868, *passim.* On Woodburn drawings, J. Wilde, *Drawings at the British Museum*: Michelangelo and His Studio (1953), p. vii. On Ruysdael from Monro of Novar sale 1867 (to Carfax at Knowles sale 1908), *Daily Telegraph*, 30 May 1908. Also on Knowles's pictures, chap. 9, n. 13.
[53] Basil Clarke, *Parish Churches of London* (1966), p. 61.
[54] Knowles to Hewlett, undated (WPL).

About this time, in 1867, Knowles may have had an entrepreneurial finger in Henry Hewlett's new appointment as Keeper of Land Revenue Records, a post recently created for a Crown specialist in antiquarian law, which he held until succeeded in the 1890s by his son Maurice. (For instance, there is a letter of February 1867 to Hewlett from Knowles, offering to do 'anything in the business line' for him, such as 'seeing Redgrave', possibly J. E. Redgrave, a Crown lands official Knowles had dealt with over the St. James's Street building, and another letter delightedly thanking Hewlett for a bottle of wine.) Nipping about to put a word in the right ear was a skill he already had.[55]

By 1868 Knowles had come to know Dean Stanley, whether through Tennyson or the Borradailes or Clapham acquaintance with the Bradleys, or by eager conversation over some antiquity in the Dean's beloved Westminster Abbey, or over Stanley's book of early 1868 on the Abbey; or Knowles may have sought spiritual reassurance in the dark months of 1864, Stanley's first year as Dean of Westminster. 'His social gifts, his stores of anecdotes, his quick perception alike of the serious and of the ridiculous, his ready sympathy, his power of apt quotation . . .the marvellously expressive countenance' of 'the little eager Dean', were not the only traits that will have attracted Knowles to Stanley, whose portrait in words we have from Stanley's friend and successor George Bradley and, as follows, from Stanley's relation Augustus Hare:[56]

Every phase of opinion, every variety of religious belief . . . were cordially welcomed in the hospitalities of the Deanery . . . especially on Sunday evenings after the service in the Abbey. . . . It was with the fancy that . . . he could make the Abbey the great temple of reconciliation, that the most heterogeneous preachers were invited by Arthur Stanley to make use of its pulpit—preachers from the very north and south and east and west of opinion.

This delight in reconciling or at least defining opposites appealed to Knowles intensely. Among his papers when he died were four pages of notes on the Dean's Whit Sunday sermon in 1868,

[55] Knowles to Hewlett, 18 Feb. 1867 and another undated (WPL).

[56] G. G. Bradley, *Recollections of Arthur Penrhyn Stanley* (1883), p. 101; Augustus J. C. Hare, *Biographical Sketches* (1895), p. 75. Knowles was to commission Arnold's stanzas on Stanley's death for *NC* Jan. 1882 (with 'Abbey by the westering Thames' an odd view of an eastward-flowing river).

notes suggesting in their detail that the Dean allowed him to copy this sermon on the theme of love for one's neighbour, 'that Charity which is greater than faith & hope'. (Yet we may suppose that for someone with Knowles's interest in the great stage of the world about him, 'the greatest of these' was Curiosity.) The appeal of the Dean's way with history to someone of strongly associative cast of mind can be guessed from passages in a lecture Stanley gave some years earlier at Exeter Hall on 'The Study of Modern History', its theme the study of London:[57]

It is the peculiar compensation to the inhabitants of a city like this, that what others gain from the study and enjoyment of Nature, you may gain from the study and enjoyment of History . . . the mere fact of [London's] grandeur—of its vast size—of the ceaseless stir and excitement of its daily and hourly life—is an assistance to the comprehension of History. . . .It raises us out of ourselves—it gives us a consciousness of nearness to the great pulses of national life.

One reason for Knowles's ultimate success as a London editor was that, with his associative mind, he was by early naturalization a Londoner. He grew with Victorian London, helped to make it, and was increasingly fascinated by 'a consciousness of nearness to the great pulses of national life'. Hewlett, who loved the country-side of south-east England and preferred to live out of London, was to write for him three articles on the 'county characteristics' of Surrey, Sussex, and Kent, describing felicitously in August 1885 the character of the Reigate region where Knowles was born. Knowles's own instincts for ten months of the year were devotedly urban: in June 1875 expostulating to Huxley, 'No man who is worth anything ought to be *allowed* to be out of Town at this time of the year', in October 1888 glad to be back in 'dear smoky old London', in June 1892 bemoaning to Gladstone the seaside convalescence that prevents him from going through the Season as 'maddening—in the face of the delicious Dissolution excitement!'[58]

Meanwhile, a fortunate meeting in 1867 engendered a famous

[57] Canon Stanley to YMCA at Exeter Hall, 31 Jan. 1854 (pamphlet in Leicester University Library's English local history collection), pp. 5–6.
[58] Henry Hewlett, 'County Characteristics: Surrey', *NC*, Aug. 1885, p. 274. Knowles to Huxley, 9 June 1875 (Huxley Papers, Imperial College). Knowles to Gladstone, 15 Oct. 1888, 23 June 1892 (Gladstone Papers, BL as chap. 7, n. 50 below).

house, the one commission its architect can have wholly enjoyed. With Aldworth there were no speculators, no shareholders, no board of directors, no church quarrels, but an inspiring client and site, a high uncommercial prestige, and a consciousness of nearness to the mainsprings of poetry and ideas. Knowles's talents could begin to find their range.

6

Turning-point: Aldworth and the Metaphysical Society

'Once, as we stood looking at Aldworth just after its
completion, he turned to me and said, ". . . That
house will last five hundred years." I answered him,
"I think the English language will last longer," '
Knowles, *Nineteenth Century*, January 1893

READERS OF TENNYSON who look down their noses at
historians taking his house apart for visual sources or
crediting his architect with its strange devices, may
reflect as the poet did upon critics looking for allegory in *The
Idylls of the King*: 'they are right and they are not right.' The house
was the poet's own fantasy, stimulated and then translated into
stone during 1867-8 by a lively new friend. The partial inter-
locking of this process with the founding of a Metaphysical
Society in 1868-9 has been little noted: the two processes are
usually described by different hands. In the context of both came
a parallel process that in this connection cannot be ignored, the
new uprush of Tennyson's poetry during 1868-9; the *Idylls* since
1859 had been brewing only beneath the surface. The context in
which the poetry emerged ought to be defined—without
pressing influences too hard—by recognizing the precipitant role
played by the building of the house and the accompanying
stimulus of much metaphysical conversation.

In the summer of 1867, for the first time in James Knowles's
adult life, came a sudden release of contagious exhilaration. Now
he could begin to find his role as one of those necessary catalysts
who sometimes rise up in the vicinity of people more creative
than themselves. The dedication of his book to the Poet Laureate in

1861 having led to desultory correspondence, he had dared to call upon him in the autumn of 1866. Now they met again—partly by chance—and the ensuing circumstances, crystallized by Knowles's quick response to needs partly defined by himself, led to his editorial career. He was the sort of man for whom Chance often worked because he was ready to seize it when it arrived—or to nudge it his way. On his way to what has been called the higher journalism, Aldworth was his turning-point.

A VICTORIAN CAMELOT

> 'Then all the host of craftsmen . . . found out a proper site whereon to build . . . and eagerly began to lay in the foundations.' Passage marked in Tennyson's copy of 1868 edition of Knowles's *Legends of King Arthur*, chap. i (TRC, Lincoln)

Like Thackeray's house on Kensington Palace Green, Aldworth was designed and built within two years, unlike the long accretion of Strawberry Hill and Abbotsford. Yet all four houses were closer to book-illustration than to the architecture of their own time, 'homes and haunts' of literary men, evocative architecture not devised primarily by architects. Few such houses can match Aldworth on its site high on a great hill with the Sussex Weald spread out before it—sometimes the sea glinting beyond the South Downs rim, sometimes the great plain enacting Tennysonian storms, 'covered with moving mist in the dim twilight and bellowing from end to end with thunder', as Emily Tennyson put it in the family journal. She had known the stirring North Downs scenery around Haslemere before she married. In the 1860s the Surrey–Hampshire–Sussex border was still a fine and private place, which the Isle of Wight in summer, with its tourists and Bard-hunters, was not. Tennyson's books were now earning enough for the family to have two houses. It was suitable that a native of the region, born beside the North Downs, should spring up to help. What actually happened—to reassess the twice-told tale—went something like this.[1]

[1] Sources on Tennyson and Aldworth for this chapter include: Tennyson family journal MS. and Knowles's letters to Tennyson at TRC, Lincoln, and helpful information from Mrs. Nancie Campbell there; compilations by Hallam 2nd Lord Tennyson: *Materials for a Life . . .* (c. 1895) vol. III, *Memoir* (1897) vol. II, and *Tennyson and His Friends* (1911) with essay by Knowles (as chap. 5, n. 50

Early in June 1867 the Tennysons looked at land called Green-hill, south of Haslemere, at Blackhorse Copse, 'a charming ledge' on the great hill called Blackdown, overlooking 'an immense view'. It was a natural terrace with a potato patch in the middle— 'a little flat clearance in the midst of sloping coppices that covered all the southern side of the hill', Knowles described it later— rather like the woodland terraces of the Reigate 'Park-hills' where he had played as a child, twenty miles away. Henry James was to see in Aldworth's site 'a certain high guardedness or defensiveness of situation, literally indeed from the material, the local sublimity, the fact of our all upliftedly hanging together over one of the grandest sweeps of view in England'.[2] Tennyson thought the prospect 'wants nothing but a great river looping along through the midst of it'—that book-illustrators' ideal formed from popular views by Turner and Birket Foster. The potato patch lay in the manor of River in the parish of Lurgashall, and the Lord of the Manor was the Earl of Egmont (not, as sometimes said, Egremont).

About 15 June the Poet Laureate went into Haslemere, from rooms they had taken near by, on his way to see helpful friends at Shottermill, 'to know the event' of his offer to buy the property. Mrs. Alexander Gilchrist (widow of Blake's biographer), whom the Tennysons had met the year before at the Carlyles', had been making inquiries; she later let her cottage at Shottermill to Lewes and George Eliot, and part of *Middlemarch* was written there. As Tennyson walked past Haslemere Station, or stood in the station yard peering about for a carriage, Knowles and his wife arrived by train from London and were met by carriage. (The eldest Knowles sister had married into the Stilwell family of Killinghurst, near Chiddingfold, where James Stilwell owned and farmed many acres; Tennyson was to enjoy watching the haying there.[3])

---

above); Sir Charles Tennyson, *Alfred Tennyson* (1949), *Aldworth* (1977), and helpful comments to me in 1965, 1970, and 1977; Kathleen Tillotson, 'Tennyson's Serial Poem', in G. and K. Tillotson, *Mid-Victorian Studies* (1965), and understanding comments on this chapter; Christopher Ricks, ed., *The Poems of Tennyson* (1969); material kindly communicated 1971–4 by Cecil Lang from his forthcoming edition of Tennyson's Letters; and my visit to the late Mr. and Mrs. Suren at Aldworth in 1967. (The present owners of Aldworth do not receive, and this chapter nowhere intends to imply that the house is on view.)

[2] Henry James, *The Middle Years* (1917), p. 98.

[3] On Stilwell connection, chap. 3, n. 72 above. Killinghurst is about two miles north of Aldworth. Tennyson family journal, July 1871: 'We call at Mr Stilwell's

Mrs. Tennyson's journal is more expressive than any paraphrase:[4]

A. had said to him [at Farringford the previous October] as he does to most strangers I am so short sighted that I shall not know you if I meet you unless you speak to me. Speak to him Mr Knowles does. I am going in your direction & drove him to Shotter Mill . . . having been told A's errand said I am an architect. A. replied, you had better build me a house & Mr Knowles said on one condition that you take my services freely only paying the journeys. Afterwards this was agreed upon.

As happens in such cases, unkind stories were later put about that the architect as a perfect stranger came up to Tennyson on the station platform (or the Portsmouth boat) offering to build his house. Yet Knowles did perhaps know from his brother-in-law that Tennyson was looking at properties thereabouts. For what it may be worth, the man with whom an agreement was to be made for the Blackdown land—probably Lord Egmont's agent—and the innkeeper of the Winterton Arms at Chiddingfold had the same surname, Lucas.[5] The Stilwells were on the local grapevine. And so, courting the ensuing possibility in advance, Knowles caught the first train for a little visit to Killinghurst.

A week later the Tennysons, attended by Knowles, held a picnic on the site. At first the couple thought in terms of a small four-room cottage—ideas that 'gave way somewhat', Knowles recalled later, as they talked it over, and Mrs. Tennyson explained 'certain rough ideas which she could not quite express by drawing but which I understood enough to put into shape'. This was probably the occasion for certain rough sketches by Tennyson that survive (Pl. 10): 'Mr Knowles . . . looked at our sketch and plans and took them home to put them "in working form", as he said.' The Tennysons then returned to Farringford, and Knowles to his office in Gray's Inn to spend the next two or three weeks ransacking every volume of engraved plates on English and French domestic architecture within reach, doubtless ignoring all claims on his professional attention by developments then in train for

---

& A. asks to be allowed to go into the hayfield. He misses the haymaking & the harvest here at Aldworth very much.'

[4] Especially 'Speak to him Mr Knowles does'. Sir Charles recalled (*Listener*, 23 Oct. 1969) that his grandfather always said he was 'the second most short-sighted man in England'; the first will have been the albino Robert Lowe.

[5] Local directories and Tennyson family journal.

Victoria Street, Westminster, where his design for several hundred feet of frontage was in process at the time. In July, among streams of visitors descending on the Tennysons at Farringford, Mr. and Mrs. Knowles arrived, and Mrs. Tennyson spent 'a long time with him making a measured plan of Aldworth'. (Some of her Sellwood relations came from Aldworth in Berkshire, though there is no sign that Knowles went there for ideas.) Family influences may have lingered in Tennyson's mind, in an unspecific way, from Somersby Rectory and its Gothic wing added by his father—memories of heraldic gables and chimney-pieces, perhaps. Other bits of imagery in his mind's eye, before solidifying by Knowles, survive in the rough sketches preserved at Lincoln, more like client's than architect's drawing, of gables and oriels and turrets.[6]

What actually happened was that Tennyson's house developed as a fantasy on the idea of an Anglo-French manor-house. The informing idea seems to have been fixed in the period of Caxton's publication, in the precincts of Westminster Abbey on the first English printing-press, of Malory's *Morte d'Arthur*: that is, 1485, liberally construed—the year, too, of that English landmark, Bosworth Field. (And Tennyson must have liked the thought that the house was finished precisely four hundred years after Malory finished writing in 1469.) Its Englishness was to include a French strain, as the Arthurian tales did. If *Maud* helped to pay for Farringford, *The Idylls of the King* helped to pay for Aldworth (Pl. 10). On its southerly-facing height it was to be a little Camelot, 'the dim rich city' solidified, not built to the music of harps but made of real stone and slate to prick through real mist. Spenserian, of a new Gloriana's time. To dismiss it as imitation Second Empire, as many a new English house then was, is to forget that Tennyson cared little for fashion, indeed he detested the politics and literature of Napoleon III's France. In August 1870, 'We rejoice to hear of the Prussian victory . . . being all of us Prussians,' said his wife, for the generation born before Waterloo grew up in horror of Napoleon I. Yet Knowles was not one to ignore fashion: he would provide an English late-fifteenth-century stone manor-house of a generalized sort, with the steep-

---

[6] Sheet *c*. 8″ × 12″ with rough sketches probably by Tennyson, inscribed 'for Aldworth' in his wife's hand and 'by A & ET' in Hallam's hand; verso with faint plan (TRC).

roofed French skyline English architects liked in the 1860s, modern conveniences, and poetic resonance too. Bran-new, with overtones.

For a poet, the unresonant grandeur of many a bran-new Gothic country house would not do. Nor were the domestic felicities of the architects Shaw, Nesfield, and Webb yet available in the building journals, and Knowles did not move in those circles. Nearby noble houses with a patina of age—Sutton Place and Loseley, Parham and the ruins of Cowdray—were too grand for imitation here, but there were smaller ones about, such as, very near, Blackdown House, that probably suggested use of the golden local sandstone. And there was a great deal of architectural book illustration about, none of it to be pinned down precisely by source-hunters in this case. The thought-processes of eclectic architects, like those of poets, are too subliminal for rational analysis. And the client-in-charge was a poet.

The assembling of the design was probably a gradual matter; no architect's drawings are known to survive. Conveyance of the property, and freeing it from the manor of River, took several months. Knowles was busy with Albert Mansions in Victoria Street, where both he and Tennyson later had chambers. At the end of January 1868 Tennyson met Knowles at the potato patch to fix the site and returned with him to stay the night at The Hollies, the Georgian house overlooking Clapham Common where Knowles had lived since his second marriage in 1865. It was probably the Poet Laureate's first visit there, of many during the next few years. How little even Knowles could have imagined this would happen, in the early 1860s when home had been a few doors along in more modest Nelson Terrace, its horizon bounded by the parish church before his front windows and the Battersea fields in the distance from his back windows, while speculators' projects simmered in the office at Gray's Inn, and he scribbled away, venturing with very great respect to write to the Poet Laureate; or even in 1866, screwing up his courage to call at Farringford. Yet by the spring of 1867, at 35, restlessly aware of unused talents and casting about for a role in life, Knowles was ready for the wider view that Aldworth was to afford.

The site is in Sussex, about half a mile south of the Surrey line at an altitude of some 720 feet, with the summit of Blackdown rising north-easterly behind it. The original block of the house measures about eighty by fifty feet, with the main rooms ranged along the south-east side of a wide corridor proceeding right down the middle of the house from the front door; one of the senior Knowles's first country houses, at Bramley ten miles away, had a similar plan. Aldworth has two main storeys and a prominent garret: from 'the central top attic on the south front, which opened on the lead flat [over] the large bay window', Tennyson loved to step out and 'watch the changes in the great prospect spread out before him', and even royal ladies were taken up to squeeze their skirts through the window. The two-storey canted bay that supplied this platform on the terrace front is no lofty oriel, it sits firmly on the ground even though oriels sounded all very well in *Lancelot and Elaine*.[7] A plain English Gothic arcaded parapet runs along the base of the French roof and interlaces the dormers, framing fern-forms surely inspired by coal-fossils: geology, 'seal'd within the iron hills', was bound to crop up somewhere, as Knowles's first key to *In Memoriam*.

Aldworth's pinnacled and crocketed dormers, each with its shield-hung, parti-diapered gable, have their overtones. Indeed, this was an early appearance of such a feature in Victorian England (architectural historians call them François Premier dormers). Poetical overtones aside, such gables provided convenient spaces for the new proprietor to display a few sets of family coats of arms. But the overtones ought to be heard. We know that both client and architect loved Westminster Abbey: 'A. is fond of the Abbey and of strolling about it by himself,' his wife had remarked in 1866. In these dormers, reminiscence of the Aymer de Valence tomb, the Abbey nave's wall-arcade shields and the diapered wall-patterns there coalesced. Beyond that, in the jungle of meanings and sources then available, we can only fall back on what Humpty-Dumpty told Alice and surmise that certain forms meant whatever Tennyson wished them to mean. The day after fixing the site of the house in January 1868, Tennyson went from Clapham to hear his friend the Dean of Westminster preach and came away 'much pleased', carrying back to Farringford Stanley's gift of his newly published book on the Abbey, from which Hallam read aloud, doubtless with special interest the pages on Poets' Corner: Tennyson's copy at Lincoln bears his marginal marking at the page on the Chaucer and

[7] Lines 1170, 1191; first published 1859 as *Elaine*.

Spenser burials, where Stanley quotes a line of Thomas Fuller's, 'enough almost to make passengers' feet to move metrically, who go over the place where so much poetical dust is interred'. Knowles will have remembered Gilbert Scott in 1859, exhorting his fellow-architects to observe the neglected quarry of design in Westminster Abbey ('Let us make use of it!'), and we know how the elder Knowles, with his son at his elbow, had then proceeded to do so in leafy friezes on the Grosvenor Hotel. By the spring of 1868 and perhaps through Tennyson, Knowles had come to know and intensely admire Dean Stanley, whose delight in reconciling opposing opinions matched his own. There were in those days reconcilers of forms and reconcilers of opinions, and some who were, temperamentally, both.

The empty shield on the dormer gable over the front door, supported by dragons ('that tare each other in their slime', perhaps), was later explained by Knowles: '[it] had remained blank when all the rest were carved—simply because of a hesitation how best to fill it up . . . he stood spying up at it through his eye-glass for a long while, and then decided to leave it blank . . . [thinking of] the blank shield in his own Idylls, of which Merlin asks, "Who shall blazon it?" ' Misremembering, Knowles must have meant Sir Percivale's description of the twelfth stained-glass window at Camelot: that line of the *Holy Grail*, 'And blank: and who shall blazon it? when and how?' was written in September 1868 when the walls of Aldworth were going up. Early views of the house also show a carved bird standing on the roof parapet (south-east corner), 'set up as a model for approval . . . never intended to stay there. He looked at it long and curiously, and laughed and said it seemed to grow queerer, that it was a pity to take it down; and there it remained . . . in its original solitariness, to his great content and amusement, which had a touch of seriousness in it.' When client and architect share a taste for the overtones and queernesses of both words and forms, no conventional house will result.[8]

The house bears a motto (Pl. 11) on a band-course of intermittent panels carved in low relief with little leaves and flowers and tiny animals, all intertwined in an inscription suggested by

---

[8] Knowles (1911), pp. 249–50. The falcon is no longer there. To balance such fancies, the triple-bay porch, for example, was a favourite crossbred motif of early nineteenth-century eclectic architects (e.g. on Friday Grove, Clapham Park).

Mrs. Tennyson: GLORIA IN/EXCELSIS DEO/ET IN TERRA, running from south-end bay to terrace-front bay, that is, below two sides of Tennyson's first-floor study and under the bedroom where his life was to end. Such a panelled frieze unrelated to a classical order and threaded between the storeys of such a house reflects a truly catholic taste, being of classical origin boiled down from pedestal-courses of dado and apron panels, surviving (perhaps originally via the engravings of Serlio) as a series of panels much used by the French and borrowers from the French—the sort of thing English eclectic architects around 1600, or 1860, might use on anything from a chimney-piece to an office-building—as printers would for engraved title-page or chapter-head ornament. Fit receptacle—if only to the prehensile eclectic eye—for the fauna and flora of North Gothic naturalism, indeed in close-up a successful bit of synthesis, delicately designed and precisely carved, just visible to a short-sighted client from the lawn. From across the lawn it is too small-scale to be read, either as design or as inscription, unlike much brash architectural ornament of the day. Unlike the Grosvenor's bold foliage, it was for close inspection like the page of a book. Tennyson or more likely Knowles may have found some suitable engraved borders for the, now anonymous, sculptor (possibly from the firm of John Daymond) to work from. Aldworth was bookish, typographical. Even the quiet diapering on the entrance-end chimney stacks is like printers' ornament. There had been a fashion for carved ornament on the exterior of country houses in the late 1850s and early 1860s, in the wake of the great urban model, the Houses of Parliament: the heraldic panels and lettered friezes there will certainly have been in Knowles's mind, for the decoration of Barry's building was part of the background of his growing-up. With the richer sculptural ornament of the 1860s–70s in South Kensington and Whitehall, Aldworth had nothing in common.

Near the entrance porch, and originally forming a corner of the house, is the foundation stone, inscribed simply with a centred monogram in a sunk shaped panel. There is no carved quotation, as implied in the Tennyson family-journal report, of words spoken at the stone-laying ceremony in the spring of 1868. Knowles chose the day, 23 April, St. George's Day, traditionally Shakespeare's birthday. The builder, Duke of Farnham, had set up a barracks and workshops for his men, with materials brought

over the rough moor (both Tennyson and Knowles having
forgotten to arrange with Lord Egmont about a road). By June
enough had been built for the owners to inspect, and Tennyson
went again in August. 'The invariable and tormenting delays in
finishing the house . . . annoyed him greatly', but they were to
move in only a year later, in July 1869. By then the four *Idylls*
written or extended in the prolific year 1868–9 were nearly
finished, and Knowles was busily writing a commentary on the
manuscripts Tennyson lent him.[9]

In April 1869 there was a shopping expedition to London; it
was also the week of the organizing dinner of the Metaphysical
Society at Willis's Rooms. The Tennysons stayed at The Hollies:
'Mr Knowles kindly meets us in a Brougham at Vauxhall
Station' (who would imagine the Tennysons stepping into a
carriage at that surging road-junction now?) Next day Knowles
escorted his guests 'to Haywards about grates & tiles', that is,
Yates, Haywood & Co. in Upper Thames Street, marble
merchants and dealers in stoves, clocks, and works of art—
providers of the complete chimney-piece. From there he took
them 'to the Deanery to see a certain stone mantelpiece which he
admires . . . very simple & graceful & we adopt it', possibly the
one in the Jericho Parlour: a chimney-piece in the ground-floor
corridor at Aldworth might have been worked up from that plain
sixteenth-century model, with embellishments from tombs in the
Abbey ambulatory, or book illustrations thereof. It was fun for
all concerned to think they were emulating the Abbey directly.
Other Aldworth chimney-pieces are variations on one set of
themes revived especially by Pugin, with colonnettes and 'range
of stony shields' as Tennyson put it in *Gareth*, and the look of
engraved title-pages. Ceiling-mouldings simulated deeply under-

---

[9] On stone-laying: Knowles to Mrs. Tennyson, 13 Apr. 1868 (TRC); family
journal (TRC); Knowles (1911), p. 249. Duke the builder, mentioned in Knowles's
letter: in trade directories for 1867 William Duke of Farnham was the only
builder of that name in Surrey. On difficulty over a road, C. Tennyson (1949),
p. 380; on Earl of Egmont, *Complete Peerage*. A date-stone with '1869' is beside a
rear door. Knowles wrote to Mrs. Tennyson while her husband was in Switzer-
land (incomplete letter, June or July 1869, TRC): 'Did you know that the
M.S.S. of Pelleas & Leodogran (i.e. *Pelleas and Ettarre*, then partly done, and
Coming of Arthur, written in February) are in my keeping during Mr Tennyson's
absence—that I may be making notes from them for an article to come out in
some proper way & place when they come out?' (his *Spectator* letter of 1 Jan.
1870).

cut Gothic friezes of running convolvulus and grape-vine, or engraved page-borders. Tiles surrounding the Welsh Lion on the threshold were familiar types adapted by Minton in the early 1840s from the rediscovered Chapter House floor at the Abbey.[10]

A proper historian would puzzle over the staircase with its Victorianized versions of the twisted baluster, not a Gothic notion. It seems that during the shopping expedition a good deal of carved furniture of Charles II type was bought at a shop in High Holborn, chairs and tables with the barley-sugar type of legs and rungs, simply because the Tennysons liked them: one sees them in contemporary engravings of the poet in his study. New-antique furniture—very superior Wardour Street—probably inspired the form of the stair balustrade.

Aldworth was wonderfully quiet, but for occasional 'thunders moaning in the distance' from naval guns at Portsmouth. Over the years, the rumble of guns from the Solent and the bellow of storms over the Sussex Weald made their contribution to English poetry. Most years, the family returned to Farringford for Christmas when the weather on Blackdown grew bitter: 'The cold mist seems to suck the life out of one Vampire like' (Mrs. Tennyson)—that 'deathwhite mist' added in 1869 to Tennyson's *Morte* of 1842 as he turned it into 'The Passing of Arthur'. At Farringford then, 'thank God we are at home'—and 'pre-eminently home' that remained. But the change to Aldworth every year was beloved and stimulating. It is a dignified, comfortable house, superficially not far (but for those roofs) from Early Victorian 'Old English' villas and mansions 'of the Olden Time' so well regarded a generation before it was conceived, yet in no way a 'period' house. Placing the Poet Laureate upon a suitably symbolic height, it was his own miniature edition of Camelot, issued in the 'as if' spirit of Spenserian castles (such as Bolsover) built in another cross-bred age in the afterglow of the Elizabethan revival of chivalry. Aldworth was Tennyson's own fantasy on Malory, translated by an adept at metaphor. Unlike Thackeray's

[10] On shopping, Tennyson journal and directories (Yates Haywood were to supply marbles for Baron Grant's commissions, chap. 7). Advice on pre-war Deanery from the Abbey Librarian. On idea of 1869, 'arms of all the greatest Poets & philosophers' to be carved on chimney-pieces, Knowles to Mrs. Tennyson as n. 9, and Tennyson in Oct. as *Materials*, iii. 133; those shields are still blank, though it is said that little pegs under the dining-room mantel-shelf were for suspending painted wooden shields.

executant architect, who remained obscure, Tennyson's architect had an eye on further enterprises, with the same sense of timing that caused Disraeli in 1869 to write *Lothair* about a young man asking what to believe.

KNOWLES AS IMPRESARIO

> 'Metaphysics . . . have engrossed A. much of late—
> The materialism of the day has revived his interest in
> them.' Mrs. Tennyson's journal, August 1866 (TRC)
>
> 'The questions which we treat touch the very base of
> all our life in Church & State, & carry in them the
> social future . . . nor perhaps is there any spot where
> the modern fermentation of opinion could be more
> compendiously seen than in our parlour of the
> Grosvenor.' James Martineau to Knowles, 27
> October 1874, quoted by Knowles to Gladstone,
> 29 October (Gladstone Papers, BL)

Late in 1868, soon after Aldworth was roofed in, Knowles touched off the spark that fused an unusual gathering of men, who met during the next decade to discuss what they believed. Alan Willard Brown's good book, *The Metaphysical Society* (1947), saves a biographer much trouble, yet the background for Knowles's flexible intelligence still puzzles historians of ideas and his biographer can offer clues previously missing through lack of awareness of the context of his life.[11]

This little forum of troubled men grew from a 'triangular duel' of a conversation between Tennyson and Pritchard and Knowles one morning in mid-November 1868 at The Hollies. It grew partly too out of much talk between Knowles and Tennyson about the King Arthur story, and out of the writing of *The Holy Grail* in September 1868 after an almost ten-year gap in the series. Emily Tennyson doubted if the *Grail* would have been written at all but for her own encouragement 'and the Queen's wish, and that of the Crown Princess'. But the stimulus of Knowles's

[11] Alan Willard Brown, *The Metaphysical Society, Victorian Minds in Crisis 1869–80* (1947), a full account of its history, meetings, members, and issues, lists papers read and, where possible, names of those present. Brown saw some, but evidently not all, of the unsorted papers then in Eirene Skilbeck's possession. On the Society marking the change from a common to a fragmented intellectual context, see R. M. Young's article in *The Victorian Crisis of Faith*, ed. Symondson (1970), kindly shown to me by Prof. Philip Collins.

persistent keen interest helped: Tennyson told him, perhaps over half seriously, 'I know more about Arthur than any other man in England, and you know next most.' That the great poem was bound to emerge eventually had nothing to do with anyone but the poet himself. Yet the moment for quickening, and a quickener, had arrived together, with the constructive stimulus of the house.

Early in 1868, between the site-fixing and the stone-laying for Aldworth, Tennyson had begun to work out the ground-plan of the Grail poem. An article in the April *Contemporary Review* by a professor of theology on 'The Arthurian Legends in Tennyson', claiming that no epic of Arthur was possible in our day, that the first four *Idylls* were 'pictures' and no more, did not deter him.[12] That summer or early autumn (perhaps with some nudging from Knowles) the publisher of the *Contemporary*, Alexander Strahan, decided to take over and reissue in a cheap edition Knowles's youthful prose rendering of *The Story* (retitled *The Legend*) *of King Arthur*. It had been intended not only for the young but, with the rise of a new 'general reader' implied in the new Reform Act (and its coming corollary the Education Act), 'to become the introductory popular reading book on King Arthur—the Primer of the subject', as its preface explained, for other editions of Malory were too obscure, except (primly) 'where not obscure enough'. Paperbound in smaller format than the 1862 edition (just under Penguin-size, in fact), still dedicated to Tennyson, with twelve chapters instead of fifteen and no illustrations, and priced at one shilling, Knowles's new edition reached the British Museum Library in December 1868.[13] Its new preface was the embryo of articles on the *Idylls* that Knowles was to publish in 1870 and 1873, which suggests to us that, as Aldworth rose on Blackdown during 1868, he was drawing out the intentions in the poet's mind and pressing him to go on. 'We can but hope and trust', the preface said, 'that one who has the power to read aright

[12] Samuel Cheetham (*DNB*, professor of pastoral theology at King's College, London) in *CR.* Apr. 1868. Alfred Austin took this up in *Temple Bar*, May 1869, on which Knowles to Mrs. Tennyson (4 May 1869, TRC): 'the Sealskin Manifesto ... must have been revised by the "great Seal" himself', referring to Tennyson's line 'Ancient Pistol, sealskin Payne' (Ricks, p. 1229) that substituted for Shakespeare's Poins the manager Payne from Moxon's publishing firm from which Tennyson had just painfully separated. Date, beginning of *Grail* prose draft: Ricks, p. 1661, C. Tennyson (1949), p. 375.

[13] BM date-stamp 10 Dec. 1868. On the back cover Strahan advertised books by Gladstone, Stanley, and Robert Buchanan.

so great a dream may feel it laid upon him as a duty to tell the whole interpretation of it, lest any part neglected should fall to baser meanings in unworthier hands. The growing popularity of Arthurian story was welcomed as 'a wholesome sign of the times', a protest led by Tennyson 'against the low and selfish side of a too commercial life' (with a shudder no doubt by Knowles at the thought of some of his clients, and taking the word 'materialism' in an un-Darwinian sense). The preface smacks too of Tennyson on poets he disapproved of, in its call for 'putting down the pandering cry of Art for Art's sake by the far greater cry of Art for Man's sake', anticipating Tennyson's furious lines on that theme. The latent allegory that Knowles perceptively angled for, and pursued in his later articles, was that 'Arthur "the King" mysterious in birth and death . . . stands evidently for the Soul, the moral conscience, as the Round Table for the passions.' For Tennyson had just pointed out to Knowles, in a letter probably written immediately after a meeting at the building-site in August 1868 ('After you were gone it struck me that you might touch upon this in your preface'), that the *Idylls* were more than 'mere legends of Arthur' and that 'in the very title there is an allusion to the King within us'. This was the theme Knowles passed on to Dean Alford a year later.[14] In Knowles's various commentaries on the *Idylls* his skill at metaphor was to suit 'the Primer of the subject' as his hand and eye were suited to the latent allegories of Aldworth. (We never hear of the Metaphysical Society as a 'Round Table'; no one imagined that Arthur's knights spent their evenings talking.)

Knowles was to recall that when he kept urging Tennyson 'to resume his forsaken project of making a whole great poem' of it, 'he would constantly protest that it was next to impossible now to put the thing properly together. . . . Perpetual importunity, however, had its effect, and in the end he came to admit that the plan of a series of separate pictures connected by a purpose . . . as a thread connects beads, had its merits'—Knowles in his commentaries loved figures of speech. He went on: 'After many

[14] Tillotson (1965), p. 100 on Knowles and the allegorical approach Tennyson preferred: for confirmation of her conjecture that Knowles instructed Alford, see chap. 7, nn. 8, 9 below. I owe to Cecil Lang knowledge of letter (owner Gordon Ray) Tennyson to Knowles, undated but seems to follow family-journal entry, 'A. goes to Greenhill' (i.e. Aldworth), for 20 Aug. 1868, when Knowles will have been writing his preface.

discussions as to which of the legends should be chosen to complete the series, he resumed the great scheme with the Holy Grail, much of which he made in our old house or under the trees on the lawn.' Knowles was certainly being journalistic there, and more anxious to appear to be at the core of things than the facts warranted: most of the *Grail* poem seems to have been written at Farringford, though all of the prose draft may not have been; at any rate, some writing was indeed done at The Hollies in the next few years. When the series was finished, Tennyson 'would sometimes point his finger at me with a grim smile, and say: "I had given it all up long ago . . . and then this beast said 'Do it', and I did it".' That was not quite all teasing, and Knowles deservedly lapped it up. It was the beneficent side of a 'perpetual importunity' that, after the *Idylls* were done, Tennyson was sometimes to find irritating.[15]

The hob-nobbing continued. Toward the end of September 1868, the Tennysons visited the Knowleses in Suffolk, the latter having taken a house near Ipswich for a month. In October the Knowleses arrived at Farringford in time for Mrs. Tennyson and Miss Thackeray to consult him on their plans for 'a house & a restaurateur kitchen for poor ladies . . . this pitiable class of being' —one hears no more of that scheme except Tennyson's 'comical lines on our Ladies Home', probably the ones (parodying Henry Mayhew): 'Home is home, though never so homely, And a harlot a harlot, though never so comely.' Then Tennyson had to read *The Holy Grail* aloud to Mr. and Mrs. Knowles, having just read it to Annie Thackeray. Three weeks later, Tennyson was back at The Hollies, the Woolners and others came to dine, and 'nothing can be kinder than the Knowleses'.[16]

The publisher Strahan was making 'liberal offers' to Tennyson for the publication of his works, perhaps at first through Knowles on the October visit; Tennyson spent much of November at The Hollies while negotiations were begun and the *Grail* set in type for a private trial printing, a year before its publication with other poems. Knowles was busy behind scenes, seeing Strahan and the lawyer Arnold White, helping to smooth the awkward-

[15] *Memoir*, ii. 53 quotes Tennyson: 'I made most of "The Holy Grail" walking up and down my field . . . at Farringford.' My other quotations from Knowles's *Idylls* leaflet, *c.* 1896 (TRC and Knowles papers, chap. 8, n. 88 below).
[16] September visit in *Materials*, iii. 87, October visit in Tennyson journal.

nesses of the withdrawal of Tennyson's works from the Moxon firm.[17] One day during this visit Tennyson and Knowles were at Emily Eden's in Kensington, trying 'to move a table mesmerically', and Browning came in. Knowles will have been quick to mention that, as we know from his letters, he had called on the Brownings at Casa Guidi in 1854. Browning returned with them to The Hollies to hear a reading of the *Grail*, coming again the next evening to read the opening canto of *The Ring and the Book* from its first volume published that month.[18] The master of The Hollies was coming on. Browning is said to have been asked subsequently, and unsuccessfully, to join the Metaphysical Society, but his concern with the traits of individuals, the development of *a* soul, would have consorted uneasily with the Tennysonian progress of The Soul, indeed with metaphysical guesses about souls in general.

In that month of November 1868 came the General Election (and in *Punch* Tenniel's elaborate cartoons of Gladstone and Disraeli drawn up in Arthurian tournament—strange simile for the first election after electoral reform). A pairing arrangement had to be made for Tennyson's continued absence from his polling address at Freshwater, pairing possibly with Charles Pritchard the astronomer, by then his neighbour there and a Conservative, and a fellow-guest at the Knowleses' in the first week of Tennyson's stay. Sir Charles Tennyson has described how friendship with Pritchard fostered the poet's growing interest in metaphysical speculation; and we have seen how Pritchard in his earlier days in Clapham had fostered young Knowles's curiosities about the universe. Pritchard was a pioneer in stellar photography, soon to be Savilian Professor of Astronomy at Oxford, yet he thought the most important thing in life was to reconcile science with the Bible. Tennyson was deeply concerned over 'the materialism of the age' and the blind brutish progress of Darwin's 'realm of matter and law', watched by so many (as Huxley put it)

---

[17] C. Tennyson (1949) on many publishers anxious to secure rights, and Strahan introduced by Knowles; also Tennyson journal, *Materials*, iii 90 ff., 179, *Memoir*, ii. 59, 66–7; Knowles to Tennyson, 12 Jan. 1869: 'Who can be telling all the wonderful cock-&-bull stories. . . . I myself have not oped my mouth to living creature' (TRC). In 1873 Tennyson moved to the firm of Henry King and later to Macmillan. A number of surviving letters between Knowles and Tennyson have to do with the arrangement of American rights.

[18] *Memoir*, ii. 59 (cf. n. 31 below). Knowles to Hewlett, 15 July 1854 (WPL). Tennyson and Browning had known one another since 1851 or before.

with the fear of savages watching an eclipse. In August Tennyson had sought reassurance from Darwin himself. In September the writing of the *Grail* poem was impelled by a 'strong feeling as to the Reality of the Unseen'—already compressed into a short poem, 'The Higher Pantheism', that was to launch the first regular meeting of the Metaphysical Society.[19]

Knowles left various similar accounts, all written down much later and varying as to who said what, of the germinal conversation at his house that morning after breakfast. Accounts of it a generation later in biographies of Tennyson and Pritchard were based on contributions from him, not from themselves. We can surmise that the intellectual stimulus came from Pritchard, the spiritual inspiration from Tennyson, and the practical, social impetus from Knowles. A rough draft among his papers includes Arthurian references in this context, for Tennyson had been reading *The Holy Grail* aloud to Pritchard and Strahan and Knowles, apparently the night before:[20]

While King Arthur was being so much and so frequently discussed between us the mystical meanings of the Poem led to almost endless talk on speculative metaphysical subjects—God—the Soul—free will— Necessity—Matter & spirit— & all the circle of Metaphysical enquiry. . . . Tennyson said how good it would be if such subjects could be argued & debated by capable men in the manner & with the machinery of the learned Societies. 'Modern Science' he said 'ought surely to have taught us how to separate light from heat— & men ought to be able now-a-days to keep their tempers—even while they discuss theology.' I said that if he & Mr Pritchard would join such a society— I would endeavour to get it up in London.

The account Knowles gave to Hallam Tennyson continues the story:[21]

[19] *Punch*, 21, 28 Nov. 1868. *Memoir*, ii. 57, 59, 90. C. Tennyson (1949), p. 373. On Pritchard, chap. 3, nn. 3, 4 above. Current topics can be deduced from the November periodicals: Lewes on Darwin in the *Fortnightly* and the running argument over the clergy's attitude to science in the *Contemporary*; J. D. Hooker as Pres. of the British Assn. having made 'a sharp speech' on the subject in August (Owen Chadwick, *The Victorian Church*, 1970, ii. 15). 'The Higher Pantheism': n. 34 below.

[20] MS. in Knowles papers (now TRC) with series of drafts for 1893, *c.* 1896, and 1911 printings of his writings on Tennyson, reworked over and over chock-a-block; cf. also chap. 5, n. 50 above on possible memoir.

[21] Knowles on Metaphysical Society, leaflet privately printed *c.* 1896 (chap. 8, n. 88 below) for Hallam's use in his *Memoir*; the account in Pritchard memoirs also based on material from Knowles.

They agreed to join, and I at once set to work to find the other members for a proposed 'Theological Society'.

At first it was intended that no distinct and avowed opponents of Christianity should be invited, though Anglicans of all shades, Roman Catholics, Unitarians, and Nonconformists should be eligible. But it was soon felt that if any real discussion of Christian evidences was to take place, the opposition ought to be fully and fairly represented. This extension of the plan commended itself especially to Dean Stanley, whom I consulted early about it, and it was when talking over it at the Deanery one day, with him and Lady Augusta, that she suggested the name of 'Metaphysical Society' as being better than Theological Society in the altered circumstances.

In short, the Society was to be a private example of the varied platform Dean Stanley sought to provide at Westminster Abbey and that Knowles was to provide in the *Nineteenth Century* after his trial run with the *Contemporary*. None of these, whatever anyone said, was a completely 'open platform', but by invitation or selection. The old term 'Christian evidences' came out of Knowles's own young days of clinging to Paley. Now the 'opposition' included Thomas Huxley: his Edinburgh address on 'The Physical Basis of Life' was published in the *Fortnightly* that February of 1869, with seven reprintings. It was Sir John Lubbock who, in April, invited Huxley to join the new society. Soon thereafter the word 'agnostic' seems to have been used (perhaps coined), as Richard Hutton recalled, 'by Professor Huxley at a party held previous to the formation of the . . . Metaphysical Society, at Mr James Knowles's house on Clapham Common, one evening in 1869, in my hearing'.[22] It was Huxley's label for himself, among all the 'isms' of the other members, perhaps especially dissociating his own scholarly scepticism from the loose latitudinarianism of Stanley, the 'bigot for toleration' as someone said. Vital of course for the convener, the Hon. Secretary as Knowles became, to be latitudinarian too.

[22] Lubbock to Huxley, 16 Apr. 1869 (Huxley Papers, Imperial College), saying that Hutton and Bagehot were 'getting up a club or small society to discuss metaphysical & theological matters in a Scientific manner!' and asking him to 'a preliminary dinner' on the 21st. On coining of 'agnostic', R. H. Tener to *TLS*, 10 Aug. 1967, cites use in *Spectator*, 29 May 1869, p. 642, and Hutton's letter of 1881 in *OED*; Knowles's party probably sometime between 21 April dinner and 29 May issue of *Spectator*, 'previous to the formation' meaning before first regular meeting in June.

In January, when Tennyson came up again from the Isle of Wight 'on this troublesome Moxon business', Archbishop Manning and W. G. Ward, editor of the Catholic quarterly *Dublin Review*, came to The Hollies to discuss 'the claims of the various thinkers of the day to be invited to join', and there was much bustling about between Ward's house at Hampstead and Clapham Common; a far cry from the burning of cardinals in effigy on that Common in 1850. Tennyson was delegated to ask the Duke of Argyll to join; there was some intention of inviting the Duke to preside, but His Grace dreaded *viva voce* discussion of such topics, thought judicial calm impossible, and declined to take part; a year or so later, when judicial calm was proven, he was prevailed upon to change his mind. Newman, Arnold, Lewes, Mill, and Spencer all refused to join.[23]

Vast notions of the Society's scope were entertained at first, anyway by the Hon. Secretary, whose ideas for its constitution, before the dinner in April, included three clauses: 'To form a complete library of mental and moral Science and speculation', 'To compile a Dictionnaire raisonné of philosophical systems— and perhaps also a popular and simple Introduction to Metaphysical Enquiry', and 'To publish such of the papers as essays communicated to it as it might think fit.'[24] Perhaps he imagined himself installed in Somerset House (where the learned societies then were before translation to Burlington House) preparing the 'popular and simple Introduction' himself. The idea of a dictionary lingered for a while: in 1874 Knowles was to ask Huxley for a list of twenty words needing definition, from which the Society's 'committee of definitions' could select the words most urgently in need of clarifying; on Knowles's letter Huxley jotted down 'absolute', 'cause', 'certitude', etc.[25] A vehicle for the publication of papers was soon to be made of the *Contemporary Review*.

The organizing meeting or preliminary dinner was held on 21 April 1869 in one of the smaller rooms that could be hired at Willis's Rooms (the former Almack's Assembly Rooms opposite Christie's in King Street, St. James's): ten years earlier, the Liberal Party had been founded there. Now Tennyson and Knowles

---

[23] Wilfrid Ward, *William George Ward and the Catholic Revival* (1893), chap. xii. *Materials*, iii. 103; Tennyson journal, Jan. 1869. Brown (1947), p. 165.

[24] Scribbled sheet in Knowles papers (WPL).

[25] Knowles to Huxley, 31 Mar. 1874, sending notice of meeting with 'Mind you come!' (Huxley Papers, Imperial College).

went together from Clapham; this was the week of the shopping expedition for Aldworth. The original membership seems to have stood at twenty, of whom thirteen went to that meeting; three more were balloted for then, and three in June, with more in July and later (if Brown's account is slightly adjusted by a draft for a letter of 31 May from Knowles to Stanley).[26] The original list continues to be astonishing: in alphabetical order, Henry Alford, Dean of Canterbury and editor of the *Contemporary Review*; Walter Bagehot, editor of the *Economist*; Alfred Barry, Canon of Windsor and Principal of King's College, London, who had recently published a life of his father Sir Charles Barry and whom Knowles will have known from childhood; W. B. Carpenter, physiologist and Registrar of the University of London; the historian James Froude, then editing *Fraser's Magazine*; the then Prime Minister, W. E. Gladstone, who came seldom while in office but served later as chairman; James Hinton, the ear-surgeon and philosopher; Richard Hutton, the co-editor of the *Spectator*; Thomas Huxley, the agnostic biologist and defender of Darwin; Knowles, as Hon. Secretary and catalyst; Sir John Lubbock, banker, scientist, and much else; Archbishop (later Cardinal) Manning; the Unitarian James Martineau; the poet and philosopher, Roden Noel, temporarily also Groom of the Privy Chamber to the Queen; the astronomer Dr. Pritchard; J. R. Seeley, author of the bestseller life of Jesus, *Ecce Homo*; Dean Stanley; Tennyson; John Tyndall, the physicist and geologist; and W. G. Ward of the *Dublin Review*. In April the Principal of Edinburgh University, Alexander Grant, and Tennyson's brother-in-law Edmund Lushington, Professor of Greek at Glasgow, and Lord Arthur Russell were voted in; and soon Father Dalgairns of the Brompton Oratory, George Grove the editor of *Macmillan's Magazine* and future lexicographer of music, Robert Lowe the Chancellor of the Exchequer, various bishops, and John Ruskin were added; later the Archbishop of York, the lawyer James Fitzjames Stephen, Dr. Andrew Clark, John Morley the editor of the *Fortnightly*, Leslie Stephen, F. D. Maurice briefly before his death, and others; almost at the end of the Society's life, Frederick Pollock and Arthur Balfour joined; during just over a decade more than sixty names overall.

But it must be emphasized that these members were never

[26] Knowles to Stanley, 31 May 1869, draft in Knowles papers (WPL).

present all at once, some seldom came, or dropped out, or died; at the most around twenty, sometimes as few as five, are known to have attended together. The meetings were monthly, from November to July while Parliament was in session, from 1869 until the Society was dissolved in 1880. As a sample of the depths plumbed or heights scanned, the first papers read and discussed during 1869 were, as listed by Brown: June, Hutton on 'Mr Herbert Spencer's Theory of the Gradual Transformation of Utilitarian into Intuitive Morality by Hereditary Descent'; July, Carpenter on 'The Common Sense Philosophy of Causation'; November, Huxley on 'The Views of Hume, Kant, and Whateley upon the Logical Basis of the Doctrine of the Immortality of the Soul'; December, Ward on 'Memory as an Intuitive Faculty'— titles that hardly convey to us now the anxieties behind a continual debate over the borderlines between religion and science.

The ancestry of these debates was more mixed than a direct line from the Cambridge Apostles and the Oxford Essay Club, those undergraduate groups thought to have been so influential in Victorian intellectual life, although a number of the Society's members came from that direction. Actually the original conversation at The Hollies, calling for 'the manner and the machinery of the learned societies', sounds more like Charles Pritchard FRS, FRGS, PRAS. At quite another but not negligible level, we may remember that Pritchard had been one of the founders in 1841 of the Clapham Athenaeum, the sort of local society where someone like young Knowles could begin 'to think about thinking', see the value of equal opportunity for opposing opinions, and briefly create an 'enduring record' of one of the society's papers in a boyish attempt at a monthly *Clapham Magazine*. A suburban March of Mind guyed in early numbers of *Punch*, a rage for debate called 'Athenaeumania' by the *Clapham Gazette*, had characterized the two decades we call Early Victorian. Knowles's eventual Late Victorian success on a sophisticated urban level was rooted in a vigorous Early Victorian suburbanity; in the 1860s, he was betwixt and between.

There was a longer, popular urban tradition of public discussion forums in London—where the room and membership were free, but payment was made for food and drink, with a chairman in charge of the discussion—a tradition said to date from at least the mid-eighteenth century in London. (The connection of those public debates with food and drink, and a master of ceremonies, sounds as if there were some Darwinian link with the evolution of the music hall.) Yet, while religious topics had been barred absolutely in such public forums, other traits of the discussions there (or of the human race) were relevant to the ultimate fading out of the Metaphysical Society:

A man goes with certain preconceived views, and he holds them to the end, all argument notwithstanding. Such a climax as settling a point once for all seems never to occur to an habitual forum spouter. . . . Occasionally a man of scientific bent wanders into a discussion forum, and gains acquiescence of the chairman to the delivery of a speech on some scientific subject. The result is always a failure—a woeful fiasco. The clear, sharply defined yeas and nays of science do not accord with the genius of those places.[27]

The genius of those places, urban and suburban, could neither define nor reconcile the borders of religion and science. The reasons for the Clapham Athenaeum's final dissolution in 1868 were really more social than philosophical, the cohesiveness of suburban life so near London being then diminished by more efficient public transport. That that dissolution happened so near in time and place to the fertilizing talk at The Hollies was simply a bit of fate's irony. That Knowles's career was strewn with such neat ironies is a sign of his instinct for the timely issue.

It may be relevant that the new spark was struck by someone schooled in the polarities of a new profession that had been defining its own borders in the Early Victorian decades. How the heads of that profession had harped on its dualism: for example, Professor Donaldson setting up his courses at University College on architecture-as-an-art and architecture-as-a-science in 1842, glorying in the profession's 'distinctive feature from any other department of knowledge . . . essentially composed of two divisions—Imagination and Reason'. Young Knowles, after two years of exposure to Donaldson's lecture-habit of tabulating human progress as a tidy pendulum, had himself glibly held forth, in 1850 at the age of 19, on 'those great waves which from the dawn of history have periodically influenced the human race', produced in 1853 an 'instinct v. reason' paper and another on certain 'vibrations of the great pendulum of thought', and in

---

[27] *Tinsley's Magazine*, July 1870. On Clapham Athenaeum, chap. 2, n. 21 above, and *Clapham Magazine*, Nov. 1850.

1859 before the Clapham Athenaeum elaborated on the notion of science-as-analysis *v.* art-as-synthesis. Finally, in 1869, for the February issue of the *Contemporary Review*, he produced 'The Alternation of Science and Art in History' signed J.T.K. This may have been encouraged by Strahan who had just published Knowles's King Arthur book, yet the editor of the *Contemporary*, Dean Alford, had probably already been approached to join the new Society, in time to be receptive to a contribution from Knowles. And an article, in the form of a letter from J.T.K. about what was later called mental telepathy, appeared in the *Spectator* for 30 January—Hutton being another of those early-enrolled members of the Society, though Knowles had probably written letters to the *Spectator* before. These two essays at learned speculation were obviously poured out in a fever of high-minded busyness while nursing the new Society and the new house. Knowles's other professional clients can have seen little of him just then.[28]

His way of absorbing and giving off ideas is wonderfully illustrated by the 'Science and Art in History' article, which has perhaps been too much dignified in retrospect as 'neo-Hegelian', a term applicable to men like Donaldson; Knowles in his young days was neo-Donaldson, with all the era-consciousness Victorian minds were prone to. Yet this article is a quite extraordinary blend of keen nose-for-news, poetic perceptiveness, pat citing of Locke, Pascal, Schlegel, Whewell, Bunsen, etc. etc., and naïve tabulation of history as alternating periods of analysis (science) and synthesis (art), oddly like, yet the opposite of, modern theory on convergers (scientists) and divergers (artists), but more like his old professor's tables on the blackboard. Here Knowles professed to be tracing the career down the ages of an imaginary Cartophilus, personifying the wanderings of the human mind and adapted no doubt from the legend of Cartaphilus the Wandering Jew—reports of whose appearance in the world persisted in the nineteenth century, last heard of in Salt Lake City in 1868—nose for news indeed. 'There is in all directions an increase of specu-

28 On Donaldson, chap. 3, nn. 2, 5. Knowles on dualism of history: Nov. 1850, opening leader, *Clapham Magazine*; Aug. 1853, paper shown to 'vastly clever' clergyman at Broadstairs, and paper published on educating architects; Mar. 1859, paper to Clapham Athenaeum on art criticism; Feb. 1869, article in *CR*. On 'brain-waves', n. 31. Theoretically Knowles was watching over construction in Victoria Street and Battersea during 1868–9.

lation and theory, a love for broad though hasty generalizations.
. . . There are Mormonisms and spirit-rappings and ghostologies
without end. . . . There is an exhaustless appetite for new
inventions, and for abstract science made straightway tangible.'
This particular human mind was like blotting paper with litmus
sensitivity.[29]

Tennyson shrewdly remarked to Wilfrid Ward (son of the
editor of the *Dublin Review*) that no one 'ever had his brain in
his hand as Knowles had. . . . He could learn in half an hour
enough of a subject which was quite new to him to talk about it,
and never talk nonsense', though it was a bit unfair of Tennyson
to assume that Knowles was completely ignorant of philosophical
speculation before the Society was formed and only then began to
'chatter metaphysics with the best of us'; his boyhood letters
were full of unschooled 'metaphysical talk', as he had called it
when writing to Hewlett in 1853. There would seem to have
been some misquoting by Ward, for Tennyson must have said
that Knowles at first 'did not know a hypothesis from a hippopotamus'—a poet's joke—not 'concept from a hippopotamus'
as tiresomely quoted and requoted since.[30] The remarkable
conclusion to Knowles's *Contemporary Review* article reflected
Tennyson's hope that poetry might solve the riddle of the
universe: looking beyond an age of technology to 'the advent of
an imaginative cycle once more' when Cartophilus, the human
mind, might 'be about to open the golden gates of the twentieth
century to Art and Poetry and Faith'. Such optimism was not
general in 1869.

The *Spectator* piece was called 'Brain-Waves—A Theory' and
proposed the 'collection of authenticated ghost stories . . . to
throw light on one of the darkest fields of science, a field, indeed,
hardly yet claimed by science', and cited personal experiences
gathered (doubtless during that fertile November) from Browning and Tennyson and Woolner as possible evidence for 'my
crude hypothesis of a *Brain-Wave*' like an 'electric manifestation'
or series of undulations 'proceeding from every brain when in

[29] J.T.K., 'The Alternation of Science and Art in History', *CR*, x. 285–95,
Feb. 1869. 'Neo-Hegelian': Brown, p. 173.
[30] Wilfrid Ward, 'Three Notable Editors', *Ten Personal Studies* (1908), pp. 70–1.
His daughter Maisie Ward in her *Browning . . . 1861–89* (1969) and E. M. Forster
in his *Marianne Thornton* (1956), both perceptive writers, took over Ward's
recollection of something said many years before.

action' into the 'circumambient ether'. Knowles said later that the idea occurred to him in about 1851 'when watching experiments in what was then called electro-biology'. He had touched on such a notion to Hewlett in 1853, was to resurrect it in the *Nineteenth Century* in 1882 in connection with the founding of the Society for Psychical Research, and again in 1899 after Marconi's discovery of wireless telegraphy. Whether Knowles's use of the term 'brain-wave' contributed anything to popular terminology is obscure; an obituary letter in 1908 had it that Knowles had read a paper on the subject before the Metaphysical Society, which he did not, and that he 'claimed the distinction of having discovered the germ of wireless telegraphy'. What he said in 1899 was that Marconi's invention seemed to lend more plausibility to his idea: if messages could be sent from an electric battery, why not from a brain like Mr. Gladstone's? That electricity given off by the brain is now measurable would have delighted him.[31]

The brain-wave article reflects or is reflected in another early clause quietly dropped from the new Society's constitution after the organizing dinner in April: that it should undertake to 'collect trustworthy observations upon ... mental and moral phenomena'; and for that meeting only, the full name was Metaphysical and Psychological Society. The brain-wave theory was one more stage on the way of Knowles's own careering mind. It will be remembered, incidentally, that a theory of one member of the Society, Dr. Carpenter, on the brain's registration of sensory phenomena, had furnished Wilkie Collins with a clue for *The Moonstone*, published in 1868.[32] Plucking sensory phenomena out of the circumambient air was a trick of the mind Knowles had. Even if he was the only man present at the Society's meetings who had ever designed a church—a point that perhaps only Ruskin would have thought relevant, if he knew it—Knowles himself doubtless kept that sort of thing in a separate compartment of his mind. For he was not so much design-minded as idea-minded:

[31] J.T.K., 'Brain-Waves—A Theory', and editorial comment on this 'curious and thoughtful letter', *Spectator*, 30 Jan. 1869, pp. 133, 135. Table-moving at Miss Eden's, Nov. 1868 as n. 18 above, 'table-speaking' result of someone's knowledge 'directing a motion to take place', Knowles to Hewlett, 20 Sept. 1853, as chap. 3, n. 36 above. Extracts from *Spectator* letter reprinted *NC* June 1882 with article on 'Thought-reading' by Barrett, Gurney, and Myers (cf. Brown, 1947, p. 244, on founding of Society for Psychical Research), and Knowles, 'Wireless telegraphy and "brain-waves" ', *NC*, May 1899, p. 857.
[32] *The Moonstone* (1868), 2nd period, 3rd narrative, chap. x.

transplanting Ruskin's 'the oak, the ivy, and the rose' to the walls of the Grosvenor Hotel had been an idea, translating Tennyson's wizard music to the walls of Aldworth was an idea, to be running this Society was to be an orchestrator of ideas.

Before the first regular meeting was held on 2 June 1869 at the Deanery, Westminster Abbey, Knowles wrote to Tennyson on 29 May:

Yesterday I read to Hutton as you gave me leave to do 'the higher Pantheism' which gave him wonderful delight. He begged me . . . to beg of you most earnestly to let it be read—if you will not come and read it yourself. . . . It would make it [the meeting] historical he said— to open with such a piece as that. . . . He said 'it would do more to convert the Atheists than all our arguments.'

'. . . but it wants to be read in a big voice,' Tennyson replied. 'Can you make yours big enough?' (according to Knowles's quotation, among his papers, from an apparently lost letter),[33] for Tennyson did not come to the meeting. At any rate, that summer evening in the Abbey precincts—probably in the Dean s library over the western approach to the cloisters, with a great window looking into Dean's Yard—Alford, Barry, Hinton, Hutton, Huxley, Lubbock, Lushington, Manning, Russell, Stanley, Tyndall, and Ward listened to Knowles's voice, intensely expressive however light in volume, we suppose, reading 'Law is God, say some: no God at all, says the fool;/For all we have power to see is a straight staff bent in a pool.' The scientists present may have smiled gently. The agnostic view was comprehended and put aside: 'The ear of man cannot hear, and the eye of man cannot see;/But if we could see and hear, this Vision—were it not He?' The Society, too, was to end with a question mark. Of that evening, Grant Duff (who joined later) reported a friend rushing up to Lord Arthur Russell outside Dean's Yard after the meeting: 'Well, is there a GOD?' 'Oh yes . . . we had a very good majority.'[34]

[33] Tennyson to Knowles, apparently 30 or 31 May 1869, partly quoted by Knowles in NC, Jan. 1893, p. 171 ('I am not coming up . . .') without this sentence ('but it wants to be read . . .') which appears in one of Knowles's drafts (now TRC); communicated to Prof. Lang who has not found original letter. Knowles's of 29 May is at TRC. After talking with the Abbey Librarian (then Mr. Lawrence Tanner), the Dean's Library seems the likeliest room in the Deanery for this quietly historic meeting.

[34] The poem was written in Dec. 1867 (Ricks, p. 1204). Brown (1947), pp. 27, 318, lists those present. M. E. Grant Duff, *Notes from a Diary 1851–72* (1897), ii. 185.

Knowles arranged for future meetings a 'room & dinner at the Grosvenor Hotel', without remarking that that Renaissance building with its Gothic details was a symbol in itself of attempted reconciliation of opposites; while never unduly suppressing any mention of the family profession in other company, he did not flaunt it either. We can picture the eminent members ascending the hotel's middling-grand staircase beside the giant ivy-leaves of which its balustrade then apparently consisted, to their private parlour on the first floor. Dinner was more genial and clubbable than the formal debate afterward, Knowles remembered later: 'There was greater ease and freedom of speech . . . than was possible after the chairman's hammer had fallen and the paper of the evening had been read.' If no member ever succeeded in changing the views of another, any more than the spouters of the City discussion forums had, it appears that they did come to like one another more, and the clubbable gain was in mutual personal respect. The long-past architectural effort to comprehend medieval–irrational and classical–rational elements in their 'club-house' will have been noted by nobody.[35]

Little has surfaced from the discussions of papers to convey the intensity of feeling aroused at that table, except one letter written by Knowles in June 1875 to Huxley, who had been absent from an evening spent upon the subject of vivisection, or, 'The Rights of Man over the Lower Animals':

We had a famous talk last night over Lord A. Russell's paper— Gladstone was in the chair & spoke much & excellently— & Martineau was as loftily luminous & perfect as he always is when he is thoroughly roused—

Hutton was (as Gladstone said to me) in a minority of one—I was really surprised & so was Lord Arthur to find how much support Lord A received. . . .

But the greatest fun was your note to me—I read aloud so much of it as I dared & was glad I did not read quite all—for it drove Hutton into a white rage—I have seldom seen him so moved. I can't recollect

---

[35] Draft for letter to Stanley (n. 26 above) on 'room & dinner'. Such private dining parlours were on the first floor (manager). One meeting, on 11 July 1871, was held at the Westminster Palace Hotel at the other end of Victoria Street (Knowles to Gladstone, 27 June 1871, Gladstone Papers as chap. 7, n. 50), because either the Grosvenor's room was engaged or the other was closer to House of Commons. On gains in personal respect, Knowles's leaflet *c.* 1896, also Ward (1893 as n. 23 above) quoting Dalgairns and Martineau.

his epithets but he said such a letter ought to be burnt 'by the common hangman' & so forth—It made however such an effect that at the end of the evening I was called upon to read it a second time— & though the extreme trenchancy of its terms did almost stagger some—yet all were with it in spirit.

Usually the 'wonderfully genial and kindly tone' of those meetings, as Knowles told Leonard Huxley later, 'was very largely owing to your Father & to Dr Ward—who habitually hit each other at the hardest—but never with a touch of lost temper or lost courtesy'. Huxley and Manning often had 'lively but most friendly' arguments, and bishops who had expected to see 'horns & hoofs' on Huxley were 'wonderfully softened by meeting him . . . face to face for 10 years'.[36]

After the vivisection meeting, Knowles reminded Huxley that 'we are all sworn to an honorable secrecy—but this may not be held to extend to out-of-doors'; that is, disagreement between Huxley and Hutton on that matter was no secret. In general, although some papers were eventually published, and all were privately printed and circulated to members before meetings (the Hon. Secretary having a printer at his elbow from 1870 on), the talks were wholly private. As Knowles put it later, 'one cannot but lament the absence of any sort or kind of reports of the debates—tho' doubtless their value & force & charm were principally chiefly owing to this very absence of reporting & to the sense of mutual loyalty & confidence warranting quite open speech'.[37] In 1885, after the Society's demise, Hutton at Knowles's bidding described a typical meeting to readers of the *Nineteenth Century*, evoking the voices and expressions of some of the most remarkable men around that table, and a few other comments survive. Neither Pritchard nor Tennyson went to meetings

[36] Knowles to Thomas Huxley, 9 June 1875, and to Leonard Huxley, 23 Feb. 1899 (Huxley Papers, Imperial College). Hutton's propaganda against vivisection in the *Spectator* was said to be largely responsible for the limiting Act of 1876 (Brown, p. 207 n.). See *Life and Letters of Thomas Huxley*, ii. 439, Huxley to Darwin about Vivisection Commission on which Hutton sat. Here the Society came closer to current affairs than usual. Huxley's note to Knowles, read at the meeting, appears to be lost. I have seen no minutebooks, but see n. 37.

[37] Draft in Knowles's papers (now TRC). The Society's surviving minutebooks apparently bear out a wise comment on the early days of the Royal Academy: 'the minutes of any society made up of men old enough to have acquired some worldly wisdom are not usually designed to inform posterity about what actually happened' (E. K. Waterhouse, *The Times*, 13 Dec. 1968).

much: the former was at his best with only one or two people at a time, for a speculative conversation, for all his taste for learned societies, and the Poet Laureate, though his presence greatly dignified the proceedings when he did go, modestly said little; these were not poets' occasions. Frederic Harrison, only half-perceptive, thought Tennyson didn't always quite follow the arguments: Tennyson's perceptions arose instinctively, soaring away from argument. Knowles by himself, during the years he knew Tennyson best, say 1868–75, was able to meet him part-way on the instinctive plane. But Metaphysical Society meetings were not on that plane.[38]

The Hon. Secretary as impresario went to almost every meeting for ten years; as Mivart recalled later, 'the life of the society was indeed bound up' with Knowles's 'secretaryship'. He never gave a paper, probably took small part in the formal debates except for a keen word now and then, having actively incited good talk over dinner and had a busy hand in proposing subjects or inducing others to do so. The idea of such debates was to be reflected in written symposia he stage-managed in the *Nineteenth Century*. A wonderful reservoir of contributors was here for the editors present (Morley to Huxley in 1877: 'Knowles & I are going about like ravening lions').[39] Knowles's editorial career came out of the Society.

Hutton thought these occasions demonstrated 'the extraordinary fermentation of opinion in the society around us', perhaps picking up the metaphor via Knowles, to whom James Martineau had said in 1874 that nowhere could 'the modern fermentation of opinion . . . be more compendiously seen than in our parlour of the Grosvenor'. Moral and intellectual yeast, said Hutton, 'was as hard at work multiplying its fungoid forms in the men who met at that table, as even in the period of the Renaissance itself'. Yeast was a popular intellectual metaphor then—Huxley wrote about the real stuff for Knowles in the *Contemporary* in 1871. Perhaps, as Hutton did not say, the Society's effort to comprehend all knowledge was a last expression of the Renaissance idea of universal man. (Yet the Victorian

[38] R. H. Hutton, 'The Metaphysical Society, A Reminiscence', *NC*, Aug. 1885. Knowles to Miss Pritchard in her *Memoirs* of her father, p. 98. F. Harrison, *Autobiographical Memoirs* (1911), ii. 86–7; also Grant Duff to Wilfrid Ward, Tennyson *Memoir*, ii. 169.
[39] Morley to Huxley, 27 Nov. 1877 (Huxley Papers, Imperial College).

faith in discourse is still with us: for example, a Nobel conference behind closed doors in 1969, attended by a list of men whom journalists called 'a name-dropper's delight', to talk about 'The Place of Value in a World of Facts'.) 'The questions which we treat touch the very base of all our life in Church and State, and carry in them the social future to which the eye of a philosophic statesman must always be turned', said Martineau, urging Knowles to urge Gladstone to chair the 1874–5 season, in words Knowles duly passed on.[40]

Imagine today's Prime Minister, Chancellor of the Exchequer, Poet Laureate, Anglican deans and bishops and the Cardinal of Westminster, with the Warden of All Souls, Lords Annan and Snow and Clark, with assorted scientists, lawyers and editors, and our nearest equivalent to Mr. Ruskin (whoever that could be), meeting regularly ten or fifteen at a time for a private unreported dinner in a London hotel: what antennae would lurk to trap and trivialize the brain-waves. More deeply serious than many societies of its day, less random than lunch at The Athenaeum, in its privacy the Metaphysical Society was a quiet phenomenon of the 1870s that fermented from worries of the 1860s.

Beyond that table, toward the end of the 1860s, 'a vague sense of social insecurity' in English society became generally evident as trade lingered in what the *Illustrated London News* in January 1868 called 'a winter of extraordinary duration', its sap 'run down to the roots' (yet the leader-writer insisted 'that England has yet a great and beneficent work to do' and refused in a striking phrase to 'anticipate any permanent decline in her virility'). Standing armies on the Continent made even unmilitary observers uneasy; even in architectural designs hung at the Paris Exhibition of 1867 one English critic, in the *Contemporary* for October, sensed 'an unsettled state of thought and intent throughout Europe'. At home, practical men in business and the professions, and the more thoughtful artisans involved in the growth of cities and of their callings, approached the new decade with an apprehension not unlike ours in the 1970s. Many thoughtful men beside the band of thinkers at the Grosvenor Hotel faced the future with doubt. Even an Aldworth above 'the plain that then began to darken under Camelot' seemed no asylum. Tennyson's lines of 1869 on the 'last, dim, weird battle in the west' expressed a fear of 'the

[40] See head of this section.

fiercest battle the world has yet known between good & evil faith & unfaith' (family journal), seeing as Matthew Arnold did the 'darkling plain Swept with confused alarms . . . where ignorant armies clash by night'—a feeling, not confined to poets, of standing on the edge of an abyss, 'on a mountain pass in the midst of whirling snow and blinding mist' (Fitzjames Stephen). Yet for a man like James Knowles, just finding his role as impresario, however deeply the retreat of faith had worried him once, an age of anxiety was his platform: the more eminent and articulate the anxious ones the better. The meetings of 1867–9 had set him on his way, and he entered the 1870s with relish.

7

The Contemporary Review *and Bread &* Cheese

'If we architects . . . as custodians of an art whose
essential attribute it is to reflect the character of the
time, reflect this character all too faithfully . . . what
else than this could we be expected to do?' Professor
Robert Kerr to the RIBA, 18 January 1869, *RIBA
Transactions 1868–9*

In 'the existing state of commercial immorality . . .
"there is need" (as King Arthur says when he seeks
Excalibur) "of a sword that shall chastise these rebels
terribly"—I do so wish that you would draw and use
it.' Knowles to Gladstone, 31 July 1875, Gladstone
Papers, BL

A SAD LITTLE NOTE FROM THAT OTHER ARTHUR,
James Knowles's first-born, survives from these years
when his father was often importantly away at Aldworth
and Farringford:

My dear Papa
    I hope you are quite well and I bought a sword and the
strap is not long enough to go round my waist and the sword is blunt
and I have broken the handle
                    Your dear Affectionate Son
                                Arthur James

In 1870 the children were eight, seven, and four years old—
Jane's Arthur and Millicent much less cossetted by their stepmother than her own Beatrice—and there were no more. Family
limitation was a trend of the 1870s, having a good deal to do
with rising standards of living and rising social expectations
among the young professional classes with unstable incomes and

multiplying household tastes.[1] James Knowles was used to a comfortable life, modestly so in childhood, with increasing ease from his mid-teens although kept on a tight rein by his father, after the family moved to Friday Grove. Just as one of the pleasures of that stately house and of Knowles senior's statelier income in the 1850s had been the entertaining of the great on their horizon such as the Barrys, so young Knowles's suddenly expanded horizon at the end of the 1860s meant having Tennyson to stay, with the Woolners to dine one day, Browning and Alexander Macmillan another day, it meant having Manning to confer with Ward and Tennyson, Ruskin to confer with Huxley and Manning, and a party for all the original members of the Metaphysical Society, it meant taking the Prime Minister and the Poet Laureate to Richmond on a summer's day, and so on. Lion-hunting, be it ever so high-minded, costs money.

Little building went on for Flower's estate architect to attend to during 1870–2, and Knowles energetically took on an estate for another client at 'West Brighton', or Hove, a commission that was to lead to large designs for Kensington and for Leicester Square, and much perturbation of spirit and pocket. Otherwise, there were some cheap church-auxiliary buildings for his old friend George Herbert at Vauxhall; there was no fee from Aldworth; and the *Contemporary Review* was to pay poorly and irregularly. Arthur Knowles was to have an expensive education, at the new London International College, Spring Grove, Isleworth (of which Huxley was a governor), and Trinity College, Cambridge (B.A. 1885), under the same tutor the young Tennysons had had; Knowles may have put his son down for Trinity after a visit with Tennyson in November 1873 (an expedition later recalled as the day 'Tennyson took me thro' Cambridge . . . [when] he said he saw "the ghost of a man in every corner" '; although, as the party seems to have included Mrs. Julia Cameron and one of her boys, it was not such a private tour after all). The girls were to have governesses: Lily Whichelo, later E. M. Forster's mother, was one. The Knowleses' neighbour, Forster's aunt Marianne Thornton, representative of an older, more

[1] On birth control, J. A. and Olive Banks, *Feminism and Family Planning in Victorian England* (1964), pp. 82–3, 92. Child's letter in family possession. Milly told her niece that neither she nor Arthur remembered ever being picked up and held by the stepmother they acquired when they were babies.

aristocratic Clapham, was to feel sorry for the girls growing up in a 'smart journalistic' household.[2] Isabel Knowles, apparently not such an interesting person herself, went about socially less than her husband did: as wife to a strenuously busy, nervy man with many guests her plate was full, and social strenuousness away from home may have bored or even frightened her—Mrs. Gladstone and Mrs. Tennyson, at any rate, may have seemed rather daunting to her. Invitations did not always include her: in May 1872, Knowles accepting Gladstone's invitation to one of the Thursday breakfasts in Downing Street was happy to be entrusted with inviting Miss Thackeray to come, though 'her movements are almost as bird-like as her tongue and her heart'; and later on, Knowles apparently went alone to dinners given by the Gladstones. During the 1870s he came to be more and more prized as a guest: at Hawarden in 1876, 'Mr Knowles came and drew out Papa finely'; at the surgeon Sir James Paget's during 1872–6, 'the music and the talk were of the utmost excellence . . . when Miss Janotha [the singer], Mr James Knowles, and Canon Scott Holland were all there together'; and after one of Miss Thornton's 'intellectual dinner parties' in 1875 Miss Forster wrote to Miss Darwin:

Knowles so absorbed me. . . . He is wonderfully good-natured. He is a snob, but I am more and more struck with what good talk he draws out; he doesn't shine himself but there is sure to be light in his neighbourhood. . . . [He] liked talking nonsense about great people every bit as much as we did hearing him. So he went on assuring us that Manning was a really good fellow to whom he, Knowles, could speak his mind and he should insist on Gladstone doing this that and the other.

[2] On St. Peter's, Vauxhall, *Bldr*, 1 Feb. 1868, tenders column: OS 1871 Sheet LV (school between church and Pearson's art school); and MBW *Minutes* 1873, p. 552, Knowles's application for mission house in Kennington Lane opposite church (gaunt, cheap-gothic, brick four-storey), and possibly addition to Vicarage (former Vauxhall Gardens manager's house) beside the church, No. 308 Kennington Lane, where Maurice Hewlett's future wife grew up (chap. 9, n. 6). On International College, founded 1860s in cause of universal brotherhood, *ILN*, 20 July, 7 Sept. 1867, pp. 63–4, 264. Tennyson talked of showing Cambridge to Knowles in November 1872 'as he has never seen the place' (*Materials*, iii. 193), but not clear that Knowles, then with much business at West Brighton, actually went that time; on visit of 15 Nov. 1873, *Materials*, iii. 225, Emily Tennyson to Edward Lear, 27 Nov. 1873 (published by J. O. Hoge, 1974), and Knowles to Gladstone, 12 Dec. 1895, Gladstone Papers as n. 50 below. E. M. Forster, *Marianne Thornton* (1956), p. 252; Beatrice Knowles, according to her daughter, was Forster's godmother.

On such an occasion 'he also advised the company how to stop the architect Alfred Waterhouse from pulling down the old hall and court of Pembroke College'. This unsuccessful advice may have been not unrelated to an entry in the Tennyson family journal that Waterhouse was making plans for an addition at Farringford in 1871. Knowles may have had his oar in; Tennyson to Knowles, from Farringford, 5 April 1872: 'The rooms are not quite dry.... My chimney-piece is a great success.'[3]

During 1871-3 Knowles acted professionally for Huxley at No. 4 (now 38) Marlborough Place just off Abbey Road in St. John's Wood, by designing an extension for an existing cottage. The new wing (still standing as a day-hospital) was an 'uncompromisingly square face of yellow brick [now stuccoed] distinguished only by its extremely large windows ... not without character, and certainly ... unlike most London houses', Huxley's son was to say of it, 'built for comfort, not beauty; designed, within stringent limits as to cost, to give each member of the family room to get away by himself or herself if so disposed'. Knowles is not mentioned in Leonard Huxley's account; privacy suited both client and architect, for Tyndall had advanced money to help Huxley pay for it, and Knowles said less about such professional work after 1870. Nevertheless, he made the required application to the Metropolitan Board of Works for 'addition and portico', and sixteen of his surviving letters to Huxley refer to it. In the beginning (November 1871): 'I will set on about the plans this week.... I long to have a talk about your future work [for the *Contemporary*] and the "House" '; and (February 1872 to Huxley in Cairo): 'Yesterday I achieved yet another of those dinners which I extort and propose to extort from your household under cover of my professional character.' These letters, like surviving letters from Huxley to him, are delightedly warm and chatty, with an air of mutual understanding much less present in Knowles's correspondence with older great men.[4] Meanwhile,

[3] Miss Thackeray: Knowles to Gladstone, 5 May 1872 (Gladstone Papers as n. 50 below). *Mary Gladstone . . . Her Diaries and Letters*, ed. L. Masterman (1930), p. 110, 12 Oct. 1876. *Memoirs and Letters of Sir James Paget*, ed. S. Paget (1902), p. 258. Forster (as n. 2), p. 218. Farringford rooms: Tennyson journal, 23 Feb. 1871, 'Mr Waterhouse brings his plans for the new room'; original of Tennyson to Knowles, 5 Apr. 1872 (quoted by Knowles in leaflet on *Idylls* prepared for Hallam's grudging use) not known to Prof. Lang.
[4] Knowles to Huxley, n.d. (Nov. 1871) and 23 Feb. 1872 (Huxley Papers, Imperial College). L. Huxley, *Life* (1900), i. 383. The builder 1872-3 was Chappell,

Huxley's article on 'Yeast' appeared in the *Contemporary* for December 1871, cheek by jowl with Tennyson's 'Last Tournament'; fortuitously, or almost so, the editor was architect to two of that month's authors.

Ruskin certainly never employed Knowles, but he seemed to like him, even giving him two Turner drawings—one, in chalk, of King's College, Cambridge—probably during eager conversation over the monocular mode of viewing that artist. As a collector himself, Knowles knew how to draw Ruskin out. One doubts they talked of architecture much, except in vague, ironic generalities, certainly not of Ruskin Street, Battersea, for which Knowles was to design rows of small houses in 1878, his profession having become a secondary practical matter—and Ruskin's opinion of architects exploded in 1874, when he refused the Institute's Gold Medal. The old Ruskinian sources of the Grosvenor design must have been dead to Knowles for some time, and Ruskin doubtless never observed them. Most of his letters to Knowles were destroyed in this century; one brief undated note from Denmark Hill says '*Nothing* but illness shall prevent me from being at the next dinner'—for he had been elected to the Metaphysical Society in February 1870 and attended at least thirteen meetings, at three of which he read papers, before his first breakdown in 1878. His diary mentions the meetings, or 'dinner at Clapham', now and then. And he was one of Knowles's lions in the pages of the *Contemporary Review* (three articles, 1870–3) and the *Nineteenth Century* (eight, 1878–81).[5]

FIRST YEARS OF EDITING

> 'The *Contemporary Review* maintains the improvement recently remarked in it,' *Illustrated London News*,
> 9 July 1870

Journalism, like the architectural profession, was on its way up socially in the Mid-Victorian years. What is sometimes called

---

then working at Hove to Knowles's designs and soon to build for Grant in Kensington.

[5] Knowles sale, Christie's, May 1908, two Turner drawings 'presented by J. Ruskin'; also in the sale drawings by Ruskin, one of Doges' Palace colonnade. Knowles aged 21 on Turner, chap. 3, n. 25. Most of Ruskin's letters to Knowles were destroyed in the 1920s, according to E. Skilbeck; one brief note seen at the late Miss Flint's. *Ruskin Diaries*, ed. Evans and Whitehouse, ii. 706.

'the higher journalism' of the monthly reviews had become by then a loftier occupation, even when pursued full-time, than the most respectable architectural practice—partly perhaps because architects dealt more directly with their builders then writers or even editors did with their printers; but more, no doubt, because contributors to reviews came increasingly from the universities and from the upper reaches of public life. When Knowles wrote anonymously for non-architectural periodicals in the 1860s, perhaps entirely in the form of letters to the editor until 1869, even those appearances will have been precious to a non-university man. We have seen how, in his twenties, he attempted essays and reviews and hoped for two professions. After obtaining some editorial reputation, he is said to have written leaders for the *Morning Post*, although from 1872 that became more of a Conservative organ than it had been. If, as already suggested, his father was ostensibly Conservative, as one of the more dignified specimens of the deferential vote, considering his early clientele and the fact of open voting until the 1870s, still some independent craftsman's radical opinions may have sheltered silently in his breast. His son's political sympathies in the 1870s are likely to have been Liberal, although membership of the Reform Club from 1865 and of the Devonshire Club soon after it was founded by Liberals-out-of-office in 1874, like his eager seeking-out of Gladstone, will not have been solely political. Neither the *Contemporary* under Knowles nor his *Nineteenth Century* was ever a Liberal party organ—as the *Contemporary* became under Bunting in the 1880s. The principle of the 'fair field' to which Knowles had committed himself at the age of 19 in 1850 was to become the point of strain, in the religious field, with the proprietors of the *Contemporary* in 1876.[6]

The *Contemporary Review* had been founded as a monthly in 1866 by the publisher Alexander Strahan 'to be the *Fortnightly* of the Established Church', both its scholarly Christianity and its

---

[6] Fox-Bourne, *English Newspapers* (1887), ii. 345; *Morning Post* 'under the editorship of William Hardman [*DNB*: from 1872] . . . much more of a party organ than it had formerly been when James Knowles, before he commenced "The Nineteenth Century" . . . (was) among its leader writers'. Knowles needed both money and (behind-the-scenes) recognition right up to 1877 more than he can have minded the *Post*'s politics. On later acquaintance with its proprietor, chap. 8, n. 44 below. On his father's politics, chap. 2, n. 11. H. T. Waddy, *The Devonshire Club* (1919).

occasional space for comment on art and music being guaranteed by the special talents and interests of its first editor the Dean of Canterbury, Henry Alford. Strahan himself seems to have been interested in the appearance of his periodicals (in a way that Knowles was not); for example, the decorative borders at the heads of articles in the *Contemporary*, and the title-page border of horse-chestnut branches engraved by Dalziel for *Good Words*. Incidentally, the 1868 volume of *Good Words* (then edited for Strahan by Dr. Norman MacLeod) had contributions from Gladstone, Stanley, and Tennyson: Knowles and his Society did not bring these authors to Strahan's stable, whatever Knowles had to do with steering Tennyson's books there.

Editing the *Contemporary*—modern commentators sometimes forget—was expected to be a part-time affair. The Dean of Canterbury combined it with decanal duty and with his work on the *New Testament for English Readers* and other books including one on the Riviera illustrated by himself, as well as articles, hymns, and so on. He managed to attend every one of the twelve meetings of the Metaphysical Society in 1869 and 1870 (the Grosvenor being so conveniently placed beside the railway station). But early in 1870 Alford arranged to undertake a five-volume commentary on the Old Testament, and this, with a warning of failing health, led him to give up the *Contemporary*; the March issue contained a note of his resignation. When he died the following January, not all the obituaries mentioned his editorial post, there was so much else to say about him.[7]

Alford will have known Knowles by early 1869, being probably one of the first asked to join the new Society, and he included Knowles's 'Science and Art in History' article in the February issue of that year as we have seen. At the end of the year, when Tennyson's *The Holy Grail and Other Poems* was coming out, Alford consulted Knowles, who was about to review it in a letter to the *Spectator* for its issue of 1 January 1870, on his own review for the January *Contemporary*. From the Athenaeum on 16 December 1869, the day after a Metaphysical Society meeting, Alford wrote to Knowles:[8]

[7] On *CR*, *WIVP* (indexing prose only) vol. I and corrections vol. II; *Good Words* had illustrations and fiction, *CR* had neither. On Alford, *ILN* obituaries 21, 28 Jan. 1871; *Life* by Alford's widow (1873), and Augustus Hare, *Biographical Sketches* (1895); Brown (1947), p. 170.

[8] According to draft, remaining in Knowles papers (now TRC), of a copy

I wish if you can do so without inconvenience, that you would write me a letter expounding a little more of what you began last night—the exposition of A T's design in the Idylls. A new light has risen on the Grail since, & I should like to write my article in its effluence. Does the design extend over the whole? If so would you mind pointing out to me which portions of the great Lesson each Idyll takes—A very few words will do & then I can work out the rest for myself.

To this, Knowles told Gladstone on 22 January, he had replied by sending Alford 'extracts from my already-written article' for the *Spectator*. Some tongues must have wagged unkindly when the two articles appeared, for the expounder of the Poet Laureate's design to the Dean of Canterbury found it necessary anxiously to assure the Prime Minister that '*I* have not plagiarized from *him*', and to enclose copies both of Alford's request and of Tennyson's letter praising Knowles's article.[9] But Alford had been careful to say in his review that the exposition was not 'a mere invention of our own'. Occasional bouts of thin-skinned anxiety beset Knowles's way through life, not very often, but surviving instances of it, more often than not, had to do with Tennyson.

At any rate, by early 1870 both Alford and Strahan had noticed Knowles's abilities and connections. The choice of a new man must have been made not later than February, what with the announcement of Alford's resignation in the March issue and plans for April. During the quarrel that ended relations several years later, Strahan claimed that the choice had only been made to oblige Tennyson, who he said asked him to 'find some literary occupation' for Knowles.[10] Be that as it may. Consulting editor, it appears, was the term used at first, Strahan regarding himself as some sort of editorial director; it amounted to Knowles conducting his relations with authors and publisher from his own house and architectural office, and Strahan conducting the day-to-day publishing business with other periodicals and books from Ludgate Hill (later from Paternoster Row), where also was the *Contemporary*'s sub-editor. That Knowles was good for business became very clear. He said later that he had raised the circulation

---

Knowles made of Alford's letter for Gladstone, whereabouts of original unknown (Knowles may have sent it to Tennyson, but not at TRC).

  [9] Draft, Knowles to Gladstone, 22 Jan. 1870, on verso of copy of Alford's (n. 8); letter not with Knowles's others in Gladstone Papers at BL. On Knowles's *Spectator* piece, n. 37 below; on Tillotson conjecture, chap. 6, n. 14 above.

  [10] Knowles (indignantly) to Tennyson, 20 Jan. 1877 (TRC).

of the *Contemporary* from under 2,000 to 8,000: although, as we shall see, a statement made in the heat of controversy, that was said to the head of a printing firm who was in a position to know. Knowles's yearly stipend throughout was probably meant to be the £500 briefly guaranteed him in 1876, paid monthly, except when Strahan was in difficulties.[11] (Trollope's Professor Booker in *The Way We Live Now* had £500 a year for editing a literary periodical.) Knowles's chief practical reward for serving his almost seven-year apprenticeship to the *Contemporary Review* came of learning the ropes and making a few useful mistakes before launching out on his own: he gained his freedom of the craft there.

In the beginning, Knowles's success with the *Contemporary* had more than a little to do with its 'special relation' with the Metaphysical Society. During his editorship (82 issues if we count as the first the April 1870 issue, probably partly made up by Alford, and as the last the January 1877 issue, in course of printing when the new proprietors terminated Knowles's appointment in December 1876), there would appear to have been 156 contributions by Metaphysical Society members, of which 27 had been read as papers before the Society. Right away, the review's range was widened from its 'preponderance of theology' under a new subtitle, 'The Magazine of Thought'. The year 1871 was especially prolific in the publication of Metaphysical papers: Manning in February, Bagehot in April, Russell and Ruskin in June, Hutton and Sidgwick in July, Ellicott in August, Roden Noel in October, bearing out the review's new character as an 'organ of speculative thought'. But it also lived up to its title, contemporary topics treated during 1870–1 including female education, workmen's strikes, pay for Members of Parliament, imperial federation for England and her colonies, the formation of coal, and the 'religious difficulty' of the School Board (the last two by Huxley).

Knowles's first real *coup* marked the start of his second year as editor in the April 1871 issue: the first of four articles on the Franco–Prussian war by the old warhorse Mazzini, Italian patriot in exile, then nearing the end of his life. If the 'curiosity excited by the announcement' of the first article was 'somewhat disappointed

[11] On separation from *CR*, last section of this chapter. On William Gellan, subeditor through it all, E. R. Houghton in *VPN*, Nov. 1968, p. 18, and his obituary in *CR*, May 1883, p. 766 n. Knowles to McCorquodale, n. 63 below.

by the essay itself', Mazzini's 'customary strain of grave, ardent eloquence' in the subsequent articles (two of them posthumous) added new prestige to the *Contemporary*.[12] Knowles's arrangements with Mazzini must have been going on at the same time and on the same desk as Food Fund arrangements to relieve besieged Paris, the laying out of West Brighton, and emergency plans for dealing with pipe-bursts at Aldworth. His link with Mazzini, oddly enough, may have led to West Brighton: there from the spring of 1871 Knowles's clients were the City firm of solicitors Messrs. Ashurst Son & Morris of Old Jewry; in October 1870 he had published an article on Mazzini, now known to have been written by an earlier partner's daughter, Emilie Ashurst Venturi, the old Italian's literary editor.[13] But a Morris connection out of propinquity in Clapham Park and Streatham church also led to Old Jewry and West Brighton, and may have led to Mrs. Venturi in the first place. The sources of Knowles's acquaintance could be as multiply allusive and as multiply drawn-upon as the sources of his architecture.

Anonymity sometimes characterized the *Contemporary* menu. It is quite possible that an anonymous review-article in the May 1870 number was by Knowles himself: 'Nature-development and Theology', reviewing books by Huxley, J. H. Stirling, the Duke of Argyll, James Martineau, and Jacob Frohschammer, has all his brisk practical omnivorousness; and a letter he wrote to Tennyson on 4 April, mainly about Spinoza and implying a good deal of library-reading, may have been an offshoot of it. Perhaps the most celebrated pseudonymous contribution to the *Contemporary* was that of October 1871 when the poet Robert Buchanan, already one of Strahan's authors, took the pen-name of Thomas Maitland to assail 'The Fleshly School of Poetry' of Rossetti ('the disquisition of an owl upon a nightingale', said the *Illustrated London News*). Knowles felt at the time that this dealt deservedly with the 'tone of literature in [Swinburne's] set' that had depressed Tennyson so much when *Songs Before Sunrise* came out earlier in the year; and Knowles took up his own pen, again anonymously,

---

[12] Comment in *ILN* monthly 'Magazines' column provided (as did *ILN* comment on buildings) a non-specialist middlebrow reader's sounding-board: e.g. 8 Apr., 10 June 1871, pp. 343, 575; obituary of Mazzini, 23 Mar. 1872, p. 280.
[13] Boase. *CR* published articles by her on Mazzini in Oct. 1870 and Sept. 1871. The first reference to Knowles's architectural commission at West Brighton (n. 19 below) occurred in 1871.

in the cause in the *Contemporary* for May 1873 on 'The Meaning of Mr Tennyson's King Arthur' (a letter of thanks from Tennyson, saying 'very workmanly done', seems to refer to it). Yet, eventually, in the *Nineteenth Century* for some years from 1884, he was to publish Swinburne in both prose and poetry (and, incidentally, Knowles bought five Rossetti drawings after the latter's death), whereas Buchanan never appeared in the *Nineteenth Century*. The furore in the aesthetic set caused by the Maitland article can have done no harm to the *Contemporary Review*'s circulation, yet this episode seems to have caused Knowles to take the reins more into his own hands so far as insistence upon signed articles was concerned. It is true that a recurrent contributor, the journalist W. B. Rands, appeared under one or other of his pseudonyms (Matthew Browne 19 times, Henry Holbeach 8 times) in the *Contemporary* from 1868 to 1880. But whereas, during Knowles's first six months of editorship in 1870, some dozen unsigned or pseudonymous pieces appeared in the *Contemporary*, the proportion of signed articles went up noticeably after 1871. Exceptions included two in 1872 on Fenianism by 'One Who Knows'; and in 1875, Bishop Magee as P.C.W. contributed to a discussion, originating in the Metaphysical Society, on the scientific basis of morals. In June of that year, Gladstone as 'Etoniensis' reviewed three books on the Prince Consort, having offered the article to Knowles on condition that it be unsigned, apparently because it amounted to a (largely favourable) discussion of Albert's character, unsuited to an ex-Prime Minister's pen. Knowles in accepting it pointed out that it would be even more interesting 'if signed by yourself', but suggested alternatively that, if Gladstone's own initials would not be 'sufficiently insufficient', the initials 'M.P.' might be a 'sufficient formal veil'. The question of a pseudonym was still undecided after the review was in proof, Knowles declaring himself ready to comply if Gladstone preferred to be 'simply anonymous without nom de plume'; finally, after the issue was printed a hint of its authorship seems to have appeared, possibly Strahan's doing, in some 'offending circular', to the irritation of all concerned.[14]

[14] On anonymous writing see also chap. 8, n. 18. By 3 Nov. 1874 Knowles was citing to Gladstone 'our rule about the personal signature of essays' (as n. 50 below) Article in *CR* May 1870 unidentified in *WIVP*; attribution here based on style, also possibly on Knowles to Tennyson, 4 Apr. 1870 (TRC). Comment on

Knowles's *coup* at Christmas-time 1871, the first publication of 'The Last Tournament', the only one of Tennyson's Idylls to appear in a periodical, must have enhanced the *Contemporary's* prestige as well as its circulation, although the poem was deliberately depressing and not universally well received: 'Very few, we imagine, of Mr Tennyson's sincere friends desire to see any more Arthurian idylls from his hand,' said that organ for unspeculative thinkers, the *Illustrated London News.* 'However it is published there will be *some* objectors', Knowles had pointed out to the poet. A prize of a different sort, doubtless obtained through Dean Stanley, was the sermon Bishop Colenso was forbidden by higher authority than Stanley's to preach in the Abbey in December 1874, published by Knowles in his January issue to the approval of popular family weeklies such as *Punch* and the *Illustrated London News,* for according to the latter, 'The Bishop of Natal has taken the simplest means of exposing the irrationality of the persecution to which he had been subjected by publishing the sermon which he was forbidden to deliver in Westminster Abbey . . . a fine composition, concluding with an impressive passage on the duties of British colonists towards inferior races.' But church members who had preferred the *Contemporary* in Alford's day may have thought it unwise to print Colenso.[15]

To continue with Knowles's first years of editing, 1872 saw articles as untheological as Herbert Spencer's series on 'The Study of Sociology' and John Addington Symonds's translations of Michelangelo's sonnets in the *Contemporary.* The editorial device of starting discussion that provoked more discussion—keeping things going 'by self-acting machinery' as one critic put it—was already working. Huxley was usefully provocative in that way: his article on Darwin's critics, launched with great care in November 1871,[16] provoked St. George Mivart the naturalist to

'Maitland' article: *ILN,* 7 Oct. 1871, p. 343; Rossetti's reply, 'The Stealthy School of Criticism', *Athenaeum,* 16 Dec. 1871, and Swinburne's letters, C. Y. Lang, ed. (1959), ii. 161 ff. On 'tone of literature', Tennyson family journal, 26 Feb. 1871. Knowles's article May 1873, n. 38 below. On Rands, *WIVP* I, II. On Gladstone's review in *CR* June 1875: Knowles to Gladstone, 19, 22, 28 May 1875 (as n. 50 below).

[15] Knowles to Tennyson, 4 Nov. 1871 (TRC). *ILN,* 9 Dec. 1871, p. 558. On Colenso, Chadwick, *Victorian Church,* ii. 90–7; *ILN,* 16 Jan. 1875, p. 54; *Punch,* 2 Jan. 1875, p. 9.

[16] On timing of this article, n. 61 below. On 'self-acting machinery', *ILN,* 20 May 1876, p. 499.

assail him in January. A perhaps indirectly influential article, read
first before the Metaphysical Society, appeared in October 1872,
'The Special Beauty Conferred by Imperfection and Decay', by
W. R. Greg, Bagehot's brother-in-law. Greg's Ruskinian theme,
that man's perception of beauty in ruin and in imperfection, as of
the beauties of mountain scenery, had only dawned on him in
modern times—that the Picturesque, like the Sublime, could
only be appreciated by civilized minds—implied that restoring
ancient buildings is wrong: part of the point of view that was to
lead a few years later to a Society for the Protection of Ancient
Buildings. Among the ninety-odd papers on Life, Death, and the
Absolute, read before the Metaphysical Society during its eleven
years of talk, only that one dealt with aesthetics. Ruskin himself,
this being the 1870s, not the 1850s, addressed them and subsequently the readers of the *Contemporary* on the intellectual powers
of different levels of animate life, the nature and authority of
miracle, and the social policy suited to the principle of natural
selection. Greg's article is memorable in the annals of aesthetics,
of the idea of Pleasing Decay, whether William Morris read it or
not. By this time, Knowles's own early training in perception of
the picturesque was expressed in modest but determined collecting of paintings and drawings but the conservation of works of
architecture (other than Westminster Abbey) seems not to have
fired him as a cause.[17] Meanwhile, extra-editorial activities were
jostling for his attention.

PUBLIC INTERLUDE: THE PARIS FOOD FUND

'London might do for Paris a service of salvation
which would never fade away from the heart of
France. If anybody doubt this, let him read the awful
story of the four months' siege of Paris in 1590,
when there was no "London within ten hours" of it.'
J.T.K. to the *Standard*, 31 October 1870

A bundle of letters and cuttings among Knowles's surviving
papers gives some sense of a sudden swirl of public-spirited

---

[17] Greg's article: cf., e.g. John Piper, 'Pleasing Decay', *Buildings and Prospects*
(1948), p. 89. On threats to Westminster Abbey, *NC*, Mar. 1889, July 1890.
But Knowles did in April 1877 publish an important article by Lubbock on
preserving ancient monuments.

activity in the winter of 1870–1.[18] In September Napoleon III surrendered at Sedan and Prussian armies surrounded Paris. The Parisians, feeling betrayed by their own government, and warned by Bismarck what a siege could mean for their food supply, attempted in October to form a commune in the spirit of 1789. In London dismay at the spirit of 1789 was mixed with pity for French misery and anxiety to 'be kept clear of all suspicion of partisanship' (Duke of Devonshire to Knowles, in November, and Marquis of Salisbury to Knowles in January). On 31 October 'J.T.K.' wrote to the editor of the *Standard* from the Reform Club (preferable to Clapham, Gray's Inn, or Victoria Street as source of a letter to the press) a letter headed 'The Starvation of Paris':

Sir,—Count Bismarck's warning of the terrible starvation which may befall Paris . . . may surely be taken to suggest to others of the charitable some effort to provide against so supremely frightful a calamity while yet there is time.

Cannot some organization be found or formed at once in this city, to collect and store—say a week's provisions, if only of grain—at or near Dover and Folkestone, and to arrange for its instant transmission to Paris at the right moment.

Some purposeful nipping-about then went on, and J.T.K. wrote on 14 November to the *Pall Mall Gazette* (which was showing more interest than the *Standard*):

Sir.—The suggestion . . . that a week's provisions bought and stored beforehand might save Paris alive in the first dreadful days after her gates are beaten down or opened, has met with so much sympathy as to encourage me to ask your further help about it. . . . The sum required would not be large, and the object . . . is definite and practicable. But if undertaken at all, it should be undertaken well beforehand. Left to the eleventh hour, no human help could accomplish it.

The practical idea now was that stores of preserved meat, preserved milk, biscuit, and other food not needing cooking should be got ready, Knowles having first consulted commissariat officials at the War Office and Admiralty about ways and

[18] This section is mainly based on letters, drafts, and cuttings, Paris Food Fund, 1870–1, in Knowles family possession until 1973 (now WPL); also on Knowles to Tennyson, 11 Jan. 1871 (TRC), Emily Tennyson to Knowles, 5 Feb. 1871, in Knowles papers (now TRC). Stuart Wortley, Ruskin, Manning, and Thornton letters are with Food Fund papers above. Knowles's bronze medal in family possession. On banquet, *Daily Telegraph*, 19 Oct. 1871.

means, and deduced that about £100,000 would be required. From the first he offered a programme for action as well as an appeal for money. Archbishop Manning and Professor Huxley agreed to act as trustees, and Sir John Lubbock's bank, Robarts & Lubbock, to act as bankers for a Paris Food Fund: the Metaphysical Society once more proving a useful bank of public figures. The fund grew slowly; English awareness was not ready yet; Knowles's programme was too early.

In January the Bishop of Versailles appealed to England for food in a message to the *Daily Telegraph*, which published his appeal with a rousing leader on the 9th, and subscriptions began to pour in to that office. It was now much more obvious that when Paris surrendered, as was to happen at the end of the month, there would be only a few days' food left. J.T.K. immediately wrote to the *Telegraph* describing his fund, the editor commenting at the foot of this letter that the two funds should be united. Knowles then replied, over his full name, that Manning, Huxley, Lubbock, Ruskin, and himself would be pleased to form 'part of such a public committee as you have advised' and to place 'subscriptions already sent to us at its disposal'. His committee was joined in a day or so by Tennyson, to whom Knowles had written that it was 'the opportunity for which I have been waiting', and rejoicing in the *Telegraph*'s 'support in all its 190,000 copies'. The Lord Mayor was made president of the new committee, on which Manning's presence was balanced by that of the Bishop of London and the Baptist minister Dr. William Brock, with other prestigious names; the fund was to be run from the Mansion House, and the Food Sub-committee consisted of Knowles, Alderman Finnis, and young Alfred de Rothschild (whose Paris connections were useful), with Knowles in charge. Two commissioners in charge of distributing the food in Paris— on their way, via Dieppe and Rouen, with the first load of provisions on 2 February—were Lieut.-Col. Henry Stuart Wortley and George Moore the textile millionaire, Knowles Sr.'s old client, from whose warehouse in Paris they could operate. Besides their formal reports quoted in the *Telegraph*, five private notes to Knowles survive, written under strain by Stuart Wortley with rheumatism in an old wound in his arm:

[Feb. 8] We are all day at work, imagine, no horses to be got, no fuel, & everyone absorbed by the elections. . . . We have relieved through our fund thousands of starving people. . . . Imagine, no *French* labels on the condensed milk. . . .

[n.d. but refers to *Daily News* of Feb. 8] We see you say . . . we arrived on Saturday evening. Really we were within the enceinte of Paris at 11 p.m. on the Friday night. We are very proud of having been the *first train in* and do not wish that glory taken from us. . . . If you knew the difficulties we vanquished to get here first you would understand. . . .

[Feb. 16] Mr Labouchere's lies in *Daily News* of Feb. 13. Remember every English scamp in Paris has applied to try & *job* in connection with the fund—Foiled in this they turn round and abuse us! . . . If you could imagine what our difficulties have been you would wonder we have done what we have.

[Feb. 17] Thank you for your letter. . . . If you were here & saw the way we are worried and the constant snubbing we have to give every little dirty shopkeeper who tries to get a job out of us . . . *disbelieve everything you hear.* The day will come when you will have to acknowledge that we have done our best.

[Feb. 24] Thank you for your letter. 'Times' of 23rd just come—We see report of the Food Committee—Perhaps some day you will praise your *distributors*!

Knowles must have been less than tactful, strenuously aware only of the end in view, and reactions in London. Obliviousness to the difficulties of people working under him was a trait he had. But the *Telegraph* as sponsoring newspaper did publish praise of these 'able and energetic commissioners', who were thanked personally by M. Thiers in Paris and called indefatigable in a first-hand report released by the Lord Mayor's committee in London.

Knowles's role as go-between comes out in a multifarious correspondence. Mrs. Tennyson writes on 5 February to ask if food can be sent to a certain convent in the rue de Sevres where 'girls of the best families in France are educated'; Ruskin writes on 13 February to ask help for a friend's friends at St. Malo who have 'lost all in the siege'. On 17 February the Prussian Minister in London, Count Bernstorff, sends word through his son of Count Bismarck's telegram giving fuel trains precedence over food trains. Wm. Jackson & Co. send details of their 'celebrated milk biscuits', as do the proprietors of 'Captain Warren's Campaign Biscuits', and a wholesaler with a ton of Yorkshire hams ready at King's Cross. Archbishop Manning writes on 28 February on the urgency of sending seed corn for planting, and 'I will take my chance of finding you in Victoria Street tomorrow'—up all those stairs to the top of No. 16 Albert Mansions, presumably, where Knowles was often to be found at Tennyson's chambers. To the Lord Mayor, with whom Knowles and Rothschild had 'paid great attention to the subject of fuel', Knowles wrote on 6 February: 'You will begin to think it was an evil hour for your peace that you made my acquaintance—so frequent are my demands on your time & patience.' Knowles was trying to sound out the Duke of Argyll (by then a member of the Metaphysical Society) on the chance of government subscription to the fund, but was put off by the Duke's reply that the government would not do so and that he himself could not be a 'channel of communication on this matter'. In early 1871 Knowles did not yet know Gladstone well enough to press farther, though that channel was soon to be improved. A note came also from Knowles's neighbour Miss Thornton with some rumour flying about Clapham Common: she had had it from Lady Trevelyan ('Sir Charles having had to feed Ireland during the famine has been asked to arrange a plan to be laid before the Cabinet') that the government meant to provide stores for the French to buy, 'being persuaded there is no want of money . . . in Paris—I hope this may be true, for if we are going to war, we soon shall have to subscribe to our own sick & wounded I suppose'. It was a nervous time. The ensuing Paris rebellion in March was to have one delayed effect in England eleven years later in the opposition so fiercely organized by Knowles against a Channel Tunnel.

In the end, bronze medals were bestowed by a grateful City of Paris upon all concerned, and in October 1871 a splendid banquet was given at the Mansion House, where it was pointed out, not for the first or the last time, that 'the antiquity of the corporate aristocracy of the City of London dated long anterior to the Norman Conquest'; the Lord Mayor gracefully and at length described how 'the City of Paris has of late been an object of solicitude to the whole civilized world (Hear, hear)'; the Prefect of the Seine equally gracefully and lengthily described how, until help came from England, it had seemed 'que le 19me siècle n'existait plus et que le moyen age était revenu'; and the Mansion House turned to collecting contributions toward the relief of sufferers in the Chicago Fire.

ESTATE DEVELOPMENT AT WEST BRIGHTON

'. . . wealthy residents and visitors emigrated to the
sphere, where the sun sets.' From a chapter by a local
valuer in H. S. Porter, *History of Hove* (1897)

In the spring of 1871 or thereabouts, probably through South
London propinquity, Knowles found a new source of income on
the Sussex coast. In the 1850s and 1860s a William Morris,
equity draftsman and conveyancer of New Square, Lincoln's
Inn, lived in New Park Road, a part of Clapham Park that lay in
Streatham; attendance at Streatham church may have been the
neighbourly link between him and the Knowles family. A John
Morris of Blackheath was, apparently, William's brother and a
partner in the long-established City firm of solicitors, Ashurst
Son & Morris of No. 6 Old Jewry, the address William used for
his own property speculations. In 1842 an Eleanor Morris,
daughter of an elder William Morris of Blackheath and so
presumably sister of the above William and John, had married
William Stanford of Preston Manor at Brighton; their daughter
Ellen, after her father's death in 1853, became tenant for life
of his estates and when she married her husband added Stanford
to his name. In 1870 it was decided to develop the 'West
Brighton' part of those estates, with her uncle William as lessee,
a Stanford Estate Act of 1871 (and a second, Improvement
Act, in 1872) being passed by Parliament, concerning about
forty acres on the sea-front at Hove—thereupon locally called
'Morris's portion'—a one-time brick-field occupied from 1848
by the Royal Brunswick Cricket Ground, land for which
Charles Barry had once made unused designs for William
Stanford's father. It was bounded on the east by a lane adjoining
Palmeira Square and Adelaide Crescent, on the west by Clifton-
ville (which had mushroomed in the 1850s 'with the lightning
rapidity of an American city'), on the north by Church Road and
on the south by the Shoreham Road, or Kingsway, and the sea,
along which the broad promenade and the Lawns were to be
extended westward. In 1871 Knowles was brought in as architect,
made a master design for the estate (summarized in an unsigned perspective drawing now at Preston Manor), and the two
Queen's Gardens terraces on the sea-front were begun, including

a Queen's Gardens Hotel, later Prince's Hotel and Conservative Club, now Gas Board (Pl. 13). All designs, street-names, etc. were submitted for approval to a shadowy figure, apparent source of the cash, a certain 'Baron', Albert Grant. No. 7 Queen's Gardens at the corner of Second Avenue, the house where in 1889 David Sassoon was to receive the Shah of Persia, for a few years was the seaside residence of Baron Grant: he and Morris took leases on the front at first when no one else would.[19]

In 1872 William Morris's interests were incorporated as the West Brighton Estate Company with John Morris as a director, and Knowles was active on the site and at directors' meetings (said to have been usually attended only by William and himself), but in mid-1873 he was replaced by other architects and development proceeded with less expensive versions of and variations upon his designs. Not that his were lavish: he had reduced his Cedars estate terrace-house type to a sparsely ornamented basic form, depending for quality on good proportions and well-laid brickwork; for all his earlier interest in ornament, he could design for penny-pinchers without it.[20] The layout, under Morris's and Grant's control, was unimaginative, with five avenues leading north from the sea-front, The Drive (now Grand Avenue) in the centre flanked by First and Second Avenues on the east and by Third and Fourth Avenues on the west: these developers were impressed by the boring anti-picturesqueness of American cities, it seems. Yet the simple masses and varied skyline of Knowles's sea-front ranges east of Grand Avenue are effective from a distance and more agreeable close-to than the grey-brick variations built on the estate after his departure, however lacking in the Regency sparkle of the other end of

[19] Private Bill papers, Stanford Estate Acts 1871, 1872 (HLRO); directories and (with care) H. S. Porter, *History of Hove* (1897). Knowles, letter of 1882 in Park Town papers, recalls Brighton clients as 'Messrs Ashurst of Old Jewry': i.e. Ashurst Son & Morris, by then consisting of John Morris and another man (then already an old firm, it flourishes in the City today). William Morris used the Old Jewry address for his own property development, instead of his own conveyancing office. W. F. Pickering, 'The West Brighton Estate Hove', Univ. of Sussex M.A. thesis 1969, based on estate records in safe-deposit, copy in Hove Reference Library. Before Knowles's appointment in 1871 and possibly after his departure in 1873, H. J. Lanchester was estate architect (Pickering). Barry's early drawings are in RIBA Drawings Collection.

[20] But Tennyson to Knowles, 9 Jan. 1872 (Lang, ed., Tennyson's Letters, Clarendon Press, forthcoming), playfully refers to brain-waves and sea-waves playing about Knowles's new balustrade along the front.

Brighton. Toward the end of the 1890s, much red brickwork was
added on the west side of the estate, where in 1908 the King
lunched with the Sassoons in King's Gardens.[21] Westward the
course of architecture and good addresses took its way along the
Lawns at Hove, as the local valuer said. The West Brighton of
the 1870s was an unlikely background for the redemption of
Leicester Square.

BARON GRANT: WAS HE MELMOTTE?

> 'Need I descant on Baron Grant, or all his deeds
>   declare,
> Who from deep gloom made Eden bloom anew in
>   Leicester Square.'
>   J. T. S. Lidstone, *The twentieth Londoniad*, 1876

Leicester Square garden, where marble Shakespeare broods over
pigeons and crowded benches, is the only visible mark left upon
London by one of the best-known public figures of the 1870s.
Which is just as well.

Albert Grant, born Gottheimer in Dublin in 1830, emerged on
the London public scene in 1865 as M.P. for Kidderminster and
managing director of the Credit Foncier & Mobilier of England,
presumably a branch of parent companies in Paris, with offices in
Cornhill. Some years earlier, according to trade directories, an
Albert Gottheimer was partner in a firm of wine importers in
Mark Lane: the basis, perhaps, of the story that Grant was
'educated in London and Paris'. In 1865 he is said to have put up
most of the money for the building of the Galleria Vittorio
Emmanuele at Milan, that is, he floated the City of Milan
Improvements Co. Ltd, the client for that great cruciform
shopping arcade, designed by Mengoni but mainly a British
enterprise. Grant's reward was a title conferred by Victor
Emmanuel II in 1868; at that time it must have meant much to
Piedmontese pride to confer kudos in the name of Italy, and the
Galleria remains a marvellous gift to urban life. So far, so good.
Grant gave his address in 1870 as the Conservative Club and
Cooper's Hill, Egham—the latter reminding us of appropriate
lines in Denham's poem on Cooper's Hill: 'Finds wealth where 'tis,

[21] On Sassoon entertaining the Shah in Queen's Gardens in 1889, Porter's *Hove*;
on Sassoon entertaining Edward VII in King's Gardens, *Brighton Gazette* during
week 10–17 Feb. 1908.

bestows it where it wants,/Cities in deserts, woods in cities plants', and especially the last line on how soon 'Great things are made, but sooner are undone'. For Grant was a pioneer of mammoth company promoting in England, blandly issuing prospectuses for Lima Railways, Lisbon Tramways, Odessa Waterworks, the Imperial Bank of China, the Emma silver-mine, and much else in an international network of speculation of which he was only a part: for example, in the United States, the Credit Mobilier fostered transcontinental railways, corruption, and panic in a period known there now by the name of another, President Grant. The Baron's particular bit of finesse was to concentrate on lists of small investors, clergymen and widows who were only too anxious to invest; he gambled on the gambling spirit of little people.[22]

A man of 'agreeable presence and enthusiastic manners', Grant lasted about ten years. He was at his zenith in 1874, when he rescued Leicester Square, bought the *Echo* newspaper, and was re-elected to Parliament. A photograph of him shows slightly hooded eyes with an expression both cynical and sanguine, the look of a would-be connoisseur of art and men; not a strong face and not much resembling Trollope's description of Augustus Melmotte in *The Way We Live Now* with a 'wonderful look of power about his mouth and chin' in a countenance 'on the whole unpleasant'; Grant's countenance was on the slippery side. Yet Melmotte's spectacular position in the world and in the City, and his parliamentary seat, make him indeed reminiscent of Grant. Melmotte's spectacular downfall was charted in Trollope's study in Montagu Square in 1873, while financial panic was indeed spreading from Europe to New York but while Grant himself was still riding high. Melmotte's collapse, then, was a macabre prediction of Grant's more gradual downfall that was to become obvious only in 1876. The moral imagination of the novelist is wonderfully illustrated in *The Way We Live Now*, as it must indeed have seemed to keen observers as its final parts came out in late summer 1875, just as *The Times* delivered its thundering leader of 11 August against the scandals, the extravagance, and the speculations of London society. Four years before, a friend of Trollope, the painter Henry O'Neil, had dedicated to him a long

[22] On Grant, *DNB*, directories, *ILN*, obituary with photograph, 9 Sept. 1899; and on Galleria, *Bldr*, 25 Apr. 1868, pp. 297–9.

satire in verse, *The Age of Stucco* (that material having sunk to
stock prop in the allegory of modern sham), a bitter attack on the
impostures of the day and a compliment to Trollope's awareness
of them. In Melmotte, and in Lopez in *The Prime Minister*,
Trollope dramatized not only the imminent fall of such a speculator among speculators as Baron Grant, but the moral climate that
produced him.[23]

But in 1872–4, whatever one thought of parvenu financiers,
this was a successful specimen. Knowles and he were of an age,
both had 'enthusiastic manners' and a client was a client. Grant's
gift of Landseer's portrait of Sir Walter Scott to the nation—
when the nation could not find the 800 guineas it went for at
Christie's—may have been prompted by Knowles, Grant being
obviously keen to play the public benefactor and Knowles being
often at Christie's, buying pictures for small sums. Grant owned
a suitable pair of Landseers himself: 'Prosperity' and 'Adversity'.
From conversation with Knowles, too, may have come the rescue
of Leicester Square. The key to all this was Knowles's engagement
to design a baronial house at Kensington, with none of the high-
mindedness of Aldworth, but an irresistible potential fee. As we
have seen, they encountered one another on the Stanford estate
at Hove: if Grant's role there was obscure, it was clearly powerful
at first. Just the place to encounter a likeable villain, Brighton,
with its long history of oddities almost Southern Californian.
The Morris legal antennae may have tapped the network of his
operations in the City; it would be interesting to know who
Grant's solicitors were. Or, Knowles may have met Grant
through the younger Charles Barry, who was employed professionally to test the costs of the Milan Galleria. Grant seems to
have been involved at Hove before he made his first moves to
acquire land in Kensington; and the building contractor for his
new house, John T. Chappell, had already been at work on
Knowles's terraces at West Brighton (and also on Huxley's
house in St. John's Wood). Grant now bought the freehold of
about seven acres on the south side of what was then called
Kensington High Road opposite Kensington Palace. Near the

[23] Melmotte is described in chap. iv, and the Great Railway to Vera Cruz is
part of the thread (chap. ix etc.) of *The Way We Live Now*, written May–Dec.
1873, issued in parts Feb. 1874–Sept. 1875, book published July 1875 (M.
Sadleir, *Trollope Bibliography*, 1928). Dasent, *Delane*, ii. 319–21, on leader, 11 Aug.
1875. *DNB* on Henry Nelson O'Neil, 1817–80, ARA.

road were two eighteenth-century courtiers' houses, Colby House and Kensington (or Noel) House, while south and west of these was a wretched tangle of slums, originally the cottages of building-labourers and palace retainers. All were demolished in the spring of 1873, the extermination of these rookeries being hastened not only by offering the occupants housing elsewhere, but by urging them to take as much of their old woodwork (and vermin) with them for firewood as they could carry, by which inspired means much clearance was done. The two-hundred-foot frontage of the new Kensington House was placed opposite the Palace, with room behind for a lake, a skating-rink, an American bowling-alley, and a coach-house for twelve carriages fronting on Kensington Square.[24] The 'largest private residence in town' (Pl. 13) rose slowly during 1874–5, utterly symmetrical in plan with a four-storey central block flanked by three sets of wings of various heights but all relentlessly complementary, not lavishly orna-mented but depending for effect on piled-up size and expensive materials: yellowish Bath stone laced with white Portland stone string-courses, a portico of polished pink Aberdeen granite columns, great marble-paved terrace, and so on. It had the steep crested roofs required of such a building in the 1870s, no longer with any particular French relevance in London; yet on the whole, in its park, obviously intended to be a château worthy of the Credit Foncier & Mobilier of England. It was.

The great central hall commanded long marbled vistas eastward and westward, through screens of paired Corinthian columns of Italian marble and on between pairs of caryatids—representing the four seasons and supporting staircase landings—and on eastward through a picture gallery to the ballroom, westward along a broad corridor flanked by billiard-room and library to the triple dining suite. The vistas of an Egremont Castle or a Villa Monserrate, indeed. To an idealistic plan for a permanent display of busts of 'chief men of the day', a Hall of Worthies probably in the focal central hall, we owe Thomas Woolner's fine late bust of Tennyson—as we learn from Mrs. Tennyson's journal for late October or early November 1873: 'Mr & Mrs Knowles call. He wants A. to have his bust done for Baron Grant's house which he

---

[24] Descriptions of site and house: *Bldr*, 19 Apr. 1873, p. 300, and 8 July 1876, pp. 653–4; *Brit. Architect*, 11 Sept. 1874, p. 171; *Graphic*, 30 June 1877, p. 625; W. J. Loftie, *Kensington Picturesque and Historical* (1888), pp. 119 ff.

is building desiring to adorn the hall with busts of the Chief Men of the day—We know nothing but this of the Baron.' But when the portrait bust was done, according to a note in Hallam Tennyson's 'Materials' not used in the *Memoir*, Grant 'sent the bust back to Mr Woolner because he said that it was too classical, and that he thought the bare shoulders not quite proper'.[25] The poet's comment on *that*, one would like to have heard. Presumably the caryatids were well covered, or perhaps it was only contemporary nudity he minded. Dare we suggest that Woolner's bare-shouldered marble bust of James Thomas Knowles the elder, dated 1873 and installed in this century in error at Aldworth, was also intended for Grant's Hall of Worthies and similarly rejected?[26]

Aside from this surprising prudishness, Grant's household tastes were doubtless formed in the London clubs: one of the more lavish productions of the 1840s was his own, the Conservative Club, decorated internally by Frederick Sang. A member of the Sang family was busily embellishing Grant's house as the lawsuits gathered in 1876. About thirty firms in the building trades contributed to the construction and adornment of the house—and then to the roster of Grant's creditors. Knowles's own early admirations of his Grand Tour days—for 'summer and winter suits of rooms', for segmental colonnaded dining bays, for 'an architectural vista'—made him a suitable interpreter for all this, just as his father had suited the new rich of a generation before. Grant might so easily have chosen a gin-palace architect, instead of Knowles's more dignified handling. His supervision seems to have ended sometime in 1875. Suppliers' squabbles arose, said to hinge upon refusal of the architect's certificate and probably relating to the client's non-payment of suppliers' bills and architect's fees. There was one row, for example, over payment

[25] Also Tennyson journal, 8 Nov. 1873, 'A. goes daily to Mr Woolner's studio because of the bust'. Tennyson to Knowles, 21 Dec. 1873: 'You are quite in the right. Of course it was at your request as my friend, that I sat for the bust in question. I hope your client will approve of it' (MS. in possession of Dr. Gordon Ray, to be published by Prof. Lang, to both of whom I am grateful). *Materials*, iii. 224.

[26] Apparently at Friday Grove 1873–6 (house-sale particulars 1876), probably then to Russell Square, exhibited by Woolner at RA 1879, later to the Stilwells, whose descendants gave it in well-meant error to Aldworth, but it clearly portrays Knowles Sr., not the architect of Aldworth. On collaboration of Knowles Sr. and Woolner in 1871, chap. 4., n. 32 above.

for sixteen marble columns, probably the eight pairs screening the hall from staircase and vistas, and probably the same ones, twelve and a half feet high minus pedestals, that fetched 'but 74 guineas a pair' in the 1882 sale.[27] Meanwhile, there had arisen the happier case of the Leicester Square garden. The vicissitudes of this private ground, between crowded Soho and the open space of Trafalgar Square, during the lifetime of most people then living had been those of some modern bombed site: hoardings, weeds, rubbish, vandals, temporary buildings, legal tangles. Over the years *Punch* had isolated a new species of nettle, 'a real Leicestersquariensis, four feet high', and George I's statue there was slowly being reduced to a sick joke. Just as the Metropolitan Board of Works was finally in a position to attempt to acquire the garden at last for the public, in January 1874 Grant told them that *he* was about to do so, having been 'for some months past . . . in negotiation . . . for the purchase of the ground with a view to laying it out as a garden, and handing it over to the Board as a gift to the Metropolis'. Surely if Victor Emmanuel gave a barony for the Galleria, Victoria might recognize a gift like this. The gesture often called the redeeming feature of a flamboyant career wasn't meant to be made for nothing. Grant made a similar offer later in the year to improve Soho Square (not accepted), just to underscore the point.[28]

Knowles was commissioned by Grant in February 1874 to design the new layout ready for ceremonial opening in July, so with gardeners, sculptors, marble merchants, and ironmongers he had to work fast—a situation that suited his driving energy better than the longueurs of Grant's house. Moreover, it was possible to invest the public garden with idealism evoked by the central fountain with its statue of Shakespeare (Pl. 14), and by the separate busts of Newton, Hogarth, Reynolds, and Hunter who had lived in or near the Square.[29] The central figure was adapted from the monument in Westminster Abbey (designed

---

[27] *BN*, 28 Jan., 31 Mar. 1876, pp. 107, 336, and Loftie, n. 24 above.

[28] S of L vol. 34, *St Anne's Soho*, pp. 431–40; *CBA for 1875* (1874), p. 142; *Brit. Architect*, 10 July 1874, p. 28; *ILN*, 4 July 1874, pp. 4, 6.

[29] Busts in corner of garden: Newton by W. Calder Marshall, Hogarth by J. Durham, Reynolds by H. Weekes, Hunter by T. Woolner—sculpturally a dull crew. The landscaping here and for Grant at Kensington was by John Gibson Jr., best known for his work at Battersea Park.

by William Kent and carved by Scheemakers)—an adaptation doubtless inspired by Knowles's interest in the Abbey, possibly born of some talk with the Dean, and carved by Giovanni Fontana, sculptor of the Kensington caryatids. It stands detached from any background, but otherwise is virtually the same as the one in the Abbey, without masks on the base of the reading-desk and with a different quotation on the scroll in the Bard's hand. Instead of the Abbey's lines misquoted from *The Tempest*, the scroll in Leicester Square was inscribed with a line from *Twelfth Night*, IV. ii., 'There is no darkness but ignorance'. [30] Was there no lapidary tongue-in-cheek on someone's part, in so recalling the clown's assurance to Malvolio? At any rate, it was in a sense Grant's shareholders, 'more puzzled than the Egyptians in their fog', who involuntarily gave Leicester Square garden to the public of London. Long before 'It's a Long Way to Tipperary, Farewell Leicester Square' became the hit song of the First World War, the Bard on his pedestal was gazing toward the old Empire Theatre. The pedestal rises from the bowl of a fountain fed by dolphins spurting water from their heads like cherub-whales spouting; and the four busts still stand on bases like up-ended soapboxes in the corners of the garden. Within a year after the ceremony in July 1874, the baseless fabric of the mammoth promoter's vision and all his cloud-capp'd companies began to dissolve. By 1877, eighty-nine legal actions against Grant were pending.

Public curiosity about Grant's house became acute during 1876, while interior decoration still continued and rumour assigned its sale to this or that great person. Whereupon Gladstone, certainly not as a potential purchaser but as one ever ready to observe interesting phenomena, asked Knowles to show it to him; the resulting comments are unrecorded, but Knowles's reply of 26 May 1876, agreeing to meet him 'at the gates of the new House', adds 'which however I shall very shortly be ashamed to show to anybody so fearfully & wonderfully is it being "painted & decorated" '. So, structurally at least, Knowles was proud of it, although his own connection with it had ended, his fees unpaid. In October he wrote Gladstone of being 'greatly occupied with my action against Albert Grant—which collapsed suddenly & at the last moment through his paying all my claim and the lawyer's

---

[30] S of L (n. 28) doesn't mention inscription, which is hard to see, but there is much contemporary evidence for it, including *Bldr* engraving, 4 July 1874.

costs—rather than go into court', perhaps because the fees included the design of Leicester Square, and so some last shreds of prestige.[31] The house—never lived in, hired once for a ball— was demolished by Grant's creditors in 1883. He was still in difficulties at the time of his death in 1899. In the spring of 1877, just as Knowles was triumphantly bringing out his new review, Grant's collection of pictures, mostly bought *en bloc* to furnish the new house, were sold off at Christie's. Grant's last public-spirited gesture had been the loan of one of them, a Maclise, to the Royal Academy in 1875, its subject 'The Disenchantment of Bottom', catalogued with suitable quotation: 'I have had a dream, past the wit of man to say what dream it was; man is but an ass, if he go about to expound this dream.'[32]

Meanwhile, Knowles's income can have had little from the Park Town estate he had laid out in the 1860s at Battersea. Here and there in the Victoria area, however, he designed for various clients. For William Salting the collector's brother Knowles designed in 1873 the building containing Overton's fish shop and restaurant adjoining the Underground station: with its (former) turrets, Grosvenor-style medallion heads, and tiled storey-course, this once made a picturesque prospect of the westward view along Victoria Street.[33] The young Flowers and Saltings, like the surgeon Erasmus Wilson for whom he was to design a hospital in 1879, were reputable men, as different from Grant as clients as Tennyson had been from the lesser suburban speculators Knowles had dealt with in the 1860s. Victorian architects, like Victorian editors, dealt with a wide range of species of their own time.

FRIENDSHIP WITH TENNYSON

> 'His active nature I thought sometimes spurred A.T.
> on to work when he might be flagging.' Mrs.
> Tennyson in *Materials*, iii. 107 for May 1869,
> *Memoir*, ii. 110 for November 1871

In 1872 Tennyson composed the clanging war-song of the knights —'Blow trumpet, for the world is white with May. . . . Clang battleaxe, and clash brand! Let the King reign'—while striding

[31] Knowles to Gladstone, 26 May, 20 Oct. 1876 (as n. 50 below).
[32] RA winter exhibition catalogue 1875, quoting *Midsummer Night's Dream*, IV, i. From the 1882 sale, Grant's staircase is said to have gone to Mme Tussaud's (demolished during the Second World War), gate piers to Sandown Park.
[33] Application to MBW, 9 Apr. 1873, 7 Aug. 1874.

across Clapham Common. Perhaps all the way to the western end where still there is a grove of ancient whitethorn trees—not then white with may, for this was in November. Isabel Knowles wrote it down for him ('Mrs Knowles has written out the "War-song of the Knights" . . . made on Clapham Common').[34] For the three years 1870–2, Tennyson had rooms on the top floor at No. 16 Albert Mansions in Victoria Street (taking a set of chambers doubtless to avoid always having to be a house-guest on visits to London). These were the years when Knowles's friendship with him was closest. Knowles's later claim that they shared these chambers as joint-tenants needs to be taken with a grain of salt. When Tennyson was away from London during that time, Knowles wrote to him from his own office at Gray's Inn (for example, in January 1871 about the Food Fund) and the editor and architect's official address changed from Gray's Inn to No. 17 Albert Mansions only in mid-1872. For Knowles it will have been a case of stopping in to forward Tennyson's mail when the poet was not there, and friendly attendance when he was (and building at Albert Mansions still went on in 1870 to be seen to). Manning, writing to Knowles in February 1871, hoped to 'take my chance of finding you in Victoria Street'. Let us say that Knowles had a *pied-à-terre* in Tennyson's rooms there from 1870 until sometime in 1872, for one foot only. He still then addressed him as 'Mr Tennyson', though by 1875 it was 'My dear Tennyson' (as never with Mr. Gladstone).[35]

Emily Tennyson's acceptance of the Knowleses was not quite as simple as her husband's. Her gratitude for Knowles's thought-fulness and practical help in publishing and architectural matters was warmly expressed, as in her letter to him from Farringford in January 1869 after Tennyson's fifth visit in a year to The Hollies: 'as to my thanks for your goodness I hope you believe that they are as unwearied as that goodness'; for 'he gets more nervous [about business] here than with you'. In May she told

[34] *Materials*, iii. 193, 198.

[35] On Knowles's office address: Knowles to Tennyson, 4 Apr. 1870, 11 Jan. 1871 (TRC), to Cyril Flower, 15 Feb. 1872 (St. Philip's, Battersea, churchwardens' minutes), to Hallam Tennyson, 5 Sept. 1872 (TRC); Manning to Knowles, letter with Food Fund papers (WPL). 'Joint-tenant' in *Idylls* leaflet *c.* 1896 (chap. 8, n. 88 below) was for Hallam. On No. 16 Albert Mansions, chap. 5, n. 37. On mode of address, no letters from Knowles to Tennyson appear to survive from 1873–4. On nursery friendliness in 1872, see p. 158.

Hallam that 'Papa has been very cheerful' since a recent visit by
the Knowleses: 'He has a great fancy for them. I am thankful to
say that Mr Knowles has the power to encourage him in his work'
—a comment she was to make more than once. In July and August
there was the strain of settling into the new house, and some
ambivalence thereafter, when the Knowleses were enabled to
have an inexpensive holiday: writing in the family journal at Aldworth in October 1869, she mentioned that 'We have lent them
Farringford which they went in the 9th of Sept.' and 'We send
Sophia to prepare Farringford for us thinking that the Knowles
will have left according to their arrangement', full stop. Then at
the end of October Knowles arrived, 'As usual much absorbed in
the Poems. I differ from him on some points & express my
difference somewhat too warmly as I know & tell him so
afterwards'; a month later she and Knowles sat up 'until twelve
marking passages in The Lover's Tale hoping that A. may consent
to publish them'. Later, and more than once, there were pathetic
juxtapositions in the journal. In October 1871, two days free of
guests, a brief time alone with her husband, 'lifts me above the
petty cares of life. Infinite refreshment. 21st. Mr & Mrs Knowles
come.' However, 'Mrs Knowles helps A. to arrange the scattered
leaves of Tristram ['The Last Tournament'] for press. . . . Kind
people. He very able helpful & energetic.' Although, in November 1870 'the rest & refreshment of being alone' with her
husband and in October 1872 'our one day alone for a month'
appeared in the context of visits by Knowles, he was not the only
visitor: she was sharing a public character with many friends.
After ill-health ended her journal-keeping in 1874, and Hallam
took up the journal, Knowles figured in it much less often.[36]

In January 1870, Knowles's review in the form of a letter to the
Spectator on the newly published *Idylls* caused Tennyson to write
to him that it was 'the best, & indeed might be called the only
true critique on the I[dylls] . . . very succinctly & cleanly written,
& I liked it so much that I sent it by the Dean of W[estminster],
who was here the other day, to The Queen along with the
Idylls.'[37] Knowles's occasional writing at best could have the

[36] Emily Tennyson to Knowles, 22 Jan. 1869, and to Hallam Tennyson, in
May 1869 (published by J. O. Hoge, 1974); Tennyson family journal, Oct. 1869,
Nov. 1870, Oct. 1871, Oct. 1872.
[37] Tennyson to Knowles, 11 Jan. 1870 (transcript of MS. at Yale shown me by

terse, muscular quality of his own *King Arthur* book, the unornamented quality of his sea-front terraces at Hove. In the *Spectator* letter he continued his high-minded analysis of the *Idylls*, with their 'fine and wholesome moral breeze which always seems to blow about the higher realms of art', that he had begun in his preface of 1868. His comparison in 1870 of the growth of the *Idylls* to that of Canterbury Cathedral, 'as such buildings always seem rather to have *grown* than been *constructed*', echoed his remark to Hewlett on first seeing that cathedral in 1853, that it looked 'more like some piece of nature which had grown like a forest where it stood than been reared by hands': Donaldson discoursing on Gothic buildings on Tuesday nights in the 1840s, even Ruskin's early articles on architecture and scenery, had contributed to Knowles's vocabulary. In May 1873, in an un-signed article in the *Contemporary* he continued his commentary, with a side-swipe at the Rossetti circle (implying that he was still unrepentant about the Buchanan article) referring scornfully to 'a certain set' and 'women-like men' to whose fleshly gospel Tennyson had opposed an Imitation of Christ. More interesting to us are some perceptive comments on Tennyson's workmanship, uses of language and versification to achieve certain effects, some-times as of musical notes. 'And withal it is no study of Vivisection with the Poet turned into a demonstrator of anatomy—nor a string of instances of morbid introspection, but above all things a Poem.' Knowles above all things saw that.[38]

In June 1870 Tennyson, still haunted by the funeral of his friend Sir John Simeon three weeks before, heard Dean Stanley's memorial sermon on Dickens, the Sunday following Dickens's private funeral. Knowles was with Tennyson in the Abbey and wrote the unsigned account published in 1911 by the second

---

Prof. Lang has 'clearly', given as 'cleanly' by Knowles in Jan. 1893, *NC*, p. 181 n.). A little 12-page pamphlet reprint of the 1870 article (copy in Knowles papers, now TRC) is probably the form in which Tennyson had it bound with his poems to send to the Queen; and from Knowles to Gladstone, 22 Jan. 1870. On prepara-tion of this article in summer 1869, chap. 6, n. 9.

[38] On Canterbury, Knowles to Hewlett, 10 Aug. 1853 (WPL). 'The Meaning of Mr Tennyson's King Arthur', *CR*, May 1873, p. 938, was unsigned, but *ILN* noted (17 May, p. 463) that it was 'expounded apparently by authority' and Tennyson's 'very workmanly done' to Knowles (?4 May, MS. at Univ. of Virginia, transcript shown to me by Prof. Lang) must refer to it, as Prof. Tillotson in her 'Tennyson's Serial Poem' (1965) deduced.

Lord Tennyson.[39] After the service a great crowd surged toward
the Sanctuary where Tennyson stood waiting to leave, surging
solely to see him, those around him gradually realized—and so he
had to be spirited away, probably through a door in the reredos,
past the shrine of the Confessor, and out past Chaucer's tomb
before which he was himself to lie, to the old royal door. Tennyson's grandson has described how extraordinary his appearance
was, as of a figure out of the Bible, even in an era of biblical
beards, perhaps 'the most famous figure in the world' in 1870. In
the summer of 1871 (and possibly again the next summer) there
was an expedition one would like to have seen, Knowles taking
Tennyson and Gladstone to dine at Richmond; driving through
the leafy suburbs (the Thames being for the masses then), the
swarthy prophet's head looming above the monumental profile,
and opposite them a lively little figure pointing out picturesque
features of the scenery.[40]

Knowles was a conscientious man of business for a bestselling
author—one reason the *pied-à-terre* was convenient—as the
Moxon–Strahan transactions had shown. Recurrent strains
needed smoothing out (Tennyson to Knowles, January 1870: 'I
am so weary of publishers'; March 1872: 'Bother all publishers!')
and Knowles was able to take a good deal off the poet's shoulders.
So a little self-interest on Knowles's part was understandable. A
long letter of his to Tennyson, dated 4 November 1871 and
remaining only in draft, may be worth quoting for its tortuous
compunctions:[41]

I hope you received the revise of 'The Last Tournament' this morning
—Pray, still bear in mind that if you have any the least dislike to publish
it in 'the Contemporary' it is quite open to you not to do so.

[39] *Tennyson and His Friends* (1911), unsigned contribution, known to be by
Knowles. Four days earlier, Tennyson chaired the Metaphysical Society meeting
(Martineau on Causality) at the other end of Victoria Street (Brown). At Aldworth that fortnight much consultation with Knowles over 'great trouble with
the drains' (family journal). In 1870 he was indispensable.
[40] Knowles to Gladstone (as n. 50 below), undated note on Carlton House
Terrace notepaper (pencilled July 1872) saying that Tennyson was staying with
him and could Gladstone 'come & dine with him at Richmond as you did last
year'. Nothing in Tennyson papers on this, and of course Knowles may not have
been with them 'last year'.
[41] Draft in Knowles papers (TRC). Tennyson on publishers: 1 Jan. 1870 and
4 Mar. 1872 (Lang, ed., *Letters*) shown me by Prof. Lang. Although the original
MS. of Knowles's letter of 4 Nov. 1871 is not now known, it was sent, as the
reply exists (n. 42).

The fact of sending it to Osgood [for American publication] only commits you to a publication of some sort in this country. If you become finally convinced that the 'booklet' plan is the best it is by no means too late to adopt it. You know how much better I personally consider publication in the Review—but just because I am Editor of it —I have a most distinct personal unwillingness to print it there—unless you yourself are quite clear about the desirability of it. I am most honest in saying that for my own individual comfort—I would rather it was in some other Review. . . . But . . . considering your business engagements to Strahan. . . . I feel shut up to the conclusion that it must be *Contemporary* or *Booklet*—and I still for your interests prefer the former—not inattending the exceeding might which Mrs Tennyson's opinion to the contrary has for me.

However it is published there will be *some* objectors to any addition at all being made to the Idylls— & if it appears in my Review—their objections may in part be set down (perhaps even by yourself) to the fact of its so appearing. . . . I feel (much more than I am likely to make you understand) that in taking the responsibility of urging noting opinion I am (as I said before) putting my own comfort quite out of sight. I am more than glad to do so, upon one condition that you yourself finally show my opinion to deliberately prefer the Review to the Booklet. But not else—The words of Job are ended!

Tennyson replied on the 9th that, having considered all the pros and cons, he had settled that 'The Last Tournament' should appear in the *Contemporary*, which it duly did in December. Knowles was allowed to keep the manuscript as a precious autograph, 'partly because he had managed all the late business transactions with publishers so carefully', and partly because (as he told Gladstone later) he had asked for it.[42] A year later, however, he did not succeed in getting for his New Year 1873 number the Epilogue to the Queen, written in December 1872 to complete the Idylls in the imminent 1873 edition of Tennyson's poems. After considering the idea of letting it appear first in the *Contemporary*, Tennyson wrote to Knowles from Farringford just before Christmas that there would then be no time for the Queen to see it first, and that he preferred to let it find its own way 'silently among the people'—adding in a phrase that tells much: 'though possibly if you were near me you might persuade me'.[43]

[42] Tennyson to Knowles, 9 Nov. 1871 (Lang, ed., *Letters*). *Materials*, iii. 179. Knowles to Gladstone, 14 Jan. 1874 (as n. 50).
[43] Tennyson to Knowles, ? Dec. 1872 (Lang, ed., *Letters*), which also mentions

Out of Victoria Street, or Clapham, came an undated prose draft for 'Balin and Balan' dictated to Knowles 'as a trial of that way of working . . . with scarce any pause', Knowles said later. Fourteen pages stitched together as a little notebook and covered with his handwriting, headed 'The Dolorous Stroke', seems to be the manuscript from this dictation (although the title, from Malory's different version of the story, was not used in Tennyson's resulting poem). With some crossing-out, the wording is as published by Knowles, to the Tennyson family's dismay, just after the poet's death and later by them in the *Memoir* of 1897.[44] The dictation seems to have taken place sometime in 1872, after 'Gareth' was finished, perhaps in September, or in November when the war-song was written, or in July when Knowles was allowed to copy a poem out of Tennyson's notebook for his private pleasure. That copy, in Knowles's papers, of the poem beginning 'The Lord has grown as commonplace/As the peal of the parish bells', bears Knowles's note: 'A.T.—Copied out of his M.S. book of Gareth at The Hollies July 7th 1872/J.T.K.'[45]

Tennyson thought briefly of building a chapel at Aldworth, partly prompted by Knowles, but that went no further.[46] Knowles continued to be of business assistance until eased off by Hallam's instatement as his father's right hand from 1874 on; during 1875–81 Knowles took an intense interest in Tennyson's plays; and the friendship continued on a less intimate basis for the rest of the poet's life. One worried moment, in the midst of the excitement of launching the *Nineteenth Century* in March 1877, exposed Knowles's thin skin toward some thoughtless teasing on Tennyson's part, when Knowles had just paid a craftsman on Tennyson's behalf for work at Aldworth and Farringford in 1875–6. Four anguished pages went off to Hallam:[47]

---

corrections for it which Knowles was overseeing for Tennyson; Knowles to Tennyson, 25 Dec. 1872, 'I think you made a mistake . . . but I admit that I may be prejudiced' (TRC).

[44] With Knowles papers until 1978 (now TRC). On Knowles's publication in 1893, chap. 8, n. 88.

[45] Ricks, p. 1231, conjectured date *c.* 1874. Also on same double-quarto sheet of notepaper (now TRC), notes of Tennyson's talk in 1872, in February at Farringford, in July at Clapham, in October at Aldworth, which eventually filtered into Knowles's article in 1893, or drafts for it.

[46] Tennyson journal, Feb. 1872 (TRC).

[47] Knowles to Hallam Tennyson, 12 Mar. 1877 (TRC).

What on earth *did* your Father mean the other day by saying that I had
been keeping the money back 'because of my 5 per cent'? . . . before a
table-full of strangers. . . . I have acted for him as a *friend* & not as a
maker of professional income out of him *always*—I do feel horribly
sensitive about being supposed to do such a thing when I am so
carefully *not* doing it—not that I think it in the very least derogatory
to earn my 'own living in that state of life' etc—but because it would be
very derogatory to do it when you are avowedly not doing it. Burn
this . . . such a thing as he said before strangers . . . hurts me to the quick.

But Tennyson's part in the launching of the *Nineteenth Century*
that same month was kind and apt, as we shall see. Many people
remembered meeting Tennyson with Knowles at Clapham. Mr.
Gassiot showed off his voltaic battery, Miss Thornton was surprised by a visit to her infants' school. And there were garden
parties under the old trees behind The Hollies, with Tennyson
and Browning 'receiving a few favoured fellow-guests at the
entrance of a little tent on the lawn'.[48]
Meanwhile, Knowles was helping Gladstone to unburden his
mind.

AN OUTLET FOR GLADSTONE

> 'His mind refused to give itself absolutely up to any
> one study of life. Great as he was in the House of
> Commons, his vast energies needed some other field
> of activity now and then. . . . Mr Gladstone had
> eminently what the heroines of modern fiction are
> fond of calling a complex character. When he had
> spent a certain time over politics . . . then it appeared
> to him . . . that there was something else waiting at
> his hand that he could do and which he ought to
> endeavour to do with all his might.' Justin McCarthy,
> *The Story of Gladstone's Life*, 1898, pp. 284–5

Knowles was waiting at Gladstone's hand when the Liberals fell
early in 1874. Convinced as Gladstone was that the welfare of
mankind depended as much upon thinkers as upon statesmen, it
was foregone that, once he was out of office, no one periodical

[48] T. H. S. Escott, *Great Victorians* (1916), p. 313. On Gassiot, Tennyson,
Memoir, ii. 116; Gassiot had been a founder of the Clapham Athenaeum (chap. 2,
'Clapham Park', above). Forster, *Marianne Thornton*, p. 229.

could wholly contain him.[49] But Knowles had already managed to extract from him a letter to publish as a note in December 1873, disagreeing with Herbert Spencer who, Gladstone felt, had misquoted him on the subject of evolution. (It may be noted that, according to a quotation by Knowles remaining in draft with his own letters in the Gladstone Papers, Gladstone wrote to him from Downing Street on 9 November 1873 that he had 'no formulated opinion for or against evolution'.) From February 1874 until December 1876, the *Contemporary* published thirteen articles by Gladstone, the first three Homeric—a theme which Knowles welcomed with more enthusiasm than he was later to feel on the subject: '. . . reads to me like *wine* (so to speak)—so subtle & smooth so brilliant & strong', he wrote in April 1874 of the translation Gladstone sent him for May. 'Such fragments and specimens of the Great Whole, which you roughly indicated to me as being in your mind—will admirably preface the way for its gradual unfolding—for the uplifting of the veil from the ancient Greek landscape which you seemed to me to be doing while you were speaking of Homer as you conceive him & his work.' Knowles saw the way Gladstone's mind was tending in 1874; it was the beginning of a long connection. In the *Nineteenth Century* from March 1877 until October 1896, this author was to appear sixty-seven times (counting articles in two instalments as two). That is, for both Knowles's periodicals, Gladstone wrote eighty times from the age of 64 until the age of 87. The stream was not steady, thirty-seven articles for Knowles from early 1874 until early 1880, dwindling to four during the ministries of 1880–5 and 1886, then twenty-three during 1887–9, ten of them in Gladstone's eightieth year, after that only two to four times a year. Correspondence between them fluctuated accordingly, with invitations to breakfast and dine in Downing Street in between. There is much of interest in Knowles's letters now with the Gladstone Papers in the British Library.[50] He suited Mr. Gladstone very well.

[49] During the period of Knowles's editing, i.e. the last 28 years of Gladstone's life, articles by him also appeared in the *Edinburgh* (1870, one), *Quarterly* (1874–6, three), *Macmillan's* (1877, one), *Fortnightly* (1880, one), even the *Contemporary* after Knowles left it (1877–8, three, 1887–9, four), and others.

[50] Knowles to Gladstone, 1869–97, *c*. 360 letters in Gladstone Papers, BL: Add. MSS. 44231 (1869–80), 44232 (1881–97); also Add. MS. 44786, invitations,

At first, Gladstone usually preferred to write for him on classical or religious subjects rather than political subjects, though Knowles was always trying to draw him that way. Nothing came of a request in January 1876 'which has been hovering for some weeks on the tip of my pen' for an article 'on the Suez Canal shares purchase—questioning very much the dignity—& the utility of the proceeding—& the desirability of setting such a precedent for Imperial conduct'. Gladstone had already told him not to be 'an inch-and-ell man', when Knowles begged unsuccessfully for first chance at his controversial pamphlet on *The Vatican Decrees in their Bearing on Civil Allegiance* in November 1874. After the pamphlet came out, the atmosphere of Metaphysical Society meetings that winter under Gladstone's chairmanship promised to be electric if Archbishop Manning came, but he did not, although Knowles reported to Gladstone in December that he had extracted Manning's promise to come, 'if only to show at this particular juncture & season—how really and truly Catholic is the atmosphere of our Club'; and in May, Knowles said that the (by then) Cardinal's own receptions would prevent '& thus disappoint me of the wish I had that he should have "sat under you" at the Metaphysical'. Later in 1875 Knowles explained that Gladstone's translation of a Latin hymn was to head the December issue because, 'if you will suffer me to speak quite frankly about it—my main wish is *not* to give precedence to "the Cardinal"—He has an article on "Magna Charta" in the same number and it would not be at all for the interests of the Review to put his name before your own—although it is greatly for its interest (as showing our catholicity) that both names should appear'; but in the end this aim was achieved by placing Gladstone at the very back of the issue, as far from Manning as possible. The general public represented by the *Illustrated London News* thought the hymn 'respectable and tame' and that Manning on Magna Charta would 'hardly mend the matter', preferring to these a 'generally interesting' article on 'Sea-lions'. Balancing the lions with the sea-lions required editorial legerdemain.[51]

ff. 60, 87, 104, 144; Add. MSS. 44453, papers on Strahan row 1877, ff. 5–204 *passim*, and 44454, circular 1877, Strahan *vs.* King, f. 364.
  [51] Knowles to Gladstone (in order of reference), 5 Jan. 1876, 3 Nov. 1874, 28 Dec. 1874, 30 May 1875, 19 Nov. 1875 (as n. 50). The hymn is not indexed in *WIVP* with its embargo on poetry (see Appendix herewith). On *CR* December issue, *ILN*, 18 Dec. 1875, p. 611. The author of the 'Sea-lions' article was John

Gladstone's greatest success in the *Contemporary Review* was his trumpet-blast of October 1874 against over-emphasis on ritual, in and out of church. Ritual in church was an urgent public question. Knowles wrote on the 3rd: 'The rush has been so great that nobody but "the trade" has been able to get any—and "the trade" has almost literally taken them by force. . . . There have been *Seven* editions of the Review in *three* days and "the cry is still 'they come' "!' The full title, 'Ritualism and Ritual', pertained to a dread that Gladstone did not share, that ritual in the Church of England led to Rome.[52] He began by defending 'the perpetual instinct of human nature to clothe thought and act appropriately'. But, on lack of harmony between the inward and the outward state, he took up the stance of the Age-of-Stucco satirists of the day. Beauty in full harmony with purpose had been attained by the Greeks (he inevitably said), in fact the Attic Greeks had been a 'nation of Wedgwoods'. Yet most objects made in the 1870s 'we calmly and without a sigh surrender to Ugliness', and the British were the worst in this respect: 'for the worship of beauty we have substituted a successful pursuit of comfort' (going on to say, illogically, that the dress of an English woman was 'the worst in the European world', with ornament administered in 'portentous doses' to 'the house of hair built upon her head' and 'the measureless extension of her dragging train'). And then the sermon turned to architecture: 'Who shall be the rival of some English architects plastering their work with an infinity of pretentious detail in order to screen from attention inharmonious dimensions and poverty of lines?' Ritualism in architecture was 'unwise, undisciplined reaction from poverty, from coldness, from barrenness, from nakedness', that is, from Georgian baldness as Victorians saw it.[53] One

---

Willis Clark, Registrar of Cambridge University (who completed his uncle Robert Willis's great architectural history of the university).

[52] Knowles to Gladstone, 3 Oct. 1874 (as n. 50). A Public Worship Regulation Act of that year was unsatisfactory (Chadwick, *Victorian Church*, ii. 322–5, 361–2). Magnus in his biography of Gladstone took the article of October 1874 to be entirely anti-Rome; actually it was far more general, part of it showing how the applied arts in England misapplied a 'perpetual instinct of human nature'; e.g. he also broadened narrow quarrels over vestments and regalia into a condemnation of secular dress and ornament when unrelated to utility.

[53] Gladstone, 'Ritualism and Ritual', *CR*, Oct. 1874, pp. 663–81. For its 19 pages, because of their success, Strahan paid £100 (Knowles to Gladstone, 20 Oct. 1874, as n. 50) although Gladstone had offered to take less than usual (same

suspects a long preparatory talk with Knowles, and in truth the instigation amounted to a conversation of some sort mentioned in a hopeful note from Knowles on 3 September:[54]

> I have not liked to trouble you again sooner—but trust you will excuse me for now repeating my strong hope that we may have something from you for the October number of the 'Contemporary'— Especially I hope it may be something turning on those questions . . . such as you spoke to me about when last I had the pleasure of seeing you.
>
> All men seem to me now waiting for some *voice* about these matters —which stand in a heaving stagnation among many opposing currents ready to flow this way or that according as the strong breath shall blow.
>
> Forgive me if I venture to say (*personally* & not only *editorially*) how much I hope that breath may be yours.

And so, what Knowles got was one of the great generalizing articles that he saw his readers needed, and which he was already perfecting his ability to inspire. The architectural press, incidentally, was agog to hear that, since ritualism was 'the attempted substitution of the secondary for the primary aim, and the real failure and paralysis of both', therefore 'a great deal of our architecture, a great share of our industrial production has been, or is, it may be feared, very Ritualistic indeed'.

Sir George Gilbert Scott, then President of the Royal Institute of British Architects, about to begin its winter session of meetings, must have sighed. The profession was being assailed from all directions. His annual address in November had to report Ruskin's refusal of the Royal Gold Medal. The October *Quarterly* carried a Ruskinian article by John Emmett—the architect and critic who preferred reviewing buildings to reviewing books— protesting that the only hope for English architecture lay in its workmen, and agreeing with James Fergusson on the falsehoods of contemporary buildings. Fergusson himself, in the *Contemporary*'s October issue, denounced Burges's designs upon the interior of St. Paul's—although that, if we may call it so, was an

---

letter) and earlier (overdue) payments had been £92. 8s. for 22 pages in June and £105 for 26 pp. in July (Knowles to Gladstone, 3 Sept. 1874 on both); Knowles had to extract £50 for 18 pp. on Homer in March 1876 from Strahan's partner (Knowles to Gladstone, 29 Mar. 1876). On *NC* payments, chap. 8, n. 20.

[54] Knowles to Gladstone, 3 Sept. 1874 (as n. 50), with another on 6 Sept. while on holiday at Folkestone, where the article already in proof caught up with him.

intramural row. And now here was Mr. Gladstone. These dissatisfactions were not new or sudden: 'the Architectural mind is
weary and restless', the *British Architect* thought. Professor Robert
Kerr, often a sounding-board of his day, had asked in 1869 how
a profession that was bound to reflect the character of its own
time could change it.[55] The character of the time was reflected in
The Way We Live Now, in the Baron Grants, and in *The Times*'s
leaders. While the times were much worse in the United States,
recovering from civil war, and on the Continent, still so divided,
the more insular Victorian satisfactions were evaporating with the
discovery that mankind was not an island. For Knowles as an
editor, all this was grist for his mill. As an architect he was
ambivalent, in 1874 still committed to his profession for part of
his income, and still in 1876 determined enough to stay with it
to claim his Fellowship of the Institute (dated, that is, seven years
after the work he was most proud of, Aldworth).[56] But repeated
doses of speculators, even those for whom he could work
responsibly for an ungrudged return, had killed the idealism he
had once felt; the summer of 1863, with Jane's death and Woodgate's failure, had been a sort of personal watershed. Scott must
have sighed again over the following reply from the Editor of
the *Contemporary Review* to the RIBA's invitation to come and
answer Emmett's article at an Institute meeting:[57]

Dear Sir.—I am afraid I may be unable to accept the kind invitation of
the Council to attend next Monday's meeting. I should, however,
have but a very few words to say on the *Quarterly* article, which seems
to me entirely unpractical, and, indeed, puerile.

I cannot but think that the hope of English architecture lies in
common sense rather than in such sentimental antiquarianism,—in
common sense and good taste regulated by the great principle that

[55] Ruskin, *Works*, ed. Cook and Wedderburn, xxxiv. 513 ff. Both Emmett and
F. R. Conder, a civil engineer who attacked his *Quarterly* article of Oct. 1874 in
the *Edinburgh* for Apr. 1875, are identified in *WIVP* vol. I. Fergusson on Burges,
CR, Oct. 1874, p. 750; *Brit. Architect*, 16 Oct. 1874, p. 241. Prof. Kerr to RIBA
in 1869 quoted at head of this chapter.

[56] Knowles was elected Fellow 4 Dec. 1876, when his mind was certainly not
on architecture (next section) but the matter will have been set in motion some
months before; his chief sponsors were his father and Charles Barry Jr., Pres.
RIBA at the time (RIBA Librarian kindly had records searched).

[57] *Bldr*, 26 Dec. 1874, p. 1080; the sender, not the recipients, probably gave it
to the press. 'At the head of all the new professions must be placed that of the
civil engineer', T. H. S. Escott, *England* (rev. edn. 1885), p. 554.

good architecture is decorated construction, and bad architecture is constructed decoration.

A civil engineer with a cultivated taste and the general education of a gentleman, seems to me far more nearly the ideal architect for our time than the building-foreman of the *Quarterly* reviewer.

If the Institute of Architects could be joined to the Institution of Civil Engineers, it would be, in my opinion, the beginning of a very good hope for both professions; and I heartily wish that some proposal to try and bring this about could be made at your meeting on Monday.

Do you think you could get the suggestion put forward?

James Knowles

The italicized axiom dates back to the once much-quoted proposition in Owen Jones's *Grammar of Ornament* and implies that Knowles's education had ended in the 1850s; and yet, in suggesting the alliance, perhaps Knowles was, if only journalistically, ahead of his time, At any rate, his son Arthur, son and grandson of architects, descendant of generations of craftsmen, was to be a civil engineer—but only after taking his degree at Trinity College, Cambridge.

Historians of the Cockerells, the Scotts, the Shaws of Victorian architecture have to take little note of what the Kerrs, the Emmetts, even the Gladstones said. But the lesser architects, and the greater editors, reflected the character of their time. It was because Knowles was both of these that he is interesting.

A crisis arose in his editorial career in 1876, for him a year of tension in which life was conducted in a state of nervous excitement. The death of his mother in April hit him hard. Dean Stanley, who had lost his wife only the month before, came with them to Norwood Cemetery, as Knowles told Tennyson: 'The dear good Dean came to give us his hand of comfort yesterday across the grave & read as only he can read I think—nothing would have been kinder than his coming at all & I shall never forget it.' Trusting that there might be 'Light and not Darkness . . . beyond all', he wrote to Gladstone that 'sometimes it seems as if the very glory when the High Gates open to let one in blinds us who remain—at any rate makes all this world seem darker, as to a man who has gazed on the Sun's face'.[58] Over-

---

[58] On death of his mother, Knowles to Tennyson, 20 Apr. 1876 (TRC); and to Gladstone, 22, 29 Apr., 2 May 1876 (as n. 50), referring also to 'painful circumstances' for Gladstone (Lord Lyttelton's suicide, 18 April). Dean Stanley's wife, Lady Augusta, had died in March.

work and bereavement prostrated him in May, but after a week at the seaside he was able to send Gladstone seven pages of detailed comment on the proof of Gladstone's article to be printed in June as 'The Courses of Religious Thought'.[59] Knowles's own thoughts on what he called 'the really disintegrating forces now so largely at work', expressed with distaste for the 'creed of half-educated men & of workmen' that seemed to be growing 'among those classes', did not comprehend Gladstone's wider sympathies. But Knowles's comment that materialism was increasing so terribly that nothing 'short of the Plague or the Black Death or an earthquake like Lisbon's' could startle men into 'that perception of utter dependence on which religion seems to me primarily to rest' will have been congenial. One comment, marked in the margin in other ink, is an example of Knowles's quite dizzying ability to compound, or perhaps confound, ideas in a way Gladstone probably liked: 'Once let it be seen that the word matter or atom has—under the terms energy potency & so forth—had put into it all that men have hitherto felt constrained to call by other than material names (Thought—Will—Energy—Power—Cause) —and then the marvel of evolving the world as it is from such new-fangled atoms ceases & the whole theory is exploded.' Whatever one thinks of that, it soon became clear that the uneasy elements of the *Contemporary Review* were not going to hold together much longer.

PARTING COMPANY WITH STRAHAN

> 'It is my greatest wish as "Chairman" to prevent the interchange of different views from degenerating into Controversy.' Knowles to Gladstone, 9 November 1873, Gladstone Papers, BL

The publisher of the *Contemporary*, Alexander Strahan, seems to have been an unbusinesslike Scot, a shrewder judge of literary merit than of finance, with a taste for quality in printing and binding as well as insight into content. He was given to meddling in the work of his editors, and is said to have been ruinously generous to his authors. 'Although somewhat reserved he drew

---

[59] Knowles to Gladstone, 14 May 1876 (as n. 50) from Queen's Hotel, Hastings: 'creed of half-educated men & of workmen' probably reflected Conder's contempt in the *Edinburgh* (n. 55 above) for Emmett's 'inspired workman'.

men by a fascination all his own', for some found him a lovable character. His dashing spiky handwriting suggests, however, that he was not the man to deal with an independent free-lance like Knowles.[60] At first Knowles deferred to his experience, as he explained to Huxley in September 1871, with regard to the latter's article on Darwin's critics:[61]

Strahan has . . . converted me to his view about your splendid article which he is fully as much in love with as I am—namely—that we had better 'save it up' (as the children say) for our November number. In that month the world has collected itself again, & is (so he reasons) more ready to appreciate good literary food than now in its scattered & holiday making state. Besides he agrees that we ought to blow the trumpet about our prize more & louder in advance than there would now be time to do before Octr 1st. You will understand this serpentine wisdom—even if—from your high & clear latitude—you esteem it lightly.

But Knowles soon developed his own editorial judgement and stopped citing Strahan's advice except when it proved to be mistaken. The following note of 10 April 1875 to a contributor, Thomas Brassey M.P. (son of the railway contractor and later Earl Brassey, married to a Miss Allnutt of Clapham), shows Knowles at ease in his editorial chair and environs:[62]

My dear Brassey
    Mr Gladstone & Mr Lowe have promised to dine with me on Saturday next at the Grosvenor Hotel to meet two or three of my 'Contributors'—[and] the Editors of 'The Times', 'Daily News' & 'Standard' also promise to come. I should be so very glad if you happen to be disengaged.

Either there was some high strategy or some special economy in entertaining at the Grosvenor rather than at the Reform Club. (Very likely the hotel was ready to provide the private room regularly used by the Metaphysical Society at a reduced rate, especially as the management had known Knowles in his architectural-assistant's role half a generation before.) Bold as the giving

[60] Description of Strahan based mainly on F. A. Mumby, *Publishing and Bookselling* (1934), much of which Mumby said was drawn from Blaikie's *Recollections of a Busy Life*; also, more conjecturally, on Strahan's handwriting in Gladstone Papers, Add. MS. 44453 as n. 50 above.

[61] Knowles to Huxley, 22 Sept. 1871 (Huxley Papers, Imperial College). By 1874, when he published Gladstone in October, Knowles was more flexible.

[62] Kindly shown to me by Eric Smith from his Clapham historical collection.

of such a dinner was, socially and professionally, it is not comparable to the modern television interviewer inviting a prime minister to breakfast to meet celebrities the host himself has never met before. There is no reason to suppose that Knowles had not met the newspaper editors at other dinner tables already, for by April 1875 he was a frequent diner-out, if not quite yet at the most exalted tables, well on his way to them. Strahan then, so far as 'my contributors' were concerned, occupied the back seat.

During the period 1870-6, the ownership of the Strahan periodicals and book-publishing business at 56 Ludgate Hill (later 34 Paternoster Row) changed four times. Some sort of crisis came to a head in August 1876. A conference was called by McCorquodale the printer at his headquarters at Newton-le-Willows (where the present huge printing organization had begun thirty years earlier with railway printing): an 'unexpected call to Lancashire on business', explained Knowles to Cyril Flower, who was starting more building at Battersea (editorial crises, for ten years more, being so often accompanied by demands on Knowles's architectural time). On 5 August a memorandum for an agreement was drawn up between Strahan, Knowles, a solicitor named Hamilton, and McCorquodale, whose Armoury Printing Works in Southwark—to which Strahan was said to owe £35,000—were in process of taking over his publications as security and helping him to get up a limited company to pass them on to. Clause four of the memorandum guaranteed Knowles his stipend of £500 a year plus commission on profits, the total to rise to £1,000 by 1880, and secured him the editorship for six years and ultimately, perhaps, permanently. Knowles said later that on 30 August at a meeting in the City with McCorquodale and Hamilton he tried to work out an agreement between them and Strahan which they refused, not trusting Strahan. Knowles then asking for clarification of his own position and suggesting they appoint him 'sole & not joint Editor', they did so on 7 September. But other shareholders were about to be involved, and by October Knowles knew that he and his open platform were not wanted.[63]

[63] Knowles to Gladstone, 20 Oct., 2 and 6 Nov. 1876, 3 Jan. 1877; copy of agreement of 22 Aug. on clause 4 of memorandum of 5 Aug., copy of letter 30 Dec. 1876 McCorquodale to Knowles, and copy of Knowles's reply of 2 Jan., excerpts from *The Times* 15-17 Jan. 1877 and Knowles leaflet 15 Feb. 1877

For reports had been circulating among 'certain enthusiastic evangelicals' who were also rich that the *Contemporary* in Knowles's hands was in danger of being made an atheistical organ and ought to be rescued and turned to the service of Heaven (this was Knowles's version, vouched for by Guinness Rogers of Clapham, that 'considerable non-conformist' who was to write much for the *Nineteenth Century*). Hamilton informed Knowles on 27 October that Samuel Morley, the hosiery millionaire who was one of those about to form the new company, told him that Knowles was their only obstacle: they would not buy if saddled with him. In November Morley told Knowles himself, bluntly but pleasantly, that 'his own wish was to see an Editor . . . with a strong personal bias in his own direction (ex.gr. as to his own view of the Doctrine of the Atonement)', Knowles reported to Gladstone. (Earlier that year, the Metaphysical Society had devoted two evenings to discussing Huxley's presumably disparaging views on evidence for the Resurrection; they were not published in the *Contemporary*, but there may have been a leak at the Grosvenor—although the waiters were said to suppose these to be meetings of the 'madrigal society'.) In December McCorquodale sold half the shares to the new Strahan & Co. Ltd. formed under the chairmanship of Francis Peek of Wimbledon. On 14 December 1876 Peek signed a memorandum that Knowles wrote down in his presence to the effect that McCorquodale's agreement of 7 September with him was terminated; so all was cut and dried from then on. On 30 December McCorquodale wrote to Knowles from Newton-le-Willows to say that Strahan & Co. were now half-proprietors of the *Contemporary Review*, *Day of Rest*, *Peep Show*, and *Good Things for the Young*, and would manage them in future. He believed that Mr. Strahan would be glad of Mr. Knowles's assistance in the editorial department of the *Contemporary*, and 'arrangements hitherto existing will cease'. The new owners may well have had drawn to their attention the proof-sheets of an article for the January 1877 issue. The author of this article, 'The Ethics of Belief', which was to cause a famous stir among religious men, was the atheist W. K. Clifford, who dangerously

---

(Add. MS. 44231) and Strahan letters and leaflets in Add. MSS. 44453–4 (as n. 50 above): this material in the BL gives the whole sour story or as much as one can stand. Also Knowles's letter of 9 Aug. 1876 in Park Town estate papers.

believed in 'the universal duty of questioning all that we believe'. The core of the article had been presented as a paper before the Metaphysical Society in April. It would hardly be over-simplifying to say that the Society first got Knowles his appointment to the *Contemporary* and then lost it for him.[64]

He had already been seeking Gladstone's advice in October at Hawarden (where he 'drew out Papa finely' as Mary Gladstone noted), and then poured out a bold plan he had been evolving to use if he were forced out of the *Contemporary*. Also in this tense autumn of 1876, his case against Albert Grant was pending, and there was much estate detail to deal with at Battersea, let alone the nursing of two large articles of Gladstone's into the November and December numbers of the review. (The November article continued the theme of Gladstone's celebrated thundering pamphlet of September against Turkish oppression and Disraeli's Eastern policy—for Knowles had secured a political piece from him for once.) By December the great plan that had been boiling in Knowles's mind, 'to draw off with my Company of Knights from all quarters of the compass to some quite unrestricted ground', was ready. After the visit to Hawarden, Gladstone had written to him that he had not 'the protoplasm of a thought which could grow into an intention of walking with the Contemporary Review if you are driven from it'.[65] Early in November Knowles was able to tell him that Huxley, Manning, Hutton, Tyndall, Fitzjames Stephen, and 'many others' would support 'my Review which I may have to start on the principles of the Contemporary', and that he was 'now quite content to wait the event'.

Knowles was in a very virtuous position, having, as he told McCorquodale, found the *Contemporary* 'a failure (under 2000 in circulation) & by the kindness of my personal friends . . . made [it] a great success (with a circulation of 8000)'; and much of the time (this to Tennyson) 'working at it for love instead of money when Strahan was in one of his frequent difficulties & looking to the future to see my reward'.[66] To McCorquodale he repudiated

[64] On Clifford's article in *CR* Jan. 1877: Brown (1947), p. 180; Chadwick, *Victorian Church*, ii. 115.

[65] Deduced from Knowles to Gladstone, 3 Jan. 1877: 'You were so very kind as to write to me not long ago that "you had not the protoplasm . . ." ' as quoted. On drawing out Papa, n. 3 above.

[66] Knowles to McCorquodale, copy as n. 63; Knowles to Tennyson, 6 Jan.

indignantly the idea of applying to Strahan for work, 'after what you yourself and Mr Hamilton told me about Mr Strahan & which compelled me, as you know, to withdraw from my joint-editorship with him'. A good deal of angry letter-writing went on in January and February, but Knowles with legal advice left most of it to Strahan and busied himself with gathering his 'Company of Knights'. Peek and Morley and friends were undoubtedly glad to see the backs of Clifford and Huxley and Manning, with their respective views on the Atonement, but Gladstone was receiving protests from Strahan for some time—and, after a while and after all, was to 'walk with the Contemporary' now and then.

Knowles meanwhile, in a state of uplifted fervour, felt confirmed in the principles he had, as it were, brought through the battle, telling Gladstone in November[67] that:

I should have no care to edit any Review which was not *utterly impartial* —believing as I do, that full and fair and free discussion is the best way for arriving at and disseminating Truth—; and that if I personally have any opportunity for any use at all in the world it is simply that I happen to be set among so many and various and devout seekers after Truth all of whom win my respect.

I should hold it a sort of treason to endeavour to repress as to weight any one of them in the race set before him, as I believe (whether he perceive it or not) by God.

Great men and devout seekers were listening, whether Heaven perceived or not.

1877 (TRC). Yet in June 1876 Knowles had managed to spend 66 guineas on a landscape attributed to Claude in the Wynn Ellis sale at Christie's (chap. 9, n. 13).
   [67] Knowles to Gladstone, 2 Nov. 1876 (as n. 50).

8

The Nineteenth Century:
a Late Victorian Success

'The event of the month in the magazine world is, of
course, the appearance of the *Nineteenth Century*, an
event to be hailed by all who discern the importance
of maintaining a perfectly neutral ground for the free
expression of contemporary thought.' *Illustrated
London News*, 10 March 1877

THREE REBELLIONS THAT BECAME INSTITUTIONS
bloomed in the spring of 1877: the Society for the
Protection of Ancient Buildings, the Grosvenor Gallery,
and the *Nineteenth Century* review—hopeful precursors of the
'largeness of temper and lucidity of mind', the sweetness and
light, that Matthew Arnold in the *Nineteenth*'s first number said
England needed. Knowles's letters to two of the men he most
admired describe his preparations for the new review.

He took a fair view of the *Contemporary*'s new owners who had
dismissed him, and reserved his scorn for Strahan, from whom
there had been some sharp personal split. Although the loss of that
editorship 'just when it was about to repay my efforts [felt] as if
a child had been taken from me by some who only cared to sell
it', he accepted that Samuel Morley and his friends, 'scrupulously
upright men', should not see it that way.[1] But his reference to
Strahan's 'intense ingratitude' minced no courtesies: of Canon
Lightfoot (later Bishop of Durham, said to have been a tranquil
and sensible man) Knowles wrote: 'Lightfoot I greatly fear is out

[1] Knowles to Gladstone, 3 Jan. 1877 (as chap. 7, n. 50).

of reach—bitten by Strahan— & with all the poison rankling in him of that little creature's falsenesses'; and compared Strahan to 'a pitiful Albert Grant on a small scale—& now they seem likely both to "bust up" together', as still another judgement went against Grant.[2]

Knowles's experience of speculators was just then being enhanced by a murky specimen, a certain W. J. Sarl in course of taking Flower's ground in Victoria Street opposite the present Army and Navy Stores for the building of Queen's Mansions: its quite simple grid-façade, now demolished, may have been cheese-paringly based on an original design by Knowles, but just enough hints survive of Sarl's evasive doings to suggest why Knowles thoroughly withdrew long before the flats opened, and (Sir) Arthur Sullivan moved there from Albert Mansions, about the time *Iolanthe* opened.[3]

In January 1877 Strahan wrote to Knowles 'a letter so violent & offensive that Hopgood will not let me take the slightest notice of it', and this was followed by an exchange of salvoes in *The Times*.[4] Meanwhile, the rebel editor's father, the self-made silent Mr. Knowles erstwhile of Clapham Park, now of Russell Square and a 'five-figure man' (he was to leave £16,500 a few years later), made £2,000 available to his son, according to family memory, as backing for the new venture. It was a matter of pride not to have to touch it.

---

[2] On Lightfoot, Knowles to Hallam Tennyson, 20 Jan. 1877 (TRC); also Chadwick, *Victorian Church*, ii. 70. Knowles was writing to Hallam partly because a long one had just gone off to his father that day, partly to acknowledge a list of possible contributors Hallam sent. On Grant, Knowles to Tennyson, 13 Feb. 1877 (TRC).

[3] On William Sarl, developer also of Prince's Mansions in Victoria Street, Cooper's letter-books with Park Town estate papers (chap. 5, n. 32). It is possibly relevant that Grant's offices at 17–18 Cornhill had previously been those of John Sarl & Sons, silversmiths (*BN* 1857). In 1876 Knowles was arranging a meeting 'with a gentleman of very great wealth' about 'the Queen's Mansions scheme' (Knowles to Gould, 28 Apr. 1876, Park Town papers) and in 1878 he lodged a planning application for it to the MBW (*Minutes* 1878) in the name of Sarl's front man, Mote; but on completion for others in 1882, the architect was said to be one Butler.

[4] Strahan to Knowles, 10 Jan. 1877, copy sent by Strahan to Gladstone on 17 Jan. (Add. MS. 44453, BL). Knowles to Tennyson, 20 Jan. 1877 (TRC). Strahan to *The Times*, 16 Jan. 1877, Knowles to *The Times*, 17 Ian. 1877: printed copies (Knowles used his printers like a copying machine) with his correspondence in Gladstone and Tennyson papers.

QUESTIONABLE TITLE, UNQUESTIONABLE SUCCESS

'When we read in the *Athenaeum* that it was the Poet
Laureate who gave Mr Knowles the title of his new
periodical . . . one can't help remembering how the
Poet Laureate has characterised that century, in
Maud, as "the wretchedest age since the world
began".' *Punch*, 'A Questionable Title', 3 March 1877

The name of the new review appears first in a twelve-page letter
of 6 January from Knowles to Tennyson—beginning, however,
with business concerning a house the Tennysons were taking for
a few months in Wimpole Street (the 'bald street' of *In Memoriam*)
and professional comment upon some 'vilely bad work' on its
drains. Then, after describing the final separation from the
Contemporary and his suit for damages (which a year later paid
him £1,500), Knowles announced that he would, as already
proposed, 'start *as my own property* a new Review—on the 1st
of March'. The new venture was to have

such a list of promised supporters as I should think few men can have
had before—I enclose a copy of it. . . . I really think that no man ever
had such a set of illustrious friends!
    They say one & all that the new Review will be an assured & great
success & encourage me in every way to take it up—telling me the
very kindest things about myself as an Editor—(things which would
make me blush were I anything with less natural effrontery than
belongs to an Editor!)
    For a name I have—after scores upon scores of suggestions—settled
upon one which you yourself gave me and which has stood its ground
from the beginning to the end viz—
                    '*The Nineteenth Century*'.[5]

The *Echo* newspaper (no longer in Grant's hands) soon pointed
out that Knowles's title only had a life of twenty-four years,
'besides, he likes to be in advance of his age', and it ought to be
called the *Twentieth Century*. A pity, perhaps, that he forgot his own
prediction of 1869, that man's mind might be 'about to open

---

[5] Knowles to Tennyson, 6 Jan. 1877 (TRC). On 'legally & morally outrageous'
treatment (according to Fitzjames Stephen and Alfred Wills QC who read the
correspondence professionally for him) Knowles to Gladstone, 6 Jan. 1877, and
on damages paid a year later, Knowles to Gladstone, 6 Jan. 1878 (BL, as chap. 7,
n. 50).

the golden gates of the twentieth century to Art and Poetry and Faith'—yet to be supremely of his own time, and use Tennyson's suggestion, was more important in 1877. Others thought ahead, and copyright in the next century was lost to him when the time came.[6]

And, the letter to Tennyson went on, he had declined the offer from Longmans, who at first were to be the publishers, to share the ownership: 'Do you remember how you suggested years ago when the Con. Rev. was offered to me that you & I should buy it together? How I wish now that I had acted on your suggestion —You were wise & I a fool—for I found it a failure & have made it now worth £2500 per ann—& for whom? Strahan & his creditors & friends!' He then reminded Tennyson that he had promised 'when I was last at Aldworth' to be one of the new review's supporters 'if such an event occurred as has now taken place'. This meant the list of supporters (in the moral and literary, not financial, sense) Knowles was to publish as a prospectus leaflet in February, ultimately to contain 108 names. The first handwritten list circulating in January was hastily headed: 'Mr Knowles has leave to inscribe my name on the staff of any new Review which he may start on the principles of the Contemporary Rev.' Gladstone, as an experienced politician, immediately queried the word 'staff', but the others seem to have taken it in the spirit of the Twenty-third Psalm.[7] The final burden of the letter to Tennyson was to beg a few lines for the opening number (promising to request permission from King, by then Tennyson's publisher): 'Might I by any possibility for instance have the "Old Ghosts"—or your trochaic "Brunanburh"?'—a request that for us helps to date those two poems.[8] He recalled

[6] Cutting from *Echo* enclosed by Knowles to Gladstone, 13 Jan. 1877 (BL). On closing lines of article in 1869, chap. 6, n. 29.

[7] List to Tennyson 6 Jan. (TRC) headed by Manning, followed by Huxley, Fitzjames Stephen, Arnold, Lubbock, and 18 others, mostly Metaphysical Society members. List to Gladstone 3 Jan. (BL) did not start with Manning, doubtless purposely, though he was on it. Two editions of a printed prospectus with Knowles papers (WPL) had lists of 100 and 108 names, respectively, headed by Tennyson. Not all of these 'supporters' were to write for the *NC*, but with the advance orders flowing in by 13 Feb. (Knowles to Tennyson), there is no reason to think financial support was sought. By then the publisher was Henry King, Smith & Elder's successor who had been publishing *CR* and who was by then Tennyson's publisher. Gladstone's alarm on meaning of 'staff': Knowles to Gladstone, 6 Jan. 1877.

[8] This request for 'Old Ghosts' in Jan. 1877 gives the poem an earlier date than

how Tennyson's 'Higher Pantheism' had launched the opening
meeting of the Metaphysical Society, and went on:

So far as in me lies—we will have a more illustrious band round the
new Review than has been round any other in our time—but of
course it lies with *you* to do more towards helping me to realize my
purpose than with any other one man—I mean—my purpose of
collecting all of the very best & highest—for you know quite well
that it is no flattery to say your name will draw others which no other
name would do in literature.

Pardon my disgracefully long letter & put it down to the state of
rather excited anxiety in which I find myself at this birth-hour of my
new literary child. Be its Godfather I pray you. . . . Let me have one
line . . . as soon as possible to say whether I may hope for anything—
however small—for March—to be your 'Goodspeed' to my new
venture.

Permission to use Tennyson's name as supporter arrived in time
for an announcement of the new review in *The Times* on 15
January. The request for a poem was repeated in another long
letter on 20 January: 'If you will—you may now make my
fortune'—for Knowles was understandably nervous 'at embarking
on this big venture all by myself & with my own capital'. His
long letter of 3 January to Gladstone had also asked for an article
for the first number, and ended similarly: 'my fortune as an
Editor would be made'. And on the 26th 'It rests—my dear Mr
Gladstone—with yourself alone.'[9]

He even asked Tennyson, in case there should be any difficulty
about poetry copyright, if he would send something in prose, as
a letter 'saying what I have often enough heard you say informally
& in conversation about the nineteenth century—& its good &
bad outlook . . . if only a repetition in prose of what you said at
the end of your dedication of K. Arthur to the Queen—would be
simply priceless and invaluable to me—for my first number.' It
was a sense beyond fear for his own fortune that saw in those
tremendous lines in the Epilogue of 1872 what the *Nineteenth
Century's* scope could be ('for some are scared, who mark/

Ricks does (p. 1342: *c.* 1884?) if the same poem; *Memoir*, i. xi, says meant as
preface to *Becket*, which *Memoir*, ii. 193, says was started Dec. 1876. 'Brunanburh'
was based on Hallam Tennyson's prose translation published by Knowles in *CR*
Nov. 1876 (Ricks, p. 1234).
    [9] Knowles to Tennyson, 6, 20 Jan. 1877 (TRC), latter with printed broadsheet
of items in *The Times*; and to Gladstone, 3, 6, 26 Jan. 1877 (BL).

. . . Waverings of every vane with every wind/. . . And fierce or careless looseners of the faith,/. . . or Labour, with a groan and not a voice,/. . . the goal of this great world/Lies beyond sight: yet—if your slowly grown/And crowned Republic's crowning common-sense,/That saved her many times, not fail—their fears/ Are morning shadows huger than the shapes/That cast them.').

Practical postscripts to this letter added assurances that the Wimpole Street drains were being dealt with, and defects in the Queen's Road houses at Battersea were 'being taken up'— referring to Tennyson's investment in the Park Town estate.[10]

The sonnet that came eventually was the more precious for being written for the occasion. It had grand phrasing at the end ('If any golden harbour be for men/In seas of Death and sunless gulfs of Doubt'), March in the middle ('roaring moon of daffodil and crocus'), and a touch of silliness at the start (boatload of authors fleeting 'far and fast')—with prostration for Knowles in the metaphor of the 'old craft' (*Contemporary*) as 'seaworthy still'. A long agonized letter on 13 February implored a change to 'adventuring still', as less complimentary, but no change was made.[11] His 'cold perspiration of dismay' was excusable, as Strahan was now sending round libellous pamphlets to all the eminent men leaving his fold. But that was nothing compared to the two thousand orders already coming in to King for Knowles's first number: 'he drives me almost off my head by writing that he expects to sell *20,000*! of it—if not *30,000*! Of course he must be off *his* head to talk like that.' The actual number does not appear, except that on 7 March Knowles told Gladstone 'we are printing a *5th* edition of my first no.—although the first edition was 9000 strong!'[12]

It was an immediate success: for this 176-page number in its

---

[10] Epilogue 'To the Queen' (Ricks, p. 1755); on denial to Knowles for *CR* Jan. 1873, chap. 7, n. 43 above. On Tennyson's investment in Battersea, chap. 5, n. 33.

[11] Knowles to Tennyson, 13 Feb. 1877 (eight pages, TRC). Tennyson's promise to supply a poem ecstatically acknowledged on 23 Jan.; only on arrival of the sonnet did panic set in. On *NC* sonnet, Ricks, p. 1239. According to Prof. Lang, none of Tennyson's letters to Knowles for Jan.–Feb. 1877 seem to survive.

[12] Knowles to Gladstone, 7 Mar. 1877 (BL). The first number had 176 pp. (198 pp. in July). To counter it, *CR* put out a bumper issue in March, 228 pp. after an average 160. *NC* could not match *Cornhill's* initial sale, with fiction and illustrations, of 100,000 copies levelling off to 20,000 (*WIVP*, i. 554; memoir George Smith, *DNB Suppl.*: 1st no. 120,000). Further on circulation, n. 21 below.

soon-well-known green cover, with Tennyson's sonnet on page one followed by twenty-one pages of Gladstone, offered also the Bishop of Gloucester and Bristol *and* Cardinal Manning, as well as Matthew Arnold and (as consultant) Thomas Huxley, with the Metaphysical Society also represented by Croom Robertson, Lubbock, and Grant Duff, and two other authors already known to the reading public in Baldwin Brown and W. R. S. Ralston. (The February *Contemporary* had sourly observed that it was the 'common mistake of an amateur editor . . . to suppose that all he has to do is . . . "to get a lot of clever fellows together, you know" [with] the kind of editorial conceit which fancies that it can and does supply the warp and weft of success in these matters'.) Yet balance was beautifully struck in the March *Nineteenth* between poetry and morals, the Church of England and the Vatican, literature and science, Russian and Turkish home life and British imperial policy, the old power of preaching and the new power of psychology—however daunting to us its unadorned pages. The precise planning of an issue was important: the April issue could start with the Cardinal because it contained no Anglican bishops. Sometimes the most important contribution would be placed last, when hot enough off the griddle to be written and corrected up to the last minute while the rest of the issue was printing, as demonstrated by a series of letters to Gladstone during the Russo-Turkish war.

In February 1878 Russia surrounded Constantinople and Disraeli's Cabinet sent the British fleet into the Dardanelles to the aid of the Turks while anti-Russian 'jingo' frenzy arose in London. For some time Gladstone, on the other hand, had been passionately denouncing the Turks for their massacres in Bulgaria: to him the Turkish presence in Europe was the greater moral danger to the world. In February Knowles begged Gladstone for an article for March and received 'The Paths of Honour and of Shame' just in time for the presses to be held 'solely for your corrections' on 25 February, when the jingo fever in London, or as Knowles put it 'this roaring whirlwind of popular panic', was at its height. The day before, while a mob threw stones at Gladstone's house in Harley Street, Knowles had 'spent some time with Mr Carlyle . . . who has not words strong enough to characterize the "delirious jargon" of the war party headed by "that quack Dizzy" '.[13]

---

[13] Knowles to Gladstone, 6 Jan.–25 Feb. 1878 (BL): on 'roaring whirlwind'

The issue for March 1878 opened with Tennyson's stirring stanzas on the last fight of the Elizabethan ship *Revenge*, the poem's eight pages preceding General Sir Garnet Wolseley's twenty-four comparing England's military strength in 1878 with that of 1854. As the Royal Navy approached its former enemy, Tennyson read his martial lines aloud after dinner at Stopford Brooke's, worrying that their publication might further inflame the public—for he had to post the poem off to Knowles by midnight if the printer was to start with it. Oddly enough, and no doubt coincidentally, the meter as well as the spirit of the 'jingo song' launched at the Pavilion, Piccadilly Circus, about 15 February ('We've fought the Bear before, and while we're Britons true') were not so different from those of Tennyson's apparently already completed lines ('I have fought for Queen and Faith like a valiant man and true'). With Tennyson at one end and Gladstone at the other, the March 1878 issue sold 20,000 or more copies—reaching, as such things are estimated, perhaps five times that number of readers.[14]

After Gladstone's pamphlet of 1876 on the Bulgarian horrors of Turkish misrule, his address to a great meeting at St. James's Hall as the first of many speeches on the subject, and his last articles for Knowles in the *Contemporary Review*, he was able to use the platform of the *Nineteenth Century* on the Eastern Question seven times in the next two years, while also writing for Knowles on other subjects. Knowles sometimes dared to temper Gladstone's language, successfully querying the phrase 'obscene birds called critics' ('might give a good deal of offense . . . to a very hard-working if thin-skinned & conceited race of men, slow to see jokes about themselves', in a letter of 20 September 1877 about the October article on colour-sense); and again, removing

---

and on Carlyle, first of two letters 25 Feb.; second from printer's on March number held for Gladstone's corrections. *Mary Gladstone* (1930), p. 132, on mob of 24 Feb. 1878, Carlyle's blessing on the NC had already been received (Knowles to Gladstone, 26 Jan. 1877; to Tennyson, 20 Jan. 1877); Carlyle was 'accustomed to the visits of earnest young inquirers . . . was almost always kind and friendly to young men . . . [and gave] them helpful advice' (Andrew Lang in *Fraser's*, Apr. 1881).

[14] On reading at Stopford Brooke's, F. Wedmore, *Memories* (1912), pp. 47 ff. On the poem, Ricks, p. 1241. On war scare and date of jingo song, *The Times*, 14–16 Feb. 1878, *Punch*, 16, 23 Feb. 1878, and Hibbert, *Fifty Years of a Londoner's Life*, p. 100. Or was it coincidental?

'trashy' as an adjective for the metropolitan press as well as a phrase aimed at *The Times*, 'whether or not from a sense of favours to come' (letter of 29 May 1878 on an article for June comparing the liberties of East and West). Knowles could be inflaming too: Gladstone had 'counteracted so far the most deadly mischief which *"that alien"* would drag [us] into' (15 August 1877); Disraeli was 'going to annex England to his native East & make it the appanage of an Asiatic empire' (27 May 1878). The success of Gladstone's article for September 1878 on England's mission, with a thousand extra copies needed by the 3rd, caused Knowles to congratulate himself on 'having to some extent been instrumental in causing it to be written' and to point out that it proved 'how righteous it is sometimes to importune'. Much of the importuning is unrecorded, as they presumably met a good deal that summer, at least at breakfast and dinner in Harley Street in July. The 'inch-and-ell man' of 1874 was the part-time right-hand man of 1878 (for Gladstone still sent occasional articles elsewhere). 'At any rate', Knowles said on first seeing the 'England's Mission' article in August, '*now* people will not be able to say that the Liberals have no clear chart to sail by in Foreign Policy'. As the developing situation was recalled later by Justin McCarthy, 'Mr Disraeli's Eastern policy . . . forced Mr Gladstone to the front and made him Prime Minister once again.' In 1880 McCarthy was to write on Home Rule for Knowles, who had been trying to get an article on the subject out of Gladstone since early 1877.[15]

A regular (but not monthly) feature, 'Recent Science', begun in the first number over Knowles's name, was headed: 'Professor Huxley has kindly read, and aided the Editor with his advice upon, the following article.' It was a compilation, apparently of abstracts from current scientific journals, perhaps with the co-operation of learned-society librarians at New Burlington House, gone over in proof by Huxley and 'diligently excluding any expression of opinion on the part of the writers [note the plural] of the compilation', as Huxley told Tyndall who with other scientists wondered whether to resent any assumed judgements in a non-scientific periodical. Such a feature was not precisely new;

---

[15] In order of reference, Knowles to Gladstone, 20 Sept. 1877, 29 May 1878, 15 Aug. 1877, 27 May 1878, 3 Sept. 1878, 25 June 1878, 28 Aug. 1878 (all BL, Add. MS. 44231), 23 July 1878 (Add. MS. 44786); on Home Rule, n. 58 below. McCarthy, *Life of Gladstone*, p. 303.

for example, in 1863 the *Cornhill* had run a 'Notes on Science' section for a few months, and in 1866 the *Illustrated London News* started a 'Scientific News' column that subsequently ran regularly as 'Scientific Results of the Month'. But Huxley's authority over this feature and the company it kept in Knowles's pages (until November 1880, then suspended until 1892) attracted laymen of higher brows than *Illustrated London News* readers.[16]

A feature that was new in 1877 (Frederic Harrison said he suggested it) began in the *Nineteenth* for April and May: a Modern Symposium, 'simply a printed debate such as we have at the Metaphysical Society', Knowles told Gladstone; 'or amicable discussions in writing', as the *Illustrated London News* explained this 'striking feature' when it first appeared. 'Each writer will have seen all that has been written before his own remarks, but (except the first writer) nothing that follows them. The first writer, as proposer of the subject, will have the right of reply or summing-up at the end.' In other words, the 'fair field' with invited participants (the platform was open once you were on it), an orderly extension not only of the Society's verbal debates but of Knowles's own rule he had formed for the *Contemporary Review*: 'the almost invariable rule of the Review about Controversies—viz—that any sufficient champion of the other side may reply to the views of any given writer and that the original writer should have the opportunity of rejoinder but that there the Controversy must drop so far as the original combatants are concerned for fear of wearying our readers'. Sir James Fitzjames Stephen proposed the (still relevant) theme of the first symposium, 'The Influence upon Morality of a Decline of Religious Belief', dealt with after him by nine other members of the Metaphysical Society (which was itself in decline, a spent springboard: Knowles resigned in November 1879). For the reading public, with the 'Athenaeumania' of local debating societies cooling in the suburbs, this new monthly review brought discussion back to the more intellectual drawing rooms in packaged form. The ritualized shape of these first symposia in the *Nineteenth Century* did not

---

[16] L. Huxley, *Life*, ii. 16–17, with letter Huxley to Tyndall, 2 Dec. 1880: 'I was anxious to help Knowles . . . and at his earnest and pressing request I agreed to do what I have done. But being quite aware of the misinterpretation to which I should be liable . . . I insisted upon the exact words which you will find at the head of it . . . [defining] my position as a mere adviser of the editor.' On revival for Kropotkin, n. 65 below.

last, its debates becoming more spontaneous as Knowles's handling became more artful.[17]

The title page bore the legend 'edited by James Knowles'—if signed articles were to be the responsibility of authors, editorial responsibility was to be acknowledged as well. The latter was not an invariable custom among the reviews, although John Morley's name appeared on the *Fortnightly* (and George Godwin's name had appeared from 1852 on the weekly *Builder*). Signed articles were not new: most of those in *Macmillan's*, founded 1859, were signed; and in 1865 G. H. Lewes had ruled against anonymity in the *Fortnightly*.[18] Knowles was quick to adopt these customs which he did not invent. The date of issue could vary a little from the first of the month, the January number sometimes being brought forward or 'I fear we shall lose Xmas', Knowles would say. At election-time in the spring of 1880, the April number was brought out 'in time to influence votes'; in March, too, Knowles sent to Gladstone, electioneering in Midlothian, an advance copy of Frederic Seebohm's paper for the April number on 'Imperialism and Socialism' in the 'fervent hope' that Gladstone would mention it—for, said Knowles, 'if only we can connect the words *Imperialism* & *Socialism* together in the public mind. I feel we shall do much towards curing the imminent dangers of the former to this country', that is, of the armaments race to peaceful internal development and true democracy.[19]

Payment to contributors seems to have been generally at the rate of two pounds per page, more if you were Tennyson or Gladstone, less if you wrote badly and much sub-editing was needed. So far as poetry was concerned, payment could range between Tennyson's £150 in 1880 for 'De Profundis' (printed as

[17] F. Harrison, *Autobiographic Memoirs* (1911), ii. 90. Knowles to Gladstone, 26 Jan. 1877, 2 Nov. 1876 (BL). *ILN*, 7 Apr. 1877, p. 326.

[18] On rule for signed articles, *WIVP*, ii. 625, mentions four pseudonyms that got past Knowles, but of these only one is said to have fooled him, to his disgust (William Sharp's appearance in 1900 as 'Fiona Macleod') according to Eirene Skilbeck; of the others, he may have allowed Lady Blennerhassett's use of 'C. de Warmont' in 1879 and Amelie Claire Leroy's use of 'Esme Stuart' in 1893 for unknown social reasons; as for the 'young Turkish lady' who described harem life for him simply as Adalet in 1890–2, the lack of her family name must have been understandable, and perhaps was the subject of Knowles's appointment with the Turkish ambassador in Dec. 1888 (n. 45 below). The appearance of the Queen of Roumania in the *NC* in 1900 as Carmen Sylva, with a poem in German and translation by Arthur Waugh, doesn't figure in the *WIVP* prose account.

[19] Knowles to Gladstone, 18 Dec. 1877, 23 Mar. 1880 (BL).

five pages, or £30 per page) and Walt Whitman's just over $145 in 1885 for his *Fancies at Navesink* (seven poems printed on four pages, or about seven guineas per page with the exchange at $5). Translation paid less, even to Gladstone (£25 in 1894 for five odes from Horace, printed with the originals as nine pages). For prose, Gladstone usually got £4 or more per page. In 1889 Knowles increased from £2 to £3 the rate for Huxley, then in full flood of articles and soon to provide one on 'The Natural Inequality of Men'. Beatrice Potter, later Mrs. Webb, after having two guineas per page for her first article for Knowles in 1887 on East London dock life, was paid only one guinea a page in 1888 for one on the East London tailoring trade, which suggests it required editorial tailoring. It has been said of John Burns the labour leader that his writing for Knowles in 1892 needed a good deal of editing before it was readable. That would explain the fee of only £15 Knowles paid for twelve pages by Tom Mann the dockers' leader in May 1890.[20] The sliding of the scale was practical, not political (or not very). One habit Knowles learned from Strahan, which endeared an editor to his authors, was to allow any number of revises, even when resetting was cheaper; and manuscripts from trusted authors, especially in dreadful handwriting such as Huxley's, went straight to the printer and were seen by the editor only in proof—a commentary on the way printers lived then. By 1884, when the *Nineteenth*'s average circulation was said by its publishers (then Kegan Paul, Trench) to be the highest of the monthy reviews—20,000 in 1884 according to Frederic Harrison—Knowles himself could tell Gladstone, according to the latter's private secretary, that his own profits 'about equalled the salary of the Prime Minister' (if Sir Edward Hamilton heard correctly), or about £5,000. A long way from

[20] Payment (see also chap. 7, n. 53): Knowles to Huxley, 22 Apr. 1889 (Imperial College), on usual scale £2 per page except to Gladstone and Tennyson; University of Kansas holds Tennyson's receipt to Knowles for £150 dated 18 May 1880 (Lang, ed., *Letters*); Whitman was paid $145.20 (*Correspondence*, ed. E. H. Miller, 1964, iii., 402 n.); Knowles to Gladstone, 18 May 1894. A number of payments to Gladstone are specified in Knowles's letters to him, e.g. 100 guineas for 'The Irish Demand' in Feb. 1887, though other payments later inflated by rumour happen not to be specified by Knowles, e.g. 8 Jan. 1887 on gossip. Knowles to Huxley, 18 Nov. 1889 on raising him to £3; Beatrice Webb, *My Apprenticeship* (1926), p. 276; William Kent, *John Burns* (1950), p. 330. Tom Mann to Knowles, 18 May 1890 (Knowles papers, WPL), acknowledging cheque for £15 (for 'The Development of the Labour Movement', *NC*, pp. 709–20 at head of May issue).

1874 when, according to family memory, there was no money for a trip to Paris when a chance arose (out of Food Fund contacts) to obtain some articles for the *Contemporary* there. Although in April 1889 Knowles told Huxley that 'the "till" . . . is by no means bursting with any excess of receipts. . . . The success is moral much more than financial', by November he was able to say that circulation that year was 'larger & more profitable . . . than for years past'—which underlines the change in his expectations since 1874.[21]

It was in the summer of 1875 that Knowles became a guest at the brilliant parties given at Strawberry Hill by the great political hostess Lady Waldegrave; probably only partly for political reasons, since he already shared some of the literary interests and acquaintances of her husband Lord Carlingford. In the autumn of 1878 Knowles was one of the editors, with Chenery of *The Times* and several others, summoned to Chewton Priory in Somerset by Lady Waldegrave to brief her husband and herself on the Afghan situation; and during her last Season before her death the following year, Knowles was regarded as one of her regular Sunday visitors in Carlton Gardens. She, perhaps more than any other single person, helped to bring about the more open London society that was to come in the 1880s.[22] Her parties must have been one of the chief rungs on Knowles's ladder.

TWO PRACTICES ENDED

'I saw Mr Knowles yesterday . . . very busy making out his charges against Battersea.' Park Town estate proprietor, 11 October 1878 (Park Town papers)

'I have been giving the final superintendence to a great hospital scheme at Margate.' Knowles to Park Town proprietor, 6 July 1881 (Park Town papers)

---

[21] On circulation: F. Harrison to Pierre Laffitte in Paris, 6 Sept. 1884 (archives, La Maison d'Auguste Comte, a reference kindly given me by Prof. Martha Vogeler); *Diary of Sir Edward W. Hamilton*, ed. D. W. R. Bahlman (1972), ii. 743, on the dinner of 27 Nov. 1884 when Trench was present; Knowles to Huxley, 22 Apr., 18 Nov. 1889 (Imperial College). With Paris Food Fund papers (WPL) is an apparently unused document dated Paris, 22 Jan. 1874, from office of Préfet de la Seine authorizing Knowles to see six named people who are to facilitate his mission.

[22] O. W. Hewitt, *Strawberry Fair* (1956), pp. 246, 258, 260.

'I am to be examined before the Channel Tunnel Committee after Ascot, and I shall be very pleased to have a good talk with you over the whole matter.' Duke of Cambridge to Knowles, 30 May 1883 (Knowles papers, WPL)

Out of caution, or excess of energy, for ten years after Knowles founded his own review he still continued some bits and pieces of architectural practice, from about 1877 with the help of a trusted assistant, George Robson, and from 1883 to 1887 without undertaking new work, only continuing the slow design of the Park Town estate. To understand the multifariousness of his life with two professions, take 1881, the year he was 50. It began with a triumphant opening night on 3 January of Tennyson's play *The Cup*, performed by Henry Irving and Ellen Terry at the Lyceum Theatre, with the Gladstones present as guests in Knowles's box, and the very three-dimensional temple set for the second act— 'a perfect marvel of elaboration and costly artistic effect'— credited in the programme and in the press to Irving's usual designers. A week or so later, 'an announcement, which may be held tantamount to a communiqué, has appeared in the daily papers stating that the architectural revival of the Temple of Artemis . . . was designed by Mr James Knowles (the distinguished architect and editor of the Nineteenth Century)'. It was meant to represent the temple at Ephesus, a topic of learned controversy since J. T. Wood published his book on the subject three years before. The very architectural nature of Knowles's set may have owed something to the precedent of Edward Godwin's set for the Bancrofts' production of *The Merchant of Venice* some years before: published in the architectural press in 1875, inspired by Veronese's *Marriage at Cana*, and all cast in plaster. A spectacular antiquarianism of too, too solid sets characterized all of Irving's Lyceum productions, however. Irving was already one of Knowles's authors, his series of 'Actor's Notes on Shakespeare' having started in the second number.[23]

23 George Robson ARIBA became general as well as architectural assistant until his death in 1890. On *The Cup*, Knowles to Tennyson, 4 Nov., 13 Dec. 1880, 1, 4 Jan. 1881 (TRC); to Mrs. Tennyson, 27 Oct. 1880: 'I have been making drawings for Irving for the Temple Scene with which he is hugely delighted & which are now in the hands of the scene painters' (TRC). *ILN*, 8, 15 Jan., 5 Feb. 1881; *Ill. Sporting and Dramatic News*, 29 Jan. 1881; *Magazine of Art*, Feb. 1881, 'Art Notes', pp. xvii–xviii; programme and cuttings, Enthoven Collection,

For the *Nineteenth Century* the vintage year 1881 opened with 'The Dawn of a Revolutionary Epoch', that is, a call for England to lead the way to social reorganization without the dangers threatening Europe, by H. M. Hyndman, at the time a friend of Karl Marx and soon to found the Social Democratic Foundation: this and Seebohm's article published the preceding April were two sides of the same coin. Hyndman recalled later how he had talked it over with Knowles: ' "Ah," he said, "you cherish these sanguine anticipations and you may be right to do so; but, mark my words, there will be a tremendous rushing back of the pebbles on the ebb of this temporary inflow before the next flood-tide of democracy and progress sweeps in." ' The waves-of-history theory Knowles had grown up with wore well as part of an editor's mental furniture. In that year, too, Lieut.-Gen. Sir Garnet Wolseley, two admirals (Lord Dunsany and Sir R. S. Robinson), a captain on the Austrian general staff, and a barrister (H. O. Arnold-Foster) discussed England's defences in Knowles's pages, while the Hon. Maude Stanley wrote about the displacement of London's poor for urban improvements, and Ireland was discussed in all its aspects (three articles in January alone, month of late sittings at the House of Commons). There were, as well, Watts the painter on art needlework, Tennyson's fiercely pessimistic monologue 'Despair', and Ruskin's final instalment on Fiction Fair and Foul—very rude to what he called the Cockney literature of George Eliot, having written to Knowles in August that now George Eliot was in Heaven he could write her epitaph with no fear of meeting her afterward; and Canon Edmund Venables the Lincoln antiquary opened the long argument on the proper style for a new Anglican cathedral at Liverpool by recommending Wren's Great Model for St. Paul's (especially since 'London is grinding down Wren's towers and spires into Portland cement'). There were Lord Derby and Matthew Arnold on Ireland, the Duke of Manchester on free trade (but Lord Hartington seldom wrote for periodicals), the Marquis of Blandford on the reform of feudal laws, and Froude on Carlyle. Four years earlier,

---

V and A Museum. On temple at Ephesus, J. T. Wood addressed RIBA 15 Feb. 1875 and published his book in 1877. Ellen Terry, *The Story of My Life* (1908), pp. 194–9; R. Manvell, *Ellen Terry* (1968), pp. 88, 116, 153–4, 338 n. A. E. Wilson, *The Lyceum* (1952), p. 142, says sets for 44 Irving plays were destroyed in a warehouse fire in 1898. Knowles published articles by Irving in 1877, 1879, 1887, 1890, and 1892.

when Knowles departed with his pride of lions, the *Contemporary* had printed a sour little note on the ideal editor: 'His menagerie must not be all lions.' The public liked lions. As Arnold remarked at the end of his April article, this good-natured editor had all kinds of potentates pressing to speak in his review. One sees the point of the joke, remembered in the Knowles family as Huxley's, that when Knowles got to Heaven and other people were lining up to speak to the first two members of the Trinity, *he* would be buttonholing the Holy Ghost to write for the *Nineteenth*.[24]

Meanwhile, on the advertising-board luring builders to take leases on the Park Town estate at Battersea, in 1881 the manager's name was substituted for Knowles's as the man to see. From then on, Knowles gradually gave up some of his responsibilities there; although the proprietors still deferred to his long experience, his delays had been irritating the estate's officers for some time: for instance in 1879 when new drains in Robertson Street had waited upon his pleasure, 'week after week slipping by', said the cashier to the manager, while he 'has too much other business in his head of more importance to himself'. But in 1881 he was still in charge of laying out the last new streets and their sewers and furnishing basic house-designs, including a drawing of June 1881 for two slightly Dutch-gabled, red-brick houses, adjusted to the proprietors' 'Queen Anne' tastes and to an awkward site at the corner of Robertson and Montefiore Streets. In May he delivered a broadside, in the form of a spirited letter to the Flowers' cashier in the City, advising them against a liberal-minded decision they had just taken to install bathrooms in the next new houses ('. . . would be perpetually out of order & likely to injure the premises —the high pressure hot water boilers would frequently burst & might give rise to bad accidents . . . considering the class of property in question . . . must be held quite free from all responsibility.').[25] It was ingrained in a professional man of business to the owners of such an estate,to consider their interest, their five or seven per cent—however many baths he had provided for Tenny-

---

[24] H. M. Hyndman, *The Record of an Adventurous Life* (1911), p. 226. Ruskin to Knowles, 3 Aug. 1881, Cook and Wedderburn eds. *Works*, XXXVII. 372. Venables (*NC* Nov. 1881) doubtless meant the demolition of five City churches in the 1870s; the Liverpool diocese was established in 1880, a Gothic cathedral design being finally chosen in 1903. *CR* on lions, Feb. 1877, p. 518. Family story from Eirene Skilbeck.

[25] Park Town papers as cited chap. 5, n. 32.

son, for Baron Grant, and for the club where George Salting lived. At the time, Knowles was supervising the building of a new hospital wing and chapel he had designed in 1879 for an older institution founded on the importance of baths 'for the scrofulous poor', the Royal Sea-Bathing Infirmary at Margate.

The donor of the new buildings at Margate, four wards with indoor swimming-bath and separate chapel and gate-lodge clothed in the red and black brickwork and terracotta of their time, was one of the first specialists in skin diseases, the surgeon and philanthropist Erasmus Wilson, knighted in 1881 when he became President of the Royal College of Surgeons. Wilson had paid for the sea-transport from Egypt of the ancient obelisk Cleopatra's Needle. (When it was about to be set up on the new Thames Embankment in 1878, the Poet Laureate supplied at Dean Stanley's request ten lines in its honour, that partly run 'Whence your own citizens, for their own renown,/Through strange seas drew me to your monster town'; but in the end these were not engraved on the new pedestal: 'own renown' may have stuck in Wilson's throat.) Where Knowles met Wilson does not appear: at the Deanery, or through the Freemasonry of Wilson and Knowles senior, or perhaps through the surgeon Sir Henry Thompson, whose articles on cremation and other subjects he had published and to whose choice dinners he sometimes went. At any rate, the Infirmary's directors also found Knowles's delays trying, but still in November 1881 he was being consulted on layout of the grounds and thereafter on resiting of the mortuary and coal store, and interior work continuing in 1882. The name of the master plasterer, James Paramor of Margate, was to appear with the famous on Knowles's petition of 1882 against a Channel Tunnel.[26]

These were not Knowles's only building activities in 1881. In March he applied on behalf of the Army and Navy Cooperative Society Ltd. for Metropolitan Board of Works approval of an intended 'open portico' on the front of their new stores in the former distillery in Victoria Street (permission refused); that is, Knowles was then in charge of remodelling the old building for

[26] Royal Sea-Bathing Infirmary: court minutes 1877–84, MS. vol., Kent Archive Office, Maidstone; Knowles's ward plans 'were prepared by Professor Wilson's directions'. The chapel is essentially Knowles's first chapel design of 1862 for Lower Sydenham (chap. 5) translated into 1879 red brick; interior decorative scheme on theme of healing probably by a firm of church-furnishers.

that new institution the Army and Navy Stores, later altered by others. In August he applied on behalf of the Army and Navy Auxiliary Stores (subsidiary company for selling provisions, held to be objectionable in the main building) to erect 'a furnace chimney-shaft at their premises in Francis Street', that is, he was the architect of the neat red-brick building at the bend of the road, later City of Westminster College, with rusticated pilasters and tall, narrow windows (and little side-corbels within the window-reveals that must once have held a late, last set of Knowlesian 'eyelids'). The Army and Navy Stores, part of the new co-op movement, now became a sort of auxiliary club to its members, their wives and families, thus enhancing the social tone of Victoria Street. The 'Stores' could also be regarded as a military barometer, as in Knowles to Gladstone in December 1877: 'I was told the other day by the head of the "Army & Navy Stores" here that one of their colonels had just been in, busy about all preparations for active service & telling my informant that "he had had '*the tip*' that war would be certain & to act accordingly".'[27]

And 1881 was the year when Knowles arranged that Millais should paint Tennyson's portrait, now in the Lady Lever Art Gallery at Port Sunlight. Millais's son mentions the painter beginning it for Knowles, with an incident of the day when Tennyson and Knowles arrived unexpectedly for lunch. Ostensibly the picture was commissioned by the Fine Art Society who bought the copyright for engraving, so that Knowles was then able to buy the portrait from them at less than the artist got for it— which one may guess was Knowles's plan from the start.[28] For relaxation he still went to Christie's, in June 1881 buying seven drawings at one sale—four Claudes, two Rembrandts, and one attributed to Giorgione. But the final footnote to 1881, hidden in the Park Town estate correspondence, was that in November 'the doctors' were advising Knowles to drop everything and rest

---

[27] Knowles to Gladstone, 13 Dec. 1877 (BL). MBW *Minutes*, 11, 25 Mar., 12 Aug. 1881, 7 July 1882. See T. H. S. Escott's description in his *England* (1879, in 1885 edn., p. 221; quoted in my *Victorian London*, pp. 137–8.
[28] J. G. Millais, *Life and Letters of Sir J. E. Millais* (1899), ii. 141–2, or (1905), pp. 283–4. D. S. MacColl in *Burlington Magazine*, June 1908, with Emery Walker engraving commissioned by Knowles as improvement on Fine Art Society's engraving by Barlow and presented to the Queen (lady-in-waiting to Knowles, 6 July 1896, WPL). Walker Art Gallery and Royal Academy, Millais exhibition (1967) catalogue no. 101.

for a few weeks, and a very short respite in activity, not apparent to readers of the *Nineteenth Century*, took place.[29]

At least once confusion did arise. During (apparently) the rush of early autumn, he had successfully prevailed upon Tennyson to let him publish the long poem 'Despair' in his November number while at the same time giving Tennyson the impression that he was refusing the poet's offer of 'The Charge of the Heavy Brigade'—and then, early in 1882, complaining to Tennyson when he heard *Macmillan's* was to have that. A clear case of misunderstanding between the over-sensitive and the over-wrought.[30] We can sense the personal tensions of that year—the concentrated excitement of the volunteer go-between as Irving rehearsed in London and Tennyson stayed at Aldworth, the sharp assertion of authorship of the temple set when none of the eminent egos concerned remembered to drop a public word about it; the consistently deft design of the review, assembling exactly the right elements, smoothing or ruffling exactly the right feathers, while urgent details accumulated at Battersea and Margate and Victoria Street; the dashing about from The Hollies to Albert Mansions, from the Reform Club to the Deanery, where his old friend Dean Stanley died in July 1881; and always the round of dinner tables. Now and then it was all so exhausting.

But, early in 1882, Knowles was ready for his first sustained campaign to influence public opinion upon a national issue: the proposals for a Channel Tunnel. When a Channel Tunnel Act was passed in 1875 he had published no reactions in the *Contemporary*, but then came the war scares of the late 1870s. Early in 1882 the tunnel promoter, Gladstone's friend the railway owner Sir Edward Watkin M.P. and a Colonel Beaumont were trying to get a further Bill through Parliament, and Knowles sensed in his 'constituency' (as he liked to call his readers) a revival of the ancient island-fear of being yoked with the Continent. Not only was he on to a good thing, as editor and proprietor, in organizing the opposition, but he felt deeply himself—Knowles never

[29] Christie's catalogue, Knowles sale, May 1908. A 'River Landscape' drawing by Claude bought by Knowles at the Bale sale, lot 2353, for 16 guineas went for £58 at the 1908 sale, lot 19 (later Lugt Collection; Christie's bicentenary exhibition 1967, no. 48; Arts Council exhibition 1969, no. 81, 'an impressive yet poetic sheet'). Knowles to Gould, 26 Nov. 1881, Park Town papers.

[30] Tennyson to Knowles, undated (TRC); Lang places it in Jan. 1882 (letter 3 Oct. 1971). Ricks, p. 1305.

organized a cynical campaign in his life—rushing to wise old Miss Thornton 'in a perfect storm of terror about the tunnel under the channel', for though 'Britannia [was] able to rule the waves she could not manage the tunnels.' And when Watkin took Chamberlain as President of the Board of Trade and a train-load of influential people down to view the trial-workings near Dover, Knowles in one of his imaginative sweeps told her how he dreaded 'dreamy notions of universal brotherhood forcing England [he always said England, never Britain] to form one of the United States of Europe' with the Board of Trade 'as the great power amongst them'.[31] But, with due regard for the rules of controversy, he did not limit his contributors on the subject entirely to the 'French-will-be-upon-us' school.

The first blast came in February from Lord Dunsany, at the end of the number in the 'hot off the griddle' position, expounding how a tunnel under the 'Silver Streak' would weaken further the defences he had deplored the year before. Much of his article was in quotation marks as the view of an unnamed 'military authority occupying the highest position in the estimation and favour of the country' (Wolseley probably, unable to comment directly on a specific parliamentary issue, one way of dodging the anonymity problem). In March, Colonel Beaumont was allowed to reply, with a rejoinder from Dunsany, and Goldwin Smith as a civilian thought there were 'some reasons for hoping that war is gradually dying out', while John Fowler offered an engineer's alternative in huge floating railway stations or jumbo train-ferries in an 'unbroken continuity of vehicles'. April opened with 'The Proposed Channel Tunnel, A Protest': two pages of names including Lubbock, Manning, Paget, Tennyson, Browning, Huxley, Spencer, Harrison, Hutton, John Murray, and labour leaders among Knowles's contributors such as George Howell and Thomas Burt M.P. (for, as Knowles was to point out in a later pamphlet, the masses feared an invasion of Continental paupers); and a six-page editorial leader, the first article that Knowles allowed himself in the *Nineteenth Century*. He pointed out that the

---

[31] As of 1879, Knowles was saying 'we and France should stand together holding her oriflamme firmly aloft . . . the best hope for Europe . . . essential for English foreign policy' (Knowles to Gladstone, 12 Nov. 1879, BL). On Watkin, Sir Philip Magnus, *Gladstone* (1954), pp. 378, 407. Forster, *Marianne Thornton* (1956), p. 217.

public had no (other) *locus standi* from which to oppose a private bill, and that the professional heads of the fighting services were known to disapprove entirely, only etiquette preventing their signing the petition for which, quoting John of Gaunt, Knowles invited more names. In the May issue there appeared about 450 more names with so many coming in that a pamphlet was to be necessary (with another in recapitulation in 1883). In May also came four more articles, one from an officer in the Royal Engineers saying that the promoters were only speculators out for gain, whereas we would have to introduce conscription and 'change the whole nature of our institutions'. Another contributor said that England's great safeguard against invasion had always been, not the difficulty of landing here, but the trouble the enemy would have in getting home again. However, in a reply by Joseph Reinach, a French journalist, England was seen to be 'walking backwards . . . from civilisation'—Nelson and Macaulay would be ashamed of these fears, there could be no more seasickness, commercial relations could improve. Wolf, wolf, and all that. The Bill did not pass, nor the one Watkin introduced in 1888, when Knowles published another pamphlet, nor again in 1890, nor in 1907, when Knowles was still in action. John Morley, writing his farewell to editing the *Fortnightly* in 1882, observed: 'The editor of a Review of great eminence said to the present writer (who, for his own part, took a slightly more modest view) that he regarded himself as equal in importance to twenty-five members of parliament'—doubtless Knowles in a moment of euphoria that summer.[32]

Watkin had a friend in Gladstone, who was convinced of the need for a tunnel and allowed Watkin to railroad him in more than one sense, for it was in 1890 that Watkin built a branch railway to Hawarden for Gladstone's convenience (an imputation the grand old man would have minded very much, but it lingers) and it was in June 1890 that Gladstone spoke in the Commons supporting Watkin's request for permission to resume the tunnel works (Knowles to Huxley, 6 June 1890: 'I could have *shot* Gladstone yesterday'). Knowles already felt secure enough to differ with Gladstone on this subject, as in a letter of 4 November 1887:[33]

[32] John Morley, 'Valedictory', *Fortnightly Review*, Oct. 1882.
[33] Knowles to Huxley, 6 June 1890 (Imperial College); to Gladstone, 4 Nov. 1887 (BL).

May I begin by saying how proud I am of the title you confer upon me—'*the murderer of the channel tunnel*'. I can only hope I may never forfeit my claim to so honorable a distinction—& that I may deserve it for an epitaph! That *you* should raise your hand against the Sacred sanctuary of Freedom formed by Nature herself & held as such by generations of Englishmen—is to me matter of true sorrow & pity. There—so much for the 'murder'!

It apparently did not matter to him that, once the editor took a firm stand on a question, the *Nineteenth Century* was no longer 'a perfectly neutral ground' or 'utterly impartial', and his handling of controversy became more human than Olympian. During the 1890s, when the English cultural pendulum swung a little toward interest in France, younger men were puzzled by Knowles's fears—harking back as these partly did to Waterloo epitaphs in church when he was 14 and the Paris Commune when he was 40, and partly to his first taste of real power in 1882. Finally, in February 1907, a year before he died, the *Nineteenth Century and After* unfurled the banner once more with six articles including a leader that managed to cite what 'the Empress Frederick, then the Crown Princess, [said] to the present writer' on one page and what 'Victor Hugo once said to me' on the next—deploying opposition to the 'un-islanding of England' to the last drop of a name.[34] But the issue is still with us.

Another subject suddenly became an issue in 1883 and after: London's slums. Before these became a topic for excited discussion by the general public late in 1883, the question of how far the state should alleviate bad housing was already a matter for argument among informed people. In August 1882 Knowles published 'Homes of the Poor in London' by Richard Cross, who had been Disraeli's Home Secretary, responsible for the Artisans' Dwelling Acts of 1875–9, and in this article urging further action. In June 1883 George Howell the trade unionist contributed 'The Dwellings of the Poor', a useful survey of existing powers: one of the reasons why the would-be informed public liked the *Nineteenth Century* was that Knowles was good at extracting such summaries of the state-of-play from his authors. In October 1883 the *Pall Mall Gazette* took up the case of a pamphlet, *The Bitter Cry of Outcast London*, Lord Salisbury immediately took up the subject in the November *National Review*, and by 1

[34] Knowles leader, *NC*, Feb. 1907, pp. 174–5.

December not only was the *Fortnightly* ready with an article by Joseph Chamberlain but the *Nineteenth* was even more ready with four articles—a slum symposium—under the heading of 'Common Sense and the Dwellings of the Poor', by Octavia Hill, the aged Earl of Shaftesbury, Arnold-Foster, and an unsolicited workman of Southport, William Glazier. In Knowles's January 1884 number Cross wrote again, and by March Knowles had launched a Society for the Enforcement of Sanitary Laws and the Improvement of Dwellings with Lady Burdett-Coutts, Miss Hill, Lord Shaftesbury, Cross, and others on the committee and Knowles of course as Honorary Secretary—a society of which no more was heard, eclipsed by the Royal Commission then set up. It was in 1883, the year of Karl Marx's death, that Knowles approached Engels with a view to commissioning a translation of *Das Kapital*, presumably for serial publication, but nothing came of it.[35]

And so by 1883 Knowles's own opinions were being seriously consulted, not only as a deployer of other people's opinions but, as by Lady Waldegrave in 1878, as one in a position to be well informed himself. The Duke of Cambridge (perhaps with a bit of poking at first) found it useful to talk over the Channel Tunnel question with him in June. In the course of 1883, out-of-Town social life included an evening at the Earl of Lytton's at Knebworth and a weekend stay with the Earl of Pembroke at Wilton. In January 1884, along with the French and Russian ambassadors, Lord Carlingford, the Goschens, and Sir James Paget, Knowles boarded the train at Liverpool Street Station for his first weekend visit to the Prince and Princess of Wales at Sandringham. And on 15 March 1884 he escorted Octavia Hill to Marlborough House for lunch with the Princess of Wales, who took much interest 'in all connected with her Great Work among the Poor', according to the royal note so carefully preserved in Knowles's papers.[36]

A few days later in March 1884, the senior James Thomas Knowles in his 78th year died at his house in Russell Square.

[35] Yvonne Kapp, *Eleanor Marx, I: Family life 1855–83* (1972), p. 282, a reference kindly given by Prof. Martha Vogeler.

[36] Duke of Cambridge to Knowles, 30 May 1883, as quoted at head of this section and 11 June 1883 (WPL). On Knowles at Knebworth, *Gathorne-Hardy 1st Earl of Cranbrook, A Memoir* (1910), ii. 190; at Wilton and Sandringham, Hamilton's *Diary* (as n. 21 above), ii. 520, 541–3: 11 Dec. 1883, 13 Jan. 1884. Princess of Wales to Knowles, 14 Mar. 1884 (WPL).

Number 49 on the south side was then the third house west from Bedford Place, with the long staircase window of its kind on the back, and within, no doubt, as described in *Vanity Fair*, the 'arch' where the coffin rested on its way downstairs. The Royal Institute of British Architects (for most of whom old Knowles's works were by then quite out of fashion) noted the loss of this 'valuable member of our body . . . who, having passed a most laborious life in the active performance of professional duties, might well have claimed in his declining years entire rest, but who preferred to remain amongst us as an Examiner and Member of Council, where . . . his presence was always as welcome as his opinions were valuable', and his last appearance 'only preceded his death by a few days'. The *Builder* in May was even shorter, and a New York professional journal disposed of him in three sentences as the designer of the Grosvenor Hotel and the Thatched House Club whose son was editor of the *Nineteenth Century*: even to being given the club that was not his, that was the sum of his reputation in 1884. Two winters before, for the funeral of Street the great architect of the Law Courts, who had died while in office as President of the Institute, the cortege forming in Cavendish Square included nine carriages of its present and former officers, the fifth one containing Waterhouse, Knowles, Paley of Lancaster, and Worthington of Manchester: what did they talk about as they were slowly borne along Regent's Street and Whitehall to the Abbey—Scott's funeral there in '78, and Barry's in '60, probably. Old Knowles himself was buried in the family plot on the brow of the slope at Norwood Cemetery, where his wife eight years before had joined Jane's lonely stone. From what one can tell through the brambles, these are simple stones compared to some of the grandiose tombs around—*those* were for clients, but a Friday Grove of a tomb for a pragmatical architect was quite unnecessary; he had arrived already. The important thing to him at the end of his life was to watch over the standards of his profession in the spirit of its founders such as Professor Donaldson whom he so admired; his own opinions on unaesthetic matters will have carried the weight of a thoroughly practical experience, whatever the changes in fashion. And his professional status had been the family stepping-stone.[37]

[37] RIBA *Transactions* new series I (1885), president's address 3 Nov. 1884; Knowles Sr. sat on council 1852–4 and 1880–4. *Bldr*, 3 May 1884, p. 604. *Building*

Did the 'starchy old gentleman' the Hewletts remembered, greeting small grandchildren by extending two fingers with a curt 'How do', end his days as self-satisfied as he began? There was a story among his irreverent children that in his last years he drew his eldest daughter's attention to a man watching their carriage go by and told her 'I believe he knows who I am'—but by then no stranger could be assumed to know that. In a photograph of about 1871, when he was 65, newer methods of photography may not entirely account for a loss of aplomb since 1860 or an unbecomingly wistful little smile on his plain face. (The marble nobility of Woolner's bust of 1873 can, of course, be discounted.) From the time he stopped practising in 1869—except for designing the memorial at Wigton to oblige an old client—there were only charitable committees and churchwarden duties in Clapham Park, and after the lonely move with George to Russell Square, the Institute's committees in Conduit Street.[38] To much of his elder son's career after 1870 he was an outsider, proud of the fact that his offer of £2,000 was not needed to launch the *Nineteenth Century*; and how proud too, could he have known that James was to be knighted and leave twice as much money as he did. Part of James's share in his father's bequests of 1884 may have financed the younger family's removal from Clapham to Westminster, right after his father's death, as his father's removal from Bell Street to Cockshut Hill had followed the death of old Mrs. Knowles, glazier, in 1836. The Westminster lease had been secured in the autumn of 1883; after some months of repairs and redecoration, the break with the past could be made complete.

AT HOME IN WESTMINSTER

> 'Went with Mr G. to dine with J. Knowles at his new
> house in Queen Anne's Gate—a charming residence,
> full of beautiful things.' Sir Edward Hamilton,
> November 1884, *Diary*, 1972

> 'Went to Mr Knowles's ball . . . rather enjoyed
> sitting out in garden with unlimited strawberries and

(New York), May 1884, p. 95, a reference for which I thank the Avery Librarian at Columbia University. On Street's funeral, *BN*, 30 Dec. 1881, p. 893.

[38] Introduction to *Letters of Maurice Hewlett* (1926), pp. 7–8. 'I believe he knows . . .' from the late Miss Flint. On marble bust, chap. 7, n. 26. On last years of practice, end of chap. 4 above.

cream and the flabby limp figure of Oscar Wilde
mooning about.' Mary Gladstone, July 1885, ed.
Masterman, 1930

'. . . it was a perfect night and the garden full of
friends and strawberries.' Knowles to Gladstone,
July 1887, Gladstone Papers, BL

By 1883 Knowles had been running the *Nineteenth Century* for
six years partly from his study at home beside Clapham Common,
and partly from his office at Albert Mansions, Victoria Street. By
then it was clear that Clapham, for an editor with his finger on
the public pulse, was too far from the heart of things. And for
fertilizing conversations, neither his unmellowed office nor the
whispering gallery of the Reform Club (Pl. 14) would do.
Eminent contributors whose working day revolved around
Whitehall, the Houses of Parliament, or Jermyn Street could
seldom be lured all the way to Clapham to consult over luncheon,
however anxious they were to please or avid for information.
Eminent dinner guests anxious to meet other guests even more
eminent still thought twice about driving to Clapham on a foggy
night. As a constant diner-out himself, Knowles began to feel
the strain. Clapham was partly still a district of large houses well
kept by comfortable people, but for someone like him the place
was already a dormitory suburb. He could now afford financially
to consider living in central London, or rather, to consider that
he could hardly afford not to. Antennae may have been out for
some time: the usual London terrace house facing a row of the
same would never do.

In September 1883 he acquired the lease of one of the most
desirable and unusual private houses in London, one of the select
few overlooking St. James's Park: No. 1 Queen Square Place,
known as Queen Anne's Lodge (Pl. 16).[39] This had been a late
eighteenth-century rebuilding, by the father of Jeremy Bentham
the philosopher, of a cluster of old tenements beside his own house,
No. 2 Queen Square Place. The latter, known as Garden Mansion,

---

[39] A short version of this section appeared in *AR*, Mar. 1974. On early history of
Queen Anne's Lodge, S of L vol. X, *Parish of St Margaret's Westminster part 1*
(1926), p. 142. Knowles held the lease, but not the freehold, here for the rest of
his life. The same firm of developers that he contended with in 1888–90 is responsible for the present hulking block (now the Home Office) on the site.

was occupied after Bentham's day by the engineer Sir John Fowler, who still in the 1880s kept his office in part of it; and the engineer Samuel Bentham, Jeremy's brother, had been an early occupier of No. 1. The two main floors of Queen Anne's Lodge lay nine windows wide on its park front, with Birdcage Walk running at the foot of the garden. East of the garden stood the house John Stuart Mill grew up in (now 40 Queen Anne's Gate), leased by his father from Jeremy Bentham and afterward occupied by John Bowring when he was editing the *Westminster Review*. In the 1820s–30s this was a Benthamite neighbourhood, teeming with more ideas than all the rest of Westminster put together. Bentham senior had been proud to own, too, the house next door in Petty France once occupied (it was said) by Milton. Who in today's new Government blocks towering over Bentham's old ground remembers what intellects towered there?

Around the corner to eastward sat the little enclave of Queen Anne's Gate with its select inhabitants. Except for the noble tenants of Carlton Terrace across the lake and certain Whitehall offices, few other neighbours besides the Royal Family had a view of the park. To westward, beyond the remains of Bentham's garden, lay Wellington Barracks (Foot Guards) and, close to Bentham's garden wall, the Guards' Chapel—at that time Greek Revival outside and Early Christianized inside, so suitable for the Guards. The entrance front of Queen Anne's Lodge gave on to an irregular courtyard where, a few years before, certain rebuilding had taken place.

For several years Queen Anne's Lodge had been occupied by Lieut.-Gen. Sir Dighton Probyn VC, Controller and Treasurer of the Prince of Wales's Household. In March 1883 he had renewed his lease from the post-Bentham ground landlord, Land Securities Company. In September, for one reason or another, Probyn disposed of the lease to Knowles, who by then was moving in the periphery of Royal Household circles, though he might have heard of the chance from Fowler, already a contributor to the *Nineteenth Century*. Probyn, known among the Households for a certain crustiness, may have grown tired of interference with his light and air by an elephantine neighbour: the first block of the hulk of flats called Queen Anne's Mansion (singular then), begun in the mid-1870s at the corner of York Street (Petty France) and Broadway, so that Probyn's carriage-entry ran through its nine-storey gatehouse.[40] The new block enveloped only one end of the courtyard then, and existing plans for its expansion lay dormant in the early 1880s. Knowles started repairs on his new house at once, and early in 1884 the family moved in. So far as physical ambience went, this meant a change of local climate from Clapham Common's altitude of ninety feet above the river to St. James's Park at river-bank level, where winter fogs were of a concentration, of an antiquity almost, unattained by the raw suburban variety. 'The air always seems to me heavy and thick', said Henry James of Westminster in the 1880s, and noted the slum children and the unemployed sprawling in the park.[41] The slums were near enough, and Charles Booth was assessing them as James wrote, finding behind the new blocks and empty lots of Victoria Street south of Queen Anne's Lodge 'a very mixed population'. Ancient Westminster, unlike Belgravia or parts of the perimeter of Clapham Common, was no one-class neighbourhood. But its blackest courts were shielded by seemlier buildings, offending no sensibilities during the Knowleses' short drive now to church, St. Margaret's beside the Abbey (far more fashionable than the district church in Caxton Street a few yards from home). Places of public resort opposite the Abbey, Westminster Hospital and the Aquarium, were best ignored. Yet north of Queen Anne's Lodge the open horizon of the park gave intimations of Whitehall and Buckingham Palace beyond the trees. Whoever sprawled on the benches, fresh greenery in spring filled the prospect from the Knowleses' drawing-room windows. Ducks quacked on the lake and days were punctuated by distant bugle calls and bursts of military music from the Barracks, and a clatter of hooves when carriages passed along Birdcage Walk, Big Ben's deep tones rolled through the neighbourhood, and in the quiet of night even the hoots of tugboats approaching Westminster Bridge on a rising tide. But Victoria Street's traffic was out of earshot, and at least the nine storeys of Queen Anne's Mansion shut off noises from Metropolitan Line trains in the open cutting by St. James's Park Station opposite.

[40] On Probyn, *Kelly's Handbook to Titled . . . Classes* (1883), A. Ponsonby, *Henry Ponsonby, Queen Victoria's Private Secretary* (1942), p. 355, and Knowles to Hopgood, 20 Dec. 1889 (letter-book cited n. 43).
[41] Henry James, 'London', *Century Magazine*, Dec. 1888, p. 230. For neighbourhood, OS 5' sheet VII.82, 1871 and 1893; Charles Booth, *Labour and Life of the People* (1889), vol. 2 appendix and Poverty Map SW.

The *Nineteenth Century* could now be edited from Knowles's library. From there it was only a stroll over the park bridge to the War Office, then in Pall Mall, to brief the Duke of Cambridge again on the dangers of a Channel Tunnel, or to Marlborough House when summoned in March 1884 to discuss the agony of the poor, or to Christie's to consider some drawings, or up to Stallard's in Albemarle Street to sample their white port, which Knowles recommended to Gladstone in April 1891. Another short stroll away was the Abbey Deanery, then inhabited by Dean Bradley, who had lived in Clapham as a boy, and whose memories of the place and of Dr. Pritchard's school made a most readable article for Knowles's March 1884 issue. Later one of the Bradley daughters, Mrs. Alexander Murray Smith, lived in Mill's old house next door to the Knowleses. From Queen Anne's Lodge, too, one could easily step over to the Lobby and Strangers' Gallery of the House of Commons or, at certain periods, along to breakfast with Mr. Gladstone in Downing Street or St. James's Square. Knowles's clubs were just across the park, the Reform and, up St. James's, the newer Liberal Devonshire. In Spring Gardens was the office of Henry Hewlett, so close a brother now, and in Whitehall Place, the office of their old friend and Knowles's solicitor John Hopgood. The review's printers, Messrs. Spottiswoode, were farther afield in New-street Square off Fleet Street, and its publishers Kegan Paul, Trench & Co. in Paternoster Square near St. Paul's—but messengers were cheap.

Many milestones of Knowles's life lay near by. In Vincent Square, St. Mary's parsonage no longer overflowed with Jane's relations, but the little church periodically received another stained-glass window from him in her memory. Off Vincent Square in their stonemasons' yard the firm of Daymond & Son still carved away, probably still ready to admit that the Grosvenor's great friezes were their work, as a generation later they were not. The Grosvenor loomed over the still modest buildings of Victoria Station but no longer harboured the tremendous conversations of the Metaphysical Society. In Victoria Street, where Tennyson had looked out from Albert Mansions and pronounced it 'a street in hell', the Army and Navy Stores brightened the pavement. Across the park, critical young men of the 1880s occasionally singled out the grimy stone front of the Thatched

House Club as hopelessly Mid-Victorian. Around the corner from the club, opposite the then still partly Georgian premises of Christie's in King Street, stood Willis's Rooms where the Metaphysical Society was launched. In Westminster Knowles could have seen (as Tennyson told him he saw in Cambridge) a ghost in every corner. Yet editorial and social concern for the immediate future must have exorcised nearly every one.

At last, once mourning for his father (not long-drawn-out as for his mother) was over, he could entertain his choicest guests at home. By the 1880s the Grosvenor had fallen out of favour for Knowles's dinner-parties, the Reform Club being the scene of one given in August 1883 attended by Gladstone, Wolseley, Leighton the painter, Waddington the French ambassador, Hill the editor of the *Daily News*, Tyndall the scientist, and others. The parties at Queen Anne's Lodge began in November 1884 with two dinners, the guest-list on the 3rd being built around Chamberlain and that on the 27th around Gladstone. Knowles's own dining-out was such that a typical London dinner-blunder occurred (cf. *Punch* on the 'Inconvenience of Uniform Architecture in London Terraces', or Lady Jeune's 'nothing so dangerous as giving a dinner-party on the same night as your next-door neighbour'). Knowles was bidden to Reginald Brett's in Tilney Street off Park Lane, his first invitation to that house, perhaps in 1890 around the time of Brett's second article for him. Arriving in a rush as usual, Knowles thought his hostess, whom he had not before met, looked especially pleased when he was announced; assuming that Brett's absence was unavoidable, Knowles was his usual delightful self to her guests, but when he came to say good-night she (a Mrs. Hobart-Hampden, according to directories) confessed to his horror that she had not been able to bring herself before to tell him he was in the wrong house because it had been such a *coup* to have him as her guest. His daughter Beatrice arrived in their carriage from another party in time to see him burst out of No. 2 Tilney Street and into No. 1 to apologize in a frenzy of excitement. And Gladstone hearing of it afterward pronounced in high amusement, 'it could *only* have happened to you'.[42]

---

[42] Dinners: Hamilton's *Diary* (as n. 21), ii. 473, 743; Ponsonby (as n. 40), p. 269. *Punch*, 13 Feb. 1875, p. 68; Lady St. Helier, *Memories of Fifty Years* (1909), p. 189. Knowles family story from Eirene Skilbeck.

Meanwhile, on moving to Queen Anne's Lodge, Knowles had given up his Albert Mansions office and installed George Robson in some corner of the house as general dogsbody and secretary. There Robson served as loyal lieutenant in a furious losing campaign that began four years after they moved in. The Jubilee summer of 1887, with one more At Home in the garden filled with friends and strawberries, was the last carefree Season in the old setting. In 1888 the ugly cancer of the Mansion began to spread. In June Knowles suddenly became aware of plans for a new 'vast mass or cliff' next door. After a whirlwind visit to the District Surveyor's office to inspect them, he laid out his campaign, assigning a new letter-book to this issue alone, the only one of his multitudinous letter-books to survive. First he pointed out to the Metropolitan Board of Works—a dying body soon to give way to a newly created London County Council—that the proposed addition, rising to a height of 150 feet, would continue along York Street (Petty France), return at right angles toward the park and then eastward toward his house with a great range facing the park and overshadowing the Guards' Chapel. (A plan for covering the entire site, including that of his own house, with new blocks of flats had been lying in the M.B.W. office since 1877, ignored by everybody.)[43]

Knowles then proceeded to supply the First Commissioner of Works, David Plunket M.P., not only with a question to be put to him in the House but also with '(suggested) Reply', mentioning in his accompanying note that he had already shown both question *and* answer to the Speaker 'on the chance of obtaining your approval'. Next he wrote letters to the *Daily News*, *The Times*, and the *Morning Post* as an Inhabitant of Westminster protesting against the overshadowing of this historic quarter by the ugliest building in London and deploring the unlimited impudence of Limited Companies—with personal notes to each editor, that to the editor of the *Post* mentioning that he had already had a word with 'Sir Algernon [Borthwick, the paper's proprietor] in the Lobby'. Knowles then drafted a Private Bill to curb the height of buildings in narrow streets according to 'the common rule which gives an angle of 45 deg as every man's fair

---

[43] Main sources of this and next six paragraphs: Knowles letter-book, 1888–90 (WPL), also containing copies of certain letters received, taken before passing on the originals to his lawyer; and MBW case files 23744, 24348, 38442 (GLRO).

allowance of light and air on streets', and showed it to Gladstone.[44]
But 1888 as a year of crisis in London government was no time for
such a bill. The idea of expensive proceedings before a parliamentary committee soon gave way to a resolve to sue in the courts
(in general, Knowles tended to keep his lawyers busy). So deep
was he 'in defence of my own hearth and home' that an invitation
from Princess Mary Adelaide of Teck to visit with her a charity
in which she was interested had to be refused. Before departing
on holiday in August, he instructed Robson to make a model of
the existing buildings, showing how Bentham's old Garden
Mansion leaned against the west wall of Queen Anne's Lodge,
buttressing its chimneys. There in September 1888 demolition
began, 'on the other side of my library wall'.

At first, exchanges with the architect for the new blocks, as
fellow-professional, were amicable; this was E. R. Robson
(apparently no relation to Knowles's assistant), whom he had
known for some years. Knowles asked if he might be connected
with 'the electric light' intended for the new building (Robson
replying certainly if they could get rid of Fowler's office where the
generators were to go). In fact, Knowles even offered to take
shares in the new company, Queen Anne's and Garden Mansions
Ltd., if the blocks could be reduced in height and still yield ten
per cent. A purely temporary diversion, this, from dedicated
opposition to the whole scheme. But the awkward fact was that
no one had stopped the first Queen Anne's Mansion; however
much initial comment had been caused by it, the neighbourhood
had lived at peace with it for several years. Even though the new
blocks were to be yet taller, the entering wedge had been lodged,
and accepted. As cracks criss-crossed Knowles's library wall, and
trenches were dug beside the foundations of his ninety-year-old
house, his tone became querulous in a stream of summoning
notes to Hopgood across the park ('Pray come at *once*') and
sometimes telegrams to Hopgood's house since none of them was
on the telephone.

A Mansions Ltd. foreman coming civilly to shield Knowles's
skylights was sent away for not having made written application
to do so, and injunctions were threatened when the Mansions
people (they said) were only asking their aggrieved neighbour to

[44] Knowles to Gladstone, 8 July 1888 (BL). Knowles had published an article
by Borthwick two years before.

appoint his own surveyor for a discussion of damages. Just before
Knowles's case came up for trial 'the model' was sent over to
Hopgood's office with this note: '. . . pray observe—that *it must
not be put outside any cab or vehicle—but carried under cover.* It is far
too fragile and delicate to stand the accidents of external carriage.
Robson brings it in a 4-wheel cab—riding on the box himself with
the driver—and I beg of you to have it taken anywhere in the
same manner—in a 4-wheel cab all by itself—with a clerk of
yours on the box.' And so, one day in 1888, an architectural model
of the old Bentham houses passed along Whitehall inside a four-
wheeler, with two men aloft on the coachman's box.

Expert witnesses who came to view the ancient light enjoyed
by the house were shown how 'many of my best pictures were
hung in my Staircase which is lighted from that same open sky'—
for daylight meant much to a collector of pictures, whatever the
shortcomings of daylight for half the year. There were 'tremendous
blows and thrashing' as demolition was 'driven on furiously' all
night, Knowles wondering furiously if this was the 'quiet enjoyment' for which he paid £500 a year to the very people whose
agents were doing this. Dining at the Speaker's early in December,
of course he made a splendid dinner-story out of it. And a witness
arriving to inspect new fissures was held at bay while the Editor
of the *Nineteenth Century* conducted 'an appointment with the
Turkish Ambassador in my Library' (a conversation that may
have led circuitously to the articles by 'Adalet' that appeared in
the *Nineteenth Century* during 1890 on life in a Turkish harem).[45]

The court case came on. Knowles lost, and started another. All
support for his west wall was gone, and 'the Ladies of my family'
were in a state of nerves whenever the wind blew. Huxley,
remembering trouble with awkward neighbours in St. John's
Wood when Knowles was his architect there, said 'Good for you
to have a taste of it for yourself' when Knowles invited him to
'fill your malicious soul with joy by contemplating the ruins in the
midst of which this house yet survives'.[46] One sharp little engagement was proudly reported by George Robson, when a photo-

[45] Date of dinner at Speaker's in Knowles to Gladstone, 7 Dec. 1888 (BL). On
Adalet, n. 18 above; the Turkish embassy was nearby in Queen Anne's Gate.
[46] Huxley to Knowles, 30 Dec. 1888 (from letters 1886–95 privately printed in
slip form by Knowles for Leonard Huxley's use, while keeping the originals, of
which present whereabouts unknown to Imperial College archivist; other parts of
this letter in the *Life*, ii. 221). Knowles to Huxley, 1 Jan. 1889 (Imperial College).

grapher hired by Knowles to record operations was stopped by the
Mansions' solicitors with policemen and had to be rescued by
Robson, 'I saying . . . *"Dismiss your Army"* '. In January 1889,
Knowles's one relief was being able to say to E. R. Robson that
'I have been away staying at Sandringham'—where General
Probyn must have permitted himself a pitying smile.

Mollifying was now in order. The War Office, for the Guards'
Chapel, were also suing the Mansions Ltd. And E. R. Robson
may have pointed out to them that Knowles had considerable
influence, or nuisance-value, whatever their contempt for his
rights and anxieties. Possibly it was known, early in 1889, that the
Queen was horrified at what she saw from Buckingham Palace.
Not one course of brick the less was laid for the intended twelve
storeys that were to scowl over St. James's Park for eighty years.
But Knowles was now offered not only £500 in damages but a
flat in one of the new ranges with the south aspect his house was
losing and a tunnel from his cellar to the basement below the flat:
two rooms for day-time use as a study for himself and a sitting
room for his wife where they could withdraw from their busy
household for quiet enjoyment of light and air. Having never in
his life lived in a flat or chambers—but only designed them—
Knowles was aghast on inspecting the plans to see that some utter
stranger's plumbing lay on the other side of a mere three-inch
partition, so unsuitable for a lady to listen to.

Meanwhile, as the storeys rose in Queen Square Place, the
expiring Metropolitan Board of Works refused to sanction the
new building. (The precise moment in London's history chosen
for its erection probably had a good deal to do with its success.)
The new County Council's lawyers informed their own Building
Act committee that indeed these people couldn't be stopped from
exceeding a height of 100 feet until they actually did so. When
they did and the District Surveyor took the builders to court, the
magistrate ruled against him, and the L.C.C. in November 1889
concluded that it was useless to appeal. A *fait accompli* in bricks and
mortar was the strongest witness in its own defence. And subsequent legislation tempering the height of London buildings was
the slamming of the barn door. At Queen Anne's Lodge, causes
for complaint continued. In December Knowles refused to sign
a lease for his new flat with a body called Mansions Ltd. and not
Company: Hopgood must insert something to show 'that I *am*

contracting with human beings and not with bricks and mortar! There is a point beyond which the accursed slovenliness of commerce offends anybody with any sense of art—and instincts revolt', said this experienced sufferer from the limited ways of building-speculators. In April 1890 came more cracks in the library although the new cliff was not, quite, to touch the house. The last entry in the letter-book records the crash of a brickbat through a double skylight into the bath.

Surviving volumes of the *Nineteenth* for 1888–90 give no hint of the chaos out of which the 'copy' reached the printing office in New-street Square. Thereafter, during almost every Season until Knowles's death in 1908, there continued to be held at least one very grand party at Queen Anne's Lodge, overflowing through the long windows on to the lawn, overlooked by the cliff-dwellers next door. In 1891 the Wales family came, irritating young William Wray Skilbeck, by then Knowles's secretary and already in love with Beatrice Knowles, that she should dance with 'the one with the beard' (the future George V) instead of with him. After 1908, the last private resident of the house seems to have been Sir Edward Coates, Bt., M.P. and stockbroker (d. 1921), and later it became the office of the eminent civil engineer Sir Alexander Gibb (d. 1958). When Queen Anne's Lodge was finally demolished in 1971, it had ghosts of engineers and editors in every corner.

MIDWIFE TO GLADSTONE AND HUXLEY, AND TO THE ROYAL FAMILY

> 'Now for the "midwifery".' Knowles to Gladstone, 4 November 1887

> 'you have often commended me for letting men blow off all their steam in words.' Knowles to Gladstone, 17 November 1887, BL

> 'I am possessed by a writing demon, and have pretty well finished . . . another article for Knowles, whose mouth is wide open for it.' Huxley to a friend, 3 March 1889, *Life*, ii.

> 'the [working man's] naïve nonsense "leaps to the eyes"— & the object (at least my object) is to make it do so. Let us know the weapons & tactics of the

savage foes of Patience & of Science—& we may
the better beat them.' Knowles to Huxley, 20 March
1890, Imperial College

Evidence for the workings of the editorial process behind the
Nineteenth Century from the mid-1880s to the mid-1890s can be
found in the editor's correspondence with two of his most
eminent contributors. Sometimes editorial obstetrics involved
mating author and subject, as well as careful nursing into print.
And sometimes articles arose by spontaneous generation, or
combustion, the midwifery consisting only in the administering
of large doses of editorial tact.

The famous debate between Gladstone and Huxley in the pages
of Knowles's review personified for some Late Victorians the war
between religion and science. It flared up twice: in 1885-6 during
the brief period between Gladstone's second and third ministries,
and in 1890-1 during the Indian summer before his last ministry,
with rumblings in between, and other participants rushing to
join in. Much of Knowles's correspondence with the two
principals survives and reveals his hand in the middle, a steadying
more than a steering hand. Personally, he was on warm and
humourous terms with Huxley, more relaxed than his deferential
copiousness with the Grand Old Man. When the liveliest fire-
works were finally set off early in 1891, Gladstone was 81 and
Huxley was 66. Each clash was ignited by a book—the monthlies
being in part still propelled by book-reviews and counter-
reviews—and few contributions from either side had to be
invited, landing (almost) unbidden in the editor's lap.

Early in October 1885 Knowles came home from holiday
abroad to find a letter from Gladstone offering him an article.
After leaving office in June, the former Prime Minister had sailed
to Norway in August on Sir Thomas Brassey's yacht, and then in
September plunged into politics, writing a new Midlothian
manifesto in preparation for his speech-making tour during most
of November in Scotland and the general election in November/
December. But the proffered article was not political, it concerned
primitive civilization—the great man's energies being stimulated
by such swings in concentration. Knowles quickly assured him on
12 October that the subject of primitive civilization had always
fascinated him, had indeed been 'the theme of my very first
public deliverance (at a Scientific Society)'—that is, at the

Clapham Athenaeum when he was 22. Gladstone was returning
to a favourite theme, the early dawning of the human capacity
for worship as proved in the book of Genesis and reflected in
Greek myth, because he had just discovered that a French
historian of religion, Albert Réville, disagreed with him. An
English translation of Réville's little book with the big title,
Prolegomena of the History of Religions, had appeared in 1884 with
an introduction by Max Müller. Réville singled out Gladstone as
prominent upholder of the doctrine that man was naturally
religious from the start, a doctrine 'clearly contradicted by the
discoveries of historical science', being based upon a book,
Genesis, that 'cannot pass as a document relating the beginnings
of the whole human race'. By 15 October Gladstone's proof for
the November *Nineteenth* was being sent to the Bishop of
Winchester (also cited by Réville) to read at Gladstone's request;
revised proof was ready by the 22nd, and by the 29th when
Gladstone dined with Knowles at Queen Anne's Lodge publication of 'The Dawn of Creation and of Worship' was off their
minds. The next issue of *Punch* had this to say of 'The "Dawn of
Creation" and Practical Politics': 'Mr Gladstone seems . . . to be
somewhat in accord with the gentleman who, on visiting the
ruins of Jupiter's Temple, politely took his hat off, explaining that
"he considered it polite to keep in with the old *regime*, as one never
knew what turn of the wheel might bring them into power
again".' At any rate, in the November *Nineteenth* the Gladstonian
sentence unfurled itself as triumphantly as ever it did in the House
of Commons:[47]

For those who believe that the old foundations are unshaken still, and
that the fabric built upon them will look down for ages on the floating
wreck of many a modern and boastful theory, it is difficult to see
anything but infatuation in the destructive temperament which leads
to the notion that to substitute a blind mechanism for the hand of God
in the affairs of life is to enlarge the scope of remedial agency; that to
dismiss the highest of all inspirations is to elevate the strain of human
thought and life; and that each of us is to rejoice that our several units
are to be disintegrated at death into 'countless millions of organisms';
for such, it seems, is the latest 'revelation' delivered from the fragile
tripod of a modern Delphi.

[47] 'The Dawn of Creation and of Worship', *NC*, Nov. 1885, p. 706. Knowles
to Gladstone, 12, 15, 22, 24, 30 Oct. 1885 (BL). *Punch*, 7 Nov. 1885, p. 222.

Three days after publication, and a few days before Gladstone
left for Scotland, Knowles wrote to him that the article had both
'stirred up Prof. Huxley' and moved the public: 'My publishers
tell me that a second & third edition . . . have been called for.
Men feel more & more deeply about such subjects & all that they
entail than they do about most others—which I wish Mr Chamberlain could understand.' (Joseph Chamberlain at the time wrote
occasional articles for the *Fortnightly* and, although he dined with
Knowles now and then in the 1880s, had not written for him yet.)
Just over a week later, Huxley's article was in hand and, against
usual habit with the maze of Huxley's handwriting, Knowles read
it in manuscript before consigning to the printer: 'I cannot refrain
from writing one word of thanks and congratulations! You never
wrote better in your life. . . . It is as if all the fire which has been
kept in so long & smothered in uncongenial work had at length
burst out again & would burn up ill health & any other obstacle
to its own free course.' That was just what had happened. Huxley
had recently retired from all his official positions including the
presidency of the Royal Society, and was gradually finding his
way out of ill-health and depression. It now became a Huxley
family proverb that a bile-stirring dose of Gladstone was just
what the liver needed. Gladstone's assertion that the first chapter
of Genesis gave the true order of creation set Huxley off, as he
told Lord Farrer in December:

From a scientific point of view Gladstone's article was undoubtedly
not worth powder and shot. But, on personal grounds, the perusal of
it sent me blaspheming about the house with the first healthy expression
of wrath known for a couple of years . . . and I should have 'busted up'
if I had not given vent to my indignation; and secondly, all orthodoxy
was gloating over the slap in the face which the G.O.M. had administered to science in the person of Reville.

The ignorance of the so-called educated classes in this country is
stupendous, and in the hands of people like Gladstone it is a political
force . . . now I have recovered my freedom, and I am greatly minded
to begin stirring the fire afresh.

His 'The Interpreters of Genesis and the Interpreters of Nature' in
the December *Nineteenth* began by saying that in his judgement
Réville was absolutely right, but that:

he, as a foreigner, has very little chance of making the truth prevail
with Englishmen against the authority and dialectic skill of the greatest

master of persuasive rhetoric among English-speaking men of our time. As the Queen's proctor intervenes . . . between two litigants in the interests of justice, so it may be permitted me to interpose as a sort of uncommissioned science proctor. My second excuse for my meddle-someness is that important questions of natural science—respecting which neither of the combatants profess to speak as an expert—are involved in the controversy.

And the article ended by roundly declaring that 'the antagonism of science is not to religion, but to the heathen survivals and the bad philosophy under which religion herself is often well-nigh crushed'. The tone was genial, while seeming to bowl over the antagonist 'as easily as if he were a rickety nine-pin' (as *Punch* put it).[48]

At first from Gladstone, just back from his Midlothian cam-paign, there was no comment, only a letter rebuking Knowles for printing in the same issue a rather poor article on the poet Leopardi that made no reference to Gladstone's own article of 1850 on that writer. But to Knowles's direct query on 3 December, 'I should much like to know what you think of Huxley', came a reply from the midst of the election-excitement at Hawarden: 'Quoad Professor Huxley. I am very grateful for the abundant courtesy with which he has treated me, despite his overflowing scorn for reconcilers collectively—& if you have an opportunity I should be much obliged by your telling him so.' As to the scientific side of the attack, which Gladstone felt affected only a small part of his argument: 'Now my first impulse here is simply to bow my back to the lash. I am *zero* in such a question. But . . . I am bound not to recede too hastily from my ground, without examining it through the minds of others more competent than myself. . . . But in truth my leisure is at this moment like my scientific value, zero.' Looking at Huxley's article 'in its polemical aspect', he went on, however, 'I own that my fingers itch to deal with it'. And within the week he was offering Knowles a rejoinder for the January number. (The monthly-periodical interval was

---

[48] On number of editions of November number, Knowles to Gladstone, 4 Nov., 26 Dec. 1885 (BL). For a later view of Chamberlain, n. 101 below. On Huxley's 'The Interpreters of Genesis and the Interpreters of Nature', *NC*, Dec. 1885: Knowles to Huxley, 12 Nov. 1885 (Imperial College); Huxley to Lord Farrer, 6 Dec. 1885 (*Life*, ii. 115); passages quoted *NC* pp. 849, 860; *Punch*, 19 Dec. 1885, p. 289. The Dec. *NC* also contained Max Müller's 'Solar Myths' in reply to Gladstone.

exactly right for the boiling-up of considered reaction and its setting in type.) Knowles answered on the 10th 'how gladly I shall keep place for you . . . &, if you will let me say so, when antagonists like yourself & Huxley meet each other with such abundant candour & courtesy as you do—a priceless lesson is taught quite irrespective of the merits of the discussion itself'.[49]

At Hawarden on 17 December, while the Liberal majority teetered in the Irish balance, with 'great hubbub all round . . . general confusion, telegrams without end', Mary Gladstone noted that in the midst of it all her father 'despatched another "Dawn" article to *19th Century'*. By the 23rd Knowles was thanking him for prompt return of proof (Spottiswoode's compositors worked fast) and candidly confessing his own inability to see how Gladstone's case could be 'ultimately proved'—because to me, as an ordinary juryman, the weight of evidence seems overwhelming the other way'. But, said Knowles encouragingly, 'I honestly think no advocacy could go beyond the skill with which yours is exercised.' And on Boxing Day, reflecting upon his own good luck, he offered further encouragement:[50]

You have set a ball rolling which almost overwhelms me—& would quite overwhelm all the space of the XIXth Centy for a year—if I did not stand in the way. . . . I daresay you yourself hardly know the interest & excitement you have awaked by 'the Dawn of Creation' . . . the publishers had to issue six editions in six days—a thing almost—if not quite—unprecedented! And now every post brings me offers of attack & defence from all the winds that blow.

In 'Proem to Genesis: a Plea for a Fair Trial' in the January 1886 issue, the great man's temperature rose slightly over his adversary's 'exaggerations' and the Genesis account was gone over in (to us) unreadable detail. What to Huxley was 'shuffling' and to Mrs. Humphrey Ward 'no sense of critical evidence' offers slithery footing to modern readers. Sending an early copy to Huxley on 31 December, Knowles observed, 'I think you will find that your adversary lays himself *very much* open to your weapon!' and next

---

[49] With Knowles to Gladstone, 3 Dec. 1885 (BL), replying to rebuke on Leopardi and asking comment on Huxley, is Gladstone's draft for his to Knowles of 4 Dec.

[50] *Mary Gladstone* (1930), p. 373. Knowles to Gladstone, 23, 26 Dec. 1885 (BL). The January issue did not come out before Christmas this year, and printing was held up until the 28th for a postscript Gladstone was allowed to send.

day reassured Huxley that space was indeed reserved for another rejoinder in the February number. Huxley, having already described to him over lunch at Queen Anne's Lodge the gist of his own next instalment, now required the encouragement which Knowles supplied:[51]

But—do think 'once twice even three times' before you abandon what you had already written before Mr Gladstone's 'vol. 2'. It may well be that you would lift the whole matter up from the particular to the general—which is precisely what I long for. This discussion about Genesis surely derives its greatest interest from being an 'illustration' of the great controversy as to whether any special man or set of men have ever had special or *more than natural* means of Knowledge—& whether where that has been pretended to it is not possible to show that it is not *Knowledge* at all—but dreams & hopes & visions which have been put in place of it.

Perhaps Knowles's own philosophy had worked around to that. At any rate, to an editor ever looking for new conclusions of permanent value to be established in his pages, the aim was always to see matters lifted up from the particular to the general. But Huxley in his second round—which the editor sent unread to the printer on 6 January—changed his tone somewhat, for as he told Lord Farrer, while attacking Gladstone again was not really necessary, 'the extreme shiftiness of my antagonist provoked me, and I was tempted to pin him and dissect him as an anatomico-psychological exercise. . . . I laughed so much over the operation that I deserve no credit.' So what Knowles read in proof on the 14th, we can only surmise from the letter he then wrote:

Of course I find it quite 'pulverizing' & final. But—may I take my courage in both hands—& ask you to be a little less fierce & more good humoured about your vivisection? . . . I do think the extreme good humour of your former article added enormously to its weight & effect—& I do also think that anything like absence of the same sense of humorous supremacy will be at once noticed in the second article. You must wear the same easy & unruffled smile—all through . . . whatever provocation you feel—don't you agree?

And Huxley was invited again to lunch 'all by yourself, bringing the proof when you have settled it, & letting me submit to you

[51] Knowles to Huxley, 31 Dec. 1885 (Imperial College).

any of my crude hints'.[52] To which Huxley agreed, admitting
that he had lived long enough 'to know the value of moderation',
and adding: 'If I were Providence now, and had the right to deal
with the G.O.M. according to his deserts, I would not omit a
drop of vitriol; but being only a hater of iniquity, and particularly
of shuffling (which so far as I can see P[rovidence] isn't) I am prepared to put in as much alkali as may neutralize any superfluity of
acid.' So the language 'calculated to make a judicious editor's hair
stand on end' was toned down, doubtless with some hair-raising
resetting for the printer.[53] Where Gladstone had begun like this in
January: 'As I have lived for more than half a century in an
atmosphere of contention, my stock of controversial fire has
perhaps become abnormally low; while Professor Huxley, who
has been inhabiting the Elysian regions of science . . . may be
enjoying all the freshness of an unjaded appetite'; Huxley concluded his own, still most readable, article in February by
saying:

I confess that my supposed 'unjaded appetite' for the sort of controversy
in which it needed not Mr Gladstone's express declaration to tell us he
is far better practised than I am (though . . . no one would have sus-
pected that his controversial fires are burning low) is already satiated.
In 'Elysium' we conduct scientific discussions in a different medium,
and we are liable to threatenings of asphyxia in that 'atmosphere of
contention' in which Mr Gladstone has been able to live, alert and
vigorous beyond the common race of men.[54]

Where Gladstone had required 22 and 21 pages to state his cloudy
case, Huxley's two brisk articles took 12 and 14 pages. For
instance, to Gladstone's contention that the nebular hypothesis
confirmed the cosmogony of the spirit of God moving upon the
face of the waters, Huxley austerely commented (after taming):

[52] Huxley to Lord Farrer, 13 Jan. 1886 (*Life*, ii. 116). Knowles to Huxley, 14
Jan. 1886 (Imperial College).
[53] Huxley to Knowles, three letters 15–20 Jan. 1886 in privately printed set,
two used in *Life*, ii. 116 (dates may be incorrect); the one about Providence not
used, dating (i.e. Huxley's handwriting) probably unclear to printer but it is the
reply to Knowles's of 14 Jan. and probably should be dated 15 not 16 Jan.
[54] Gladstone, 'Proem to Genesis', *NC*, Jan. 1886, p. 3. Huxley, 'Mr Gladstone
and Genesis (No. I)', *NC*, Feb. 1886, p. 205. 'No. II' in February was by Henry
Drummond, a young Scottish reconciler, both evangelistic preacher and science
teacher; Knowles to Huxley, 5 Feb. 1886 (Imperial College): 'Yes, it is rather
hard to have even Drummond turn upon him & I assure you Drummond's first
version was nearly as fierce as yours.'

'I have met with no form of the nebular hypothesis which involves anything analogous to this process.' To Huxley the language of Genesis was 'vivid and admirable' as poetry only —but the adversary was no longer listening. Gladstone spent 1 February at Osborne, reluctantly recalled by the Queen to form his third, short government of 1886.

In July, even before that government was out, the Prime Minister invited Knowles to breakfast and offered one more paragraph on 'Genesis and Science', inquiring whether the rules of this controversy allowed another little rejoinder. Knowles replied that in spite of his 'usual limits of Controversy, in the case of yourself & Huxley . . . "nice customs curtsey to Great Kings" ', and that he had hoped Gladstone would be 'tempted on to a final rejoinder', but then came 'that fatal change of government which took away my hope—*for the time*.' And so in the August 1886 number there appeared a short note:

Mr Gladstone presents his compliments to the Editor of the *Nineteenth Century*, and requests, with reference to an observation by Professor Huxley on Mr Gladstone's neglect duly to consult the works of Professor Dana, whom he had cited, that the Editor will have the kindness to print . . . the accompanying letter [from Prof. Dana at Yale, saying]: 'I agree in all essential points with Mr Gladstone, and believe that the first chapters of Genesis and Science are in accord. . . . James D. Dana.'[55]

So there. During the next four years both Gladstone and Huxley took on other themes and other enemies in Knowles's pages (in forty-three articles between them) before they met one another in tournament again.

Two of Gladstone's most celebrated review articles were induced by editorial suggestion. As soon as the government of 1886 was out, Knowles began striking suggestions like matches, until in December one struck a light.

Another idea has occurred to me. . . . Tennyson's new volume is to have a Sequel to Locksley Hall in it—which will be rather a pessimistic view of the drift of things in this Country & elsewhere for the last 50 years or thereabouts. Will you write a review of the book for me— taking—as you must of course take—a hopeful rather than a hopeless view of the same stretch of time & its tendencies? It would be a splendid peg for hanging a 'Jubilee article' upon.

55 *NC*, Aug. 1886, p. 304. Knowles to Gladstone, 12 July 1886 (BL).

This Gladstone agreed at once to do for the January number, and two other suggestions in Knowles's same letter brought articles for February and March. Knowles's own view of Tennyson's poem was ambivalent, as something between a work of art and a literal report of the poet's own loss of faith (as well it could have been so soon after Lionel Tennyson's death). In two further letters Knowles set down a few ideas about the recent progress of the world, the better to set Gladstone off:

surely the growth of Sympathy amongst men—within this last half century—is as Divine a manifestation—(is it not more so?) as any miracle recorded in the Past—If I, for one, were asked the greatest glory & hope of our time—& the thing to be most noted in our Jubilee year—it would be this growth of Sympathy amongst men. . . . [But Tennyson's line] 'Demos end in working its own doom' hardly sounds even Christian does it?

You perhaps see that the Tory papers all praise the poem much more than the others. Alas! that the poison of political partizanship should enter into those fields of Enna—in which Art & Poetry & Literature might live an enchanted life. . . . Thank God—the progress of the world makes it every day more a social than a political question, what best to do with one's life—& others' lives.

There was editorial strategy, not egotism, in thus declaring his own opinions: with such tactful theorizing Knowles might begin a conversation in his own library to start his author thinking —part of the kindling process. When the manuscript of ' "Locksley Hall" and the Jubilee' arrived, Knowles wondered a little— thinking of Tennyson's old line of fifty years before, 'In the Parliament of man, the Federation of the world'—why the article modestly made no reference to Gladstone's own great idea of arbitration between Great Britain and the United States (the Geneva settlement of the *Alabama* claims in 1872). For Gladstone only said of the concept that the poet had seen 'all the way—I fear the immeasurable way—to the great result' of a world parliament. Knowles, for all his patriotism in the matter of channel tunnels, could comprehend some of the supranational quality of Gladstone's mind.[56]

[56] Knowles to Gladstone, 8, 10, 16, 26 Dec. 1886 (BL); and in the last asking if he may keep the MS. (now Add. MS. 43871) published in *NC* Jan. 1887 as ' "Locksley Hall" and the Jubilee'.

During the Golden Jubilee year only two months passed without a Gladstone article in the *Nineteenth*. The years before his
last ministry were indeed an Indian summer of mental vitality,
and it was during these years that editor and author were most at
one—and once, most at odds. Two moments of stress arose in
1887, one that Knowles handled beautifully, and one when
Gladstone floored him completely for a while. These were quite
aside from the moments during many years when the great man
would offer an article and, if Knowles were away or unable to
acknowledge by return of post, would then inquire with a hurt
air if it was, after all, not wanted—moments easily dealt with.
The well-handled difficulty concerned the Greek gods. In conversation during the autumn of 1886, Gladstone had proposed
taking up, in all the detail of which he was capable, five 'Greater
Gods' for an eventual book, if Knowles thought his readers
would like them. 'Poseidon' had been accepted for March, but
in February both proof and the usual reassurances were delayed by
Knowles's winter sojourn at Brighton, so that Gladstone, becoming anxious, let it be known that he was reviewing Greville's
diary for another periodical, which produced the reply:

Pray do not conclude that you need go 'off the rails' again . . . for the
fact that you honor the XIXth Centy as your habitual Tribune in the
Periodical Press is of extreme value to me—& an honor which I most
unwillingly surrender any part of to others . . . indeed I wish you could
consider that you have a sort of retaining fee in the way of a perpetual
petition for any subject you may think it worth while to write upon.
When I next have the pleasure of a talk with you I will suggest several
topics—& endeavour to anticipate other people's kidnapping
adventures.

Asking about the probable extent of the Olympian series,
Knowles said frankly that he would like 'to break its continuity
from time to time by other subjects *from yourself*'. In August, after
three Olympian papers in five months ('broken' by one paper on
another topic in June), Knowles looked thoughtfully at the manuscript for 'Hera' and took up his pen: 'I find that the subject does
not attract my readers sufficiently to make a prolongation of the
series desirable—I believe they would devour . . . anything else
that might interest you—but they cannot be drawn up to the
Olympian heights—I am sorry for them—& I must reluctantly

admit that you yourself were quite right in your prediction on the point.' Gladstone amicably replied that they had better end the series forthwith, and promised an article on Ireland for October, to which Knowles: 'I feel ashamed at taking advantage of your magnanimity about it—but the temptation to give the whole world what it will eagerly read—instead of a corner of the world its amusement—is too much for me.' But still when returning 'Hera' ('so as not to interfere with any other arrangements for her') and sensing that the old man's feelings might be hurt, Knowles remarked reassuringly that such papers had a 'technical & professional interest' not quite suited to the *Nineteenth*: 'So far as I could possibly go I would go—& will go—in that direction— and I have the idea that I can go further than many others. Nobody could be so interested as I am in retaining to the full the central pillar of my temple from the building of it. But I *dare* not go *too far* into this Homeric world.' And 'Hera' appeared in the *Contemporary* the following February.[57]

The misunderstanding that was not amicable concerned, appropriately, Ireland. In the October 1887 number Gladstone reviewed or rather denounced *A History of the Legislative Union of Great Britain and Ireland* by Thomas Dunbar Ingram, an Irish historian who wrote from a strongly Unionist point of view and was sure to be infuriated by his reviewer. Knowles had been publishing articles on various sides of the Irish question for some years, seeking out papers on Home Rule before Gladstone adopted the idea. In its widest sense of local self-government, not only in Ireland, to stem the deluge of business at Westminster (today they call it devolution), Knowles had been proposing the subject to Gladstone in March 1877. In November 1879 he wrote to him: 'I seem to have a feeling that this Irish land question contains still much of real grievance & sorrow, which might perhaps be taken up by the Liberal Party with the effect of obscuring & putting away the sentimental part of the Home Rule cry'; and in February 1880 he was glad to assign to Justin McCarthy the subject of 'The Common Sense of Home Rule' on which Hugh Childers had said he was too lazy to write, and brought out the April issue with McCarthy's second instalment 'in time to influence votes' in the general election. Knowles himself by the end of 1886, like so many men in intellectual and

[57] Knowles to Gladstone, 14 Feb., 7, 10, 16 Aug., 10 Sept. 1887 (BL).

professional circles, was leaning toward Unionism, though he put it to Gladstone diplomatically: 'I am—for one—a Home Ruler—but also a Unionist . . . [one of] the multitude of us who would vote for Home Rule at once when the fear of ultimate separation was taken away from us', though by 1889, the Home Rule idea went 'much against the grain' of 'us Unionists'. Knowles's own abiding view of Ireland was expressed in his will: trust investments for his widow to be made only in England or Wales, not Ireland. The new literary interest of the 1890s in Celtic poetry, a young men's trend, passed the *Nineteenth Century* by. Meanwhile, in October 1887, Gladstone was allowed by Knowles to call Ingram 'this easy-going fabulist', one to whom 'the gift of language seems to have been given in order to hide the truth', with a 'want of all Irish feeling' and a 'blank unacquaintance with Irish history', a man of 'bold inventions' and 'overmastering prejudices'.[58]

Not surprisingly, Ingram wrote a vehement reply, published in December. 'I shall be curious to know what you think of it', said Knowles to Gladstone in November. He was soon to know. For Ingram now accused his critic of 'unveracity'. This was a different sort of warfare from the arguments over Genesis with Huxley. Gladstone could be equable over lack of appreciation for Homer. Accusations of 'unveracity' over Ireland were another matter (and still another the insults he had heaped upon Ingram, apparently). A week of intense letter-writing ensued:[59]

[G to K, 1 Dec.] I was not before aware that the N—— C—— was meant to be the vehicle of language such as [Ingram] employs: in particular of the charge of falsehood, which is the only meaning known to me for the word unveracity! . . . viewing the level to which you have allowed the controversy to descend, and on which I cannot be a party to it, I certainly could not make any reply to you for insertion.

[K to G, 3 Dec.] . . . hurts me to the quick . . . how grieved I am to have passed such a word . . . since it strikes your mind as it does. I had entirely forgotten it. . . . [Reminds G that he magnanimously] rather

---

[58] Knowles to Gladstone, 7 Mar. 1877, 26 Nov. 1879, 16 Feb. 1880, 24 Dec. 1886, 11 Oct. 1889 (BL). Last will, 1904. Gladstone, 'Ingram's *History of the Irish Union*', *NC*, Oct. 1887, pp. 453, 462, 469 ('a denunciation rather than a review', wrote Lord Brabourne in 'A Review of a Review', *Blackwood's*, Nov. 1887).

[59] Gladstone's drafts for his letters to Knowles of 1, 6, 8 Dec. 1887 (one for the 4th missing) are with Knowles's replies of 3, 5, 7, and 8 Dec. 1887 (BL, as chap. 7, n. 50 above).

urged me *not* to interfere with it editorially lest Ingram might complain that he had been mutilated. . . . I considered also that you had yourself . . . hit him very hard. . . . Please recollect how hard it is for me as an Editor to know sometimes how far, in protecting the character of my Review, I am justified in making any writer in it appear more of a gentleman than he may happen to be.

To Gladstone's letter of 4 December defining the one and only meaning of unveracity, Knowles's answer of 5 December was a long, worried brandishing of dictionaries, attempting to distinguish between *in*veracity as falsehood and *un*veracity as only inaccuracy, and continuing:

Fifthly—Although I cannot even on the most careful consideration blame myself for any Editorial lapse in the enforcement of Order upon either side—I repeat my very great personal regret that you should have had any annoyance in the matter. It would be an ill return indeed for the years of kindness you have shown to me and my work not to do my utmost to meet your feeling.

And he asked if Gladstone would like him to insert in the next issue a note signed by himself as editor. To which Gladstone replied on 6 December: 'There would be no use I think in my troubling you further: but I dissent throughout . . . [seven dictionaries] are wholly at variance with you', and such a note letting him appear *in forma querentis* 'would in no degree meet my view', but he hoped it would make no difference whatever 'in our personal relations'. There was then a little argument over Talleyrand's epigram about language concealing men's thoughts, after which communication lapsed for more than two months. The great man's next article on Home Rule followed 'Hera' into the *Contemporary* for March. But at the end of February, during the tense parliamentary session of early 1888, he dined at Queen Anne's Lodge; a day or so later, a copy of 'that wonderful Japanese book on Birds which you admired when dining here' was obtained for him; and it soon appeared that a momentous review article had been discussed.[60]

In March Knowles confirmed his proposal that Gladstone should review for the *Nineteenth Century* Mrs. Humphrey Ward's new novel on the crisis in belief, *Robert Elsmere*. Yet in the same

[60] Knowles to Gladstone, 20, 22 Feb., 3, 16 Mar. 1888 (BL). The Gladstones had just taken No. 10 St. James's Square for the session.

letter, Knowles admitted that, after reading further into 'its exorbitant & egregious length' himself, he doubted whether he would have spoken quite so warmly of the book: 'However, for the sake of its great subject & the very considerable ability of its appreciation of the currents of our time, I still send it to you in the hope that you may think it worth a notice in my Review (which would "make" the author).' So far as making the author's name was concerned, it may be noted that the novel reached a third edition before Gladstone's review came out in May, and that the author's uncle Matthew Arnold, before he died in April, had described to her the members of Lord Pembroke's house-party at Wilton 'all reading it, and all talking of it'.[61] Gladstone was soon putting to Knowles earnest questions about the circumstances and temper of the author, whom Gladstone had not yet met, and so her family connections with the Arnolds and Huxleys and her husband's position as art critic for *The Times* were duly explained. Knowles's personal assessment of her would seem to have been that of a fellow dinner-guest, since she was not writing for him yet:[62]

As to her 'temper', I find this very difficult to answer—She strikes me as very *prim* & rather like a married old-maid in some ways. . . . She evidently has the power of hiding what she really feels—a sort of natural reticence—but her eyes are, as evidently, observing, like quick birds, all that is going on in the ways & feelings of others. . . . I fancy she would take honest & capable criticism well & gratefully & would not only be but feel all the better for it, & like the critic none the less— She easily wakes up to enthusiasm in talk on *subjects*—& in this respect —as in many others reminds me more or less of George Eliot. . . . As to 'her standing'—that I really & honestly think at the present moment rests with yourself. If you can & will expand what you sketch in out-line . . . I believe it will confirm her in a position towards which she is tending in literature—of considerable eminence—if not something even more than that.

This view shows a certain element of Knowles's opinion of intellectual women in general that seems to have reinforced his campaign against female suffrage a year later (however quick he

[61] Knowles to Gladstone, 16 Mar. 1888 (BL). Mrs. Humphrey Ward, *A Writer's Recollections* (1918), p. 235.
[62] Knowles to Gladstone, 2 Apr. 1888 (BL).

was to commission articles from clever women). He thought the book itself 'a new confirmation of the way in which the "enthusiasm of humanity" has got hold of our Century' (and suggested that an article on Savonarola, which he had been unsuccessfully working on Gladstone to write, would make a wonderful pendant to it). A few days after this preparation, Gladstone met Mrs. Ward at Oxford, as described in her *Recollections*, to discuss her hero's stormy way to truth in two intense interviews, 'tremulous with interest and excitement'. During this month before publication, tongues wagged to the *Pall Mall Gazette* that Knowles had privately been begging for the review, and he wrote to Gladstone asking him not to believe that he had had any hand in the rumour. 'Upon principle, & *as a matter of business* I very carefully avoid speaking to anybody about any negotiations or hopes I may have as to forthcoming articles . . . a complete mystery to me where & how these wretched gossip-mongers pick up their miserable crumbs!' Former prime ministers did not discuss best-selling novelists' sense of sin every month in the year.[63]

Meanwhile, in April 1887, Huxley had been dealing with the Duke of Argyll's article in Knowles's March issue. The Duke was proud of his presidency of the British Association a generation before in 1856, but fearful of what he called 'the muddy torrent of bad physics and worse metaphysics which has been rushing past us under the name of Darwinism' since that period. Huxley's urbane essay in demolition caused Knowles to 'gasp in delight' as he read it in proof: 'Poor Duke—he has bearded the lion at last & got his reward.'[64] For Huxley, neither Gladstone nor the Duke of Argyll (any more than the bishops he took on with equal gusto) was a qualified scientific opponent, yet their articulateness and their eminence made them ideal targets in a laymen's periodical (Knowles to Huxley: 'When are you going to take your next shy at the Duke?' and again, 'How about another turn at the bishops?'). But their opposition related to the past. Another sort of adversary appeared a year later, after publication of

[63] 'An Appeal against Female Suffrage', *NC*, June–Aug. 1889. Knowles to Gladstone, 16 Mar., 2 and 9 Apr. 1888 (BL).
[64] Duke of Argyll, 'Professor Huxley on Canon Liddon', *NC*, Mar. 1887. Huxley, 'Science and Pseudo-Science', *NC*, Apr. 1887. Knowles to Huxley, 18 Mar. 1887 (Imperial College).

Huxley's 'The Struggle for Existence' in February 1888, an adversary whose objections had relevance for the future—Peter Kropotkin.

When the Russian geographer, writer, and anarchist Prince Kropotkin returned to England in 1886 after three years in French prisons, he was more famous as an agitator than as a scientist. And during those three years articles by him had been coming out in the *Nineteenth Century*. The first, on Russian prisons, which appeared in January 1883, the month of his trial at Lyons, would have had to be written before his arrest in December; perhaps all four of his Russian-prison series published between then and March 1884 were written in England in 1882. Three more articles that appeared during 1885, on Finland, on a possible Afghan war, and on geography, may have been written in Clairvaux prison. Kropotkin was to tell Lady Knowles after her husband's death that they had first met in 1886. The articles published during 1883–5 must have been obtained through an intermediary, possibly H. M. Hyndman who wrote occasionally for Knowles during 1878–85 and who said later that he had introduced Kropotkin to him. The first article Knowles published by Kropotkin after his release from Clairvaux dealt with French prisons, in March 1886, and thereafter several articles by him appeared in the *Nineteenth* every year. In 1892 Knowles revived for him the 'Recent Science' column, defunct since 1880 when Huxley and Knowles both became too busy to put it together. In December 1894, for instance, Kropotkin summed up the latest research on earthquakes, diphtheria, and flying machines under that heading, and this feature continued to appear one to three times a year until in 1908 Kropotkin told Knowles's successor that he was unable to keep on with it. He had remarked to a friend in 1893 that he was 'writing for a salary on scientific matters, which are frightfully boring to me, and are absorbing my time and annoying me'—like any good popular writing on technical subjects (rarer then than now) it required careful library work, and like all brain-taxing hack-work was both bread-and-cheese and burden.[65]

---

[65] On 'Recent Science' 1877–80, n. 16 above; Kropotkin's letter of 1893, G. Woodcock and Iavakumovic, *The Anarchist Prince* (1950), p. 239. Kropotkin to Lady Knowles, 18 Feb. 1908 (WPL). Hyndman, *Record*, p. 267. Kropotkin to Skilbeck, 20 July 1908, Knowles papers (WPL).

Kropotkin's three best-known books, *Fields, Factories and Workshops* (1899), *Mutual Aid* (1902), and *The Great French Revolution* (1909), germinated as *Nineteenth Century* articles from the latter 1880s on, the last growing from his centenary article on the Revolution in 1889. He needed the money these brought in, but more than that he needed the enthusiastic understanding with which Knowles encouraged him to express his ideas, a support that Knowles was willing to give because Kropotkin was interesting and because his scientific training gave an edge to his writing. Kropotkin's anarchism, becoming in England more intellectual than militant, seemed an acceptable, even glamorous eccentricity in London. For the English serious reading public, the fact that his essay of 1887, 'The Scientific Bases of Anarchy', should appear in the *Nineteenth Century* made writing about anarchy, at any rate, a respectable utopian pastime. Yet, despite Kropotkin's benign, scholarly appearance and quiet life in the suburbs, and his learned contributions to *The Times* and the monthly reviews, the word anarchy was inseparable from the thought of violence. It may be an indication of the breadth of Knowles's sympathies, reinforced by editorial *savoir-faire*, that Kropotkin felt like saying to Knowles's widow: 'I always considered him, notwithstanding our different opinions in some political matters, as one of my best personal friends in England. I always knew that in any hard moment of personal or political life I would find in him . . . a wise, sympathetic adviser.' Kropotkin's aristocratic background may have eased his way here, as well as his newsworthiness and his own qualities.

It is true that, as Frederic Harrison pointed out later, Knowles resolved almost from the start to give the labour movement a fair field. Labour was news. Not every author concerned to help the underdog by writing in the *Nineteenth Century* probably found Knowles personally so warm as Kropotkin did. Beatrice Potter (later Mrs. Webb) did, at first anyway. H. H. Champion, son of an officer and a gentleman, apparently did. Tom Mann and John Burns may not have, partly because they needed help in expressing themselves on paper. Hyndman was not an easy man; Knowles did indeed publish his 'Dawn of a Revolutionary Epoch' in 1881, but by 1890 was privately referring to him as a 'poor fool', one of the Socialists' 'silly tail of sentimentalists', although this was said to Huxley, who did not care for Socialists. If there was something

of the chameleon in Knowles's professional make-up, there was
the independent vein of Surrey iron too. Like most people, he
carried a portmanteau of old opinions along with him. When
in November 1887 he expressed to Gladstone his private contempt
for 'the Democracy', calling the masses on Bloody Sunday in
Trafalgar Square 'an ocean of filthy hyaenas', it was not only the
successful man's fear of the mob but that long line behind him of
self-reliant country-town craftsmen, unsympathetic toward
street-rabble, rick-burners, and the underdogs dealt with by
overseers of the poor. On that frightening Sunday in November,
he walked across the park, perhaps to the roof of Hewlett's office
in Spring Gardens, to hear for himself the masses demonstrating
in support of free speech. As custodian of his own selective 'open
platform', he came as a critical spectator, unlike William Morris
marching in company with his fellows there. Whether or not
Knowles saw some of them clubbed down by the police, the
'outrageous disgrace' to him—or so he put it to Gladstone—was
that 'such miserable scum should shout the sacred name of
Freedom & not be paralysed "out of the blue"'. His self-
employed Reigate ancestors had been trained to shore up,
enhance, and renew existing structures for an existing order.
Knowles senior on his way up can have had little but disdain for
Chartists.[66]

Yet a year before Bloody Sunday, writing to Gladstone in
December 1886 about Tennyson's pessimism as we have seen,
Knowles thought 'the growth of Sympathy amongst men
within this last half-century . . . the greatest glory & hope of our
time'—was this just belated Victorian optimism, mixed with
awareness of Gladstone's cloudy sympathies? It may have been the
loosening of social barriers to professional men and the greater
mingling of the middle and upper classes in Knowles's own career,
rather than sympathy downward, that he partly meant, and
partly the wider availability of education, not least through
periodicals. He had done his bit in 1860 to encourage self-help in
the Acre Lane reading-room, though not in the slums of Westminster when his father-in-law Abraham Borradaile ministered

---

[66] On *NC* a neutral zone for prince and ploughman, F. Harrison, 'Retrospect',
NCA, Oct. 1918, summarizing first 50 vols. 1877–1901. The first two labour
articles in *NC*, by Joseph Arch and George Potter, appeared in January 1878. On
Hyndman, Knowles to Huxley, 20 Jan. 1890 (Imperial College). On Bloody
Sunday, Knowles to Gladstone, 17 Nov. 1887 (BL).

there. As architect to the Flower estates he laid out hundreds of house-plots on new building land for comfortable investors to let to poor (but not too poor) tenants. As a shrewd editor he was running articles on slums well before the *Bitter Cry* pamphlet of 1883, and brought out Beatrice Potter's article on East London dockers' lives two years before the great Dock Strike of 1889. Practical concern for solving obvious problems and editorial concern for balancing his monthly menu prompted him constantly to seek out articles on social troubles. Times were changing, but his nose for news was still sharp. Frederic Harrison lifted matters up 'from the particular to the general' in the way Knowles liked in 'The new Trades-Unionism' written in the immediate aftermath of the Dock Strike:[67]

Thirty years ago the old orthodox Economy was dominant; it received the superstitious veneration of the whole capitalist class. . . . To-day the . . . Gospel, or the Sophism, of Supply and Demand, absolute Freedom for Individual Exertion, and so forth—all this is ancient history. 'We are all Socialists now', cries an eminent statesman [Harcourt] in jest or in earnest. And the jest has earnest in it, if we take Socialism to mean, not the substitution of some communistic utopia for the old institutions of capital and labour, but rather the infusion of all economic and political institutions with social considerations towards social ends.

That generalized attitude (and no more) would seem to have been what an editor with a feeling for his times meant by 'growth of sympathy' and 'more a social than a political question, what best to do with one's life'. Dr. Guinness Rogers discussed 'The Middle Classes and the New Liberalism' in the October 1889 number, Harrison on the new trade unionism opened in November, followed by the Duke of Marlborough on 'The New Tories' and Montague (Cookson) Crackanthorpe on 'The New National Party'; with the vogue for the new-this and the new-that of the early 1890s, Knowles was a bit ahead. Other journalists might tell him in 1891 to join 'the New Journalism' (on the subject of the Elgin Marbles),[68] but on the brink of the 1890s he knew the journalistic strength of the New Radicalism. If his father had foreseen that his son would publish Harrison's remark that Supply and Demand in plain English meant 'May the devil take the

---

[67] Harrison, 'The New Trades-Unionism', *NC*, Nov. 1889, p. 721.
[68] *Anti-Jacobin*, 4 Apr. 1891, a reference from Professor Vogeler.

weakest!' and that this was no longer acceptable to public opinion, one wonders whether the unneeded £2,000 would have been offered.

So when Kropotkin was distressed at the 'survival of the fittest' programme in Huxley's 'Struggle for Existence' article early in 1888, feeling that there is no infamy in civilized society, or in the relations of the whites toward the then so-called lower races, or of the strong toward the weak, which would not find excuse in this Darwinian formula, he was enabled to express himself because 'Two persons only supported me in my revolt against this misinterpretation of the facts of nature.' One of these was H. W. Bate, secretary to the Geographical Society. The other, 'Mr James Knowles, with his admirable perspicacity, at once seized the gist of the matter, and with a truly youthful energy encouraged me to take it in hand', as Kropotkin put it in his memoirs ten years later.[69] Out of that gist came the 'Mutual Aid' articles, seeking to show that co-operation evolved as naturally as competition among animals and men—as the Metaphysical Society's reconcilers in the 1870s would have been glad to hear. These articles were published in the *Nineteenth* during 1890–6. The date of the book which they became, 1902, is sometimes attached to the Mutual Aid theory, but Kropotkin first resolved to treat the idea in the spring of 1888.

Late in 1889, the climate of social questioning following the Dock Strike also induced Huxley to begin for Knowles a series planned as six 'letters to working men'. That title was dropped to 'escape any appearance of incitation' and the four resulting articles were published from January to May 1890. Beforehand Knowles explained to Huxley his principles on the titling of articles:

I especially want working-men to read the [first] paper & I feel sure that [the name] Rousseau or Rouseau-ism . . . would make no impression on most of them—I want to call the article 'On the Natural Inequality of Men' or some such true as well as arresting 'text'—as you know I always like to give the titles to my articles—if only because as Editor I only can guard against their clashing in the same number.

As for Huxley's title for March, 'Capital and Labour' was found to be better as 'Capital the Mother of Labour'—less dry, less

[69] Kropotkin, *Memoirs of a Revolutionist* (1899, reprint 1971), p. 499.

suggestive of 'political economy & all sorts of dull words [which] would repel many who most of all need to read' it.[70]

Huxley's second clash with Gladstone in Knowles's pages arose seemingly spontaneously after long smouldering, over the truth of the New Testament story of the Gadarene swine, the miracle of 'the possessed pigs' as a test of Gospel authority. This time it was less a case of specialized scientific knowledge against layman's knowledge, more a matter of clear thinking *versus* muddled thinking in the treatment of historical evidence. 'My object . . . in the whole business has been to rouse people to think', Huxley told Knowles in April 1889. He had brought this controversy upon himself by referring, in an article on agnosticism ·in February, to the destruction of other people's pigs as a misdemeanour and a bad example, a point immediately taken up by Dr. Henry Wace, Principal of King's College, London, to Huxley's glee:

Wace has given me a lovely opening by his profession of belief in the devils going into the swine. I rather hoped I should get this out of him.

I find people are watching the game with great interest, and if it should be possible for me to give a little shove to the 'New Reformation', I shall think the fag end of my life well spent.

To which Knowles agreed that 'the man who can swallow all that herd of swine & the devils inside them can surely swallow anything, & in the witness-box would be held discredited by the jury'; and was glad that Huxley liked Mrs. Ward's 'New Reformation' dialogue (her answer to Gladstone), Knowles insisting it was only by coincidence that her article appeared in the same (March 1889) number as Wace's: perhaps the 'Stars in their courses are fighting for the new Reformation. Do not you however', said Knowles to Huxley, 'abstain from helping the Stars. If any living man can give it a shove—you can,'[71]

Knowles perhaps helped to bring about the eventual detailed discussion in Huxley's 'Keeper of the Herd' article of December 1890, while reading in proof Huxley's rejoinder to Wace for the April 1889 number. The argument being about agnosticism and belief, could not the details of 'discrepancies in the Swine narratives' be left out? The rejoinder, he thought, would be more

[70] Knowles to Huxley, 13 and 16 Dec. 1889, 19 Feb. 1890 (Imperial College).
[71] Huxley to Knowles, 28 or 29 Feb. 1889 (*Life*, ii. 223, and privately printed version); Knowles to Huxley, 1 Mar. 1889 (Imperial College).

effective without them, after the 'high arguments' preceding them:

You have lifted one up to the real summits of the matter—to such a degree—that the intrusion of the Swine at all . . . is I think to be regretted, as tending to draw a herring across your own great hunt. . . . They are not worth so much, especially at such a crisis, & you have already drowned them over & over again. Think of this editorial & sympathetic criticism with such indulgence as you can. . . . [Hoping] your artistic sense would confirm mine, that the proportions of a picture would be so much better. . . . It is the old story—the secret of Art is to know *what to omit*.

The resulting article concluded with about two pages on 'the Gadarene pig affair': how much detail these were cleansed of is impossible to tell, but they contain the kernel of Huxley's argument a year and a half later. Another little dose of editorial tact tempered Huxley's article on agnosticism for June 1889, with a suggestion that he alter

the illustration of turning the water into wine—which is so sacred in so many eyes—that upon your own right & kind principle of avoiding as much as possible what may hurt good people—I feel sure it had best be passed over.

The greater, as you say, includes the less—but sometimes it *is* much better and kinder to let people find that out for themselves—when once they have got the 'principle' put into them.

To which Huxley agreed, adding: 'I had my doubts, but it was too tempting. All the teetotallers would have been on my side.'[72]

The essays for working men then intervened, early in 1890. As soon as these ended in May, another clerical target offered itself: the old-guard (Tractarian) reaction to a new volume of essays, *Lux Mundi*, written by a group of churchmen anxious to come to terms with the modern world. Huxley's offer of a 'tilt at "Lux Mundi"' for July was welcomed by Knowles with joy. In 'The Lights of the Church and the Light of Science', Huxley pointed out that the question of biblical historical accuracy was just as awkward for the new reconcilers as for the old guard. For the new reconcilers were 'raked alike by the old-fashioned artillery of the Churches and by the fatal weapons of precision with which

---

[72] Knowles to Huxley, 17 Mar., 20 May 1889 (Imperial College). Huxley to Knowles, 22 May 1889 (*Life*, ii. 227).

the *enfants perdus* of the advancing forces of science are armed'. It was the contrasting of weapons of precision with old-fashioned artillery that upset Gladstone, just concluding a series of articles for *Good Words* that were to come out in November as a book, *The Impregnable Rock of Holy Scripture*. As soon as Huxley's *Lux Mundi* article came out in July, Knowles told him that 'Gladstone is in great wrath with you & would I believe go at you if I urged him (which I don't)—& in defence of his own position in "Good Words" '. (This wrath will have been oral as the Gladstones were near by in St. James's Square.) And Knowles asked Huxley to lunch to consult about 'the actual state of the whole campaign'—Huxley's great flow of articles for him being in mid-flood. After Knowles's usual pause for rest and *villegiatura* out of London from mid-August to mid-October, campaign planning was resumed. Space was to be kept for Huxley to review Gladstone's book, promising 'opportunity for some lively hitting', as soon as the book was available. An impatient note came from Huxley in mid-November (misdated 1888 by Knowles later for Huxley's son, but clearly of 1890 from its contents), decorated with one of Huxley's little pen-sketches, of a winged demon riding a leaping pig (Pl. 15), while the reviewer awaited his review copy, duly sent on the 18th. On 27 November, while dealing with Huxley's proof as press-time drew near, Knowles commented that he would have liked to omit—if there had been time to ask Huxley, which there was not—certain concluding references to Gladstone's Home Rule policy, as of dubious Gadarene relevance, feeling that to show political *animus* was to weaken an otherwise overwhelming force of destructive criticism, as the moral was obvious 'without being ticketed so plainly'. For, after briskly dealing with the whole Gadarene dilemma and describing Gladstone's way with it as 'the extreme need of a despairing "reconciler" drowning in a sea of adverse facts', Huxley had unkindly added: 'Mr Gladstone . . . may possibly consider that the union of Gadara with the Decapolis by Augustus was a "blackguard" transaction, which deprived Hellenic Gadarene law of all moral force. . . . I do not agree with him, but leave the matter to the appreciation of those of our countrymen, happily not yet the minority, who believe that the first condition of enduring liberty is obedience to the law of the land'—and he then added insult to injury by quoting Balfour as

Chief Secretary for Ireland on Gladstone's critical methods in the
Parnell crisis. As Knowles went on to say, 'the article is quite a
crusher & I am only sorry that it falls upon him just at the moment
when he is already politically crushed. . . . Mrs O'Shea must be
a strong Unionist!' For that was the month of the O'Shea
divorce-suit revelations and the end of any chance of Irish
reconciliation via Parnell.[73]

Late in December Knowles told Huxley, 'you are to have the
"G.O.M." down upon you in February—He has just written to
say that he has changed his mind about replying to you in
"Good Words" & would prefer to do so in the XIXth', after a
bit of needling apparently. To Gladstone Knowles said he thought
there might be 'several weak places in [Huxley's] line of battle',
and that 'I shall be excessively interested to see if you attack him
at what seem to me to be the weakest points'. (Which didn't
necessarily conflict editorially with expressions used to cheer
Huxley on, 'being myself entirely with you in the controversy',
'anxious to see your position strengthened', and so on, the month
before.) The Duke of Argyll now stepped in with 'Professor
Huxley on the War-Path' in the January 1891 number: 'such a
war-whoop against yourself as will lift your hair up!' Knowles
had told Huxley in December while also mentioning to Gladstone that he had 'forewarned Huxley of it & told him in
the language of the streets "to keep his hair on"'. Hairy
metaphors are not so new as we think. The Duke's article
attacked Huxley's geological attitudes towards a universal Deluge
with such a mixture of geology, religion, and 'diluvial invective'
that little reply was possible, so that he was encouraged to rake up
some more old accusations in the April number: 'I almost
hesitated to publish some of his remarks about you,' said Knowles
to Huxley. 'But I reflected that if he did choose to give himself
away in an access of bad taste & bad temper, it was really more
his affair than anybody's', for this time the arbiter could count

[73] For a summary of the Lux Mundi excitement in the Church of England in
summer of 1890, when Huxley's 'The Lights of the Church and the Light of
Science' (*NC*, July 1890) was only a blast from the sidelines, see Chadwick,
Victorian Church, ii. 101 ff. Knowles to Huxley, 19 May, 8 July, 27 Oct., 27 Nov.
1890 (Imperial College). Huxley to Knowles, 18 Nov. 1890: read as 1888 on copy
printed by Knowles for Leonard Huxley, but referring to Gladstone's *Impregnable
Rock* published Nov. 1890 and offering article that was to appear as 'The Keepers
of the Herd of Swine', *NC*, Dec. 1890; his reference to Home Rule on pp.
978–9 of the article.

upon his favourite not minding what the enemy said. Meanwhile, in February, Gladstone unbent enough to confess that in his book he had accused Huxley of imputation against Jesus instead of only against the New Testament account, before devoting twenty pages to their remaining differences.[74] Five days after publication of that, Huxley's reply was in Knowles's hands for the March issue. Gladstone had held him up in his book for besmirching the character of Jesus, where Huxley had only said he didn't believe a word of the biblical story: and now Gladstone gave an 'offensive travesty' of Huxley's views before making 'attenuated reparation'. But after a bit more on demoniac swine and on political chieftains' controversial methods outside their own field, Huxley proceeded to 'lift matters up from the particular to the general': behind the question as to whether the nineteenth century was to adopt the demonology of the first century lay the whole credibility of the Gospels and 'the prodigious fabric of Christian dogma' built upon them:[75]

We are at the parting of the ways. Whether the twentieth century shall see a recrudescence of the superstitions of mediaeval papistry, or whether it shall witness the severance of the living body of the ethical ideal of prophetic Israel from the carcase, foul with savage superstitions and cankered with false philosophy, to which the theologians have bound it, turns upon their final judgment of the Gadarene tale.

Faced by this tremendous argument Gladstone seemed only to be bothered by the thought that his apology for misrepresenting his opponent might have been shabby. To which Knowles replied:

It is impossible for me not to answer quite frankly your magnanimous question about the 'apology' made in your February article . . . it did strike me as *grudging* . . . and I delight in your desire to make it more ample & hearty—which only a noble controversialist would do. Of course it was a tremendous imputation & one which must have made Huxley feel very sad . . . such a stigma from yourself must have been very wounding.

[74] Knowles to Huxley (in order of reference), 31 Dec., 27 Nov., 9 Dec. 1890, 26 Mar. 1891 (Imperial College). Knowles to Gladstone, 29 Dec. 1890 (BL). Argyll, 'Professor Huxley on the War-path', *NC*, Jan. 1891; Gladstone, 'Professor Huxley and the Swine-Miracle', *NC*, Feb. 1891; Argyll, 'Professor Huxley and the Duke of Argyll', *NC*, Apr. 1891.
[75] Huxley, 'Illustrations of Mr Gladstone's Controversial Method', *NC*, Mar. 1891, p. 466.

And he suggested a short letter for the April number, where its two dignified paragraphs followed and contrasted with five irritable pages from the Duke of Argyll. As Knowles pointed out to Huxley, it showed Gladstone 'as really great-natured for all his faults & sins . . . the sort of thing which always wins me to his personality, however much I may resist his politics'. The final comments were Huxley's, in a postscript to his article in the June number: Gladstone was gracefully thanked with a gentle allusion to 'the misadventures which arise when, as sometimes will happen in the heat of fence, the buttons come off the foils'; and the Duke, for having used the 'products of defective knowledge, multiplied by excessive imagination', received quite as much correction as was good for him.[76]

In Huxley's campaign for clear thinking there was one more foray, three months before he died in June 1895. 'Since you have forsaken the Constable's Beat,' Knowles wrote encouragingly in February, 'the loose characters of thought have plucked up too much courage.' Only the first half of a long review of Balfour's recent book *The Foundations of Belief* was ever published, as 'Mr Balfour's Attack on Agnosticism' in the March issue. Knowles was unable to persuade Huxley's widow that the un-corrected proof of the second half should be published as it had been left before illness closed in. But there was no unpleasantness in the refusal and the affection between Knowles and the Huxleys is obvious in a correspondence that continued (not on that subject) until Knowles's death.[77]

Royalty also found Knowles's tilting ground useful. In 1897 he gave an airing to the issue of Schleswig–Holstein: 'Europe's lucifer match' (or one of them), that thick neck between Denmark and Germany where the Kiel Canal linking the Baltic to the North Sea had been opened in 1895 (when Gladstone watching the parade of German ships murmured 'this means war'). In the May 1897 number appeared 'The Schlesweg–Holstein Question

---

[76] Knowles to Gladstone, 12 Mar. 1891 (with which, in Add. MS. 44232, is Gladstone's revised draft of 18 March for letter published in April *NC*, p. 690. Huxley, 'Hasisadra's Adventure', *NC*, June 1891, postscript, pp. 924–6.

[77] Knowles to Huxley, 9 Feb. and five other letters Feb.–Mar. 1895; to Mrs. Huxley, 16, 20 Aug., 11 Oct. 1895 on this subject, eleven others to her 1897–1908, and three to Leonard Huxley 1898–9 (Imperial College). Huxley to Knowles, Feb.–Mar. 1895: 3 telegrams, 9 letters (7 quoted in the *Life*, ii. 398–400) printed by Knowles for Leonard's use as n. 46 above.

and its Place in History' by Max Müller, who wrote fairly often
for Knowles, and with a head-note saying that it had been
'submitted to and approved by the highest possible authority
upon the facts, who vouches for the correctness of this version of
them'. The authority was Prince Christian, husband of the
Queen's daughter Princess Helena—as confirmed by seven letters
from them in Knowles's papers.[78] The Prince's brother was Duke
Frederick of Schleswig–Holstein, who had joined Germany
against France in 1870, and whose daughter was married to Kaiser
Wilhelm II. Müller, living in Naples, waived seeing proofs and
left their correction to Prince Christian, whose letter of thanks to
Knowles for all his interest—and luncheon at Queen Anne's
Lodge—rather implies that the article had been commissioned at
the Prince's suggestion.

And so there appeared in the December number 'The Danish
View of the Slesvig–Holstein Question' by A. D. Jorgensen, late
historian and keeper of the state archives of Denmark, and headed
thus: 'The following reply to Professor Max Müller's article in
the May number of this Review is published at the desire of an
exalted Personage in this country, interested in the Danish side of
the question, who considers that Professor Max Müller's views
are incorrect and inconsistent with historic truth. The author died
before he saw the proofs, which have been submitted to and
approved of by the same exalted Personage.' The personage was
the Princess of Wales, daughter of Christian IX of Denmark, son
of a previous Duke Frederick of that controversial territory—that
is, she was Prince Christian's first cousin as well as sister-in-law.
Proof-sheets stamped 'Second Revise' remaining in Knowles's
papers were obviously corrected by her (rare though surviving
letters from Alexandra now are, several short notes from the
years 1884–99, in a handwriting like partly unravelled knitting,
also remain in Knowles's papers for comparison).[79] The corrections here consist mainly of altering Schleswig to Slesvig and
removing the word 'pro-German' for Müller's views as empha-
sizing the obvious. The article itself vigorously concluded that
Müller's paper was 'a slap in the face to the whole Scandinavian
race' and that according to him both the Prince and the Princess
of Wales were Germans, but that it was doubtful if 'the English

[78] Knowles papers, WPL.
[79] Knowles papers, WPL.

nation will relish the idea that the next heirs to the throne of Great Britain are Germans!' Anti-German feeling was already growing in England. There also remain a series of letters of October and November from Francis Knollys of the Household: the Princess' name had better not appear, but the heading 'can be made as *pointed* as you like'. And Knowles was invited to spend the last weekend in November at Sandringham—as reward for arrangements that had no doubt begun in conversation at Marlborough House.[80] Thus in 1897 he acted as umpire between the Danish branch and the German branch of the Royal Family, and it will be noted that his eventual knighthood from Edward VII was the KCVO, which is given for service to the sovereign.

MISUNDERSTANDINGS WITH THE TENNYSONS AND OTHERS

> 'Whom the Gods love, die young, the proverb told;
> The meaning is—they never can grow old;
> However long their list of labours past
> God-given youth is with them to the last.'
> Lines made by Knowles in August 1890 for
> Tennyson and Gladstone, in Knowles to Gladstone,
> 28 September 1890, BL

In the late summer of 1890 for two months, Knowles took Holmbury, Frederick Leveson Gower's house with beautiful views near Leith Hill in Surrey; renting a furnished country house in one of the southern counties being his frequent habit for the annual family holiday. Tennyson came over from Aldworth for two nights in August, just past his 81st birthday, himself in an Indian summer 'wonderful in vigour', as Knowles described it to Gladstone:[81]

[80] Knowles papers, WPL. During this visit to Sandringham, the Princess gave Knowles a small painting, a seascape signed 'Alix' (note of gift and date in Knowles's hand on the back), still in his family's possession.

[81] Knowles to Gladstone, 28 Sept. 1890 (with spelling 'Labors'); poem sent to Gladstone again on request 25 Apr. 1891, dedicated 'primarily to Tennyson, Watts, & yourself', with spelling 'labours' (BL). Knowles to Huxley, 17 Sept. 1890, also praised Holmbury 'where we are making our "villegiatura" . . . in the midst of the loveliest country in the S. of England' (Imperial College); 'I can just make out Aldworth windows through a telescope from here,' he told Hallam Tennyson, 12 Aug. 1890 (TRC).

He walked all round & to the top of Holmbury Hill—up to the
Roman Camp & straight down that excessively steep declivity which
falls from the Camp down as it were on to the roofs of this House—
and this just after a heavy rain which made all the ground slippy!
And he told me poems which he has made within the last week or two
fresh and lovely as he wrote at 35!!

On the Saturday, the Poet Laureate read aloud or rather chanted
'The Passing of Arthur', and next day also 'The Lady of Shalott',
as recorded by Beatrice Knowles in her copy of the 1880 edition
of his poems ('Read by the Bard on August 23rd . . . on Sunday
August 24, 1890 at Holmbury). It was a friendly summer, for in
early July Tennyson and his elder son had spent several nights
with the Knowleses in London—the poet reading aloud part of
Maud (fourth stanza, part two, according to Beatrice's note) 'at
Queen Anne's Lodge . . . when the Duchess of Teck came'
(between 12 and 1 on her way to open a home for Bryant & May
match-girls, according to the Duchess's note to Knowles on the
4th). And also on one day Tennyson read the Sleeping Beauty
section of 'The Day-Dream' to Lady Brownlow and Lady
Pembroke after he had looked at Burne-Jones's 'Briar Rose'
paintings of the subject at Agnew's.[82]

During that July visit in 1890 occurred the touching meeting
between the two grand old men at Queen Anne's Lodge, after
Tennyson refused at first to meet the author of Home Rule.
Sir Charles Tennyson, writing about his grandfather in 1954,
placed this meeting in 1886 (perhaps partly because Gladstone
wrote to Tennyson explaining his view on Home Rule in April
1886, or partly because someone, Hallam or Knowles, mis-
remembered; April was the month when Lionel Tennyson died,
and although Tennyson did come to stay with Knowles that July,
Gladstone was then busy with the demise of his government).
Lady Tennyson's letter of 7 July 1890 summed it up: 'Mr
Gladstone being very anxious to see my Ally who however did
not dine downstairs but Mr Gladstone went up and brought him

---

[82] *Tennyson's Works*, published by Kegan Paul 1880, inscribed probably in her
father's hand, 'Beatrice Isabel Knowles from her loving Papa & Mamma Xmas
1880' when she was 14; pencilled in, here and there, notes on readings 'By the
Bard' in 1887 and 1890 at Queen Anne's Lodge and Holmbury, and on verso of
frontispiece a signed photograph of Tennyson (book in Beatrice's daughter
Eirene Skilbeck's possession until her death in 1969, since lost). Duchess of Teck
to Knowles, 3 and 4 July 1890 (WPL).

down after dinner and was very delightful.' And they spent the rest of the evening talking of Homer and Browning. Queen Anne's Lodge with its pleasant atmosphere, its pictures and other works of art—but not so many books, oddly enough—was a place of reconciliation in 1890.[83]

Tennyson still usually gave Knowles new volumes of his poems as they came out, as late as April 1892 (*The Foresters*). In the *Nineteenth Century* Knowles had published four of Tennyson's poems in 1877 and one each year from 1878 to 1883, with then a gap until the late sonnet for the Duke of Clarence in the February 1892 issue; Tennyson's Jubilee poem for April 1887 went to *Macmillan's Magazine* and Knowles had one from Swinburne (who now became his most constant poet, besides writing some good prose criticism for him). The summer of 1882 may have been the last time Knowles was invited to stay with the Tennysons ('if you *can* come you will make us happy'). Hallam remarked in 1883 that in London his father most liked to stay at the Deanery with the Bradleys; on his last visits to London in 1891 and 1892, however, he stayed with G. L. Craik, editorial manager of Macmillan's, by then publishing his books. But Tennyson with Hallam did stay at Queen Anne's Lodge in July 1886, with excursions to the theatre and the Colonial Exhibition to distract his sadness. And according to Beatrice Knowles's note, there was also a visit to Queen Anne's Lodge in October 1887, when the Bard read the 'Ode on the Death of the Duke of Wellington' and 'Boadicea' aloud by request. At some time, according to family legend, there was a play-reading there by Henry Irving and Ellen Terry of *Becket*, when Ellen Terry 'wept buckets'. Knowles's last period of acting as Tennyson's man of business had been in the autumn of 1875, smoothing the way with Irving and Mrs. Bateman and the lawyers for performance of *Queen Mary*. Thereafter, Hallam took over. Hallam seemed to honour Knowles as an influential man and his senior, calling on him on 17 December 1889, as Knowles reported to Gladstone, 'to thank me for my little letter in "the Times" today', in which Knowles urged that Mrs. Browning's remains should be brought back from Italy to rest beside her husband in Westminster Abbey. Tennyson's last

[83] Sir Charles Tennyson, *Six Tennyson Essays* (1954), p. 68. Emily Tennyson to Anne Weld, 7 July 1890, *The Letters of Emily Lady Tennyson*, ed. J. O. Hoge (1974).

stay at Queen Anne's Lodge was the one in July 1890. Knowles may have entertained him briefly in the summer of 1891 in a crowd of guests; a year later Knowles himself was convalescing at the seaside. The last happy meeting in the old warm way, without other guests, besides Hallam, will have been the visit to Holmbury in August 1890.[84]

In October 1892 Tennyson died at Aldworth. At the funeral in the Abbey, the great men who were his pallbearers did not include Knowles. But he was already busy gathering poetical tributes for his December number. We have the corrected proof-sheets for seven poems, by Huxley, F. W. H. Myers, Roden Noel, F. T. Palgrave, Aubrey de Vere, Theodore Watts, and Knowles (though not for Swinburne's which appeared in January). These poems in December, though heartfelt, are of the cloudy cloying kind and not very good, save for a few lines of Huxley's poem (the Abbey speaking: 'Bring me my dead!/. . . And lay him gently down among . . ./The thought-worn chieftains of the mind:/Head servants of the human kind') and some lines in Knowles's poem, called 'Apotheosis', imagining—of all the Gladstonian notions—the Greek gods descending into Westminster Abbey, and concluding:

> Great Bard, dear Friend! thy welcome by the gods
> Is our sole comfort for the loss of thee;
> They will be happier in their golden clime
> And Heaven, when we reach it, more like Home.

He did, at least, have a sense of form and of direct speech (and marked up twelve proof-sheets before he got it right). He added a footnote that Tennyson would have relished: 'As the grave was being hewn out of the hard rock-like foundations of the Abbey, it was filled continually with sparks of fire struck from the stone and flint.' A week after the funeral, Knowles wrote to Mrs. Huxley: 'Last night I dreamed that the dear & grand old Bard came to me "from the region of his rest"—greater better stronger & more loveable than even in life—and talked with me as a man talketh with his friend. It was quite a lift & comfort to me.'[85]

[84] On *The Foresters*, Knowles to Tennyson, 1 or 2 Apr. 1892 (TRC). Beatrice Knowles, note (as n. 82) 1887. On Mrs. Browning, Knowles to Gladstone, 17 Dec. 1889 (BL).

[85] Proof-sheets of poems published Dec. 1892, Knowles papers (TRC), accounting for pp. 831–44 missing from *WIVP*. Knowles to Mrs. Huxley, 19 Oct. 1892 (Imperial College).

'Aspects of Tennyson, No. II' appeared in the *Nineteenth Century* in the January 1893 number (with other instalments by various authors in December, February, March, May, and October), this one being 'A Personal Reminiscence' by Knowles, cut down before publication, of which the longer version survives in proof. Knowles proudly sent two copies of the January number to the second Lord Tennyson and his now 80-year-old widowed mother. There was an immediate reaction: they were very upset. The precise wording of an angry letter Hallam sent Knowles can only be surmised from a series of half-drafted replies in Knowles's papers. Hallam as now the only son wished to be first biographer. He regarded some of the material Knowles had used as family property. The article was indeed personal, and it had come out rather smartly for an age—in the more dignified periodicals at least—less used to personal instant-journalism than we are. Lord Tennyson and Knowles managed to shake hands at the Lyceum Theatre in February, after a performance of *Becket*, but the feelings that erupted in January must have been long coming, to judge by letters from both sides. Lady Tennyson writing to relations on 15 February (in a letter imperfectly published in 1974), defined the family attitude:

We don't think that it is treachery in Mr Knowles but simply that there are such defects in his character that he is not conscious that it is treachery.

He is the cleverest man we any of us have known—with that sort of cleverness which can adapt itself to the moods of men or work upon them in differing moods—'Ma non ragionam'.

He has been hospitable & kind in his way & both Hallamee & I are glad that he shook hands with him coming out of the Lyceum the other evening—for we must forget the grievous wrong he has done & try to repair it as best we may, must we not?

Or, to paraphrase Dante (*Inferno*, III. 51), let us not speak of such people.[86] The handshake at least muted the unpleasantness of Hallam's initial charges of illegal conduct and his refusal to answer

[86] Proof-sheets for Knowles's article, under correction Dec. 1892, are with his papers at TRC; also drafts, Knowles to 2nd Lord Tennyson. Lady Tennyson to Anne and Agnes Weld, 15 Feb. 1893 (TRC): comparison of photocopy of original with version in Hoge's 1974 edn. (n. 83) shows several discrepancies. By '(ma) non ragionam . . . di lor ma guarda e passa', Dante meant 'Let us not speak of these . . . but look and pass' (for help with this line I am grateful to Dr. A. G. Alessio of the University of Leicester).

Knowles's indignant replies. Someone had offered to mediate between them, possibly Dean Bradley, although the Deanery was near enough not to need the letters to an unknown mediator for which furious drafts survive in Knowles's papers: Hallam 'the greediest and most jealous of small-minded men . . . was always miserably jealous of his great Father's affection for me' and so on.[87]

Nothing is sourer than old hurt feelings, but at least these dim pencillings do tell the nub of the trouble: Knowles's publication, with his article, of 'The Dolorous Stroke' prose draft for 'Balin and Balan' dictated to him in 1872—surely not even Hallam could suppose that was 'copyright property belonging to him!' He might just as well 'lay claim to all the notes on his poems which the Bard from time to time dictated to me—avowedly for me to make public use of in explanation of passages in his poems which I individually asked him to clear up'. For the Bard had co-operated in this note-taking, not only in aid of Knowles's preface of 1868, his *Spectator* article of 1870, and his *Contemporary Review* article of 1873 on the *Idylls*, but in allowing notes to be taken on conversations ranging over all the poems. As Dr. Gordon Ray has observed, with Knowles's jottings before him, we come very close to Tennyson in them. Whether Knowles was justified in being quite so quick off the mark in releasing both the 'Balin' draft and the sheaf of precious hoarded commentaries on *In Memoriam* that he put into his article, is now hard to judge, or the precise amount of special pleading in the statement that 'I was the first man Hallam asked to help him about his Father's life . . . [and] I put at his service all that I myself might say in the XIXth, and much more . . . not yet published.' Matters lapsed until a chance meeting at Marlborough House in 1896, after which it was apparently grudgingly arranged between them that Knowles should furnish some material in privately printed form for Hallam's use; e.g. two leaflets which Knowles prepared, one on *The Idylls of the King* and one on the Metaphysical Society, from which, in the end, Hallam quoted sparingly (because Knowles gave him no original papers, only printed versions vouched for by himself; the little 'Balin' draft has remained in Knowles's

---

[87] Drafts in Knowles papers (TRC), one starting 'It is very kind of you to offer to bring poor Hallam to a better & friendlier state of mind as regards myself. But I think it would be quite hopeless.' Numerous drafts for Knowles's article also remain.

papers until now, when it goes at last to Lincoln). A letter which
Knowles had printed in the *Idylls* leaflet for Hallam, written by
Tennyson to Knowles on 5 April 1872 about 'Gareth', did get into
a footnote (*Memoir*, ii. 113n.) without the introductory explanation: '. . . he was so anxious about misprints that, for greater
security against errors, he caused the proofs of them to be sent
to me as well as to himself', and so on. A more significant
omission from the *Memoir* was 'The Christ at Ammergau' poem
printed in the *Idylls* leaflet, having been cut from the 1893 article.
Perhaps Hallam omitted it (one is only guessing) because its use
was hedged about with covenants by Knowles, in whose hand the
dictated manuscript was written and in whose hands it remained.
In 1955 Knowles's granddaughter found it (now at Lincoln) in
his papers and with the Tennyson family's permission published
it in the *Twentieth Century*: a bitter poem, suited to the twentieth
century, 'chanted out in his great voice . . . quite impromptu' on
the fourth floor in Victoria Street in 1870. The poem in privately
printed form was lying among the Tennyson family papers from
about 1896.[88]

The article of 1893 was reverent without being obsequious,
and no loyal humorous family need have objected to it—but
families are seldom humorous in such situations. More communication beforehand would have been far more seemly, but
Knowles apparently acted on the supposition that that would
stop him entirely, and a bit of journalist's ruthlessness seemed
called for. This was *his* knowledge of Tennyson and he wanted
people to know it was his. Full of Tennyson's relaxed comments
on life and poetry, the article was more literately and perceptively
written than the family *Memoir* eventually assembled and pub-

[88] 'The Dolorous Stroke' (chap. 7, n. 44 above) published with Knowles's
article (*NC*, Jan. 1893, pp. 175–80), then in Hallam Tennyson's *Memoir* (1897, ii.
134–41). Most of pp. 182–7 of the 1893 article consist of Tennyson's comments,
drawn out by Knowles, on *In Memoriam*. On earlier authorized note-taking,
chap. 6, n. 9. Pair of four-page leaflets (*c.* 1896) on *Idylls* and Metaphysical Society
prepared and privately printed by Knowles for Hallam (rather than give up
original material), copies at TRC and in Knowles papers. 'The Christ at
Ammergau': unpublished proof-sheets for 1893 article (n. 86); *Idylls* leaflet p. 3;
Twentieth Century (1955), CLVII. 2–3; Ricks, p. 1220. Knowles to 2nd Lord
Tennyson, 2 Nov. 1896 (TRC), with notes for peaceable reply on the back. Dr.
Ray's acute observations on Knowles's annotated copy of the *Poems* (vol. iv,
1872) in his possession were delivered in his Sedgewick Memorial Lecture at
the Univ. of Brit. Columbia, Vancouver (1968), kindly shown me by Prof. Philip
Collins.

lished in 1897. To be sensitive enough to get under the skin of a poet meant inevitably being sensitive enough to mind terribly the fuss that resulted. Knowles said to Huxley in May 1893, with regard to a proposed monument at Freshwater, 'The children of his mind were not of clay—& when he died—the clay part of his family lost its charm for me.'[89] He knew that they had found him tiresome for a long time. And equally he knew that the Bard, most of the time, had not found him so. Family appreciation, mixed with understanding amusement, for Knowles's contribution to Tennyson's work had to wait for Tennyson's grandson.

And so it was a tense time during the early 1890s in Knowles's early 60s, partly due to the Tennyson imbroglio, partly to confusion in his own editorial office, and partly to trouble with his health, to which he was ever attentive. His faithful assistant George Robson died in the autumn of 1890. Walter Frewen Lord, a journalist who in 1888 had married Millicent Knowles, then attempted to step in; it was unkindly said elsewhere in the family that he had aimed from the first to be the editor's heir but could not provide the selfless handling of details required by his exacting father-in-law, with whom he did not get on. In February 1891 Knowles bemoaned to Huxley the muddle caused by his own regular winter stay at Brighton after Christmas. For two years around this time it is said that Henry Hyde Champion, socially acceptable as a major-general's son for all his sometime socialist opinions, served as Knowles's sub-editor (not assistant editor, for on the *Nineteenth Century* there was no such creature) possibly in the publisher's office—from mid-1891 Sampson Low Marston in Fetter Lane—or at Spottiswoode the printer's, whose reader 'has never yet I think failed me' in the matter of corrections, Knowles told Huxley in November 1890. One can only say that first Robson—followed briefly and clumsily by Lord—and finally Skilbeck filled the position of what Knowles liked to call his secretary at Queen Anne's Lodge.[90]

[89] Knowles to Huxley, 2 May 1893 (Imperial College).
[90] Knowles already referring to 'my secretary' in February 1886 to Huxley. On Robson's death, RIBA records. On Lord, family information; he continued to contribute to the NC. On Champion, W. Kent, *John Burns* (1950), pp. 24, 52, quoting Burns's diary for 2 Jan. 1892 on Champion installed (but not where; one doubts that Burns dropped in to see him at Queen Anne's Lodge); *WIVP*, ii. 625, citing *The Times* obituary 1928 ('sub-editor . . . just before going to Australia'), makes him 'assistant editor' 1890–1 and 1892–3: the English journalist's term sub-editor is not always clear in America.

William Wray Skilbeck had been at Trinity College, Cambridge, with Arthur Knowles in the 1880s. He was born at Surbiton, his father a solicitor with City connections, his mother a Donaldson from Edinburgh, his first cousins on her side eventually including a general, a bishop, and a master of a Cambridge college. Skilbeck was a large, tall man, capable and sensible: an obituarist describing Knowles as 'rather a frail man, under the middle height', added that he 'therefore took to big muscular Christians' who afforded him 'a sense of protection'. Skilbeck married Beatrice Knowles in May 1894, having served as Knowles's secretary for about three years first. Years later he described to his daughter how his heart would sink, after a hard editorial day with his father-in-law, on arriving home to find his mother-in-law's carriage standing before his own door: Isabel Knowles, after running her husband's demanding household since 1865, had her way of being exacting. Skilbeck found his protection in a good sense of humour. When he succeeded Knowles in the editorial chair, he made it very much his own during the eleven years until his death early in 1919.[91]

Knowles explained his shaky health to Gladstone (in January 1890 when he was 58 and Gladstone was 80):

If ever you reach my age—which I doubt your doing on account of your inveterate youth—you may come to know how precarious is some men's tenure of strenth—I am able . . . to get through the work which 'cometh to me daily'—but the margin left over seems to grow smaller—& especially at this time of year & under the malign influences of cold & darkness—so much so that it is always doubtful whether I can undertake a long journey until the actual time for taking it arrives.

It was usually pretty much a case of over-expense of nervous energy with him, but in December 1891 he came down with typhoid—then a fashionable disease—with 'nearly 2 months in bed', and in June 1892 hired Lord Chichester's country house, Enbrook at Sandgate near Folkestone, for a few weeks on doctor's advice rather than go through the London Season. At some time in 1893, perhaps in September, he seems to have had a very slight stroke: the only witness is an undated note among his papers, until recently attached to a pad of notes that relate to the prospect

[91] Information from his daughter, her cousin Cuthbert Skilbeck, and obituaries *NC* 1919, pp. 201, 595–608 (Moreton Frewen on muscular Christians, p. 600).

of a maid's giving notice on 2 October and to the *Nineteenth*'s menu for October 1893 and after. In rough block letters the note reads: TURN ME ON MY RIGHT SIDE SEND FOR DR MACLAGAN ALSO FOR JOHN HOPGOOD I THINK CLEARLY BUT CANNOT PRONOUNCE ANY WORDS GET ME AN ALPHABET OF LARGE LETTERS & A POINTER SO THAT YOU MAY FOLLOW WHAT I SPELL. It is not a death-bed note, for Knowles outlived his solicitor by six years and then died too suddenly to write notes. It is touchingly practical, his mind darting to the parlour-game cardboard letters as a medium for communication. His next appearance was in a perky note to Huxley on 14 November, saying he had been out of town, so the seizure was not serious.[92] He soon had a son-in-law to lean on, or rather to direct, and from then on it seems that he loved his life and rode it calmly for fourteen years more.

In the 1890s, as a man of strong feelings who had safely arrived in a position of influence and could so afford to vent them occasionally to his friends, Knowles had several *bêtes noires* besides the second Lord Tennyson (who really deserved the dislike far less than some of the others). One of the *Nineteenth*'s staunchest authors, Frederic Harrison, became one briefly for advocating the return of the Elgin Marbles to Greece: Knowles published this article in December 1890 and a reply by himself the following March, meanwhile expressing his feelings privately to two trustees of the British Museum ('sentimentalist rubbish . . . a rhetorician about Art—not a *lover* of it . . . a sinful breach of trust to . . . send to a place which may be eaten up in the great Eastern complications any day!' to Gladstone in January; 'what do such jackanapeses troubling & tomfooling about among those glorious gods' to Huxley in March). Harrison in great annoyance replied in the *Fortnightly*, concluding that Huxley must have written Knowles's article ('His yells are fearful! But he pays me the greatest compliment I ever received . . . [he] believes *you* wrote *my* article!'). Harrison then abstained for three years from the *Nineteenth Century* to which he nevertheless peaceably then returned.[93]

There were various peripheral *bêtes noires* such as the journalist

---

[92] Knowles to Gladstone, I Jan. 1890, 9 Feb., 23 June 1892 (BL). Knowles papers (WPL). Knowles to Huxley, 14 Nov. 1893 (Imperial College).
[93] Harrison, 'Give Back the Elgin Marbles', *NC*, Dec. 1890. Knowles to Gladstone, I Jan. 1891 (BL); to Huxley, 4 and 26 Mar. 1891 (Imperial College).

W. T. Stead, especially and understandably for his new digestive *Review of Reviews*, as in Knowles's letter to Huxley in January 1890:[94]

That filthy ex-convict Stead, I see, states publicly that he obtained your approval of the précis which he made for his stolen-goods truck the 'Review of Reviews' before he published it—I will not trust myself to say what I think & feel about the incredible impudence of this unconscionable cad in all his ways & works . . . filching my copyright . . . [your approval] struck out of my hand one of the chief weapons I could have used to protect myself against this indiscriminate pirate, by invoking the law . . . [for] living upon other people's brains.

But Knowles's chief *bête noire* in the mid-1890s was Canon Malcolm MacColl the contentious pamphleteer, a bull-dog Scot, below middle height like Knowles but with a massive head, a man of immense energy and enthusiasm, an admirer of Gladstone, fond of being on confidential terms with great men and of being a private go-between on great questions, loving a fight: it was foregone that Knowles should dislike him. 'Your ferocious little Canon . . . a pocket Torquemada' he called him to Gladstone when planning a set of articles on the 'Eastern Question' (MacColl's speciality) for the *Nineteenth*'s December 1895 number. Knowles told Gladstone in October that 'I have really been compelled to decline him as a combatant in my pages, out of respect for the Queen's peace in India & elsewhere', but decided instead to print the correspondence between MacColl and himself at the end of the December issue. ('He can't differ without difference of temper [a tendency that] already needs repressing . . . in my own case', Knowles had said of a travelling companion in 1854.)[95]

Revelations in September 1896 of more Turkish massacres of Armenian Christians brought out all of Knowles's old campaigning spirit, it was like old times in 1877 when both Tennyson and Gladstone had written on oppressed Montenegro for him and

---

[94] Knowles to Huxley, 20 Jan. 1890 (Imperial College).
[95] Knowles to Gladstone, 17 Oct. 1895 (BL); 'Canon MacColl on Islam: a correspondence', *NC*, Dec. 1895. On George Herbert in 1854, Knowles to Hewlett from Florence as chap. 3, n. 57. On MacColl, G. W. E. Russell, ed., *Malcolm MacColl, Memoirs and Correspondence* (1914). Sir Algernon West, for one, did not 'value very highly' MacColl's authority for a story, and general indignation with MacColl 'was pleasant hearing' to him (*Private Diaries*, ed. H. G. Hutchinson, 1922, pp. 316, 331).

even MacColl had reserved his spleen for the Turks. On 7 September, from a holiday hotel at Tunbridge Wells, Knowles sent a trumpet-call of a telegram to Hawarden: 'If I can get up symposium against that assassin the Sultan for next Nineteenth would you open it by a page of denunciation and appeal I am asking Swinburne for a furious sonnet against him but you only can be Peter the Hermit to a final Crusade against the Turk.' Gladstone wired back willingly, in the spirit of Tenniel's *Punch* cartoon, 'Who said Atrocities?' But, on the 11th, Swinburne wrote to Watts-Dunton: 'My *dear* Walter What *can* our worthy friend Knowles be thinking of?... *I* enter myself... for the anti-Turkish cursing-and-swearing stakes!' (William Watson was already contributing quite enough anti-Turkish verse to the *Spectator*), so no furious sonnet. By the 17th Knowles was assembling a set of symposiasts for his October number: Guinness Rogers for the Nonconformists, Lord Meath for the 'conservative philanthropists', John Burns for the radicals, and Anthony Salmoné, professor of Arabic at King's College, London, for the 'young Turkey party', with Gladstone's 'malediction to wind up with' so that there would be 'tempests of talk & hurricanes of hysteria', Knowles prophesied happily. On 24 September, Gladstone speaking as an individual delivered a great speech at Liverpool against the Sultan, his last public speech. Next day he told MacColl that he had based some of his article for Knowles, without specifying his source, on information MacColl had got for him from Lord Salisbury, then Prime Minister. The cause of the Armenian revolutionaries and the Young Turks was furthered a little. And MacColl abused Knowles roundly to Gladstone in ruder and less literary terms than Knowles had used of him.[96]

It was Gladstone's last article for Knowles, but they exchanged pleasant letters in December, and in May 1897 the old man sent Knowles his latest volume of *Gleanings*, largely consisting of articles he had written for the *Nineteenth Century* as had been true of earlier volumes. Knowles then wrote to him in May with a request for a few words of homage to the Queen on her Diamond Jubilee for his June issue: 'There is no other subject of the Queen

[96] Knowles to Gladstone, telegram 7 Sept., letters of 17, 22, 26 Sept. 1896 (BL). Swinburne to Watts-Dunton, 11 Sept. 1896, Lang, ed. vi. 114. Russell, ed., *MacColl* (n. 95), correspondence with Gladstone, Sept.–Oct. 1896.

—nay no other living Man—who could propose such a "Senti-
ment" (as our Grandfathers would have called it) with such
absolute & unique & appropriate Grace.'[97] Gladstone had last
seen the Queen at Cannes in March when she was not gracious.
Knowles should have sensed what their relations were; at any
rate, nothing came of this request. A year later, the last of
Knowles's great Victorian war-horses was gone.

TURN OF THE CENTURY: *AND AFTER*

> 'By & bye the artists & prophets will arise, and show
> us that—as Tennyson once said to me—"Poetry is a
> great deal truer than fact"—We are all now busy
> trying to discover & tell each other what the facts
> are—& I venture to repeat my belief that for doing
> this the Periodical Press in its widest sense may be
> made the most valuable of all instruments.' Draft
> *c.* 1892–3 for a reply by the Editor of the *Nineteenth
> Century* to a toast to Literature (WPL)

In 1895 Knowles began to think about the change in title he would
need five years hence. Someone else had already secured copyright in the obvious one. Since 1877 three publications had been
lodged in the British Museum Library under the name of the
Twentieth Century: one of 1877–8 'edited by a Comprehensiona-
list', either fugitive-crackpot or bought out by the next, a single
number of 1891 published by George Newnes, presumably bought
in turn by a William Graham who registered a typescript under
that title in 1894–5. Of various notes in Knowles's papers for a
title he could use, one is dated in October 1895; these ideas were
rather feeble: *Nineteen Hundred*; *Nineteenth Century: a Sequel*, or,
a Survival.[98] Recognizing that the twentieth century was in many
ways going to have the nineteenth century with it for years to
come, he finally settled on the *Nineteenth Century and After* for the
new era to begin in January 1901 (although some young men
inevitably said it ought to be the *Middle Ages*).

He also thought of a visual symbol to reinforce the new title
(Pl. 15), the two-headed Janus-symbol of an old man's profile
looking backward and down joined to a young woman's profile
looking forward and up. (Whether the long-haired youthful part

[97] Knowles Gladstone, 20 May 1897 (BL).
[98] Knowles to papers (WPL).

is necessarily female—considering Knowles's dislike of women's suffrage—is a doubtless unintentional ambiguity.) The design was drawn by the artist Edward J. Poynter, Director of the National Gallery from 1894 and President of the Royal Academy from 1896. In 1901 Knowles said the source of the design was a Greek coin, and he had indeed mentioned to Mrs. Huxley in 1896 that he was collecting these. But one can guess what started the idea in his mind, for in the *Studio* for February 1896 an article on Poynter's work reproduced a similar design, one of his early drawings of 1860 for the painted ceiling of Waltham Abbey, drawn under the direction of the architect William Burges in imitation of zodiac-symbols on the thirteenth-century painted ceiling at Peterborough Cathedral. Poynter was an artist very much in the late-classical tradition, whatever the gothic setting for that design. One doubts that Knowles bothered to know of the gothic prototype at Peterborough. Nevertheless, the result on his title page was of suitably cross-bred origin, a late flash of reconciliation between the gothic and classical traditions.[99]

To open his first number of the new century he chose a young poet recently acclaimed for a first book of poems, Stephen Phillips. 'Midnight, the 31st of December 1900' is no better than occasional verse, shadowed by the Boer War although with some depressing lines removed in proof: the lines 'On the street with embarrassed procession and heaven of vapours,/With a sun that is turned into blood' and 'Then the deed that is crime in a man shall be a crime in a nation/To murder, to steal, or to lie' (sounding like some tired 'Last Tournament') were removed, but the result was unmemorable. And Phillips's acclaim did not last. To tell the truth, even in the days when Knowles could command—or beg—poems from great poets, they did not often send him great poetry. It may be argued that Tennyson's and Arnold's best work was done before 1877, one could not open a new number of the *Nineteenth* and expect to find a *Tithonus* or a *Dover Beach*. And Swinburne's Jubilee poem in 1887, for instance, is not much more than occasional verse. One may indeed prefer Whitman's *Navesink* poems, that Knowles placed in the middle of the August 1885 number rather than at its head where his other poets

---

[99] Poynter's drawing for Knowles is with latter's papers (WPL). His drawing of 1860 for Burges, *Studio*, Feb. 1896, also *AR*, Jan. 1897, p. 7. Peterborough Cathedral nave ceiling, *c.* 1220, includes a Janus head.

usually appeared, apparently because he was not sure enough of Whitman's reputation in England. His judgement, or rather his use, of poetry was guided by a journalist's calculations. However, since a valuable series of reference volumes have indexed every page of the *Contemporary Review* and the *Nineteenth Century* up to 1900 *except* the pages containing poetry, a list of the handful of poets published by Knowles has been included at the end of this book. It would be odd indeed to suppose that Arnold and Swinburne wrote only prose for him or that he published nothing by Tennyson, or that the twenty-two pages occupied by 'The Last Tournament' had been censored by some quite other Index. The descent to Stephen Phillips, too, has its interest.[100]

During the Boer War, Professor Carroll Quigley has found, a group of Sir Alfred Milner's young men in London, reporting to Milner in South Africa, attempted to influence the content of Knowles's review towards more campaigning for Army reform and for Imperial federation. Knowles had already published articles on both subjects as far back as 1891, but was ready to oblige and formed a Committee for Administrative Reform. One of the plotters was Henry Birchenough, later knighted, married to one of Dean Bradley's daughters. Birchenough even wrote to Milner in August 1900, according to Professor Quigley, reporting that he was 'getting a stronger hold' on Knowles and was taking 'some share in the conduct of the Review' to the extent of bringing out the September number 'as a sort of holiday engagement' (presumably in Skilbeck's absence). Knowles was a close friend of the Bradley family, anyway, and Birchenough eventually acted as one of his executors. But one cannot help feeling that Knowles was less malleable than Milner's men hoped, since he was becoming very pro-Chamberlain and the Empire anyhow.[101] Yet the attempt to manipulate him is interesting. The letters to Milner with their air of skulduggery probably reflect the dedication within the 'Kindergarten' more than the editorial climate in London. How far one thought the *Nineteenth* might be

[100] Proof of Phillips poem in Knowles papers (WPL). For poetry published in *CR* 1870–6 and in *NC* 1877–1908, see Appendix.
[101] Letter from Prof. Quigley, Georgetown University, Washington D.C., 6 Sept. 1972, kindly offering this information of which I was unaware. Knowles to Mrs. Huxley, 6 Jan. 1904: 'Let us hope & pray that "Joe" may be spared until he has launched us as an Empire. I hope you are as much for him as I am' (Imperial College).

swinging to the right still depended partly on which article in which number one was reading at the time, as well as partly on the conservative inclination of most Englishmen then which it mirrored. It continued to be alertly informative on a wide range of subjects of the day. (In 1902 we see 'Why Not a Motor-car Way through England?'.) The monthly reviews still had a status unimaginable now, although to one brought up with the *Atlantic Monthly* and *Harper's Monthly* before the last war it is just barely imaginable. Even other editors were not too envious to grant that Knowles was 'head and shoulders, editorially speaking, above any of his three rivals', Bunting of the *Contemporary*, Courtney of the *Fortnightly*, and Maxse of the *National*.[102] Knowles's qualities and peculiarities are summarized in the next and final chapter. The present chapter has described his creation in the context of his life and especially as revealed in his (for the most part previously unpublished) letters to Tennyson and Gladstone and Huxley. It would be impertinent (and quite possibly mistaken) to assert, like Max Beerbohm on another subject, that more definitive studies of the *Nineteenth Century* review will be written by far less brilliant pens than mine. But this book is about its creator.

---

[102] Harry Quilter, ed., *What's What 1902*, p. 1076.

9

A Wonderful Medium
of Communication

'Like the portraiture of wisdom in ancient sculpture,
we should have one face ever contemplating the past,
and another always studying the demands of the
future.' Gilbert Scott, *Remarks on Secular and Domestic
Architecture* (1858), p. 265

'Every human being is a vanful of human beings, of
those who have gone before him, and of those who
form part of his life.' Tennyson quoted in *Memoir*,
i. 323 n.

IN DECEMBER 1903, while staying at Sandringham as guest
of the King and Queen, Knowles received the KCVO.
Edward VII delighted in conferring honours, and always did
it very nicely, this time apparently on the kindly spur of a moment
that arrived in the following artless manner. On the Sunday
night, on their way in to dinner, Knowles paused to admire in a
cabinet the badge of the eight-year-old Victorian Order. Immediately the King exclaimed, 'This should have been done before',
called for a sword to be brought, and knighted him on the spot;
and, finding Knowles in the library later, writing the news to his
wife, said, 'Nonsense, wire her'. A yellow carnation presented by
the Queen on this occasion was incorporated in a design Knowles
drew up for a coat of arms that remains among his papers. It
meant a good deal, just short of a century after his father's birth
in the glazier's cottage in the reign of George III and seventy-two
years after his own birth there in the reign of William IV—and
fifty years since his first professional arrival as a Mid-Victorian
ARIBA, just over forty since publication of his Arthurian book,

and twenty-seven since the founding of the *Nineteenth Century*. The name of his service to sovereign and nation was the name Tennyson had suggested for his review. That the new order of chivalry was Late Victorian was just right. He had about four years more in which to enjoy the elevation.[1]

Also in 1903 Knowles bought the freehold of two houses facing the sea on the high eastern cliff at Brighton, Nos. 3 and 4 Percival Terrace, to make into a second home for winter absences from the black fogs of London, and to replace the use of other men's houses for August-to-October sojourns. The newly joined double house, today a nursing home, stood next door to a house occupied by Herbert Spencer until his death in 1903. That grand and difficult old man having told Knowles 'that he did not think there was *any drawback* to it', Knowles reported to Mrs. Huxley, 'you will agree that from him that was a very strong recommendation'.[2] Percival Terrace is one of those bright, precise, Early Victorian parades of white-stuccoed bow-fronts, ranged at the edge of the English Channel. Knowles's granddaughter recalled the top-floor nursery where from a child's height only sea was visible, as from an ocean liner's enclosed upper deck. And she remembered, too, going down to say goodnight to him in his study, how he would whirl her in his desk-chair with a series of sudden stops when she had to shout out—in the right order—the names of the railway stations on the Brighton Line from London (starting of course with the one beside the Grosvenor Hotel). Brighton was a suitable terminus for a man born alongside the clatter of the Brighton coaches—not that Reigate will have occurred to him in 1903. One previous summer in search of salt air he and Isabel spent a week or so at the Lord Warden Hotel at Dover and each day went off on the ferry to France and back, 'crossing the Channel every day & thus getting a refreshing breeze as we rush thro air & water at 20 miles an hour'—how many well-off elderly Victorians thought of spending a week of hot weather doing that?[3] Knowles's life was seldom sedentary.

Inevitably its upward progress drew sour comment from envious contemporaries. He was never elected to the Athenaeum

---

[1] On this investiture there are various versions, of which this one has the ring of truth.

[2] Knowles to Mrs. Huxley, 6 Jan. 1904 (Imperial College).

[3] Knowles to Mrs. Huxley, 20 Aug. 1895 (Imperial College). Memories from the late Eirene Skilbeck of visits when she was 2 to 5 years old.

(although Huxley's 'I shall be in town on Monday next to vote at Athenaeum' in February 1894 suggests a move in that direction) and he never made *Who's Who* (which suggests hostility somewhere when that was revived in 1896), but the *Dictionary of National Biography* was to include him. Successful self-propelled men with a 'power of attaching distinguished persons' generally have a few enemies, and as *The Times* on his death was further to say, 'he was soon seen everywhere, and though some people resented this ubiquity . . . and some failed to understand how a man who was an authority neither in literature nor in politics could wield such literary and political influence, the influence was undoubtedly there'. At the time it was inevitable that a journalist's calculations were seen to be operating. especially by fellow-operators such as T. H. S. Escott, editor of the *Fortnightly* after Morley and author of a number of books analysing contemporary England, who wrote in 1885 anonymously as 'a Foreign Resident' and so more waspishly than when he signed his name:

Mr Knowles . . . has the same craze for social omniscience which I have repeatedly observed among the private secretaries of Ministers or the more aspiring of Foreign Office clerks. The world is his oyster; society his happy hunting-ground. . . . If you are worth knowing from Mr Knowles's point of view, it must be either because you can help him with his magazine, or because you know some person else who may be useful for that purpose. He is . . . an acute, calculating little man, always, as a look at him is enough to tell you, engaged in mentally reckoning as to whether A. or B. or C. can forward his enterprise, and, if so, up to what point.

Of course such another could see the wheels going round in such a well-tuned precision instrument; but it was not (as Escott probably hoped to imply) a commonplace instrument. For Knowles was by temperament so at ease with people, and by training so skilled in surveying his levels, he could approach almost anyone as an equal—and was kindly received too in quarters where social equality made little difference, as much by Newman at his Oratory as by Irving in his dressing-room, because they saw that he had his eye on impersonal issues—'his eye on the object' as one admirer put it. Which of course included securing names like Newman and Irving for his front cover. There were those who found him tiresome, as Lady Frances

Balfour and Sir William Richmond the painter did on the boat train in 1888: 'Knowles of the *XIX Century* was on board, and did his best to bore us both'; one of them at a time he might have coped with. An editor with twelve issues a year to fill could never leave his lookout for interesting material.[4]

Some of his own relations saw little of him, although his brother's harmless eccentricities seem to have been humorously tolerated by him to the extent of cheerfully acknowledging the relationship when a duchess at one of Knowles's parties asked who was 'that extraordinary person in the corner'. Their sister's family the Stilwells saw far more of George, a big talented, lazy, amusing man who could 'paint well', 'sing like Caruso', and recite 'all of Shakespeare', and who wore peculiar clothes (never since, alas, described) with tremendous panache and dyed his bald spot black as well as his remaining hair. Children loved his company, as when for the Hewlett boys 'a day at the Crystal Palace with Uncle George' was the best of treats that Friday Grove afforded. For he was unself-consciously himself—arriving late for a wedding, he went down the aisle on all fours so as to attract less notice, thereby attracting a great deal; and, when about to render a song on a visit to the Stilwells, first removing his teeth and putting them down on the piano beside him, while all including the servants waited with bated breath for this to happen. George Knowles 'never did a thing', all the male energy in the family went into his elder brother; and when George died in 1909, he left only effects worth less than £2,000.[5]

Their nephew Maurice Hewlett looked rather like his Uncle James, and his eyes had the same 'piercingly direct gaze'. Maurice contributed briefly to the *Nineteenth Century* while carrying on his father's profession as archivist to Crown lands, before his

[4] On Athenaeum Club, Huxley to Knowles, 16 Feb. 1894 (private copy printed by Knowles for L. Huxley). *DNB Suppl.* entry on Knowles was written by Sir Sidney Lee. *The Times* obituary, 14 Feb. 1908, p. 12. Anon. [T. H. S. Escott], *Society in London by a Foreign Resident* (1885), pp. 289–90. On Newman, n. 9 below. On Irving, F. Wedmore, *Memories* (1912), p. 169, on meeting Knowles in Irving's dressing room; also chap. 8, n. 23 above. 'Eye on the object' called Goethe's phrase by Wedmore on Knowles in *NC*, Apr. 1908, p. 692, more recently used by Arnold in 1866. Lady Frances Balfour's autobiography (1930), ii. 181, quotes own letter 11 July 1888.

[5] Family lore; and will George Henry Knowles, died 1909 when of Colville Gardens, North Kensington, previously of 34 Soho Square; according to his great-niece Miss Flint, not queer in present-day meaning but pleasantly eccentric, delightfully himself. On the Stilwells, chap. 3, n. 72.

pseudo-medieval novels made him an Edwardian success. (The verdict of certain country-bred cousins on Maurice was: 'no, we didn't like him, he wasn't kind to animals'—a view repeated with vigour in the 1960s.) It was at Queen Anne's Lodge that he met his future wife Hilda Herbert, daughter of Revd. George Herbert, Knowles's contentious travelling companion of 1854; as time went on, Hilda Hewlett preferred piloting fast cars, and eventually aircraft, to family life.[6] Maurice's father Henry Hewlett died in 1897, when the packet of letters James had written to him while they were young was returned to sender. Thanks to the long spread in time from these early letters and the early travel journals to the quantities of later letters preserved among other men's papers, we can see our subject more nearly in the round than a life represented only by the letters of its success. For him there were less than sure-footed moments even then.

We find him in October 1878, at Lady Waldegrave's in Somerset, reporting for Gladstone's approval on a first visit to Wells Cathedral, on the 'almost Greek-like breadth' of the west-front sculpture, 'cramped although it is with northern shackles', and making the sensitive comparison that art historians were perhaps not yet making: 'There always seems to me a curious connection of feeling between the best 13th century work & the best Greek work—I don't know whether you can follow what I mean'; and then, spoiling this nice perception, 'Excuse me for troubling you with such crude things.'[7] Still at 47 he sometimes lacked *gravitas*. By the time Tennyson and Gladstone had gone, he had more of the poise of a public figure himself. Then, one young admirer was Sydney Phelps, a writer of tales and verse from about 1900, remembered by Skilbeck's daughter in the First World War years as an intense chain-smoking, modern woman, who had revered Knowles as 'a poet, an artist, and a statesman'. And Oscar Wilde wrote to him admiringly in 1881. For Knowles was kind to the young, if they were interesting. They saw more to admire in him than a market for their work: 'A man of singularly upright character and of simple and generous disposition . . . faithful throughout a long life to the ideals with which he

[6] On Maurice Hewlett, *Letters* (1926), and chap. 2, nn. 25, 29 above; on Hilda Hewlett, Mrs. Belloc Lowndes, *The Merry Wives of Westminster* (1946).

[7] Knowles to Gladstone, 17 Oct. 1878 (BL). But Knowles will have heard and read the classicist Cockerell on Wells.

started . . . who defended the cause of good literature and serious thinking at a time when both were threatened by their counterfeits,' said the *Westminster Gazette* in 1908. 'One would never claim before him to knowledge one did not possess,' Sydney Phelps thought.[8] There would seem to have been times, for those from whom he demanded rigorous standards of statement or performance, when admiration was easier from a distance.

Knowles's mind was 'comprehensive' (Wedmore), 'the best informed in Europe' (Kropotkin), it could 'learn enough of a subject in half an hour . . . and never talk nonsense' (Tennyson), but it was not deep. In April 1879, we find him asking Newman, of all people, 'why my yesterday's confession of faith as to the ultimate moral sanction being "the truest & highest happiness of the greatest number of conscious beings" appeared to you almost shocking in its insufficiency—as it seemed to do?' A monumental failure of understanding there, not only to offer the utilitarian greatest-good-of-the-greatest-number to someone so steeped in the mystery of the Church and the sinfulness of human existence, but to offer it just at the emotional moment when the cardinalate had been conferred. Nevertheless, in 1877 Newman had given the *Nineteenth Century* his blessing and regretted that his bishops' disapproval prevented him from contributing to it, though in 1884 he allowed Knowles to publish his article on 'The Inspiration of Scripture'. On Cardinal Newman's death in 1890, Knowles asked, unavailingly, for somes lines as epitaph from Tennyson. Choosing to address the request through Hallam, with whom he tried to keep up some sort of relationship, Knowles in this letter said of Newman:

His figure which stands in our century as if one of the early Fathers had strayed into it—is surely full of pathos & suggestion—(He ought to have lived in Alexandria). He said to me once—'*It will be a very very long time before the English people listens to dogma again*'—This was when I was talking with him about the chances of the return of Catholic thought & power in this Country. If your Father could have seen him as he said this with his far-away mystical gaze into eternity, he would have struck his figure into the immortality of poetry then & there—

[8] Sydney K. Phelps, 'Personal Reminiscences of Two Editors', *NCA*, Mar. 1927. Oscar Wilde, *Letters*, ed. R. Hart-Davis (1962), p. 80; Knowles published essays by Wilde in 1885, 1889, and 1890. *Westminster Gazette* obituary, 14 Feb. 1908, also remarking on his 'very striking facial resemblance to Sir George Trevelyan', for whom he was sometimes mistaken.

his face was so wistful & so holy— & it seemed so sad that such a soul should be in such bonds—Yet perhaps after all they were not *bonds* but supports—'where is he who knows?'

This letter is labelled 'very curious'—the unimaginative Hallam perhaps mistaking the flash of empathy for conversion. Knowles once startled the clergy at Cardinal Manning's table by suggesting that 'if the Papacy would adopt the scientific principles of Positivism, it would effect the conversion of the world'. But it was not conversion he was after, it was conversation.[9]

Newman's biographer Wilfrid Ward, whose father the Catholic philosopher W. G. Ward had been an active member of the Metaphysical Society, and who himself knew Knowles, probably caught his qualities best, as those of:

a wonderful and most universal medium of communication between different men and between thinkers of all schools and the public. In conversation he had the very happy art of finding the subject on which different members of the company could and would talk freely, and of himself putting in the right word, and, as it were, winding up the clock. He used to be compared to Boswell; but I think this comparison materially inaccurate. Knowles was a far stronger man as well as more business-like and methodical. . . . [Boswell's] creative power as of the novelist was different from Knowles's gift which was a more practical one.

And Ward saw that (despite the Channel Tunnel affair) Knowles did not wield such political power as Delane's with *The Times*. It was Delane, not Knowles (to correct some misquoting in 1951), whom Ward said the Queen of Holland called *le quatrième pouvoir de l'État Britannique*.[10] We may also recall that, while Knowles and his father had effected an interesting meeting between styles of

---

[9] Knowles to Newman, 5 Apr. 1879, *The Letters and Diaries of John Henry Newman*, eds. C. S. Dessain and T. Gornall, vol. 29 (1976), p. 97 n.: also vol. 28 (1975), pp. 160, 224. Knowles to Hallam Tennyson, 12 Aug. 1890 (TRC) from Holmbury, just before or just after Tennyson's visit there. F. Harrison, *Autobiographic Memoirs* (1911), ii. 89.

[10] Quoted as applying to Knowles by Goodwin, introduction to *Nineteenth Century Opinion* (1951), from Wilfrid Ward, 'Three Notable Editors—Delane, Hutton, Knowles', *Ten Personal Studies* (1908), pp. 68–76 on Knowles with Ward's woolly summarizing remarks pp. 76–7 ('the man who set a review on foot which became from its first number one of the most successful in the country performed the greatest feat' was Knowles; 'As a great political force in the country . . . the man whom the Queen . . .' was Delane). On comparison to Boswell, n. 14 below.

architecture and left some sturdy proofs of it behind them, they did not sway the path of Victorian design by very much. Yet the Grosvenor Style and the Metaphysical Society were proofs of the deep Mid-Victorian longing for reconciliation between hostile forces, part of the perpetual tightrope strung between opposite poles by the anxious human race. It was in directing thirty years of the *Nineteenth Century*'s monthly survey of the world in between, that Knowles showed powers originating, as Frederick Wedmore put it, 'in the gifts of his own nature'. 'None knew so well as his earliest colleagues in the task how entirely the result was the work of the energy, the boldness, the versatile tact, and the genial sympathy' of its editor, Frederic Harrison (forgiving past differences over the Elgin Marbles) was to say.[11]

Charm of personality is a gift for the fugitive present, only half-preserved in the recorded testimony of others. Bishop Welldon thought it a 'genius for friendship', Knowles 'unsealed the lips of others', 'He was the best possible conductor of social intercourse' (conductor: a good word, in both the electrical and the musical sense). Lady St. Helier remembered, in Carlyle's 'little court of devoted friends and admirers' at the end of his life, Knowles's sympathetic deference to the old man's prejudices; that is, only partly so that he could next day say, 'as Carlyle said to me yesterday . . .' too. And there is a jaunty little note to 'My dear B.f.' from the old Duke of Cambridge, George III's last-surviving grandchild (d. 1904), a friend since he and Knowles had settled the Channel Tunnel together in 1883, inviting him to 'quite a small party' next day. John Walter Cross remembered how Knowles's 'grey-blue eyes . . . could kindle instantaneously in sympathy or become steely in antipathy . . . and there was always, too, the iron hand underneath the velvet glove'. Meeting him on the bridge in St. James's Park in December 1907, a few weeks before Knowles's death, Cross thought that while he looked thin, all the keen many-sided vigour of mind and quick sympathy were there: at 76 still the unretiring editor. For one thing, he had always watched over his own health—a habit, apparently, from early years with a doting mother, when the family moved house three times and his father was much away—

---

[11] Wedmore and Harrison in 'James Knowles: A Tribute from Some Friends', *NCA*, Apr. 1908, pp. 692, 694, and Harrison's retrospective survey of *NC* 1877–1901 in *NCA*, Oct. 1918.

and references to the after-care of small ailments recur in his letters.[12]

Art was his refuge from the world. Many guests recalled the paintings at Queen Anne's Lodge—in the dining room Watts's 'Rider on a White Horse', a Claude landscape from the Wynn Ellis collection, Millais's portrait of Tennyson—and in another room a Ruysdael 'Bleaching Ground' and a Cappelle seascape, Turner watercolours on the stairs, and somewhere a landscape attributed to Reynolds (rare in his work, but of good provenance); also Leighton's strenuous last 'Clytie' before which the painter had lain in state in his coffin, a late portrait of Gladstone painted by Troubetzkoi for Knowles, and the little seascape signed 'Alix', gift of Princess Alexandra. And he had some fine drawings, including nine attributed to Rembrandt, eighteen to Claude, and a pair of lovely Fragonards. *The Times* reporting the three-day sale of Knowles's 'few things' as he had airily called them, in the auction rooms he had frequented for over forty years, noted in him 'all the *flair* of the genuine connoisseur', although some attributions have since changed. The 443 lots at Christie's brought about £10,192, less than the family had hoped: Millais's Tennyson was no prize in 1908, nor was Turner likely to bring in much then.[13] But the *Nineteenth's* contributors remembered 'many a confabulation in the tranquil and hospitable ground floor' of Queen Anne's Lodge—'beautiful in itself', with a 'beautiful

---

[12] Welldon and Cross in 'Tribute', *NCA*, Apr. 1908, pp. 683–4, 688–90, also Welldon, p. 685, on intolerance of vulgarity. Lady St. Helier, *Memories* (1909), p. 154. Undated note from Duke of Cambridge in Knowles papers (WPL).

[13] The Claude (chap. 7, n. 66) is now considered to be by a gifted contemporary imitator, in M. Röthlisberger, *Claude Lorrain: The Paintings* (1961), no. 256, fig. 354, pp. 521, 541; bought for 600 guineas at Knowles sale 1908 for National Gallery of Scotland. The Millais (chap. 8, n. 28), not reaching its reserve of £3,000, was bought-in in 1908; during Lady Knowles's illness in the war, it was sold to the Port Sunlight gallery for £1,500 (family information). Reynolds landscape from the collection of Reynolds's niece Marchioness of Thomond via Samuel Rogers, Wynn Ellis, and de Zoete (sale 1885 when Knowles paid 8 guineas), loaned 1886 and 1903 to RA, sold 1908 to a dealer for 410 guineas. Leighton's 'Clytie', the larger of two of this subject, is now in India (R. and L. Ormond, *Leighton*, 1975, no. 396). On portrait of Gladstone (for which Knowles had tried to get F. Sandys, Knowles to Gladstone, 30 Oct. 1885, BL), Lord Ronald Gower, *Old Diaries* (1902), July 1893 on Troubetzkoi sketching Gladstone at dinner at Queen Anne's Lodge; now at Scottish National Portrait Gallery. On seascape by 'Alix', chap. 8, n. 80. Christie's sale catalogue, 27–9 May 1908; *The Times* and *Daily Telegraph*, 30 May 1908. Also on Knowles's collecting, chap. 5, n. 52, chap. 8, nn. 28, 29.

outlook on St James's Park', and 'full of beautiful things'. His parties were 'amongst the pleasantest in London' (except for certain dinners built around Gladstone's conversation that were too long for the other guests: those will have been the occasions for comparison to Boswell).[14] Once Knowles's influence grew and this house was his, with all he held to be interesting within reach, and once the Queen Anne's Mansions row and the tussle with the Tennysons were over, no wonder old tensions relaxed and he could enjoy his eminence. Even if old anxieties were reflected in an insistent intolerance of vulgarity, noted in one obituary and expressed in a scribbled translation from Horace's *Odi profanum vulgus* found in his papers, that was a dislike all too easy for an elderly man to indulge at the heart of London society around the turn of the century. (It may or may not be odd that, so far as I know, two such frequenters and observers of London society as James Knowles and Henry James seem not to have mentioned each other: which one was wary of the other, or was it mutual?)

Incidentally, the rediscovery of the eighteenth century by artistically inclined people in the 1880s is mirrored in a light-hearted scheme by Knowles and Princess Mary Adelaide, Duchess of Teck, for a 'minuet dinner' at Queen Anne's Lodge, with rehearsal beforehand since, she pointed out: 'the young people will be so shy, that *we* shall have to put *our best foot* forward to show them what *real dancing* is like'. As if either she or her host dated from the minuet era; but 'drawing-room dances' had already been featured in some of the more cultivated periodicals by then, just as some architects were already proceeding by way of the Queen Anne Revival toward a revived Georgian style. In the pages of the *Nineteenth Century*, the opening volume of Lecky's *England in the Eighteenth Century* had been reviewed in 1879, Harrison wrote on the period in 1883, Gladstone held forth on Lecky in 1887, Kropotkin on the centenary of the French Revolution in 1889. Next we find Knowles in 1890 presenting the

---

[14] Hamilton's diary 1884 as chap. 8, n. 21 above. 'Dinner too long', Matthew Arnold, letter to his sister, Dec. 1877, in *Poetry and Prose*, ed. Bryson (1954), with name of host cut out but pretty clearly Knowles (Archibald Forbes, second chief guest, having just written for him on Bulgaria): 'An evening of Bulgaria', said Arnold, 'is too much.' And Gower (n. 13 above) noted length of dinner in July 1893. These occasions were arranged to draw out Gladstone's discourse, hence the Boswellian comparison noted by Ward (n. 10 above).

novels of Jane Austen as his favourite authoress to young Princess
May of Teck, the future Queen Mary, who had never read them
and thanked him prettily, also for a portrait of Marie Bashkirtseff
(whose journal Gladstone had reviewed for Knowles the year
before)—fruits of a truly varied dinner conversation.[15]

Oddly enough though, or perhaps not oddly at all, his love of
owning pictures did not extend to owning books: 'For I am not a
book-buyer, but always think the ideal Library should consist of
the fewest books possible,' he said privately in the 1890s. In fact,
more publicly, he was prepared to doubt whether 'our age' was
propitious for books, so much was happening, so many facts were
cast before us every day, that interpretation was becoming more
and more the peculiar role of periodicals. He 'once even went so
far as to suggest to a venerable Vice-Chancellor that Chairs of
Periodical Literature might be good for our universities', but,
said Knowles, 'I still see the sphinx-like smile of that Vice-
Chancellor in reply'.[16] There the editor was ahead of his time. In
some other ways he was a conservative Englishman of his time,
detesting the works of Zola (while seeing there was genius in
them), detesting the Paris of the 1889 Exhibition, especially the
Eiffel Tower, buying nothing (so far as we know) by French
Impressionist painters.[17]

When Tennyson said Knowles 'had his brain in his hand', he
meant that talent for quick absorption, as it were through the
pores or nerve-ends, that Franklin Roosevelt for example was to
have. Old Knowles must have had it—without his son's personal
magnetism—to rise up from the Bell Street workshop as he did.
It was not imagination but osmosis, drawing up ideas as a plant
draws up nourishment. It is a talent likelier to produce great

[15] Duchess of Teck to Knowles, 21 June 1889, party called off according to hers
of 15 and 21 July (WPL). H. Sutherland Edwards, 'Drawing-Room Dances',
illustrated by Hugh Thomson, *English Illustrated Magazine*, June 1884. Princess
May of Teck to Knowles, 20 July 1890 (WPL).

[16] Knowles to Mrs. Huxley, 28 Mar. 1896 (Imperial College). Draft in his
hand for a reply to a toast to literature (Knowles papers, WPL), perhaps intended
for a Royal Literary Fund dinner but apparently undelivered, possibly due to
illness 1892–3, or later when his nephew Maurice was on the committee; the
Fund's archivist has no record of Knowles as a speaker.

[17] Knowles to Gladstone, 26 Apr. 1888, sending copy of Zola's *La Terre*: 'If
you can get over certain horrible coarsenesses & profanities in it . . . I think you
will find it a simply marvellous realistic picture' (BL). As Harrison was to point
out, Knowles was 'anxious to give a really European character to his Review',
and the *NC* menu was not insular.

editors and great politicians than great architects, though it may produce interesting architects. And so the obituarists summed up a man who was a wonderful medium of communication, a man with a genius for friendship and a keen awareness of the needs of the moment, with both velvet glove and iron hand. From those independent forebears, the vein of Surrey iron. As Tennyson also said, every one of us is a vanful of people, of those who went before us and of those who become part of our lives. The Janus-head looking forward and back was the perfect figurehead for the *Nineteenth Century and After*, yet the *Nineteenth Century* at its best was edited with a piercing eye for the present. Knowles was never 'foolishly far off from the "Zeit-Geist" ' (a scornful comment of his in 1877 when that term was fresh in England); instead, he followed the prescription he had posed for himself in 1855: 'then I have but to know the character of my own age & fearlessly apply my science'.[18]

Sir James Knowles died very suddenly, with no diminution of powers, early in the morning of 13 February 1908 at his Brighton house. One of many telegrams of condolence to his widow came from Queen Alexandra ('your dear husband who was such a friend of mine'). He left £31,000—and the monthly review, good for another half-century or so, in the end as the *Twentieth Century* and far beyond his ken. At the funeral service in St. Peter's, Brighton, and at the memorial service in St. Margaret's, Westminster, the 'Hallelujah' Chorus and 'Crossing the Bar' were sung. The gallant epitaph in the Extramural Cemetery at Brighton reads: I THANK GOD FOR MY LIFE.

---

[18] Knowles to Gladstone, 13 Dec. 1877 (BL), Arnold having used (or been assigned by the editor) the term *Zeitgeist* in a title for Knowles in *CR* in 1876. On scribblings of 1855, chap. 3, n. 69 above. Finally I should like to thank Mr. and Mrs. Antony Dale for photographing Knowles's gravestone for me.

Buildings designed by the Knowleses

Dates of design, not execution

J. T. KNOWLES SR., FRIBA 1847

c. 1833   Unknown house in Hampshire near the sea.

1835   Competition designs for the Houses of Parliament; perspective view in Victoria and Albert Museum.

1835–7   (Possibly rebuilding at Kingswood Warren, Surrey, in castellated style, with conservatory, assigned in Brayley's *Surrey* to a T. R. Knowles.)

1837   Bramley House or Park, Surrey, rebuilding for Capt. the Hon. George Francis Wyndham, subsequently 4th Earl of Egremont (demolished).

1838   'Egremont Castle' nr. Orchard Wyndham, Williton, Somerset (not built) for 4th Earl of Egremont; drawings in RIBA Drawings Collection.

Blackborough, Devon, large pair of houses for the Earl of Egremont and the Rector, and church.

Designs possibly for Gatton Park, Surrey, for Earl Monson (probably partly built); drawing in U.S.A.

1838–   Williton, Somerset, designs for rebuilding the church (not used) and the vicarage (Eastfield); rectories at Rewe, Kentisbeare, and Silverton, Devon, for the Earl of Egremont.

1839–   Silverton Park, Devon, for the Earl of Egremont (demolished); drawing in RIBA Drawings Collection.

c. 1839   Dangstein, West Sussex, for Capt. James Lyon (demolished).

c. 1840   House on Reigate Heath for Henry Lainson (demolished).

1842   St. John the Evangelist, Redhill, Surrey (demolished), endowed by Earl Somers.

1845   Friday Grove, Clapham Park, for himself, and later houses west of it for leasing (demolished).

1846   Pair of houses, Durand Gardens, Lambeth.

1850   Competition design for Great Exhibition 1851.

1850–3   General Dispensary, Manor Street, Clapham.

1852   Warehouse, St. Paul's Churchyard, City of London, for Messrs. Cook (demolished).

1854 No. 15 Kensington Palace Gardens, Kensington, for George Moore.

Office building and auction rooms, east corner Fleet Street and Chancery Lane, for Edmund Hodgson (demolished); drawing in Hodgson family possession.

1858 'International Hotel', Strand, Wellington, Exeter, and Burleigh Streets, for a consortium of developers (not built).

1859 Grosvenor Hotel, Victoria Station, for the Grosvenor & West-end Railway Terminus Hotel Co. (with his son's assistance, built 1860–2).

Palacio (or Quinta or Villa) Monserrate, Sintra (formerly Cintra), Portugal, for Francis Cook (built 1863–5); drawings in Cook family possession.

1862 Furzedown, Streatham, alterations and additions for Philip William Flower.

c. 1863 Large shop for William Tarn, Newington Causeway, Elephant and Castle, Southwark (demolished).

1865 Hedsor, Buckinghamshire, for 4th Baron Boston.

1860s Broomfield, Stanmore Hill, Middlesex.

Roydon Hall, Kent, alterations for Edwin Cook (and possibly earlier for William Cook).

Walton Grove, Walton on Thames, additions for Paul Cababe.

(Possibly Nos. 14–25 Oakley Street, Chelsea.)

(Possibly No. 119 Cannon Street, City, for J. Travers & Sons.)

(Possibly No. 117 Harley Street, former 45-A Upper Harley Street, corner of Devonshire Street, Marylebone, for Alfred Jones.)

1872 Fountain, Wigton market-place, Cumberland, with reliefs by Thomas Woolner, for George Moore.

J. T. KNOWLES JR. (JAMES KNOWLES), ARIBA 1853, FRIBA 1876

1855–9 Assisting his father.

1860– Cedars Estate, Clapham, twin terraces of houses facing the Common, detached villas on Cedars Road (most demolished), and road layout for Alexander Jones. St. Saviour's church added 1862 (demolished) for Revd. W. H. H. Bowyer.

1861– Champion Hall or Champion Park estate, Lower Sydenham, church of St. Michael and All Angels (demolished), villas (not built), and road layout for William Woodgate.

Club and/or chambers, later Thatched House Club, Nos. 85–6 St. James's Street, Westminster, for William Woodgate.

1862– Park Town Estate, Queen's (Queenstown) Road, Battersea, road layout and railway bridge, workmen's houses (about half of the ultimate 1,300 by him), and St. Philip's church for P. W. Flower and other proprietors.

c. 1862 (Possibly block of offices and chambers Nos. 61–73 Victoria Street, corner of Strutton Ground, for a developer, possibly the builders Holland & Sons.)

c. 1865 (Probably alterations, The Hollies, Clapham Common, for his own use.)

1866 St. Stephen's, Clapham Park, for the Revd. George Eastman (rebuilt).

London Joint-stock (now Midland) Bank, Nos. 123–4 Chancery Lane, alterations and refacing.

1867– Albert Mansions, Victoria Street, and stables, Spenser Street, Westminster, terrace of 19 blocks of flats (demolished except block at west end) and ' separate mews layout (demolished) for P. W. Flower and other proprietors.

Aldworth, Sussex, for Alfred Tennyson.

1868– School at St. Peter's Vauxhall, added to Pearson's church and art school; mission house opposite the church on Kennington Lane (1873), and possibly alterations to vicarage for Revd. George Herbert.

1871 Extension to No. 4 (now 38) Marlborough Place, St. John's Wood, for Thomas Huxley.

West Brighton estate, Hove, Sussex, sea-front terraces and other houses, with road layout, for William Morris, Albert Grant, and other proprietors (only partly built to Knowles's design).

1872 Kensington House, Kensington, for Albert Grant (demolished).

1873 Block of offices and shops, including Overton's fish shop, bounded by Victoria Street, Terminus Place, and Underground station, for W. G. Salting (altered).

1874 Leicester Square, Westminster, layout for Albert Grant.

1879 Royal Sea-Bathing Infirmary, Margate, hospital wing (four wards and swimming bath), chapel, and gate lodge for (Sir) Erasmus Wilson.

1880 Temple stage-set for Tennyson's *The Cup* (performed January 1881 at Lyceum Theatre) for Henry Irving.

1881   Building in Francis Street for Army & Navy Auxiliary
       Stores and alterations to main building on Victoria
       Street (demolished) for Army & Navy Cooperative
       Society.

1883   (Probably alterations, Queen Anne's Lodge, Westminster,
       for his own use, demolished.)

1903   (Possibly alterations, Nos. 3–4 Percival Terrace, Brighton,
       for his own use.)

Index to poetry published by Knowles

(to supplement *Wellesley Index to Victorian Periodicals* I & II)

CONTEMPORARY REVIEW
(*none published by Alford 1866–70*)

1871, vol. 19, Dec., pp. 1–22, Tennyson, 'The Last Tournament'.
1875, vol. 27, Dec., pp. 160–2, Gladstone, translation with Latin original, 'Hymnus Responsorius'.

NINETEENTH CENTURY

1877, vol. 1, Mar., p. 1, Tennyson, prefatory sonnet.
         May, p. 359, Tennyson, 'Montenegro'.
         June, p. 547, Tennyson, 'To Victor Hugo'.
    vol. 2, Aug., pp. 1–2, Tennyson, 'Achilles over the Trench'.
1878, vol. 3, Mar., pp. 425–32, Tennyson, 'The Revenge'.
1879, vol. 5, Jan., p. 1, Arnold, 'S.S. Lusitania'.
         Apr., pp. 575–82, Tennyson, 'The Defence of Lucknow', with dedicatory poem to the Princess Alice.
1880, vol. 7, May, pp. 737–41, Tennyson, 'De Profundis'.
1881, vol. 10, Nov., pp. 629–40, Tennyson, 'Despair'.
1882, vol. 11, Jan., pp. 1–8, Arnold, 'Westminster Abbey'.
    vol. 12, Sept., pp. 321–3, Tennyson, 'To Virgil'.
1883, vol. 13, Mar., pp. 357–8, Tennyson, 'Frater Ave atque Vale' with Latin version by E. C. Wickham, Greek version by G. Ridding, and Catullus' ode from last line of which Tennyson took his title.
    vol. 14, Sept., pp. 357–60, Gladstone, 'Senti, Senti, Anima Mia', translation into Italian of Cowper's hymn 'Hark my soul! it is the Lord' (no. 260, *Hymns Ancient and Modern*) signed 'W.E.G. August 1883' (full name on contents page).
1884, vol. 16, July, pp. 1–2, Swinburne, 'On a Country Road' (to Chaucer).
1885, vol. 18, Aug., pp. 234–7, Whitman, *Fancies at Navesink*, seven poems ('The pilot in the mist', 'Had I the choice', 'You tides with ceaseless swell', 'Last of ebb, and daylight waning', 'Proudly the flood comes in', 'By that long scan of waves', 'Then last of all').

1887, vol. 21, June, pp. 781–91, Swinburne, 'The Jubilee 1887'.

1888, vol. 23, Mar., pp. 317–20, Swinburne, 'March: an Ode'.

1892, vol. 31, Feb., pp. 181–2, Tennyson, 'The Death of the Duke of Clarence'.

vol. 32, Nov., pp. 831–44, Huxley, Myers, Noel, Palgrave, de Vere, Watts, and Knowles, 'To Tennyson: the Tributes of His Friends'.

1893, vol. 33, Jan., pp. 1–3, Swinburne, 'Threnody: Alfred, Lord Tennyson'.

vol. 34, Oct., pp. 501–3, Swinburne, 'The Palace of Pan'.

Nov., pp. 839–48, Lord de Tabley, 'Orpheus in Hades'.

1894, vol. 35, Feb., pp. 217–19, Dudley C. Bushby, 'Eleusinia'.

Mar., pp. 523–4, Swinburne, 'Elegy'.

May, pp. 701–9, Gladstone, translation of five 'Love Odes of Horace', with the originals.

vol. 36, July, p. 1, Swinburne, 'Carnot'.

Aug., pp. 315–16, Swinburne, translation of Delphic Hymn to Apollo.

Dec., pp. 1008–10, Swinburne, 'To a Baby Kinswoman'.

1895, vol. 37, Feb., pp. 367–8, Swinburne, 'A New Year's Eve' (on death of Christina Rossetti).

vol. 38, July, pp. 1–2, Swinburne, 'Cromwell's Statue'.

Nov., pp. 713–14, Swinburne, 'Trafalgar Day'.

1896, vol. 40, Sept., pp. 341–4, Swinburne, 'The High Oaks, Barking Hall, July 19th, 1896' for the poet's mother's birthday.

1897, vol. 42, Oct., pp. 602–13, Lily Wolffsohn, translation, 'Specimens of Italian Folk-song'.

1898, vol. 43, Feb., pp. 169–70, Swinburne, 'Barking Hall, a Year After'.

Mar., pp. 448–56, Lord Burghclere, 'Specimen of a Translation of the Georgics in Blank Verse', I. 311–514.

vol. 44, Sept., pp. 341–7, Stephen Phillips, 'Endymion'.

1899, vol. 45, Jan., pp. 90–1, Swinburne, 'Prologue to "The Duchess of Malfy"'.

vol. 46, Oct., p. 521, Swinburne, 'After the Verdict, September 1899' (Dreyfus).

1900, vol. 47, Feb., pp. 275–8, Lord Burghclere, translation from *The Georgics*, II. 458–542.

Apr., pp. 612–16, Carmen Sylva (Queen of Roumania), 'Westminster Abbey', in German, with translation by Arthur Waugh.

NINETEENTH CENTURY AND AFTER

1901, vol. 49, Jan., pp. 2–6, Stephen Phillips, 'Midnight—The 31st of December 1900'.

Feb., p. 197, Sir Theodore Martin, 'Victoria the Good: A Sonnet'.

June, pp. 988–97, 'Three Scenes from M. Rostand's *L'Aiglon* translated into English verse by Earl Cowper'.

1902, vol. 52, Aug., pp. 177–8, Swinburne, 'The Centenary of Alexandre Dumas'.

Dec., pp. 1016–21, Lord Burghclere, translation from *The Georgics*, III. 440–566.

1908, vol. 63, Mar., p. 341, the late Sir James Knowles, 'The Gods of Greece (in a cabinet of Greek coins)'.

Note. J. A. Symonds's translations of 23 Michelangelo sonnets in *CR* Sept. 1872, being embedded in an article, are indexed in *WIVP* vol. 1.

Index

Abbotsford, 198
Adalet, 284n, 306
Ady, Mrs Henry, 90, 99
Afghan situation, 119, 286
'Agnostic', 214
Albert, Prince Consort, 85, 166, 238
Aldred, draper, 26
Aldworth, Sussex, ix, 23, 37, 149, 181, 182, 196, 197–207, 208–10, 216, 222, 226, 228, 229, 237, 260, 266, 336n, 366, Pl. 10, 11
Alexandra, Princess of Wales (later Queen), 296, 308, 335–6, 352, 360, 363
Alford, Henry, 210, 216, 219, 222, 234–5
Alhambra, Spain, 55–6, 148
Allnutt family, 77, 100, 171, 269
Anonymity, see Pseudonyms, Signed articles
Apollo Belvedere, 69–70, 94
Apothecaries, 13, 14n
Arabic, see Islamic
Architects, 39–40, 80–2, 118–19, 121, 190, 228, 232–3; see also Builders, Clients, Competitions
Architects', Builders', & General Insurance Co., 40
Architectural Association, 61, 79, 82, 121
Architectural foliage, see Foliage, architectural
Architectural Magazine, 43, 84, 117, 118
Architectural Museum, 53–4
Architectural Photographic Society, 53
Architectural Publication Society, 40, 82
Argyll, Duke of, 215, 237, 244, 323, 332, 334
Arnold, Matthew, 194n, 215, 227, 274, 280, 288–9, 322, 349–50, 368
Arnold-Foster, H. O., 288, 296
Art galleries, 72, 77–8, 144–5; see also Knowles, James Thomas Jr.: art collecting
Arthurian theme, 210, 235; see also Knowles, James Thomas Jr.: Story of King Arthur; Malory, Sir Thomas; Tennyson, Alfred: Idylls of the King
Ashurst Son & Morris, 237, 245, 246n
'Athenaeumania', 31, 283
Athenaeum, 75, 119, 276
Athenaeum, Clapham, see Clapham: Athenaeum

Athenaeum Club, 353–4
Athenaeum, Manchester, see Manchester: Athenaeum
Austen, Jane, 362
Austin, Alfred, 176, 209n

Baalbek, 135
Bagehot, Walter, 214n, 216, 236
Bagni di Lucca, 39, 111, 144
Balfour, Arthur, 216, 331–2, 334
Balfour, Lady Francis, 354–5
Banks, Robert, 36, 52
Barry, Alfred, 216, 222
Barry, Sir Charles, 17, 23, 24, 25, 26, 28–9, 36, 38, 39, 40, 41, 43, 45, 52, 62, 97, 113, 139, 142, 144, 155, 167, 216, 229, 245, 297
Barry, Charles Jr, 249, 266n
Barry, Edward, 58, 88
Bartholomew, Alfred, 23–4, 28, 81
Bashkirtseff, Marie, 362
Batalha, Portugal, 148
Bate, H. W., 328
Battersea: Park Town estate, 64, 167, 175, 177–9, 185, 187, 188, 232, 254, 272, 279, 286–7, 289, 366; St. Philip's, 185–6, 366
Beaumont, Col., 292, 293
Beckford, William, 143–9 passim
Bennett, James Samuel, 146
Benson Logan & Co., 24
Bentham, Jeremy, 299, 305
Bentham, Samuel, 300
Bernstorff, Count, 243
Bidder, George Parker Jr, 171
Birchenough, (Sir) Henry, 350
Bitter Cry of Outcast London, The, 295, 327
Blackborough, Devon, 21, 22n, 23, 41, 52, 364
Blackdown House, Sussex, 202
Blandford, Marquis of, 288
Blashfield, J. M., 50
Blennerhassett, Lady, 284n
Boer War, 349–50
Bologna, window tracery, 55, 136
Booth, Charles, 301
Borradaile, Revd Abraham, 127; and Mrs Borradaile, 193
Borradaile family, 127n, 180
Borradaile, Jane Emma, see Knowles, Mrs James Thomas Jr.

Borthwick, Sir Algernon, 304, 305n
Boston, 4th Baron, 152–3, 365
Boswell, James, 358, 361
Bosworth, Thomas, 30, 53, 64, 74–5, 79, 82, 126, 163–4, 166
Bowring, John, 300
Bowyer, Revd and Mrs W. R. A., 183–4, 365
Bradley, George Granville, 62, 194, 302, 338, 341, 350
Brain-waves, 86, 220–1, 246n
Bramley Park, Surrey, 20–1, 21n, 203, 364
Brassey, Thomas (later Earl), 269, 309
Brett, Reginald (later Lord Esher), 303
Brighton, Sussex, 4, 17, 146, 149, 189, 249, 343, 353, 363, 367; St. Peter's, 17, 363; see also Hove
Broadstairs, Kent, 82–5, 117, Pl. 4
Brock, William, 242
Brooke, Stopford, 281
Broomfield, see Stanmore
Brown, Alan Willard, 208, 216, 217
Brown family, Rotherhithe, 13–14
Brown, Ford Madox, 76
Brown, Jones & Robinson, The Foreign Tour of Messrs, 87, 103
Brown, Susannah, see Knowles, Mrs James Thomas Sr
Browne, Matthew, see Rands, W. B.
Browning, Elizabeth Barrett, 111, 338
Browning, Robert, 111, 212, 220, 229, 261, 293, 338
Brownlow, Lady, 337
Buchanan, Robert, 237–8, 257
Builder, 23, 39, 40n, 78, 79, 81, 85, 118, 121, 122, 125, 127, 172, 176, 284, 297
Builders and contractors, 33, 81; see also by name
Building News, vii, 122, 134n, 137, 142, 160, 176, 188
Bulgaria, see Eastern Question
Burdett-Coutts, Lady, 296
Burges, William, 170, 265–6, 349
Burghclere, Lord, 369–70
Burgos Cathedral, 55
Burns, John, 285, 325, 343n, 347
Burt, Thomas, 293
Bushby, Dudley C., 369
Butterfield, William, 155
Byron, Lord: *Childe Harold*, 70, 93, 143, 145; *Manfred*, 93

Cacabe, Paul, 153, 154n, 365
Cambridge Apostles, 217
Cambridge, Prince George, Duke of, 287, 296, 302, 359
Cameron, Mrs Julia, 229
Canterbury Cathedral, 83, 84, 257
Cape Colony, 75, 76
Cappelle, Jan van de, 360

Carlingford, Lord, 286, 296
Carlyle, Thomas, 113, 119, 199, 280, 281n, 288, 359
Carpenter, W. B., 216, 221
Catholicism, Roman, 36n, 70, 92, 95, 263–4, 280
Cattermole, George, 171
Caxton, William, 161, 201
Cedars estate, see Clapham
Cement: patent metallic sand, 9, 20–1, 24, 36, 40–2; Keene's and Martin's, 140; Portland, 134; see also Stucco
'Cenci, The' (Guido Reni), 77, 95
Chamberlain, Joseph, 293, 296, 303, 311, 350
Chambers, William, 152–3n
Champion, Henry Hyde, 325, 343
Champion Park, see Sydenham
Channel Tunnel, 36, 244, 287, 290, 292–5, 296
Chappell, John T., 231–2n, 249
Château roofs, 139, 169, 175, 202
Chiddingfold, Surrey, 120, 200; see also Stilwell
Christian, Prince and Princess, 335
Christie's, see London: Christie's auction rooms
Cintra (mod. Sintra), Portugal: Villa or Palacio Monserrate, ix, 27, 49, 57, 58, 140, 143–50, 250, 365, Pl. 8
Circulation: *Contemporary Review*, 235–6, 272; *Cornhill*, 279n; *Nineteenth Century*, 279, 281, 285, 286
City, see London
Civil Engineer & Architect's Journal, 40
Civita Vecchia, 88
Claflin, Tennessee (Lady Cook), 150n
Clapham Gazette, 31, 67, 217
Clapham Magazine, 65–71, 119, 217
Clapham, Surrey (now So. London), 18, 27, 28, 30–2, 48, 51, 59, 73, 92, 109, 187, 299, 301; Athenaeum, 30–1, 32–3, 64, 68–9, 87, 123, 217–18, 310; Cedars estate, 126, 127, 167–71, 365, Pl. 7; Churches, 33, 70, 72, 75, 76, 172, 183–5, 188, 365, 366, Pl. 12; Clapham Park, 35–8, 72, 151, 153, 184–5; Dispensary, 45, 102, 364; Friday Grove, 24, 34–8, 59, 62, 73, 78, 140, 169, 187, 204n, 229, 364, Pl. 3; Grammar School, 62; The Hollies, 31, 111, 167, 188, 202, 206, 208, 211–12, 214–15, 218, 255, 261, 366, Pl. 16; Literary and Scientific Institution, 30, 87, 120n; Nelson Terrace, 30, 127–8, 160, 202; see also *Clapham Gazette*, *Clapham Magazine*
Clark, Dr Andrew, 216
Claude Lorrain, 100, 108, 273n, 291, 292n, 360
Clayton, John, 58

Clients, architects', 19, 25–6, 39, 81n, 254
Clifford, W. K., 271–2, 273
Cobbett, William, 3, 4, 139
Cockerell, Charles Robert, 11, 18, 25, 40
Colenso, J. W., 239
Collins, Wilkie, 221
Colls, Messrs, 185
Colour, on sculpture and buildings, 97, 104, 119, 134–5; 'structural polychromy', 134, 190
Comets, 74–5, 76, 85
Companion to the British Almanac, 141, 188
Competitions, architectural, 17, 41n, 57, 86, 122–3, 139
Contemporary Review, 68, 69, 159, 209, 215, 216, 219–20, 225, 226, 229, 232–40, 257, 258–9, 262–5, 268–73, 274, 276, 277, 279, 280, 283, 286, 289, 292, 319, 321, 351; *see also* Circulation, Fees, Open platform, Signed articles
Cook, Edwin, 144, 365
Cook, Francis, 1st Bart, 27, 49, 77, 144–50 *passim*, 193, 365
Cook, Francis, 4th Bart, ix, 146n
Cook Sons & Co. warehouse, *see* London: Cook warehouse, St. Paul's Churchyard
Cook, William, 27, 30, 46, 49, 144, 364, 365
Cooper's Hill, Egham, 247
Cornhill, vii, 170, 279n, 283
Correggio, 94, 192–3
Cowper, Earl, 370
Cowper, William, 84, 368
Crackanthorpe, Montague, 327
Craik, G. L., 338
Credit Foncier & Mobilier, 247, 248, 250
Crimean War, 87, 99, 109
Cross, John Walter, 359
Cross, Richard, 295, 296
Crown Estate (former Office of Woods & Forests), 50, 174, 194
Crystal Palace: 1851, *see* London; 1854, *see* Sydenham
Cubitt, Lewis, 169
Cubitt, Thomas, 30, 35, 39, 62, 138n, 169
Cundy, Thomas, 138n

Daily News, 269, 303, 304
Daily Telegraph, 242–3
Dalgairns, Father, 216
Dana, James D., 316
Dance, George, 148n
Dangstein, Sussex, 22, 364
Daniell, Thomas and William, 29, 148; *see also* India, views of
Dante, *Inferno*, 340
Darwin, Charles, 212–13
Daymond, John & Son, 142, 151, 176, 205, 302
Deepdene, Surrey, 12, 24, 52
De Grey, Earl, 41

De Keyser, Polidore, 35
Delane, John Thadeus, 83, 358; *see also Times, The*
Derby, Earl of, 288
De Vere, Aubrey, 339, 369
Devisme, Gerard, 145
Devonshire Club, 233, 302
Devonshire, Duke of, 241
Dialectics, Victorian, 63–4, 80, 83, 84, 85–6, 108, 115–16, 123, 124, 129, 142, 194, 204, 218–19, 223, 225–6, 288, 349, 359
Dickens, Charles, 54–5, 57, 73, 82, 84, 85, 105, 106, 126, 257
Dictionary of National Biography, 61n, 354
Disraeli, Benjamin, 39, 57, 208, 212, 272, 280, 282
'Dolorous Stroke, The', *see* Tennyson, Alfred
Donaldson, Thomas Leverton, 32–3, 40, 59, 61, 63–4, 72, 82, 84, 85, 100, 117, 218–19, 257, 297
Doughty House, *see* Richmond
Doxat, Henry, 171
Doyle, Richard, 87
Drainage, 141, 152, 160, 171
Drawings: architectural, 10, 16, 17, 21n, 22, 23, 24–5, 27, 51n, 55, 58, 74, 113, 126, 132, 146, 147, 175n, 245, 364–5; Old Master, 95, 192–3, 291, 360; by Turner and Ruskin, 232
Dublin Review, 215
Duke, Messrs, 205
Dulwich Gallery, 78
Dumas family, 171
Du Maurier, George, 161
Dunsany, Admiral Lord, 288, 293
Dyce, William, 162, 188n

Eastern Question, 263, 272, 280, 281–2, 361n
Eastman, Revd George, 184–5, 366
Eaton, Charlotte, *Rome in the 19th Century*, 14n, 70
Ecclesiologist, 28, 41
Echo, 248, 276
Eclecticism, 23, 25, 28, 29, 52, 53–4, 55–6, 63, 129, 139, 202, 204–5; *see also* 'English' style, Grosvenor style, Opportunism
Economist, 216
Eden, Emily, 212
Edward, Prince of Wales (later Edward VII), 127, 192, 296, 308, 352
Egmont, Earl of, 199, 200, 206
Egremont Castle, Somerset, 21, 22n, 147, 250
Egremont, 3rd Earl of, 20
Egremont, 4th Earl of, 19–21, 22–5, 26, 33, 364

Elgin Marbles, 327, 345, 359
Eliot, George, 199, 288, 322
Ellicott, Bishop C. J., 236, 280
Elmes, James, 47
Emmett, John T., 27, 265
Enbrook, Sandgate, Kent, 344
Engels, Friedrich, 296
Engineers, civil, 266n, 267
'English' style, 43, 56, 58, 124–5, 129, 133, 142, 176–7; *see also* Eyelid motif, Grosvenor style
Environment, influence of, 68, 84, 117
Ephesus, Temple of Diana, 287
Escott, T. H. S., 354
Evangelicals, 33, 72, 271
Evelyn, John, 32, 89
Exhibitions: *see* Leeds, National Exhibition of Works of Art, 1868; London: Great Exhibition (Crystal Palace) 1851, Great Exhibition 1862; Paris: Exhibition 1855, Exhibition 1889; Sydenham: Crystal Palace 1854
Eyelid motif, 55, 136, 146, 152, 169, 181, 291, Pl. 7
Eyre, Sir James, 40n, 92

Farringford, Isle of Wight, 198, 207, 231, 256
Fees and profits: architects', 229, 249, 251, 253; editors', 229, 236; writers', 264–265n, 284–5; proprietors', 277, 285
Fergusson, James, 136, 146, 148, 265
Fine Art Society, 291
Fisher family, Reigate glaziers, 6, 7n
Flint, Miss (granddaughter of Isabella Knowles), viii, 19n, 34n, 355n
Florence, 90, 110–11, 137
Flower family, 179, 182, 254, 270, 275, 327
Flower, Philip William, 151, 167, 177–81, 186, 229, 365, 366
Fluëlen, Lake Lucerne, 111
Foliage, architectural, 91, 108, 110, 112, 115–17, 124, 125–6, 135, 137, 138, 140, 143, 151, 154, 176, 204–5, Pl. 6, 7, 9
Fontana, Giovanni, 253
Fonthill, Wilts, 149
Forster, E. M., 220n, 229, 230n
Fortnightly Review, 216, 284, 294, 351, 354
Foster, Birket, 199
Fowler, (Sir) John, 293, 300, 305
France: *see* Channel Tunnel; *Château* roofs; Knowles, James Thomas Jr., European attitudes; Napoleon; Paris, buildings; Paris Food Fund
Francis, Messrs, 42
Fraser's Magazine, 75, 216
Freemasonry, 15, 16n, 290
Friday Grove, *see* Clapham
Frohschammer, Jacob, 237
Froude, James, 216, 288

Gadarene swine, 329–31, Pl. 15
Gale, Samuel Emly, 9, 10, 11
Gassiot, John Peter, 30, 73, 261
Gatton Park, Surrey, 15, 21–2, 364
Gellan, William, 236n
Genesis, Book of, 6, 310–16
Genoa, palaces, 36, 52, 59, 102
Geology, vii, 28, 63, 64–5, 75, 76, 101, 111, 203
Gibson, John (architect), 55
Gibson, John (landscape gardener), 252
Gibson, John (sculptor), 97
Gilchrist, Mrs Alexander, 199
Girgenti, 104–5
Gladstone, Mary, 230, 272, 298–9, 313
Gladstone Papers, viii, x, 262–3n
Gladstone, William Ewart, 66, 119, 140, 212, 216, 223, 230, 234, 244, 253, 255, 258, 261–8, 269, 287, 303, 361; and Channel Tunnel, 292–5; and Tennyson, 336–8; and the Queen, 347–8; portrait, 360n; in *Contemporary Review*, 238, 261–8, 368; in *Nineteenth Century*, 262, 284–5, 369, and, on Eastern Question, 263, 272, 280, 281–2, 346–7, 361n; Ireland and Home Rule, 282, 319–21, 331–2, 337; debates with Huxley *et al.*, 308–23, 329–34; on *Robert Elsmere*, 321–3; 'Locksley Hall Sixty Years After', 316–17; letters from, 262, 272, 320–1; letters to, 72, 102, 195, 208, 235, 253, 258n, 261–5, 267–8, 271, 273, 277, 278, 279, 283, 284, 291, 302, and under sub-headings above
Gladstone, Mrs W. E., 230
Glass buildings, 20n, 41n, 58, 59, 94, 121, 153
Glazier, William, 296
Godwin, Edward, 287
Godwin, George, 40, 284
Goodwin, Michael, 61n, 358n
Good Words, 234, 331
Goschen, Rt. Hon. G., 296
Graham, William, 348
Grant, Alexander, 216
Grant, 'Baron' Albert, 246, 247–54, 266, 272, 275, 366
Grant Duff, M. E., 22, 280
Grapevine, 20, 51, 168, 200
Gravestone, Anglo-Danish, 47, 74, 75
Gravestones, *see* Knowles family
Gray's Inn, *see* London: Raymond Buildings
Great Eastern, S.S., 130
Great Western Hotel, Paddington, *see* London: Great Western Hotel
Greenhill, *see* Aldworth
Greenwich, Painted Hall, 78
Greg, William Rathbone, 240
Grieg, Edvard, 98

Griffith & Farran, 164
Grissell, Thomas, 50–1
Grosvenor Hotel, *see* London: Grosvenor Hotel
Grosvenor style, 129–30, 133, 136, 142–3, 146, 147, 150, 152, 155, 176, 359; *see also* Eyelid motif
Grove, George, 30, 62, 216

Hall, Revd John, 185–6
Hamilton, Sir Edward, 285, 298
Hampton Court, 78
Hankey, Thomas Alers, 30, 59
Hardwick, P. C., *see* London: Great Western Hotel
Hardwicke, *see* Yorke
Hare, Augustus, 194
Harris, Henry, 168ff
Harrison, Frederic, 225, 283, 285, 286n, 293, 327, 345, 359, 361
Harrison, Miss, of Clapham, 184
Hedsor, Bucks, 152–3, 176, 365, Pl. 13
Hemans, C. I., 95
Herbert, George, 77, 88, 93, 95, 98, 111, 127, 229, 356, 366
Herbert, Hilda, *see* Hewlett, Mrs Maurice
Herbert, William, 30, 77, 88
Hesketh, Robert, 27
Hewlett, Henry Gay, 65, 87, 302, 326; writings, 69–70, 73–4, 126, 195; travels with, 87–101, 112–13; marriage, 126–7, 188; letters to, 65–101, 110–14, and 120–3 *passim*, 189–90, 193, 194, 220, 221, 356
Hewlett, Mrs Henry Gay, *see* Knowles, Emmeline
Hewlett, Isabel, *see* Knowles, Mrs James Thomas Jr.
Hewlett, Maurice, 38, 65n, 194, 355–6
Hewlett, Mrs Maurice (Hilda Herbert), 230n, 356
Hill, Octavia, 296
Hinton, James, 216, 222
Hobart-Hampden, Mrs, 303
Hodgson, Messrs, 10n, 45, 51, 54–7, 118; *see also* London: Hodgson auction rooms
Hodgson, Barnard, 171
Hodgson, Edmund, 54, 365
Hodgson, Sidney, 57
Holbeach, Henry, *see* Rands, W. B.
Holiday, Henry, 119
Holidays: seaside, 17, 73, 82, 120, 353; shooting, 114, 120; country-house renting, 211, 256, 336, 344, 353; *see also* Brighton, Broadstairs
Holland & Sons, 366
Holland, Henry, 148n
Holland, Queen of, 358
Hollies, The, *see* Clapham
Holmbury House, Surrey, 336–7, 339

Home Rule, *see* Ireland
Hope, Thomas, 43
Hopgood, John, 65, 68, 275, 302, 305–6, 307, 345
Horace, 102, 361, 369
Hotels, 57, 130, 141
Household Words, 84
Hove (West Brighton), Sussex, 229, 237, 245–7, 249, 366, Pl. 13
Howell, George, 293, 295
Huggins, Samuel, 112, 116
Humboldt, Alexander von, 68, 78–9, 84, 137
Humphery, John, 171
Humphreys, Henry Noel, 43, 112, 116
Hutton, Richard, 214, 216, 217, 222–5, 236, 272, 293
Huxley, Leonard, 224, 231, 306n, 331
Huxley Papers, viii, x, 306n
Huxley, Thomas, 140, 195, 214, 215, 216, 217, 222, 223, 224, 225, 229, 231–2, 236, 237, 239, 242, 249, 269, 272–3, 280, 285, 286, 289, 293, 294, 306, 345, 346; house for, 231, 366; debates with Gladstone, 308–16, 325, 329–34, 339; and Duke of Argyll, 323, 334; and Kropotkin, 323–4, 328; and Labour movement, 328–9; poem on Tennyson, 339, 369; sketch by, Pl. 15; *see also* Nineteenth Century: 'Recent Science'
Hyndman, H. M., 288, 324, 325

I'Anson, Edward Jr., 30, 33, 39, 40, 48
Illustrated London News, 31, 39, 43, 47, 57, 58, 74, 165, 166, 226, 237, 239, 263, 274; 'Magazines' column, 237n, 'Science' column, 283
Imhoff, H. M., 96
India: marbles from, 148; views of, 29, 57–8, 146, 148; influences from: *see also* Islamic art
Indianopolis, State Capitol, 155
Ingram, Thomas Dunbar, 319–20
International College, Spring Grove, Isleworth, 229, 230n
International Hotel, *see* London: Strand, hotel design
Ireland, 282, 319–20, 331–2, 337
Irving, Henry, 59, 60, 287, 338, 354, 366
Islamic art, 55, 91, 102, 103, 136, 140, 146–9 *passim*; *see also* India

Jackson, Wm & Co., 243
James, Henry, vii, ix, 199, 301, 361
Janus-symbol, 348–9, 363, Pl. 15
Jekyll, Gertrude, 21
Jeune, Lady, *see* St. Helier, Lady
Jingo fever, 1878, 280–1
Johnson, Dr Samuel, 15n

Jones, Albert, 168, 365
Jones, Alexander, 166, 168–9, 365
Jones, Owen, 55–6, 97, 136, 138n, 148, 267
Jorgensen, A. D., 335

Kata Phusin, *see* Ruskin
Kegan Paul, Trench & Co., 302
Kelk, (Sir) John, 132
Kentisbeare, Devon, 21, 364
Kerr, Robert, 40, 64n, 152, 155, 228, 266
Kew Gardens, lodge, 151
Killinghurst, *see* Stilwell
King, Henry, 212n, 277, 279
Kingswood Warren, Surrey, 364
Knebworth, Herts, 296
Knollys, Sir Francis, 336
Knowles family: at Reigate, 2, 4–10, 115, 326; at Kingston, 2, 5, 6; in Clapham Park, 38; James and Thomas as family names, 2, 5, 6; patternbooks owned by, 10, 19n, 32, 33n, 43n, 79; gravestones, 3, 8–9, 297, 363
Knowles, Arthur, viii, 128, 187, 228, 229, 267, 344
Knowles, Beatrice (Mrs W. W. Skilbeck), 158, 189, 228, 230n, 303, 337, 338, 344; annotated copy of Tennyson's *Works*, 337n
Knowles, Emmeline (Mrs Henry Hewlett), 14, 34, 38, 122, 126–7, 188
Knowles, George (Greek views), 38, 98
Knowles, George Henry, 14, 33, 34, 38, 49, 62, 77, 98, 355
Knowles, Isabel, *see* Knowles, Mrs James Thomas Jr. (Isabel Hewlett)
Knowles, Isabella (Mrs James Stilwell), viii, 14, 34, 38, 120, 121n, 199
Knowles, Israel, 6, 7, 46
Knowles, (Sir) James, editor, *see* Knowles, James Thomas Jr.
Knowles, James Thomas Sr. (1806–84): described, vii, 18–19, 34, 58, 61, 62–3, 75, 135, 275, 362; life in Reigate, 11–18, 112; life in Clapham, 18, 30–8, 45, 229; architectural career, 12, 16, 17, 18, 20–9, 33, 34–8, 40–60, 77, 125–6, 129–55, 168, 178, 297; list of buildings, 20n, 364–5; patternbooks, 10, *see also* Loudon, J. C., Bartholomew, A.; influence of his son, 60, 129–30, 135–7, 142–3, 152, 176; own house and office, 14, 16, 18, 22, 33, 34–8, 44–5, 188–9; politics, 11; social progress, 15, 25, 36, 37–8, 53, 60, 80, 189, 229, 297, 326; portraits, 44, 154, 251, 297, Pl. 1; old age and death, 38, 153–5, 275, 296–8; *see also* Eclecticism
Knowles, Mrs James Thomas Sr. (Susannah Brown), 13, 16, 34, 38, 267
Knowles, James Thomas Jr. (Sir James Knowles KCVO 1903, 1831–1908):

characterized, vii, 16, 34, 86, 87, 96, 159–60, 189, 195, 197, 202, 211, 217, 219–20, 221–2, 227, 230–1, 235, 243, 251, 259, 266, 267, 268, 290–3, 326–7, 340, 344, 352–63, Pl. 1, 14, and frontispiece; autobiographical notes, 61, 71–2, 87; childhood, 3–4, 14–15, 16–17, 18, 229, 359; education and travel, 33, 44, 51, 61–3, 71–125 *passim*, 190, 267; religious feeling, 72, 76, 91, 92, 101, 108–9, 114, 186, 188, 193; marriages, 38, 115, 127, 187, 188, 193, 228, 230; architectural career, 113, 115, 121, 126, 127, 159–60, 166–88, 190, 196, 198–208, 229, 231–2, 237, 245–6, 249–54, 258n, 266–7, 276, 277, 287, 298–91, 304; list of buildings, 365–7; influence on his father: *see* Knowles Sr. above; own house and office, 127–8, 169–70, 188–9, 255, 298–308; editorial career, 65–71, 117, 235, 266; *and see Contemporary Review, Nineteenth Century*; art collecting, 77–8, 95, 192–3, 249, 273n, 291, 306, 360, 362; stage design, 60, 287; social progress, 78, 80–1, 92, 189, 212, 217, 229–31, 232, 286; social attitudes, 268, 284, 285, 288, 293, 295–6, 308–9, 325–9; anxieties, 38, 80, 235, 260, 356, 360n, 361; politics, 233, 319–20; European attitudes, 36, 98–9, 240–4, 292–3, 295, 317, 362n; knighthood, vii, 336, 352–3; old age and death, 114, 344–5, 361, 363. Writings: early essays, 67–9, 78–81, 115–24, 219n, 233; *Story (Legend) of King Arthur*, 160–6, 209–10; 'Brain-waves' article, 219, 220–221; 'Alternation of Science and Art' article, 219–20, 234; article on *Idylls* 1870, 234–5, 256–7; 'Nature Development and Theology', 237; article on *Idylls* 1873, 238, 257; *Morning Post* leaders, 233; Channel Tunnel leaders, 293–5; article on Tennyson, 1893, 260, 340–3; privately printed leaflets, 341–2; poems, 336, 339, 370; posthumous essay on Tennyson, 64n, 257, 258n. *See also* Tennyson; Gladstone; Huxley; Channel Tunnel; Dialectics, Victorian; Fees and profits; Metaphysical Society; Open platform; Opportunism; Paris Food Fund; Signed articles
Knowles, Mrs James Thomas Jr. (Jane Borradaile), 127, 159, 160, 187, 188, 193, 228
Knowles, Mrs James Thomas Jr. (Isabel Hewlett, later Lady Knowles), 188, 189, 193, 228, 229n, 230, 256, 344
Knowles, Julia (Mrs C. C. Dumas), 14, 34, 38, 171, 184
Knowles, Maria (Mrs James, d. 1836), 11–12, 16n, 18, 298

Knowles, Millicent (Mrs Walter Frewen Lord), 187, 228, 343
Knowles, Susannah, *see* Knowles, Mrs James Thomas Sr. (Susannah Brown)
Kropotkin, Prince Peter, 324–5, 328, 357, 361

Labour movement and attitudes to working class, 126, 268, 284, 285, 288, 293, 295–6, 308–9, 325–9
Lainson, Ann, 14, 26
Lainson, John and Henry, 26–7, 364
Lambeth, Durand Gardens, 33, 364; *see also* Vauxhall
Landseer, Sir Edwin, 249
Lang, Prof. Cecil, viii, 164n, 188n, 199n, 210n, 251n
Layamon's Brut, 165, 191
Lecky, W. E. H., 361
Leeds, National Exhibition of Works of Art, 192–3
Legg, Henry, 44
Leighton, Frederick (Baron), 303, 360
Leopardi, Giacomo, 312
Leroy, Amelie Claire, 284n
Lewes, George Henry, 199, 215, 284
Lifts, 141, 177
Lightfoot, J. B., 274–5
Liverpool, Brown Library, 121
London: the magnet, 12, 16, 17, 37, 195; discussion forums, 217–18, 223; ideal house, 170, 189; slums, 295–6, 301; suburbs, 36, 142; *and see* Battersea, Clapham, Lambeth, Richmond, Rotherhithe, Streatham, Sydenham, Vauxhall. Buildings: Albert Gate houses, 138, 169; Albert Mansions, Victoria Street, 179–183, 201, 202, 244, 255, 275, 302, 304, 366; Army and Navy Stores, 181, 290–1, 302, 367; Bank of England, 140; British Museum, 12, 23, 39, 58, 78, 148, 192; Buckingham Palace, 12, 22–3, 24, 39, 140; Cannon Street, 47, 153, 365; Chancery Lane bank, 189–90, 366; Christie's auction rooms, 77, 249, 273n, 291, 303, 360; Cleopatra's Needle, 290; Conservative Club, 247, 251; Cook warehouse, St Paul's Churchyard, 46–9, 144, 364, Pl. 4; Covent Garden Opera House, 58–9, 88; Crown Insurance, New Bridge Street, 137; Dorchester House, 52; Great Exhibition (Crystal Palace) 1851, 41, 50, 73, 364; Great Exhibition 1862, 133, 141, 151, 160, 170; Great Western Hotel, Paddington, 58, 132, 133, 139, 141, 147; Grosvenor Basin, 131, 133, 180; Grosvenor Gallery, 274; Grosvenor Hotel, Victoria Station, 13, 24, 55, 60, 79, 117, 126, 129–43, 146,

147, 169, 170, 176, 222, 223, 225, 269, 302, 303, 365, Pl. 5–7; Guards' Chapel, Wellington Barracks, 300, 304, 307; Harley Street, 168, 280, 365; Hodgson's auction rooms, Chancery Lane/Fleet Street corner, 45, 51, 54–7, 90, 118, 365, Pl. 5; Houses of Parliament, 17, 97, 142, 205, 364; Kensington House, 64, 99, 105, 229, 249–52, 366, Pl. 13; Kensington Palace Gardens, 36, 50–3, 365; Knowles Court (Do Little Alley), 7, 46; Leicester Square, 229, 247, 248, 249, 252–3, 366, Pl. 14; Lyceum Theatre, 59, 60, 287, 340, 366; Marlborough House, 78, 123, 296, 302, 336, 341; Marlborough Place, St John's Wood, 231, 366; National Gallery, 17, 39, 78; Oakley Street, Chelsea, 153, 365; Oriental Baths, 180–1; Overton's fish shop, Victoria, 254, 366; Pavilion Theatre, 281; Prince's Square, 172; Queen Anne's Lodge, Queen Square Place, viii, 298–308, 314, 338, 339, 360–1, 367, Pl. 16; Queen Anne's Mansions, Petty France and Broadway, 300–1, 304–8; Queen's Mansions, Victoria Street, 275; Raymond Buildings, Gray's Inn, 16, 18, 22, 44–5, 58, 65, 172, 182; Reform Club, 23, 24, 37, 52, 140–1, 144, 159, 189, 192, 233, 241, 290, 302, 303, Pl. 14; Russell house, Park Lane, 175; Russell Square, 31, 38, 296–7; St. Margaret's, Westminster, 301, 363; St. Mary's, Vincent Square, 127, 302; St. Paul's Cathedral, 43, 47–8, 49, 90; Soane Museum, 27n, 78; Soho Square, 189, 252; Spenser Street, 181; State Paper Office, 17; Strand, hotel design, 57–9, 133, 138, 139, 142, 365, Pl. 5; Tarn's shop, Elephant and Castle, 150–1, 176, 365; Temple Church, 148; Thatched House Club, 174–7, 188, 302–3, 366, Pl. 9; Travellers' Club, 17, 139; University College, 33, 61, 63, 64n; Victoria Station, 131–2, 141–2, 143, 180; Victoria Street/Strutton Ground corner, 81n, 366; Westminster Abbey, 107, 125, 138, 170, 176, 187, 194, 201, 203–4, 214, 222, 240, 257–8, 338, 339; Westminster Cathedral, 180, 183; Westminster Palace Hotel, 141, 223n; Willis's Rooms, King Street, 174, 206, 215, 303; Wimpole Street, 276, 279
London County Council, 304, 307
Longfellow, H. W., 97
Longmans, 277
Lord, Walter Frewen, 343
Loudon, John Claudius, 15, 19, 37, 43, 58, 84, 118, 147
Lowe, Robert, 200n, 216, 269

Lubbock, Sir John, 214, 216, 222, 240n, 242, 280, 293
Lucas, Mr. (land agent), 200
Lucas, Messrs (builders), 51, 58
Lunatics Society, 71–2
Lushington, Edmund, 216, 222
Lux Mundi, 330–1, 332n
Lyell, Sir Charles, *Principles of Geology*, 101, 104
Lyon, Capt. James, 22, 364
Lytton, 1st Earl of, 296
Lytton, Bulwer, 1st Baron, *Pelham*, 83, 84

Macaulay, Rose, 150
Macaulay, Thomas Babington, 32, 119, 294
MacColl, Canon Malcolm, 111, 346–7
Macdonald, Lawrence, 96
Macleod, Fiona, *see* Sharp, William
Macmillan, Alexander, 229
Macmillan, publishers, 212n; *Magazine*, 216, 284, 292, 338
MacPherson, Robert, 98
Magee, Bishop W. C., 238
Magna Graecia, 104
Magnus, Sir Philip, 264n
Maitland, Thomas, *see* Buchanan, Robert
Malory, Sir Thomas, 128, 161, 162, 163, 201, 207
Manchester: Athenaeum, 52; Royal Insurance, King Street, 175; warehouses, 46, 48
Manchester, Duke of, 288
Mann, Tom, 285, 325
Manning, Henry E. (Archbishop, later Cardinal), 20, 66, 92, 215, 216, 222, 224, 229, 230, 236, 242, 243–4, 255, 263, 272–3, 280, 293, 358
Mantell, Gideon, vii, 28, 30, 64, 69, 70, 71
Margate, Royal Sea-Bathing Infirmary, 286, 290, 366
Marlborough, Duke of, 327
Marot, Grand, 139
Martin, John, 77, 84
Martin, Sir Theodore, 370
Martineau, James, 208, 216, 223, 225–6, 237
Marx, Karl, 288, 296
Maurice, F. D., 216
Mayhew, Henry, 211
Mazzini, Giuseppi, 99, 236–7
McCarthy, Justin, 261, 282
McCorquodale, George, 270–3
Meath, Lord, 347
Melmotte, Augustus, 248–9
Mental telepathy, *see* Brain-waves
Messina, Sicily, 108, 112
Metaphysical Society, ix, 31, 69, 72, 77, 136, 140, 142, 186, 197, 208, 212–18, 221–6, 229, 236, 238, 240, 242, 244, 263, 269, 272, 280, 283, 303, 328, 359
Metaphysics, 85, 208, 220

Metropolitan Board of Works, 181, 231, 252, 304, 307
Michelangelo, 91, 96, 192, 239, 370
Milan, Galleria Vittorio Emmanuele, 247, 249
Mill, John Stuart, 72, 182, 215, 300, 302
Millais, (Sir) John Everett, 170, 291, 360
Milner, Sir Alfred, 350
Milton, John, 300; *Paradise Lost*, 84, 86, 100, 105
Minton tiles, 207
Mivart, St. George, 225, 239
Monmouth, Geoffrey of, 161
Monreale, Sicily, 103
Monserrate, *see* Cintra
Monson, Earl (d. 1841), 15, 21–2, 364
Moore, George, 50, 51, 52–3, 154, 242, 365
Morley, John, 216, 225, 284, 294
Morley, Samuel, 271, 273, 274
Morning Post, 233, 304
Morris, William, 162, 240, 326; *see also* Pre-Raphaelites
Morris, William (speculator), 245–6, 249, 366
Mount Etna, 106–8
Moxon, Edward, 212, 215, 258
Müller, Max, 310, 312n, 335
Murray Guides, 88, 98
Murray, John, 293
Murray Smith, Mrs Alexander, 302
Muspratt, Edward, 185
Myers, F. W. H., 339, 369
Myers, George & Sons, 172, 183

Naples, 100, 102, 109, 110
Napoleon I, 36, 120, 201
Napoleon III, 201, 241
Nash, John, 146
Nash, Joseph, 58
Neapolitan Steam Navigation Co., 88
Nesfield, William Eden, 151, 202
Newman, John Henry (Cardinal), 215, 354, 357
Newnes, George, 348
Nineteenth Century, vii, viii, 68, 69, 90, 221, 225, 232, 233, 260–1, 262, 271, 274–89, 292–6, 299, 302, 306, 308–36, 338, 339–44, 345–51, 353, 355, 357, 359, 363; poetry, 338, 349–50, 368–9; 'Recent Science', 69, 282–3, 324; titling of articles, 328–9; *see also* Circulation, Fees, Open platform, Signed articles
Nineteenth Century and After, 348–51, 363, 370
Noel, Roden, 216, 236, 339, 369
Norwood Cemetery, 267, 297

O'Neil, Henry, 248–9
Open platform ('fair field'), 65, 68, 119, 214, 233, 270, 295

Opportunism, vii, 72, 190, 198, 221–2, 295; *see also* Eclecticism, Grapevine
O'Shea, carver, 124, 148
O'Shea, Mrs, 332
Overend-Gurney crash, 189
Overseer of the poor, 15
Oxford: Essay Club, 217; Exeter College, 172; Museum, 124, 148; Union, 160, 162

Paestum, 109–10, 170
Paget, Sir James, 230, 293, 296
Palermo, 102–4
Paley, E. G., 297
Paley, William, *Natural Theology* ('Evidences'), 73, 214
Palgrave, F. T., 135n, 339, 369
Pall Mall Gazette, 241, 295, 323
Papworth, John B., 33n, 77
Paramor, James, 290
Paris, buildings: Exhibition 1855, 138; Exhibition 1889, 362; Hôtel du Louvre, 59, 131; New Louvre, 139, 151
Paris Food Fund, 237, 240–4, 286
Park Town estate, *see* Battersea
Patternbooks, architectural, 10, 12, 15, 24, 29, 55, 137, 200, 202
Paxton, (Sir) Joseph, 41n, 42, 121
Payment, *see* Fees
Payne Knight, Richard, 107, 108
Pearson, John Loughborough, 27, 29, 127, 230n
Peek, Francis, 271
Pembroke, Countess of, 337
Pembroke, Earl of, 296, 322
Pennethorne, James, 55, 175n
Pentillie, Cornwall, 29
Pepys, Lady Emily, 182, 183n
Pepys, Samuel, 32, 167
Periodicals, vii, 362; *see* separate titles
Peto, Samuel Morton, 39, 50
Petworth, Sussex, 20, 21, 23
Pevsner, Sir Nikolaus, x, 124
Phelps, Sydney K., 356–7
Phillips, Stephen, 349–50, 369–70
Picturesque, The, 23, 37, 84, 108, 117, 152, 240
Plant ornament, *see* Foliage, architectural
Plunket, David, 304
Plymouth, Elliott Terrace, 154n
Pollock, Frederick, 216
Pontypool Town Hall, 86
Pooter, Mr, 82
Posilippo, 100
Positivism, 358
Potter, Beatrice (Mrs Sydney Webb), 285, 325, 327
Poynter, Edward J., 349, Pl. 15
Pozzuoli, 100–1
Pre-Raphaelites, 71, 160, 162

Pritchard, Revd Prof. Charles, 30, 62–3, 72, 74n, 76–7, 79, 191, 208, 212–13, 216, 217, 224–5, 302
Probyn, Lt-Gen. Sir Dighton, 300, 307
Pseudonyms, 237–8, 284n
Pugin, A. W. N., 53, 58, 206
Punch, 31, 38, 63, 73, 82, 83, 161, 174, 212, 217, 239, 252, 276, 303, 310, 347
Pyne, W. H., *Royal Residences*, 24

Quarterly Review, 265
Queen Anne Revival, 152, 289, 361
Queen Anne's Lodge, *see* London

Rands, W. B., 238
Raphael, 78, 90, 91, 95, 192
Ray, Dr Gordon, 191n, 251n, 341, 342n
Redgrave, J. E., 194
Redhill, Surrey, 26, 27; St. John's, 19n, 22, 27–9, 364, Pl. 12
Reggio, 108
Reigate, Surrey, 3–5, 7–9, 11–13, 14–18, 20, 21–2, 26, 31, 93, 195, 199, 353; Bell Street, 4, 5, 7, 8, 11, 13, 14, 15, 16, 18, 37, 112, 362, Pl. 1; Cockshut Hill, 4, 18; Colley Manor, Reigate Heath, 26–7, 364; parish (later grammar) school, 7, 12, 62; Park Hills, 3, 18, 93, 199; St. Mary Magdalene's, 3, 8, 9, 13, 15, 125–6, 154; *see also* Redhill
Reinach, Joseph, 294
Reni, Guido, 77, 95, 192
Review of Reviews, 346
Réville, Albert, 310
Rewe, Devon, 21, 22n, 364
Reynolds, Sir Joshua, 360
Richmond, Sir William, 355
Richmond, Surrey, Doughty House, 27, 49, 77, 144–5
Roberts, Henry, 42
Robertson, G. Croom, 280
Robinson, Admiral Sir R. S., 288
Robson, E. R., 305, 307
Robson, George, 287, 304–5, 306–7, 343
Rogers, Guinness, 271, 327, 347
Rome, first day in, 88–90; Basilica of Constantine, 93; Baths of Caracalla, 99; Borghese gallery, 94; Corsini Chapel, St. John Lateran, 22; Farnese Palace, 93n, 96; Forum, 91; Nero's House, 99; St. Peter's, 89, 90, 92, 95, 96; Vatican, 90–1, 94–5; Victor Emmanuel monument, 25; Villa Medici, 52
Roosevelt, F. D., 362
Rossetti, D. G., 237–8, 239n, 257
Rotherhithe, 13–14, 26
Rothschild, Alfred de, 242, 244
Roumania, Queen of, 284n, 369
Royal Academy, 22, 24–5, 27, 44, 60, 126, 132

Royal Institute of British Architects, 16, 18, 38–9, 40–3, 63, 64n, 74, 79, 81, 82, 86, 135, 265–7, 297; early use of 'Royal', 39n; library, 53, 55, 56n, 139
Roydon Hall, Kent, 144, 153, 365
Ruskin, John, 41, 54, 71, 79, 90, 92, 100, 103, 110, 115–16, 119, 121, 140, 147, 242, 243, 265; as Kata Phusin, 84, 117, 257; influence, 135, 136–7, 138, 147, 176, 222, 232; Metaphysical Society and, 136–7, 216, 226, 229, 232, 240; in *Contemporary Review* and *Nineteenth Century*, 232, 236, 240, 288
Russell, Lord Arthur, 216, 222, 223, 236
Russians, 89, 109, 280; *see also* Crimean War
Ruysdael, Jacob van, 193, 360

St. Crispin's Day, 15
St. Helier, Lady (previously Lady Jeune), 303, 359
St. Louis, Mo., Wainwright Building, 138
Salisbury, Marquis of, 241, 295, 347
Salmoné, Anthony, 347
Salting, George, 177
Salting, Severin, 178–9
Salting, William, 254, 366
Salvin, Anthony, 154
Sampson Low Marston, 343
Sandringham House, Norfolk, 296, 307, 336, 352
Sang, Frederick, 251
Sarl, W. J., 275
Sassoon family, 246, 247
Schleswig-Holstein, 334–6
Scott, Sir George Gilbert, 42–3, 54, 119, 130, 133–4, 142, 170, 172, 176, 183, 186, 192, 204, 265, 297
Scott, Sir Walter, 73, 120, 198, 249
Seebohm, Frederic, 284, 288
Seeley, J. R., 216
Senior, Nassau Jr., 186
Serlio, 205
Shaftesbury, Earl of, 296
Shakespeare, William, 84, 252–3, 287
Sharp, William, 284n
Shaw, Capt. E. M., 48
Shaw, John, 58
Shaw, R. Norman, 155, 202
Shelley, P. B., 95, 99
Sidgwick, Henry, 236
Siena, Palazzo Spannocchi, 139
Signed articles, 237–8, 284, 293
Silverton Park, Devon, 21, 22–5, 42, 140, 364, Pl. 2; rectory, 21, 364
Simeon, Sir John, 257
Sintra (mod. sp.), *see* Cintra
Skilbeck, Eirene, vii–viii, 34n, 284n, 342, 353
Skilbeck, William Wray, 308, 343–4, 350
Smiles, Samuel, 50, 52–3

Smirke, Sir Robert, 25, 79
Smirke, Sydney, 40, 148
Smith, George & Co., 175
Soane, Sir John, 17, 20n, 140, 148n, 170
Socialism, *see* Labour movement
Society for Protection of Ancient Buildings, 240, 274
Somers, Earl, 27
Somersby, Lincs, 201
Somerville, Mrs, 111
Southey, Robert, 143, 161
Spectator, 216, 219, 220, 347
Spence, B. E., 96
Spencer, Herbert, 215, 217, 239, 262, 293, 353
Spenser, Edmund, 181, 201, 204, 207
Spinoza, B., 237
Sponge's Sporting Tour, Mr (Surtees, R. S.), 145
Spottiswoode, Messrs, 302, 313
Stand, All Saints, 29
Standard, 240–1, 269
Stanford Estate, *see* Hove
Stanford, John, 14, 17
Stanley, Arthur Penrhyn, 159, 194–5, 203–4, 214, 216, 222, 234, 239, 256, 257, 267, 290, 292
Stanley, Lady Augusta, 214, 267n
Stanley, Hon. Maude, 288
Stanmore, Middlesex, Broomfield, 153, 365
Statham, Heathcote, 176–7
Stead, W. T., 346
Stephen, James Fitzjames, 216, 227, 272, 283
Stephen, Leslie, 216
Stilwell family, 12n, 199, 200, 355; *see also* Knowles, Isabella
Stirling, J. H., 237
Strachey, Sir Edward, *Miracles and Science*, 113
Strahan, Alexander, 166, 209, 211, 212n, 213, 219, 233–4, 235–6, 237, 238, 258, 264–5n, 268–73, 274–5, 277, 279, 285
Strawberry Hill, 198, 286
Streatham, Surrey, 35–6; Furzedown, 151, 152n, 178, 365; St. Leonard's, 36, 76, 188n
Street, George Edmund, 186, 297
Strickland, Samuel, 51, 153
Stuart, Esmé, *see* Leroy, Amelie Claire
Stuart Wortley, Lt-Col. Henry, 242–3
Stucco, 57, 96, 100, 104, 249; *see also* Cement
Studio, 349
Sullivan, Sir Arthur, 182, 275
Sullivan, Louis, 138
Swaylands, Kent, 172
Swinburne, Algernon C., 237–8, 239n, 338, 339, 347, 349–50, 368–70

Sydenham, Kent: Champion Park and St. Michael's, 172–4, 365; Crystal Palace, 55, 97, 136, 173, 355
Sydney Lodge, Hamble, Hants, 20n
Sylva, Carmen, *see* Roumania, Queen of
Symonds, John Addington, 239, 370

Tabley, Lord de, 369
Taine, Hippolyte, 117
Tarn, William, 150–1, 176, 365
Teck, Princess Mary Adelaide, Duchess of, 305, 337, 361
Teck, Princess Mary of (later Queen Mary), 362
Tenerani, Pietro, 96
Tenniel, John, 170, 212
Tennyson, Alfred (1st Lord), viii, 84, 103, 124, 135, 349–50, 352, 357, 362–3, 366; *1850s*, 64–5, 72, 108, 115, 116–17, 143–4; *1860s*, 37, 162–6, 185, 187, 188, 190–2, 197–216, 220, 222, 224–5, 226–7, 229, 234–5, 254; *1870s*, vii, 123, 158, 171, 179, 182–3, 225, 229, 230n, 231, 232, 235, 242, 246n, 250–1, 254–61, 267, 276–81, 290; *1880s*, 47, 60, 284–5, 287, 291, 293, 316–17; *1890s*, 336–43; sketches by, 158, Pl. 10; bust by Woolner, 250–1; portrait by Millais, 291, 360n; in *Contemporary Review*, 368; in *Nineteenth Century*, 369; *Morte d'Arthur*, 162, 207; *In Memoriam*, 64–5, 108, 124, 203, 341; *Maud*, 114–15, 201, 276, 337; *Idylls of the King*, 116–17, 123, 126, 142, 160–1, 166, 197, 201, 203, 204, 206, 207, 208–13, 232, 234, 239, 256–7, 258–60, 337, 342; *The Cup*, 287, 292, 366; *Becket*, 338, 340; *Queen Mary*, 338; 'Ode on the Death of the Duke of Wellington', 47, 338; 'The Higher Pantheism', 213, 222, 278; 'The Last Tournament' (only Idyll published in periodical), 239, 256, 258–9, 350, 368; 'The Dolorous Stroke', prose draft, 260, 341; 'The Lord has grown as commonplace', 260; 'Old Ghosts' and 'Brunanburh', 277; sonnet for *Nineteenth Century*, 279–80; 'The Revenge', 281; 'De Profundis', 284; 'Despair', 288, 292; 'Charge of the Heavy Brigade', 292; 'Locksley Hall Sixty Years After', 316–17; 'Christ at Ammergau', 342
Tennyson, Emily (Lady), 165, 182, 191, 198, 200–1, 205, 208, 230, 243, 250–1, 254, 255–6, 259, 337–8, 340
Tennyson, Hallam (2nd Lord), 251, 256, 260, 338, 339, 340–3, 345, 357
Tennyson, Lionel, 317
Tennyson Research Centre, viii, 198n
Tennyson, Sir Charles, ix, 199n, 200n, 258, 337, 343

Ten Thousand a-Year, 32, 68
Terry, Ellen, 287, 338
Thackeray, Anne, 211, 230
Thackeray, W. M., 198, 207–8; *The Newcomes*, 88; *Vanity Fair*, 297
Thomas, G. H., 165n
Thompson, Sir Henry, 290
Thomson, James, 84
Thorne, James, 188
Thornton, Marianne, 186, 229–30, 244, 261, 293
Thorowgood, William, 184–5
Tidey, Henry, 44
Tillotson, Prof. Emer. Kathleen, ix, 199n, 210n
Times, The, 83, 248, 266, 269, 275, 278, 286, 304, 322, 354, 358, 360
'Tinted Venus', 97
Tite, William, 39, 82
Tivoli, 100
Tracery, window, *see* Eyelid motif
Travers, Joseph & Sons, 153, 365
Trevelyan, Sir Charles, 244
Trevelyan, Sir George, 357n
Trollope, Anthony, 170, 248–9; *The Way We Live Now*, 236, 248, 266; *The Prime Minister*, 249
Troubetzkoi, Pierre, 360
Turkey, *see* Eastern Question
Turner, J. M. W., 78–9, 84, 100, 199, 232, 360
Twentieth Century, vii, 276, 342, 348
Tyndall, John, 216, 222, 231, 272, 282, 303

Utilitarian principles, *see* *Westminster Review*

Vauxhall (Lambeth), 107; St. Peter's, church, schools, vicarage, 127, 229, 230n, 366; Vauxhall Gardens, 96, 127
Venables, Canon Edmund, 288
Venice, 111–12
Venturi, Emilie Ashurst, 237
Verdi, Giuseppi, 98
Vernacular classicism, 123–4, 155
Vestier, M., 104
Victorian architecture, 43, 125, 129; *see also* 'English' style, Grosvenor style
Victorian Order, 352–3
Vivisection, 223, 224n
Vulliamy, Lewis, 48, 52

Waddington, William, 303
Waldegrave, Countess, 286, 296, 356
Walpole, Horace, 89, 198
Walters, Edward, 48
Walton Grove, Surrey, 153, 154n, 365
Ward, Mrs Humphrey, 313, 321–3, 329
Ward, Maisie, 220n

Ward, Nathaniel B., and Wardian case, 94, 113
Ward, Wilfrid, 220, 358
Ward, William George, 215, 216, 217, 222, 224, 229
Waring, John B., 45, 55, 56n, 139
Warmont, C. de, *see* Blennerhassett, Lady
Warton, Joseph, 117n
Water closets, 21, 141, 169, 177
Waterhouse, Alfred, 132n, 140–1, 175, 231, 297
Watkin, Sir Edward, 292–4
Watson, William, 347
Watts, George Frederic, 288, 336n, 360
Watts (by 1896 Watts-Dunton), Walter Theodore, 339, 347, 369
Waugh, Arthur, 284n, 369
Webb, Beatrice, *see* Potter, Beatrice
Webb, Philip, 155, 202
Wedmore, Frederick, 357, 359
Welldon, Bishop, 359, 360n
Wellesley Collection (drawings), 95, 192
Wellesley Index to Victorian Periodicals, viii, 284n, 350, 368
Wellington College, Berks, 58, 172, 173n
Wellington, Duke of, 47
Wells Cathedral, 356
West Brighton, *see* Hove
Westminster, *see* London
Westminster Gazette, 357
Westminster Review, 19n, 27, 68, 300
Whichelo, Lily (later Mrs Forster), 229
White, Arnold, 211
Whitman, Walt, 285, 349–50, 368
Who's Who, 354
Wigton, Cumb., fountain, 53, 154–5, 298, 365
Wilberforce, Bishop Samuel, 184, 185
Wilde, Oscar, 299, 356, 357n
Wilkins, William, 17, 21, 29

Willis, Prof. Robert, 29, 264n
Williton, Somerset, 21, 27, 364
Wilson, Sir Erasmus, 14n, 254, 290, 366
Wilton House, Wilts, 296, 322
Wireless telegraphy, *see* Brain-waves
Wolffsohn, Lily, 369
Wolseley, Lt-Gen. Sir Garnet, 281, 288, 293, 303
Women's suffrage, 322–3, 349
Wood, J. T., 287
Wood, Shakspere, 93–4, 97
Woodgate, William, 166, 171n, 172–7, 178, 187, 365–6
Woodyer, Henry, 55
Woolf, Virginia, *Orlando*, 176
Woolner, Thomas, 53, 154–5, 211, 220, 229, 250–1
Working class, *see* Labour movement
Wornum, Ralph, 123
Worthington, Thomas, 297
Wren, Sir Christopher, influence of, 42–3, 45, 58, 90, 123–4, 135, 138, 288; *see also* Vernacular classicism
Wright, Thomas, 162
Wyatt, James, 24, 148
Wyatt, Matthew Digby, 38
Wyatt, T. H., and D. Brandon, 55
Wyndham, George Francis, Capt. RN, *see* Egremont, 4th Earl
Wynn Ellis: collection, 273n, 360; warehouse, 48

Yates, Haywood & Co., 206
York, Duke of (later George V), 308
Yorke family, Earls of Hardwicke, 8n, 9n, 15, 20
Young, G. M., 72

Zeitgeist, 363
Zola, Émile, 362

1. Bell Street, Reigate, Surrey, postcard *c.* 1900 (*top*); Knowles Sr., in 1860, born in Bell Street 1806 (*left*); Knowles Jr., *c.* 1877, born in Bell Street 1831 (*right*; both, Clapham Antiquarian Society)

2. Silverton Park, Devon, by Knowles Sr. 1839–45; view *c.* 1892 (*top*, National Monuments Record); long section for hall *c.* 1840–3, sheet *c.* 28″ × 38″, (*bottom*, RIBA Drawings). See pp. 22–4

3. Friday Grove, Clapham Park, by Knowles Sr. 1845: sale-catalogue view 1876 (*top*, BM Maps); two views of hall during demolition 1895 (*bottom*, Clapham Antiquarian Society). See p. 36

4. Broadstairs sketched by young Knowles in August 1853 (*top*, sketchbook in
family possession). See p. 82. Messrs. Cook's warehouse, St. Paul's Churchyard,
Illustrated London News, 25 March 1854 (*bottom*). See p. 47

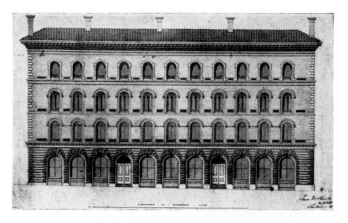

5. Drawing by Knowles Sr. for Edmund Hodgson 1854 for
Chancery Lane front, sheet *c.* 22″ × 36″ (*top*, W. Hodgson,
photo RIBA). See p. 55. Design for an International Hotel,
Illustrated London News, 3 April 1858 (*centre*). See p. 57.
Design for the Grosvenor Hotel as intended, *ILN*, 7 July 1860,
central roof feature not built (*bottom*). See p. 60

6. Grosvenor Hotel at Victoria Station, by Knowles Sr. with Knowles Jr.,
1858–62: view before 1900 (*top*, National Monuments Record); original
window-tracery, *Building News*, 20 March 1863 (*bottom*). See p. 136

7. Grosvenor Hotel, frieze and cornice, north-east corner, in 1964 (*top*, National Monuments Record). See p. 138. Window-tracery, Cedars Estate, Clapham Common North Side, by Knowles Jr. 1860 (*bottom*, National Monuments Record). See p. 169

8. Monserrate, Sintra (former Cintra), Portugal, exterior in 1965 (*top*,
A. Hamilton-Fletcher); rebuilding designed by Knowles Sr. 1858–9, completed
1863–5: preliminary drawing 1858, sheet *c.* 20″ × 33″ (*bottom*, Sir Francis Cook,
Bart.) See pp. 146, 150

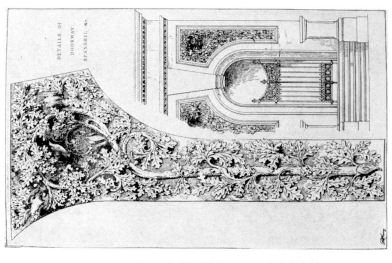

DETAILS OF
DOORWAY
SPANDRIL, &c.

9. Thatched House Club, St. James's Street, Westminster, by Knowles Jr. 1861–4: street view and detail of foliage carving, *Building News*, 9 September 1864. See p. 176

10. Sketch by Tennyson (June 1867?), sheet *c.* 8″ × 12″ inscribed 'for Aldworth' by Mrs. Tennyson and later 'by A & ET' by Hallam Tennyson (*top*, see p. 200, Tennyson Research Centre, Lincoln). Aldworth, Sussex, by Knowles Jr. for Tennyson 1867–9, as in the poet's lifetime, *Memoir* (1897), ii. 208 (*bottom*).

See p. 201

11. Aldworth, three details of carved frieze on the south face, executed possibly by a carver from the firm of John Daymond during the period 1868–77 (National Monuments Record). See pp. 204–5

12. St. John Evangelist, Redhill, Surrey, by Knowles Sr. 1842–3, *Westminster Review*, 1844 (*left*). See p. 27. St. Saviour's, Cedars Road, Clapham, by Knowles Jr. 1862–4, *Clapham Gazette*, 1862 (*right*). See p. 183

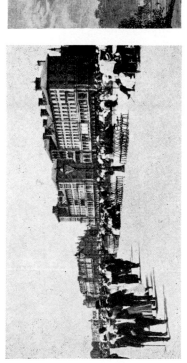

13. Hedsor, Buckinghamshire, by Knowles Sr. 1865–8, early photograph (*top*, Clapham Antiquarian Society). See p. 152. West Brighton (Stanford) estate, Hove, Sussex, sea-front terraces rear right by Knowles Jr. 1871–2, postcard *c.* 1910 (*left*). See p. 246. Kensington House by Knowles Jr. 1873 for Alfred Grant, *Graphic*, 30 June 1877 (*right*). See p. 250

14. Fountain by Giovanni Fontana in Leicester Square, layout by Knowles Jr.
1874, *Builder*, 4 July 1874 (*top*). See p. 252. Knowles on the alert at the Reform
Club, rear centre at the right of third column from left, *Punch*, 28 November
1885, detail (*bottom*)

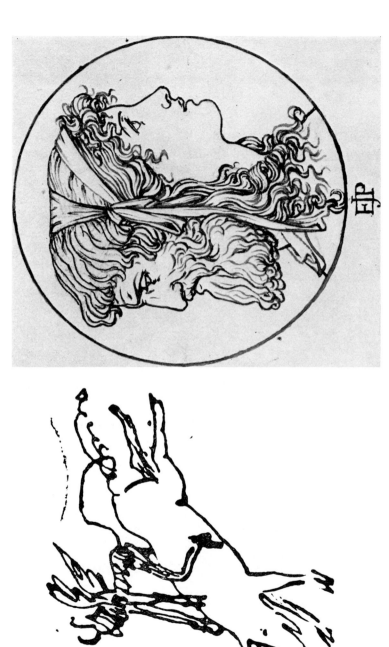

15. Demon and Gadarene pig sketched by Huxley on letter to Knowles, 18 November 1890 (*left*, from privately printed page in Knowles and Huxley papers, Westminster Public Library and Imperial College, original unknown). See p. 331. Original drawing by E. J. Poynter PRA *c.* 1896 for title page from 1901, *Nineteenth Century and After*, used without medallion and initials (*right*, Knowles papers, WPL). See p. 348

16. The Hollies, Clapham Common North Side, double house left and centre, gate piers and wall probably added by Knowles: where the Metaphysical Society was founded in 1868 (*top*, author). See p. 188. Queen Anne's Lodge, No. 1 Queen Square Place, Westminster, *c.* 1900, garden front, doorcase probably altered by Knowles: where the *Nineteenth Century* was edited 1884–1908 (*bottom*, family photograph). See p. 299